FOR DUMMIES
BESTSELLING BOOK SERIES

Final Cut Pro® HD
For Dummies®

KT-234-634

Cheat Sheet

File Menu Commands

Command	Keystroke Combination
New project	Shift+⌘+N
New sequence	⌘+N
New bin	⌘+B
Open	⌘+O
Save project	⌘+S
Save project as	Shift+⌘+S
Import files	⌘+I
Close active window	⌘+W
Close active tab	Control+W
Quit	⌘+Q

Edit Menu Commands

Command	Keystroke Combination
Undo	⌘+Z
Redo	Shift+⌘+Z
Clear	Delete
Cut	⌘+X
Cut with ripple delete	Shift+X
Copy	⌘+C
Paste	⌘+V
Paste Insert	Shift+V
Find	⌘+F
Find Next	⌘+G
Selected Item Properties	⌘+9
Select All	⌘+A
Deselect All	Shift+⌘+A

Windows Menu Commands

Command	Keystroke Combination
Viewer	⌘+1
Canvas	⌘+2
Timeline	⌘+3
Browser	⌘+4
Audio Meters	Option+4
Effects	⌘+5
Favorites	⌘+6
Trim edit	⌘+7
Log and Capture window	⌘+8
Standard window layout	Control+U

The Tool Palette

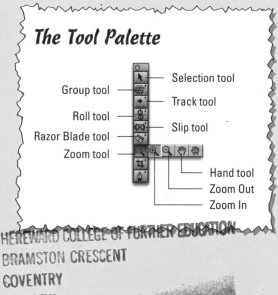

- Group tool
- Roll tool
- Razor Blade tool
- Zoom tool
- Selection tool
- Track tool
- Slip tool
- Hand tool
- Zoom Out
- Zoom In

For Dummies: Bestselling Book Series for Beginners

Final Cut Pro® HD
For Dummies®

Editing Commands

Command	Keystroke Combination
Mark in point	I
Mark out point	O
Clear in and out points	Option+X
Place marker	M
Delete marker	⌘+~
Mark clip	X
Select edit point	V
Insert edit (from Viewer)	F9
Overwrite edit (from Viewer)	F10
Fit to fill (from Viewer)	Shift+F11
Superimpose (from Viewer)	F12
Add edit	Control+V
Lift edit	Delete
Ripple delete	Shift+Delete
Make subclip (from Viewer)	⌘+U
Match frame	F
Snapping On/Off	N
Clip links On/Off	⌘+L
Default video transition	⌘+T
Set clip speed	⌘+J
Render selection	⌘+R
Sequence settings	⌘+0

Navigation Controls

Command	Keystroke Combination
Play forward	Spacebar or L (repeat press for speed)
Play backward	J (repeat press for speed)
Forward one frame	Right arrow (→)
Back one frame	Left arrow (←)
Forward one second	Shift+→
Back one second	Shift+←
Next edit	' or down arrow (↓)
Previous edit	; or up arrow (↑)
Next marker	Shift+↓
Previous marker	Shift+↑
Beginning of sequence	Home
End of sequence	End or Shift+Home
Zoom in	⌘++ (Note: That's the command key and the plus key together.)
Zoom out	⌘+-

For Dummies: Bestselling Book Series for Beginners

Final Cut Pro® HD

FOR

DUMMIES®

by Helmut Kobler

WILEY

Wiley Publishing, Inc.

Final Cut Pro® HD For Dummies®

Published by
Wiley Publishing, Inc.
111 River Street
Hoboken, NJ 07030-5774
www.wiley.com

Copyright © 2004 by Wiley Publishing, Inc., Indianapolis, Indiana

Published by Wiley Publishing, Inc., Indianapolis, Indiana

Published simultaneously in Canada

For general information on our other products and services or to obtain technical support, please contact our Customer Care Department within the U.S. at 800-762-2974, outside the U.S. at 317-572-3993, or fax 317-572-4002.

Wiley also publishes its books in a variety of electronic formats. Some content that appears in print may not be available in electronic books.

Library of Congress Control Number: 2004107897

ISBN: 0-7645-7773-5

Manufactured in the United States of America

10 9 8 7 6 5 4

1B/QX/QZ/QU/IN

WILEY

About the Author

Helmut Kobler is a Los Angeles-based filmmaker who has recently finished his latest project — the sci-fi action adventure *Radius*. (You can see scenes from *Radius* in many of this book's figures.) Helmut's a confessed Mac addict (he writes many features and reviews for *MacAddict* magazine, in fact) and has been using the Mac since 1987. In a past life, he directed and produced award-winning video games for PCs and the Sony Playstation.

If you want to know more about Helmut's film *Radius* — and the 2-disc DVD that it's featured on — visit the Web site, at www.radiusmovie.com.

Dedication

For Mom, for everything.

Author's Acknowledgments

At Wiley Publishing, I'd like to thank acquisition editor Tiffany Franklin, for bringing me into this project; project editor Christopher Morris and copy editor Rebecca Whitney, for helping to hone my work to *For Dummies* standards; and technical editor Dan Brazelton, for some helpful enlightenment. And, of course, a big THANK YOU to Apple's Final Cut team, for making such a world-class product!

Publisher's Acknowledgments

We're proud of this book; please send us your comments through our online registration form located at www.dummies.com/register/.

Some of the people who helped bring this book to market include the following:

Acquisitions, Editorial, and Media Development

Project Editor: Christopher Morris

Acquisitions Editor: Tiffany Franklin

Copy Editor: Rebecca Whitney

Technical Editor: Dan Brazelton

Editorial Manager: Kevin Kirschner

Media Development Specialist: Angela Denny

Media Development Manager:
Laura VanWinkle

Media Development Supervisor:
Richard Graves

Editorial Assistant: Amanda Foxworth

Cartoons: Rich Tennant, www.the5thwave.com

Composition

Project Coordinator: Courtney MacIntyre

Layout and Graphics: Andrea Dahl, Lauren Goddard, Joyce Haughey, Michael Kruzil, Heather Ryan

Proofreaders: Laura Albert, David Faust, John Greenough, TECHBOOKS Production Services

Indexer: TECHBOOKS Production Services

Publishing and Editorial for Technology Dummies

Richard Swadley, Vice President and Executive Group Publisher

Andy Cummings, Vice President and Publisher

Mary Bednarek, Executive Editorial Director

Mary C. Corder, Editorial Director

Publishing for Consumer Dummies

Diane Graves Steele, Vice President and Publisher

Joyce Pepple, Acquisitions Director

Composition Services

Gerry Fahey, Vice President of Production Services

Debbie Stailey, Director of Composition Services

Contents at a Glance

Table of Contents

Introduction

*W*elcome to *Final Cut Pro HD For Dummies!* The Final Cut Pro digital video editing program lets you capture raw video and audio (such as dialogue, sound, and music) on your Macintosh and assemble these elements into polished productions that are ready for the Internet, a CD-ROM, a DVD, television, and even the big screen.

Thanks to Final Cut Pro's impressive features, reasonable price, and manageable hardware requirements, it has quickly become a favorite tool among many professional editors as well as a new breed of independent filmmakers who are producing their films — from start to finish — right from their desktops.

Just to be clear: You may think that this software, with a name like Final Cut Pro HD, works only with high-definition (HD) video — that is, video that is shot on special HD cameras and can be displayed only on fancy HDTV sets that are just beginning to make their way into mainstream homes. Nothing could be further from the truth! Final Cut Pro HD can work with all sorts of video formats, from digital video (DV) shot on inexpensive consumer cameras to high-end HD. But Apple chose to give Final Cut its HD tag to call attention to the fact that this software is especially adept at working with HD video, which is a hot commodity these days in many professional circles (for example, in high-end documentaries, television shows, and even some feature films).

About This Book

This book is written for two kinds of people. On one hand, it's for beginners who have no experience with Final Cut or digital video editing in general, but it's also for those who have done digital editing with another program — maybe Adobe Premiere, Avid Xpress or Media Composer, or even Apple's own iMovie — and who just need to know which button to press or which menu item to choose to get things done.

Regardless of which camp you fall into, I think that you will appreciate this book for its down-to-earth, nontechy explanations. *Final Cut Pro HD For Dummies* shows you what you're most likely to need without overwhelming you with every last nuance of each obscure feature. When you turn to a chapter or a topic heading, I tell you what's most important to know about that topic right off the bat, and then I throw in some finer details to round out your grasp of it. The result? You will be up and running with Final Cut Pro in as little time as possible.

Of course, Final Cut Pro can look a bit intimidating at first glance — when you launch the program, you're faced with lots of different windows and palettes and extensive menu choices — but don't let that complicated exterior throw you. Using Final Cut Pro is like driving a car: Despite all the sophisticated gadgets (environmental systems, GPS locators, night vision, and entertainment centers, for example) that are built into cars these days, all you really need in order to go anywhere is the gas, brake, and steering wheel. And so it goes with Final Cut Pro: Despite all its features, you can start editing very quickly by using just a few simple tools. (Just 20 to 30 minutes with this book should get you to this point.) After that, you will have some confidence and can add to your skills at your own pace.

Speaking of adding skills, the following items summarize some of the ground that I cover here. By the end of this book, you will know how to

- Equip your Macintosh so that it runs Final Cut Pro smoothly.

- Bring in media clips (pieces of video, audio, and still pictures) from different sources, such as videotape, a microphone, a music CD, or QuickTime media files. This media is the raw material you use to build your productions.

- Organize your media clips so that you can find them quickly and easily.

- Arrange your video clips in time so that they tell the story you want to tell.

- Add multiple audio tracks for dialogue, music, and sound effects.

- Add animated, stylized text for captions, opening titles, and closing credits.

- Color-correct video to look its best.

- Remove scratches, pops, and other noise from audio.

- Use powerful filters to stylize the look of your video as well as the sound of your audio.

- "Composite" different video clips to create montages or special effects (for example, place an actor shot against a blue screen in an entirely different setting).

- Create a polished, professional-sounding soundtrack for your final project.

- Record your final movie to videotape or save it as a QuickTime file (for DVD, CD-ROM, or Internet distribution).

In other words, you can be a movie-making machine in no time!

How to Use This Book

I don't expect you to read this book from cover to cover. For starters, you probably don't have the time to read 400-plus pages, and even if you did, you would surely suffer from information overload!

Instead, I recommend this approach: Think about what you want to do with Final Cut Pro, and then use this book to fill in any know-how you're missing. If you're completely new to digital video editing (or editing in general), you should read closely from Chapter 1 and keep going until you have your bearings. On the other hand, if you have digital editing experience, you're likely to skip around, grabbing whatever you need and then moving on.

The point is, conform this book to your style of learning and your level of expertise. I wrote it with that kind of flexibility in mind so that you can get the most out of it with the least amount of effort.

One more thing: I recommend picking up this book occasionally and browsing through it for nothing in particular. You may be surprised at how much useful info you can pick up just by randomly skimming headings and flipping through pages!

Foolish Assumptions

I made some (possibly foolish) assumptions about you as I wrote this book. I assume that you either don't have video editing experience or that your experience is with a program other than Final Cut Pro. (Maybe you have done some editing with other programs, such as Adobe Premiere or Apple's easy iMovie.) Either way, you'll feel right at home here.

I also assume that you're working with the latest version of Final Cut — the HD variation. If you have the slightly older version (4.x), you can download a free update to Final Cut Pro HD by visiting the Apple Final Cut site, at www. www.apple.com/finalcutpro.

Finally, I assume that you have mastered the basics of using a Mac outfitted with the OS X operating system. Your expertise should include opening and saving files in the Mac standard dialog boxes and navigating your hard drive files with the Mac Finder, for example — pretty straightforward stuff.

How This Book Is Organized

This book is organized to follow the basic workflow you use while editing. Part I gives you a bird's-eye view of the entire editing process so that you understand each step you take to bring your projects over the finish line. Part II shows you how to import and organize the video and audio media your projects will use, and Part III shows you how to edit all that media into the story you want to tell. Part IV shows you how to add to your project all sorts of polish and pizzazz — such as titles, transitions, custom music, and special effects — and Part V covers your options for saving your final movie to either tape or digital video files. Finally, Part VI, the Part of Tens, offers tips on becoming a better Final Cut editor.

 You'll find bonus chapters for this book at the *For Dummies* Web site, which you can reach at www.dummies.com/go/finalcuthd. This bonus material touches on a collection of Final Cut Pro topics that aren't required reading but that can make your editing work much easier in the long run.

The following sections take a closer look at each part of this book.

Part I: First Things First

Part I is a quick introduction to the world of Final Cut Pro and digital video in general. I explain how Final Cut Pro can help you make movies, commercials, documentaries, and all sorts of other video content, and I briefly cover what's new in Final Cut Pro HD. I also take you step by step through the Final Cut workflow and give you a quick tour of its interface. Next, I help you get up and running for the first time: I cover hardware requirements, show you how to connect all your hardware components, advise you on locking in your general settings, and show you how to create and manage Final Cut Pro document files, called *projects*. Finally, I explain this brave new world called HD (high definition), which Final Cut Pro HD is designed to bring to your desktop. HD video is the most exciting thing to happen to film and videomaking since digital editing was invented, and I give you a crash course in everything you need to know about working in HD (if you ever choose to take the plunge!).

Part II: Importing and Organizing Your Media

Part II shows you how to capture, import, and organize all the media you want to use in your Final Cut projects (that is, video, dialogue, music, sound effects, still pictures, titles, and more). I show you how to capture (some say *digitize*) media from videotape by using a digital video (DV) camera or deck that you have connected to your Mac. I also show you how to bring media into Final Cut that's from sources other than videotape — video or audio files that are already on your hard drive, songs from a music CD, and graphics from Photoshop, for example.

Finally, I show you how to name, annotate, and organize all these different media clips in the Final Cut Browser window (the central repository for all your media) so that you can easily find them when you need them.

Part III: Editing Your Media

Part III is where the rubber meets the road; it shows you how to arrange all your project media in time so that it tells the story you want to tell. I start with the basics of editing video and audio — that is, how to move clips to the Final Cut Timeline and then how to resize those clips, cut them, or move them in time. I cover lots of ground here, but by the time you finish Chapter 7, you will be able to edit most meat-and-potatoes projects. Later in Part III, I round out your new skills and give you finer control over the Timeline — the heart of your editing universe — and I tackle the more advanced editing features of Final Cut Pro. You don't need to know these advanced topics to accomplish most editing tasks, but they can ultimately give you much more control over your work.

Part IV: Adding Pizzazz

Knowing how to edit media clips is only half the fun in Final Cut Pro. The software offers tons of other tools that let you add polish and pizzazz to your projects. In Part IV, I show you how to use *video transitions* — a neat feature that lets you smoothly blend one video clip into another. I tackle how to use the new Final Cut Pro LiveType program to create the kind of slick, animated title effects you see in hip commercials. I cover the program's audio mixing tools, which let you quickly set the volume levels for all your audio tracks so that all your dialogue, sound, and music blend nicely. I explore the new Final Cut Pro Soundtrack program, showing you how to build a custom soundtrack from a huge library of prerecorded loops (little pieces of music that can be repeated — or "looped" — over and over again). I cover the vast array of Final Cut Pro video filters, which let you stylize and correct off-colors in your video. Finally, I go over some handy compositing skills so that you can animate and blend video clips (like the stylish image montages you see at the beginning of TV news shows).

Part V: Outputting Your Masterpiece

After you're finished editing and adding extra pizzazz, you're ready for Part V, which focuses on outputting your movie to its final media destination. I have all your bases covered, showing you how to record your finished masterpiece to videotape (for tape duplication or broadcast) and how to use the new Final Cut Compressor program to save your finished movie to a QuickTime digital file that's custom-encoded for lots of different digital destinations, from DVDs and CDs to the Internet.

Part VI: The Part of Tens

What's a *For Dummies* book without the Part of Tens? In this part, I offer tips for managing projects (especially long ones) in Final Cut Pro so that you don't get overwhelmed by all the media clips you have to work with. Finally, I serve up some simple things you can do to become a more capable Final Cut Pro editor, from honing your creative and technical know-how to upgrading your current Mac setup.

Remember that you'll find three bonus chapters on the *For Dummies* Web site, at www.dummies.com/go/finalcuthd. These chapters tackle some Final Cut Pro topics that you don't necessarily need to master, but that can make life much easier. For example, I explore the finer details of the Final Cut Pro rendering engine, which is helpful if your project calls for adding special effects and filters to your video and audio. I also show you how to customize the Final Cut interface to your liking (arranging windows, creating custom button collections, and changing keyboard commands to suit your style). Finally, I show you how to consolidate your finished projects so that you can painlessly remove unused media from your hard drives (old media can take up lots of valuable space!) and save your important media clips.

Icons Used in This Book

The Tip icon provides extra information for a specific purpose. Tips can save you time and effort, so they're worth checking out.

Always read text marked with the Warning icon: This icon emphasizes that dire consequences are ahead for the unwary.

This icon flags information and techniques that are a bit more techy than other areas of the book. The information here can be interesting and helpful, but you don't need to understand it to use the information in the book.

This icon, a sticky note of sorts, highlights information that's worth committing to memory.

Contacting the Author

If you want to get in touch with me — to say hello or offer feedback — feel free to drop me an e-mail. You can reach me at director@k2films.com.

Part I
First Things First

In this part . . .

Part I is a quick introduction to the world of Final Cut Pro and digital video in general. I explain how Final Cut can help you make movies, commercials, documentaries, and all sorts of other video content, and I describe what's new in Final Cut Pro 4 and HD. I take you step by step through the Final Cut workflow and give you a tour of the Final Cut interface. I discuss hardware and software requirements and how they affect the quality of the video you can capture and record again. I show you how to connect all your major hardware components, give you an overview of the numerous Final Cut settings, and show you how to manage Final Cut document files (called projects). Finally, I introduce you to the exciting world of HD video — chances are, you won't be editing in HD yourself, but like many of us, you may find yourself daydreaming about its possibilities!

Chapter 1

Introducing Final Cut Pro

*I*magine for a moment: You're a big-time director on the set of your latest movie. You have just called your last "Cut!," the A-list actors have gone back to their mansions, and the crew is dismantling the million-dollar sets. You lean back in your director's chair, close your eyes, and breathe a deep sigh of relief, knowing that the film is finally finished. You can, at last, relax.

Yeah, right! In fact, this show is *far* from over. Although you may have some amazing footage, the fat lady won't sing until you have edited it all into a polished film. Enter Final Cut Pro.

Understanding the Purpose of Editing

Editing video or film is a bit like writing. When you write (or when *I* write, at least), you start by putting all your ideas on paper — good or bad — so that you can see what you're working with. Then, you arrange the *best* ideas in a logical order so that they say what you mean, as clearly and efficiently as possible.

It works the same way when you're editing digital video. First, you scrutinize all the footage you shot on set (usually, a lot). Slowly, you figure out which shots to keep and which ones to send to the proverbial cutting-room floor. You may remove a shot for any number of reasons: an actor's performance, technical problems, or the fact that you can see a crew member's foot in the frame. Next, you arrange your "keeper" shots, one by one, so that they begin to tell a story, and you bring in your dialogue, music, and sound effects to make the project complete.

In this book, I call your footage *video,* whether you originally shot it on film or videotape. This term keeps things simple because digital footage is generally treated the same after it's in Final Cut, regardless of its origins. (In a few cases, footage originally shot on film has some distinctions, but I note them when appropriate.)

Exploring the Capabilities of Final Cut Pro

Final Cut lets you do all this editing work on your Mac. To be a little more specific, when you're "behind the wheel" with Final Cut, you can do the following:

- **Capture:** Capture video or audio media from digital videocameras and video decks, CDs, microphones, and existing digital files onto your hard drive. (Let me say it again: Don't let the name Final Cut Pro HD fool you; sure, Final Cut works great with HD, or high-definition, video, but it's still just as adept with standard def video — the kind of video displayed on most televisions today, and captured by nearly all video cameras).

- **Organize:** Organize all your media files so that you can easily find them. (A project may use hundreds of different files.)

- **Edit:** Edit your footage, which is almost as easy as cutting and pasting text in a word processor.

- **Add audio:** Add audio to your movie — whether it's dialogue, voice narration, music, or sound effects — and control the volume for each audio element.

- **Create transitions:** Create transitions, such as fades and wipes, between shots.

- **Add text titles:** Titles can range from the classic white-text-on-black title cards to animations with all sorts of pyrotechnics.

- **Add effects:** Enhance video and audio with tons of effects filters and color-correction tools.

- **Composite:** Create impressive visual montages by *compositing* (combining) multiple shots into one. This process is similar to the one in the popular Adobe After Effects program.

- **Create a final product:** Record your polished masterpiece to videotape or export it to digital files destined for DVD, CD-ROM, or the Web.

Appreciating nondestructive editing

One of the great things about Final Cut Pro is that it's a *nondestructive* editor, which means that no matter what you do to your video and audio inside the program, the original media files on your hard drive are never changed or erased (okay, almost never; see the following Tip paragraph). Suppose that you have a bunch of video files on your hard drive, and you bring them into Final Cut to edit them together. Although it may seem as though you're cutting this media into different pieces, resizing it, and even deleting it, that's not the case. When you're editing, you're really just creating and moving a bunch of digital pointers to the media on your hard drive. The pointers tell Final Cut what parts of the media you want to play in your final movie (in other words, play Clip A for three seconds and then play part of Clip C for two seconds, for example). Thanks to this approach, you can work and experiment, knowing that you aren't hurting your precious media.

With Final Cut Pro HD, you can alter or erase your original media files within the software in only *one* way, but you really have to go out of your way to do it, and safeguards prevent accidental goofs. I explain this feature — just one of the many useful things Media Manager can do for you — in Bonus Chapter 3, on this book's companion Web site. (For more on this Web site, refer to the Introduction.)

Final Cut Pro versus the competition

Plenty of other editing programs are available these days: Adobe Premiere, Avid Media Composer, Avid Xpress Pro, and SpeedRazor all come to mind.

What makes Final Cut Pro so special? Four things:

- ✔ **It's brimming with features:** Final Cut Pro not only delivers the big power features that sound great on the back of the box, but also gets tons of details right — the little, thoughtful things that help you work smoothly, in a way that suits your personal style.

- ✔ **You don't need a supercomputer or expensive proprietary hardware to run Final Cut Pro:** You can build your editing system around many fairly modern Mac versions (as long as yours has a G4 processor — see Chapter 2 for more info) and everyday peripherals, such as capture cards and FireWire hard drives, for example. Now, with Final Cut Pro HD, you can even edit high-definition video (usually, the realm of the most advanced and pricey editing systems) on everyday Macs (see Chapter 3 for more about Final Cut's HD capabilities).

✔ **At $1,000, Final Cut Pro is affordable:** Admittedly, many people wouldn't put the terms *affordable* and *$1,000* together, but before Final Cut Pro came along, you had to pay several thousand dollars for software that did the same thing. So, relatively speaking, $1,000 is the equivalent of a blue-light special — with the bonus that you don't have to fight off angry hordes of shoppers, because Apple has plenty of copies to go around.

✔ **Final Cut Pro is hugely important to Apple Computer:** Final Cut Pro has sold many new Macs in the past few years, and Apple thinks that it can sell many more in the years ahead. (For example, major movie studios and commercial production companies are beginning to switch to Final Cut Pro instead of sticking with the former standard, Avid.) So Apple is very serious about continually and aggressively improving this gem. Here's a case in point: Final Cut has had four major revisions in about three years. Now, that's commitment!

New in Final Cut Pro HD (and the earlier version 4)

Speaking of improvements to Final Cut, lots of great ones are in the new HD update as well as in the earlier version 4. (Officially, Final Cut Pro HD is known as version 4.5.) Some are little tweaks that polish off the editing experience, and others are big-ticket additions to version 4 and the newer HD update that make a big, big difference in the kind of work you can do. Here are some of the program's more exciting features:

✔ **FireWire HD video editing (new in version HD):** Final Cut has been able to edit HD (high-definition) video since version 3, but only with expensive, highly specialized hardware, such as HD capture cards and huge hard disk RAIDs (basically, big collections of hard drives that work together to quickly read and record the tons of data that HD has, till now, required). Final Cut Pro HD is the first version of the software that can edit DVCPRO HD, a new, exciting form of HD video. I explain this format in detail in Chapter 3. This format delivers, in a nutshell, the supersharp, high-resolution quality of HD but doesn't require the use of expensive equipment (like capture cards and elaborate RAID drives) to edit on your Mac. In fact, you could edit (with some limitations) DVCPRO HD video on mere-mortal systems, like a PowerBook or an iMac, if you want. In other words, Final Cut Pro HD brings HD to the masses.

✔ **Soundtrack music making (new in version 4):** The new, stand-alone *Soundtrack* program that's included with Final Cut lets you compose custom music for your movies using short, prerecorded musical loops (drumbeats and tons of other instrumental riffs). No musical experience required!

✔ **Hot text effects with LiveType (new in version 4):** Final Cut ships with a new application named LiveType (see Figure 1-1) that lets you animate text and apply all sorts of special effects: glows, particle effects — you name it, LiveType has it. LiveType ships with tons of predesigned animations and styles so that if you're in a hurry, you can whip up good-looking titles in minutes. If you invest a little more time, you can also customize the animations and effects to an amazing degree, creating type that is truly unique to your project.

✔ **QuickTime video compression (new in version 4):** Compressor is another stand-alone program that makes it easier to encode (that is, to compress) your Final Cut movies as QuickTime digital files. For starters, Compressor features a long list of predetermined settings that you can apply to movies, depending on the delivery medium they're destined for. (For example, Compressor has settings for encoding movies for DVDs or for downloading by 56K modems or faster DSL modems on the Internet.) These predetermined settings take much of the guesswork out of encoding your video. Also, Compressor has a fantastic batch-processing mode; it can encode your Final Cut project into lots of different formats all at once while you go down the street and get a latté.

✔ **Real-time rendering (new in version 4):** Final Cut 3 introduced real-time previews of transitions (fades, for example), color corrections, and some other special effects, saving you from having to render those effects before seeing how they looked. (*Rendering* is the process by which your Mac has to calculate how an effect should look before the effect can be played.) But this feature had some limitations:

  • Final Cut 3 could offer these real-time previews for only a handful of effects.

  • You could see those previews only on your Mac's screen, not on a TV monitor, which many editors prefer to watch.

  • When you were finally ready to record your movie to tape, you still had to render all the effects the old-fashioned way.

But with Final Cut 4, all that changed: It can give you real-time previews of *any* effect imaginable (and combinations of effects, too — even if you're editing high-end HD video, care of Final Cut's HD update). In many cases, you can also view these effects on a TV and output them to tape without rendering — it all hinges on how fast your Mac is.

✔ **Customizable interface (new in version 4):** Finally, Final Cut now gives you full control over its interface. Have you ever wished that a certain function had a keyboard shortcut or a different keyboard shortcut than the one now assigned to it? Well, that's no problem — you can now assign any Final Cut function to a keyboard shortcut of your choosing. What's more, the Final Cut main interface windows (like the Canvas, Viewer, and Timeline) now let you install custom icons that call up just about any feature in the program, saving you time from hunting for them on menus.

Figure 1-1:
The new
LiveType
application
can do
amazing
things with
text titles.

Going with the Final Cut (Work) Flow

Final Cut Pro starts to make sense when you understand how you use it from start to finish. Let me summarize its workflow in four easy steps:

1. **Capture and import all the media — that is, video, audio, and still pictures — that you want to use in your project.**

   This media can come from a camera, video deck, music CD, DVD-ROM disc, or other digital file already on your hard drive. The media shows up in the Final Cut Browser window, where you have easy access to it. Each piece of media you bring into the Browser, by the way, is called a *clip*.

2. **Move your media clips to the all-important Final Cut Timeline window.**

   You use the Timeline to place, move, and otherwise edit clips so that they tell the story you want to tell.

3. **Add pizzazz in the form of titles, transitions (such as fades, dissolves, and wipes), custom music, and more advanced special effects, such as color corrections.**

4. **Record your project to videotape or export it to a QuickTime digital file.**

   You make QuickTime digital files if you're aiming for digital distribution, such as the Internet, CD-ROM, or DVD.

It's true: Final Cut Pro brims with many windows, dialog boxes, menus, and check boxes, but all this *apparent* complexity really boils down to these four easy steps. Keep that in mind, and you can see that this isn't rocket science.

Taking a Grand Tour of the Interface

After you have gotten a grasp of the Final Cut Pro workflow, you can expand your expertise by taking a tour of its interface — namely, its toolbar and its Browser, Viewer, Canvas, and Timeline windows, as shown in Figure 1-2. Keeping track of all these elements can seem daunting, but you soon see that there's not much to them and that they do in fact work together in an intuitive way. *Trust me.*

Browser window   Viewer window   Canvas window

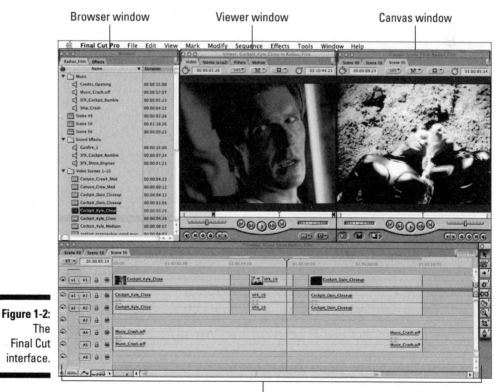

Figure 1-2:
The
Final Cut
interface.

Timeline window

By the way, you can arrange the Final Cut Pro windows differently on your screen from the way they're arranged in Figure 1-2. To get your screen to look like my screen shot, choose Window⇨Arrange⇨Standard from the menu bar at the top.

The Browser

The *Browser* is the central storage depot for all the media clips your Final Cut project uses. Just think of the Browser as a big file cabinet. When you want to work with a file (that is, a clip of media), you open the cabinet (or the Browser window) and grab whatever you need.

Although the Browser has lots of features, you really need to know only these basics: When you import a piece of media into your project (either from your hard drive or by capturing it from videotape), the media automatically appears in the Browser as a *clip*, as shown in Figure 1-3. You can also create, within the Browser window, *bins*, which store groups of related media clips and help you keep your media well organized. (Bins work much like folders on your hard drive.)

Bin icon

Figure 1-3:
You can
view items
in the
Browser in
Icon view or
in List view
(just like in
your Mac's
Finder).

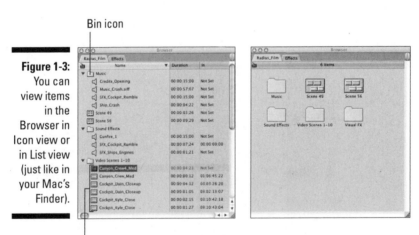

Clip icons

Besides housing clips and bins, the Browser window is the home of any sequences you create for your movie. A *sequence* is a collection of clips that you have edited together in the Final Cut Timeline window. (I get to the Timeline in a moment.) You can edit your movie into a single sequence or, for longer-running projects, such as a two-hour feature, you can create each major scene in its own sequence because shorter sequences are a bit easier to navigate and work with.

The Viewer

After you have media clips in the Browser, you can use the Viewer window to watch and listen to them before you move them to the Final Cut Timeline. To open a clip in the Viewer, just double-click its name or icon in the Browser window. Notice that the Viewer displays tabs at the top of its window and that clicking a different tab shows you different things in the Viewer. For example, the Video tab shows you a clip's video, and the tab right next to it shows you a clip's audio, as a sound waveform. The two other tabs let you control special effects and motion effects that you can apply to any clip, although this section stays focused on the basics for now.

Playing with play controls

The Viewer sports an assortment of buttons and other gizmos, but focus for now on its play controls, as shown in Figure 1-4. You can click the Play button to play your clip forward (another click pauses your clip) or use the Viewer Jog and Shuttle controls — also shown in Figure 1-4 — to move forward and in reverse at different speeds. As a clip plays, you see the Viewer playhead move across the *scrubber bar,* frame by frame. You can click anywhere in the scrubber bar to move the playhead to that point, or click and drag the playhead anywhere else.

Figure 1-4:
The Viewer lets you preview either video or audio clips (shown as waveforms) before bringing them to the Timeline.

Shuttle   Scrubber bar

Play/Pause button   Jog

The ins and outs of Ins and Outs

Besides playing clips, you use the Viewer to edit clips in a basic way by setting *In* and *Out points.* (In fact, you also use these points in other Final Cut windows, but they're "regulars" in the Viewer.) As shown in Figure 1-5, In and

Out points let you isolate only the part of a clip you're interested in before bringing it to the Timeline. Suppose that you have a great clip, except that the first four seconds suffer from a shaky camera and the last five seconds prominently feature the leg of a crew member. Because you don't want to bring the entire clip to the Timeline, you can use the Viewer to set an In point at the clip's first good frame (right after the camera shake) and an Out point at the last good frame (before the leg shows up). Then, Final Cut knows to use only the frames between those points. (I cover the basics of In and Out points in Chapters 4 and 7.)

In point   Out point

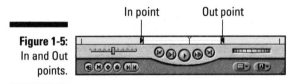

Figure 1-5:
In and Out
points.

The Timeline

The Final Cut Pro Timeline window lets you arrange *when* your media clips play in time. To better understand the Timeline, think of it as a sheet of music. Rather than place musical notes one after another on the page, you place clips of video and audio, and you tell Final Cut how long to play each one — for example, show a black screen for two seconds, play video clip A for four seconds, and then play clip B for three seconds.

So, how does the Timeline work? I talk about its many nuances throughout this book, but check out Figure 1-6 for the basics. Stretching across the top of the Timeline is a bar with notches and numbers that looks like a ruler. But those numbers aren't measurements of distance — they're measurements of time, increasing from left to right (for example, 5 seconds, 10 seconds, and 15 seconds). As you edit, you move your media clips to the Timeline (solid-colored rectangles represent clips on the Timeline) and position them under a time value. That's exactly where, in time, the clips play in your story.

One other feature to note about the Timeline is that it's divided into rows, which are called tracks. *Tracks* make it possible to stack media clips on top of each other so that they play at the same time. For example, if you want dialogue clips, music clips, and sound effects clips to all play at the same time, you place those clips at the same time value on the Timeline, but on different tracks (you can easily create new tracks yourself).

Anyway, the Timeline features tracks for video clips (the video track is labeled V1 in Figure 1-6) and tracks for audio clips (labeled A1 and A2 in the same figure). Some of your media clips come with video and audio linked together in the same clip, in which case Final Cut Pro shows the clip in the Timeline video *and* audio tracks. Other clips carry just video or audio; for example, you can see in the figure that the video clip labeled FX14 has no corresponding audio along with it.

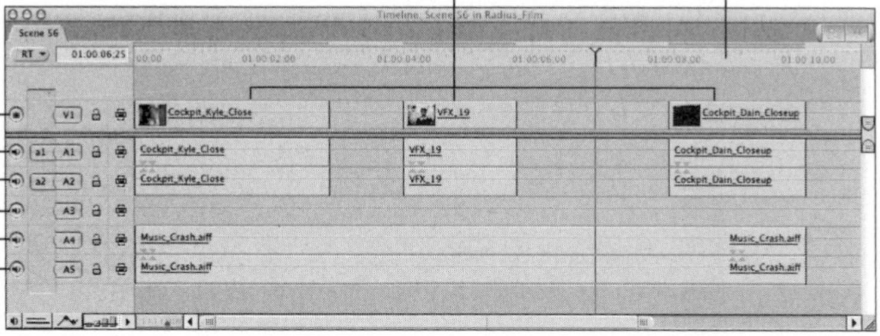

Video track   Clips on the Timeline   Ruler

Figure 1-6:
Clips on the
Timeline,
playing at
0 seconds,
4 seconds,
and 8
seconds
into this
movie-in-
progress.

Audio tracks

The Tool palette

After you move media clips to the Timeline, you can edit them — that is, make them last longer or shorter in time, cut them into smaller pieces, and rearrange them until they tell your story. Enter the Final Cut Pro Tool palette, as shown in Figure 1-7, which offers a host of tools that you can select (just click 'em) and use to edit your clips in all sorts of ways. The tool you find yourself using the most is the standard Selection tool (the plain arrow at the top of the palette), which you use to select and move media clips on the Timeline. To be honest, you can edit an entire movie with this tool alone, but the palette's other tools make that work much easier. Some of the handy ones let you select huge groups of clips at one time, cut clips in two, or quickly magnify your view of the Timeline so that you can better see what you're doing. You get to know all these tools soon enough.

When you see a little black triangle in the upper-right corner of a tool icon, more tool icons are hidden underneath it. These additional tools are all related but do slightly different things. Just click and hold down the mouse button on one of these icons, and the hidden tools pop up for you to choose.

The Canvas

After you have edited your video and audio clips on the Timeline and want to see (and hear) how they all play together, turn your attention to the Final Cut Pro Canvas window. The Canvas is where you watch your movie-in-progress as you have arranged it on the Timeline.

As you can see in Figure 1-8, the Canvas looks much like the Viewer. You *do* have the same play controls, but the Canvas has some differences. (For example, you can perform some basic edits on the Canvas rather than on the Timeline.) For now, all you need to know is that the Canvas lets you play, move forward, pause, and rewind through your Final Cut Pro movie. Sit back and enjoy your show!

The icon menu expands.

Selection tool

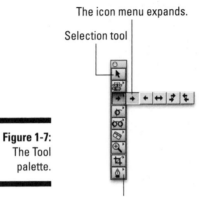

Figure 1-7:
The Tool
palette.

Click and hold over a button
to see more tool icons.

Figure 1-8:
The Canvas
window
plays
the clips
you have
arranged on
the Timeline.

Play/Pause button

Chapter 2

Getting Started

. . . .

In This Chapter

▶ Choosing the best Mac for Final Cut Pro

▶ Setting up your hardware

▶ Running Final Cut Pro for the first time

▶ Working with projects and sequences

▶ Adjusting settings and preferences

. . . .

*B*efore you can get into the fun of capturing and editing your media in Final Cut Pro, you have to get a few preliminaries out of the way. For example, you have to figure out what hardware you need to accomplish your editing goals, if you haven't already done so. You also have to configure the various Final Cut Pro settings to work with your particular hardware setup. (Tons of settings are available, but Final Cut Pro makes them fairly manageable.) Finally, you have to kick off a new project, which is where the editing magic begins.

Hardware Requirements

If you already have your Final Cut Pro system assembled, you may want to skip to the "Getting Started" section, later in this chapter. But, if you're still deciding what you need in order to build a workable editing system, or if you have questions about how you can expand the system you already have, read on.

A fully functional Final Cut Pro system needs the following two things:

✓ **A halfway-decent Mac:** For your purposes, a half-decent Mac meets the following minimum requirements:

- A 350 MHz G4 processor or any G5 (although some features, such as real-time effects and music composition, don't work unless you have a faster machine — for example, a 500 MHz PowerMac or a 667 MHz PowerBook).

- 384MB (megabytes) of RAM.

- A hard drive with between 1GB (gigabyte) and 15GB of free space for the Final Cut Pro application and all its secondary software (music loops and fancy type effects, for example).

Your Mac needs to run the OS X operating system (version 10.3.2 or better; nope — OS 9 doesn't work). Your system also needs to have a built-in FireWire port, which lets you connect video devices to your Mac.

✔ **A videocamera or playback deck:** You need a camera or deck to play existing video footage in Final Cut Pro so that the footage can be captured to your Mac's hard drive. If you want to record your final projects to videotape, this equipment is essential, too. The kind of videotape format you're working with determines the kind of video tape deck you use. Many different formats exist (HD, DigiBeta, and DV, for example), but the majority of Final Cut Pro editors work in the DV format because it provides excellent (though not perfect) quality and because DV equipment is affordable and easy to set up. You probably use DV as well (which stands for Digital Video, as you may have guessed), so that's what I assume for the rest of this chapter and throughout the entire book.

These few requirements are all that you need to get started with Final Cut Pro, but within them you have plenty of different options to consider. For example, is your ideal Mac a laptop or desktop model, and how should it be configured so that you can get your work done comfortably? (The Final Cut Pro system requirements are bare minimums. You probably want a faster CPU, more RAM, and a bigger, faster hard drive than Final Cut Pro officially requires.) Also, although all you *need* is a Mac and a camera or deck for editing, you may appreciate extra components, such as a DVD burner (to record your finished movies to DVDs) or a television monitor so that you can watch your movie in progress on a real TV rather than on the small window on your Mac.

You need a much more robust Mac if you want to edit HD video. Because HD is such a professional format, I don't assume that you're working with this kind of media; if you're considering it (or want to leave the option open), though, you need a Mac with a processor of at least 1 GHz or faster (two processors are even better) and 1GB (gigabyte) of RAM.

Selecting and Configuring a Mac

Final Cut Pro demands more hardware firepower than a word processing program or Internet browser demands, but you don't need a top-of-the-line Mac to run it. In fact, Final Cut Pro runs decently on many Macs made since 2000 (the only requirement is that the Mac has a G4 processor, also known as a CPU). The following list describes some Mac models you may want to consider, and it reviews what you need in terms of RAM, hard drives, monitors, and more:

- **PowerMac:** The stylish, upright Apple tower known as the PowerMac is the crown jewels of the Mac line. It sports the fastest CPU (a dual CPU, in some cases), the largest hard drive, the highest amount of memory, and the capability to drive two or more video displays at one time. A PowerMac also offers expansion card slots that let you add a high-end video capture card or high-speed hard disk controller (but these extras aren't necessary for editing DV video and may be wasted if you work in the DV world). If your top priority is building a high-performance editing workstation with lots of room to grow (for example, to tackle HD video), a PowerMac is the way to go. Even so, you can easily get a great deal from Final Cut Pro without going for this top-of-the-line Mac.

- **PowerBook:** The Apple PowerBook has become so good that it can handle tons of editing work without breaking a sweat. A PowerBook isn't as feature-packed as a PowerMac (for example, it has a smaller hard drive than a desktop machine and no expansion card slots), but don't underestimate the benefits of tucking your editing system in a small shoulder bag and taking it wherever you go! You can also work around the PowerBook's limitations: You can boost memory; attach a second, bigger screen; and add more storage via external FireWire hard drives (or by replacing a PowerBook's internal hard drive with a bigger one). The only thing you can't upgrade is a PowerBook's CPU, but this machine features a fast G4 processor (and maybe even a G5 by the end of 2004), which is usually fast enough.

- **iMac/eMac:** You can also build a fine DV editing system around either the iMac or a budget eMac. These systems also have fast G4 processors, and although they can't accept expansion cards or work with two monitors at once, you can easily live without such frills.

- **iBook:** An iBook has the same portable appeal as a PowerBook, but is typically much easier to afford. On the other hand, you have some tradeoffs to make: for starters, an iBook has a smaller screen than a PowerBook (it displays fewer pixels overall), which means that you see less information on-screen at any one time. For example, you see fewer clips in the Browser or Timeline window on an iBook and have to scroll those windows more often to see all their contents. This limitation isn't a deal killer, and I have done plenty of editing on iBook screens and had little difficulty, but a PowerBook screen is more comfortable nonetheless. What's more, you can't attach external monitors to an iBook (like the 23-inch Apple Cinema Display flat screen), giving yourself more screen real estate, which is a nice option that the PowerBook offers. Finally, an iBook has a G4 CPU that runs considerably slower than a PowerBook CPU. It's still fast enough to handle basic editing comfortably, but if you plan to create lots of effects in your editing, be prepared to wait a little longer for your iBook to crunch all the numbers that those effects require. Still, for bargain-basement editing, an iBook is a great little deal.

CPU speed

The brain of your Mac is its *central processing unit* (or *CPU*), and a CPU's speed is typically measured in megahertz (MHz) or gigahertz (GHz); 1 GHz is roughly 1,000 MHz. The faster your Mac's CPU, the faster Final Cut Pro runs, but how fast is fast enough for your purposes? The answer depends on the kind of editing work you're doing.

If you're primarily doing "cuts-only" editing, in which most of your work is simply cutting up media clips and arranging them on the Timeline with a cross fade or other transition, even a G4 CPU running at 400 MHz or 500 MHz can do the job. (However, I don't recommend something as slow as the Apple 350 MHz requirement.) Things may certainly feel peppier on a faster machine — a 700 MHz or 800 MHz iMac with a G4, for example — but the difference doesn't make or break your productivity.

On the other hand, when you do a variety of effects work in Final Cut Pro (tons of transitions, color correction, motion graphics, or compositing lots of images, for example), your Mac's CPU can make a big difference. All those effects have to be *rendered* (calculated), and how fast they're rendered depends almost entirely on the brute strength of the CPU. (Very fast Macs, like the new Apple G5 PowerMac or top-of-the-line G4 PowerBook, render previews of these kinds of effects in real-time; others may have to take a moment to render them.) Again, the same thing applies to working with HD video: You want a Mac with a CPU of at least 1 GHz (dual processors are better); and you would be better off with the newest G5 processor (which offers many other speed improvements beyond the measured, numerical speed of the CPU itself).

Memory (RAM)

I recommend that your Mac have at least 512MB of RAM to run Final Cut Pro well. (*RAM* stands for random-access memory, and it's also simply referred to as *memory.*) Technically, the software can run with only 384MB of RAM, but then you can't use the Final Cut Pro real-time rendering features or its cool Soundtrack application (which lets you score music to your picture). Also, with only 384MB of RAM, your Mac's OS X operating system frequently uses your hard drive to temporarily store data that would normally be placed in RAM (this is called *virtual memory*). While OS X writes this data to your hard drive, Final Cut Pro pauses for a moment, and this pause can get annoying.

When you run Final Cut Pro with 512MB of RAM, you see few, if any, of these pauses, and you also have enough room to keep a few other applications open at the same time (for example, e-mail and Web-browsing software).

If you want to run Final Cut Pro with other memory-hungry applications open at the same time (typically, photo or effects programs, such as Adobe Photoshop and After Effects), you need to stock your Mac with 768MB or even 1GB of RAM. These big "apps" demand lots of memory themselves, and if they're running at the same time as Final Cut Pro, you may start to see those annoying pauses again.

Disk storage for DV video

DV video can eat up a ton of hard drive space. You need about 13GB of space for every hour of stored DV video. Unless you're doing short commercials, music videos, or home movies, you probably need to add more drive space than an internal hard drive offers. Fortunately, one of the nice things about working with DV video is that you can use affordable hard drives to store it. (Working with video in other formats, such as uncompressed video captured from a DigiBeta or HD tape, demands very fast and expensive drives.) Your options come in the following two basic flavors:

✔ **An internal ATA drive:** This drive can replace your main system drive (if you're using an iMac or Mac laptop) or be added to the main system drive (in the case of a PowerMac, which can accommodate extra drives in addition to your main system drive. *Note:* The new PowerMac G5 uses a Serial ATA drive, whereas other Macs use Ultra-ATA drives. You can find cheap drives through many mail-order businesses.

✔ **An external FireWire drive:** This drive plugs into your Mac's FireWire port. Most Macs made since 2000 have them. (If yours doesn't, you can usually buy an add-on card that adds this port.)

A drive's rotational speed, measured in revolutions per minute (rpm), can affect how smoothly Final Cut Pro captures and plays back video; in other words, a slow drive may not be fast enough to capture video in real-time without missing frames (a big no-no) or to play all the frames in a clip smoothly. A drive that's rated at 4200 rpm is pretty slow (these drives are standard in Mac laptops), and a couple of years ago, I would have said to avoid them at all costs. Still, newer 4200-rpm models have improved and are adequate, though not great, for video work. You may still encounter dropped frames occasionally, especially when Final Cut Pro tries to play back real-time renderings of video effects.

To be safe, I recommend using drives that run at least at 5400 rpm; 7200 rpm is ideal, but if you're buying an internal drive for a laptop or one for a small, portable FireWire case, 5400 rpm is a pretty safe bet as well.

If your Mac has a FireWire 800 port (a next-generation version of the original FireWire port, which Apple now calls FireWire 400), you can get FireWire drives that transfer data to and from your Mac twice as fast as original FireWire drives. I talk more about FireWire 800 issues in a moment.

When you're in the thick of editing, you can often give your hard drive quite a workout by saving and deleting media files. This data is written on a spinning magnetic disk inside your hard drive, and over time the disk's surface starts to resemble a patchwork of areas that contain data and nondata areas. At this point, your drive is said to be *fragmented.* The result of this fragmentation is that when your hard drive reads or writes data, it has to work harder to find data or to find room to store data. This searching slows drive performance significantly and can lead to missing frames when recording or reading data. To counter this tendency, you can *defragment* your drive by using software such as Norton Utilities, which is available from retail stores or online at www.symantec.com.

The official documentation for Final Cut Pro recommends not capturing your audio and, particularly, video to the hard drive where you installed the operating system and software applications (also known as your *boot drive*). That means having two hard drives to work with — one for your operating system, applications, and documents and the other for your captured media files. Otherwise, using only one hard drive can fragment the drive more quickly and lead to other minor headaches, so you may want to factor this advice in while you decide how much hard drive space you need. On the other hand, I have created plenty of DV video projects while capturing video to my main system drive (the boot drive) and had no problems. So, you may want to take Apple's advice with a grain of salt.

Monitors and LCDs

When you're running Final Cut Pro, the most important factor regarding a monitor or LCD screen is not its physical size, but, rather, its pixel resolution. This isn't to say that a physically bigger screen isn't easier on your eyes (it is), but the display's resolution determines how much information you can see on-screen at the same time (the more pixels, the better). For example, the resolution determines how many media clips you can see on the Timeline or in the Browser without scrolling.

The lowest screen resolution that works with Final Cut Pro is 1024 × 768 pixels, which is what you get with most 15-inch monitors (like those found on many iMacs) and the LCD screens on iBooks. Although this resolution isn't exactly spacious, it's workable, especially if you learn to use the Final Cut Pro keyboard commands to quickly call up overlapping windows or to zoom in and out of the Timeline.

Any screen resolution higher than 1024×768 is gravy. I recommend a 19- or 20-inch monitor running at 1280×1024 resolution or one of the Apple Cinema Display LCD screens, which run wide-screen as high as 1920×1200 resolution (and will duly impress family, friends, and neighbors). But some editors prefer to use two monitors at the same time. (One monitor usually displays the Final Cut Pro Timeline, Viewer, and Canvas windows while the other monitor hosts the Browser and secondary windows, such as the Tool Bench, Favorites, or Effects.) To use two monitors, you need to install two video cards in your Macintosh or use a video card that offers output for two simultaneous displays (some PowerMacs ship with these 2-for-1 cards installed). A PowerBook also lets you attach a second display to use in addition to its LCD screen.

Not all monitors and LCD screens are created equal! Different models from different manufacturers vary in sharpness and brightness, which can make a difference when you're staring at the small text in Final Cut Pro all day long. The Apple Cinema Display has a good reputation, but it can be a bit more expensive than other models, so if you're considering a non-Apple brand, you may want to use an online search engine, such as Google, to find reviews and feedback on the model you're considering.

Doing DV? You need a FireWire port

If your Mac meets the other Final Cut specifications, make sure that it has a FireWire port. The *FireWire* interface is used to hook your Mac to a DV camera or deck so that you can capture video and audio from DV tape or record your finished movies to tape. You can also use a FireWire port to hook up fast and affordable hard drives for storing DV video, so it's very important!

All new Macs feature one or two FireWire ports (you can easily get by with one port because FireWire devices can daisy-chain from one to another into your Mac's single port), and many models have featured FireWire since 1999 or 2000.

Apple is now including a next-generation FireWire port, called FireWire 800, in some of its machines (in addition to a standard FireWire 400 port). This new FireWire port can transfer data between your Mac and other devices (like new FireWire 800 hard drives) two times faster than the original FireWire standard (now called FireWire 400). That's great news, but FireWire 800 isn't essential for editing DV video in Final Cut Pro. FireWire 800 is helpful for drives designed to handle uncompressed video (good news for high-end professional work), but the Mac's original FireWire 400 port is fast enough for hard drives that capture and play back DV video. And, DV camera makers are also likely to stay with the FireWire 400 interface because it suits their needs as well.

DV videocameras and playback decks

Just for the record: You don't *have* to connect a DV camera or deck to your Mac to run Final Cut Pro. I just assume that you need one to capture video for your project and later record it to tape. If this isn't the case (for example, if someone else has given you an external FireWire drive with digital video files already on it), you're free to load Final Cut Pro without any DV equipment attached.

The easiest way to capture video into Final Cut Pro (and to record it to tape) is to simply use any DV videocamera as a playback or recording deck, because these cameras have all that functionality built in. The second option is to buy a dedicated DV deck, which works just like a VHS VCR, except that it uses the same DV tapes that DV cameras do. (If you're taking this route, check out the Sony offerings.)

Why go for a dedicated deck if your camera can fill that role anyway? Well, your camera isn't built to the same industrial-strength standards as a dedicated deck is, so if you're going to play, capture, and record hundreds of hours of footage, you may wear out the camera (that's why I always buy those extended warranties for my DV cameras). Also, if you work with other people, you never know whether someone may be using your camera out in the field when you need it to pinch-hit as a deck. On the other hand, DV decks can be pretty pricey, and most people find that using their DV camera as a deck is just fine.

Either way, getting a DV camera or deck working with your Mac is quick and painless. All you need is a single FireWire cable (typically, a 6-pin to 4-pin connector, which costs about $15 at computer or electronics stores) to hook the camera or deck to your Mac's FireWire port. Final Cut Pro senses that the camera or deck is connected and knows how to control it without further ado.

Final Cut Pro may not work perfectly with every model and brand of DV equipment. For example, a particular camera may not always respond precisely when Final Cut Pro tries to control its rewind and fast-forward functions. Although these kind of annoyances are rare, you can sidestep them by making sure that your DV camera or deck is fully supported by Final Cut Pro. Apple keeps a list of such supported equipment online, at `www.apple.com/finalcutpro/qualification.html`.

Other optional hardware

Although your Final Cut Pro system doesn't require the following goodies, you may want to add them, depending on your needs and tastes:

✔ **Television monitor:** Adding a television to your Final Cut Pro setup is a good idea if you're creating movies to be seen on a TV rather than on a computer display. You can see your media clips and edited movies on TV as you work, be able to do more accurate color correction, and notice subtle problems in your video that are tougher to spot in the small video window on your Mac. Any TV with either RCA (also known as *composite*) or S-Video input jacks works fine. To find out how to set up your TV with Final Cut Pro, see the section "Connecting and preparing all your hardware," later in this chapter.

✔ **DVD burner and authoring software:** One of the coolest aspects of digital media is that you can record your movies to DVDs and then play them in most consumer DVD players. If this news floats your boat (and how could it not?), you need a DVD-R drive. If you have a newish Mac, you may already have one of these drives built in (Apple calls its DVD-R drive a SuperDrive and includes it with many newer machines), along with the free iDVD software to author your DVDs with fancy menus and other features.

If your Mac doesn't come equipped with a DVD-R drive, you can get an add-on drive from companies such as LaCie or FireWire Direct, but you have to use the bundled DVD authoring software that comes with those drives (which is not as good as iDVD) or splurge for Apple's top-of-the-line DVD Studio Pro, which now costs $499.

✔ **Keychain memory or CD-R(W):** To be safe, back up your Final Cut Pro project files (not your media files — just the project files that describe what to do with those files) somewhere other than on your hard drive. You can burn projects to a CD if you have a CD-RW drive (most Macs do), but another convenient option is to buy some *keychain* memory, which is basically a memory chip attached to a FireWire or USB connector (it can fit in your pocket or on a keychain). Just plug the memory into your Mac's port, copy files to it, and store the chip in a safe place.

✔ **Final Cut Pro keyboard:** Post-Op sells a keyboard with Final Cut Pro functions printed directly on its respective keys (obviously, in small print). Some editors like working with this keyboard because it spares them from having to memorize many of the Final Cut Pro keyboard shortcuts. (Although Final Cut ships with little stickers you can put on your keys yourself — a much cheaper, though not as pretty, alternative.)

✔ **Turbocharged mouse:** You can buy a multibutton mouse (some with a built-in jog shuttle, trackball, or flywheel) and program those extra buttons to perform Final Cut Pro operations with a simple click. Using these handy devices can save lots of time when you're editing.

✔ **Speakers or headphones:** The built-in speakers on your Mac aren't good enough to play all the nuances in high-quality audio (or highlight any problems that should be corrected). To upgrade your audio, you have a few options. If you're hooking up a TV to your Mac, choose a TV with stereo speakers. Otherwise, connect a pair of speakers to your Mac or invest in a high-quality pair of headphones.

Getting Started

After you have installed the Final Cut Pro software on your hard drive, you need to take a few steps to configure Final Cut Pro to work with your hardware and the video format you plan to use.

Because the majority of Final Cut Pro editors work in the DV realm, I focus on setting up your system to work with DV equipment and DV video. If your Final Cut Pro system is based on another format (for example, if you're using a third-party capture card hooked to an analog Beta SP deck), check out that capture card's documentation for steps to connect everything and to establish working settings for Final Cut Pro.

Connecting and preparing all your hardware

Before loading Final Cut Pro, you need to connect and prep all your hardware. ***Note:*** The following steps work whether you're using a DV camera or DV playback deck, but I assume that you're using a DV camera:

1. **Connect your DV camera to the FireWire port on your Mac, using a FireWire cable (most likely, a 6-pin to 4-pin variety).**

   The Mac may have more than one FireWire 400 port, but either works fine. (Use a FireWire 400 port, even if your Mac also has FireWire 800.)

2. **Turn your camera on, and make sure that it's in Play mode.**

   Your camera can either record or play back video. You want it to be in playback mode, so look for a switch or dial on the camera that says *VCR, VTR,* or *Play,* and make sure that the switch is enabled.

3. **Connect and turn on your FireWire hard drive, if you have one.**

   If you want to use an external FireWire hard drive with Final Cut Pro, turn it on as well, and make sure that it's hooked to a FireWire port on your Mac. If your Mac has only one FireWire port (which the DV camera requires), connect your disk drive to that single port and then connect the camera to the drive's second available FireWire port. (Most disk drives feature two FireWire ports so that you can link multiple FireWire devices in a chain.)

You may also want to add a television to your setup so that you can watch your Final Cut Pro video on a TV screen rather than on the smaller window on your Mac. How you achieve this depends on your DV camera and your TV, so I can't give you step-by-step instructions. However, some general guidance is as follows:

1. **Identify the camera's Video/Audio Out connector.**

   Most DV cameras have a Video/Audio Out connector, which sends the video and audio signal in your camera to an attached device (like a TV). Depending on the brand and model of the camera, this connector consists of a single connector or three connectors (one for video and two for stereo audio, like your stereo system offers).

2. **Identify the TV's Video/Audio In connector.**

   Most TVs have Video/Audio In connectors — usually, on the rear of the TV — that can receive a video or audio signal from an attached device (like a VCR or videocamera). On TVs, you usually find three connectors for each kind of device you can attach (one connector for video and two for stereo audio).

3. **Use cables to connect the Video/Audio Out connector on your camera to the Video/Audio In connector on your TV.**

   The type of cables you use depends on the kind of connectors your camera and TV have. The most common cables are called RCA (also known as *composite*) cables. Many DV cameras include the necessary cables to connect a TV and your DV camera, or you can buy these cables at an electronics store.

   You don't have to connect your DV camera directly to a TV. Instead, if you already have a VHS VCR (which is probably already hooked up to your TV), you can connect your camera to the VCR so that the video or audio signal goes through the VCR to the TV. Another benefit of this setup is that you can record your Final Cut Pro movies to your VHS VCR. (See Chapter 17 for more details.) If you opt for this setup, look on your VCR for the Video/Audio In and Out connectors, and connect the VCR to your camera.

4. **Switch your TV to Video mode.**

   Try this last step after you have launched Final Cut Pro and can display some video in either the Viewer or Canvas window. To see Final Cut Pro video on your TV, you need to switch your TV to one of its video channels (which show signals coming from the TV's Video In jacks rather than from its antenna or cable connection). How you do this depends on your television setup (and whether you have connected the TV to a VCR, cable box, or some other device). Look on your TV or remote control for a button that says TV/Video, and press that button. If you see a video clip displayed in the Viewer or Canvas windows, you're in business. If not, try pressing the button repeatedly, or press your Channel Up and Down buttons after pressing Video. If this strategy doesn't work, check out your TV manual to see how to switch to the TV's video input channels. Also, make sure that you have your DV camera and TV connected properly.

If your TV doesn't display video after you load Final Cut, try choosing View⇨ External Video⇨All Frames, and make sure that the All Frames option is checked. If it is, and you still get no video, try choosing View⇨Refresh A/V Devices. Still nothing? Finally, try View⇨Video Playback, and make sure the option "Apple FireWire NTSC" is selected. If none of these options works, make sure that your camera is connected properly to your TV and Mac.

Launching Final Cut Pro

With your hardware ready and raring to go, use the Mac's Finder to find the Final Cut Pro HD application on your hard drive (it should be in the Applications folder) and double-click the Final Cut Pro HD application icon. Final Cut Pro begins to load all sorts of files and modules, but if you're running it for the first time, the software prompts you for a few important settings.

The quickest way to load Final Cut is to add its icon to your Mac's Dock (as shown in Figure 2-1), which lets you launch the software by simply clicking its icon in the Dock. From the Mac's Finder, just drag the Final Cut Pro HD application icon from its window to the Dock to add it there. (Don't worry: You're not moving or affecting the original application file on your hard drive.) If you ever want to remove Final Cut from the Dock, just drag its icon outside the Dock again and the icon disappears.

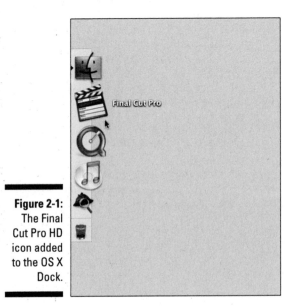

Figure 2-1:
The Final
Cut Pro HD
icon added
to the OS X
Dock.

Choosing an initial setup

When Final Cut Pro loads for the first time, it opens a Choose Setup dialog box, as shown in Figure 2-2, which prompts you for two important settings: Easy Setup and Primary Scratch Disk. The following sections explain what each setting means to you. (***Remember:*** These settings aren't carved in stone — you can easily change them later.)

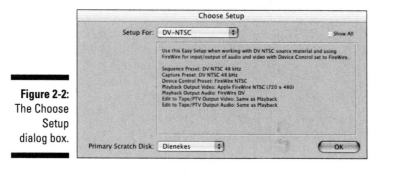

Choose Setup

Setup For: DV-NTSC ▢ ☐ Show All

Use this Easy Setup when working with DV NTSC source material and using FireWire for input/output of audio and video with Device Control set to FireWire.

Sequence Preset: DV NTSC 48 kHz
Capture Preset: DV NTSC 48 kHz
Device Control Preset: FireWire NTSC
Playback Output Video: Apple FireWire NTSC (720 x 480)
Playback Output Audio: FireWire DV
Edit to Tape/PTV Output Video: Same as Playback
Edit to Tape/PTV Output Audio: Same as Playback

Primary Scratch Disk: Dienekes ▢ (OK)

Figure 2-2:
The Choose
Setup
dialog box.

Easy Setup

An *Easy Setup* is a collection of settings that Final Cut Pro applies to your movies, based on the media format you want to work with and the kind of hardware you have. You can tweak settings individually (I show you how, later in this chapter), but, for now, start by choosing one of the following four common Easy Setups from the Setup For pop-up menu:

- ✔ **DV-NTSC:** Use this setting if you want to capture and edit video in the DV format, using video equipment (that is, camera, deck, and television) based on the NTSC television signal. If you're working with equipment bought in North America, this is your option.

- ✔ **DV-PAL:** Use this setting to capture and edit video in the DV format, using equipment based on the PAL TV signal (a European format).

- ✔ **DVCPRO HD:** Use one of these Easy Setups if your project will use media in the DVCPRO HD format. As you can see, DVCPRO HD comes in different flavors, so make sure to pick the one that matches your particular requirements. See Chapter 3 for more about DVCPRO HD.

- ✔ **OfflineRT-NTSC:** This option still uses a DV camera or deck (NTSC-compatible) to capture video on a DV tape, but Final Cut Pro further compresses the video by using Photo JPEG technology. The result is that your compressed media takes only one-tenth the disk space of standard DV video (making the most of cramped hard drives, particularly on laptops). Although the Photo JPEG image quality doesn't match that of DV (because of more compression artifacts and less frame resolution), it's often good enough for rough-editing purposes. When you're ready to record your final project to tape or disk, you want to use the higher-quality DV format, of course. That's no problem: Just switch the Final Cut Pro Easy Setup back to DV-NTSC, recapture only the media that your movie uses (Final Cut Pro knows exactly where to find that media on your DV source tapes), and then record your finished movie with the better-looking DV footage. You can find out more about using Offline RT in Bonus Chapter 3 on the *For Dummies* Web site (see this book's Introduction for the site's URL address).

✔ **OfflineRT-PAL:** This option is just like OfflineRT-NTSC, except that it's for European equipment based on the PAL TV signal.

If you don't know which of the many Final Cut Pro setups to choose, the two can't-go-wrong defaults are DV-NTSC (if you're working with NTSC gear) and DV-PAL.

If you're using a different media format than DV (for example, DVCPRO HD or uncompressed standard-definition video being captured from a high-end deck), or if you have some special requirements for your DV footage (perhaps a film-like frame rate of 24 frames per second), you should use a different Easy Setup. In the Easy Setup dialog box, select the Show All check box, and you see many more options in the Setup For pop-up menu. If you still don't find an Easy Setup that's appropriate for your work, you have to manually tweak some settings. See the section "Adjusting Your Project and Sequence Settings," later in this chapter, and consult the manual for any special hardware you're using for hints on the settings you need.

After you choose an initial setup for Final Cut Pro, you probably never need to tweak those settings again, as long as your hardware setup and video and audio requirements don't change. But, if they do, you can easily change the settings again by choosing Final Cut Pro HD⇨Easy Setup and choosing a new option from the Setup For pop-up menu. Remember that changing the Easy Setup doesn't affect settings for movies (that is, Timeline sequences) that you have already created — only new movies.

Primary scratch disk

The *scratch disk* is the hard drive where Final Cut Pro saves all your captured video and audio (and other files, such as rendered media). If your Mac has only one hard drive (that is, your internal system drive), that drive is automatically your scratch disk. But, if you have multiple drives, you can specify which one serves as your scratch disk by choosing it from the Primary Scratch Disk pop-up menu.

You can change your scratch disk at any time by choosing Final Cut Pro HD⇨ System Settings and using the Scratch Disks tab. (See Chapter 4 for more information about setting a new scratch disk.)

When you're finished making your choices in the Choose Setup dialog box, click OK. Final Cut Pro opens a new project for you, and you're ready to get down to business.

If you don't have your video deck or camera hooked up as Final Cut Pro loads, you see a dialog box indicating that Final Cut Pro can't find the device. This isn't a big deal: If you want the device to be used at this time, just make sure that it's properly set up and click the Check Again button. But you don't need this equipment to edit video, so if you don't care whether it's turned on, just click the Continue button.

Working with Projects and Sequences

After you have established your initial setup, Final Cut Pro automatically creates a new, untitled project, which in turn includes a new, untitled Timeline sequence, as shown in Figure 2-3. In other words, you're ready to roll! Before you move forward, though, I cover a few things about projects and how to manage them.

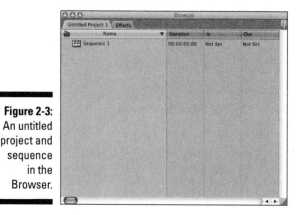

Figure 2-3: An untitled project and sequence in the Browser.

A *project* is a Final Cut Pro document file — like a Word or Photoshop document file that you create in those applications — that you can create, save, close, and open again, like any other document on your hard drive. A typical Final Cut Pro project contains the following two elements, which are unique to it:

✔ Any media clips (video, audio, and still pictures) that you capture or import into it

✔ One or more Timeline *sequences,* which are collections of the project's media clips that you have edited in the Final Cut Pro Timeline window

Generally, you create a new project for each movie or other unique, stand-alone program you're working on. For example, if you're a big-time Hollywood editor, you would have a project for each of the films on your plate. And, within those projects, you would create multiple Timeline sequences to break each movie's edited clips into smaller, more manageable pieces. For example, you may create a Timeline sequence for each major scene in a film.

Final Cut Pro lets you have multiple projects open at the same time. Each open project is represented in the Browser by a tab, and these tabs are displayed at the top of the Browser window. As you can see in Figure 2-3, each tab lists the name of each open project (or says Untitled Project, if you haven't saved the project yet).

It's a good idea to save a project immediately after you create it. It's best to get used to this now. It will save you a lot of headaches later.

Saving and autosaving projects

To save an untitled project (like the one that Final Cut Pro automatically whips up for you when you first launch the software), follow these steps:

1. **Choose File⇨Save Project As from the main menu.**

2. **In the Save dialog box (as shown in Figure 2-4), type the new project name in the Save As text box.**

Where pop-up menu   Horizontal scrollbar

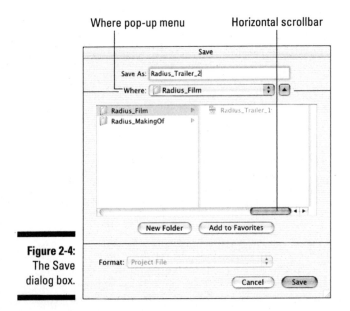

Figure 2-4:
The Save
dialog box.

3. **Select the folder to which you want to save your project.**

   Click the folders in the file selector box to see their contents. Use the horizontal scrollbar to move your view of the folders back and forth, or click the Where pop-up menu to see the current folder hierarchy that's selected.

4. **Click the Save button.**

   After you save a project, its new name appears on its tab at the top of the Browser window.

When you save a project, you automatically save all the sequences that are a part of that project. You can't save individual sequences — just projects.

After you have chosen File⇨Save Project As to save your project the first time (giving it its name), you can save the project by choosing File⇨Save Project or pressing the familiar ⌘+S. This action saves the project using the name you have already given it. If you want to save the project using a different name, again choose File⇨Save Project As.

Setting up the Autosave feature

Final Cut Pro also includes a nice Autosave feature that automatically makes a backup copy of your project, at time intervals you choose.

Imagine that you have worked on a project for an hour and Final Cut Pro suddenly crashes before you save your work manually (it has been known to happen). But, if the Autosave feature is enabled, much of your work may still be intact. You just have to load up the last version that Final Cut autosaved.

To make sure that the Autosave feature is turned on, choose Final Cut Pro HD⇨ User Preferences. Look for the Autosave Vault settings on the General tab (as shown in Figure 2-5), and make any adjustments you want. You can set how often Final Cut Pro autosaves your open projects, how many versions of an autosaved project are kept on your hard drive, and how many projects get the autosave treatment.

Final Cut Pro keeps your autosaved backups in a folder named Autosave Vault, which you can find in the Final Cut Pro Documents folder, in your Home folder's Documents folder. Within the Autosave Vault folder are subfolders for each of your projects, and within these subfolders are your backup files, in case you want to load one manually (or delete old ones that are taking up space). These backups use the same name as your original project (long filenames get shortened a bit), but they append the date and time of the autosave at the end of the filename. By default, Final Cut Pro keeps as many as 40 successive backups per project. Again, you can tweak this value via User Preferences.

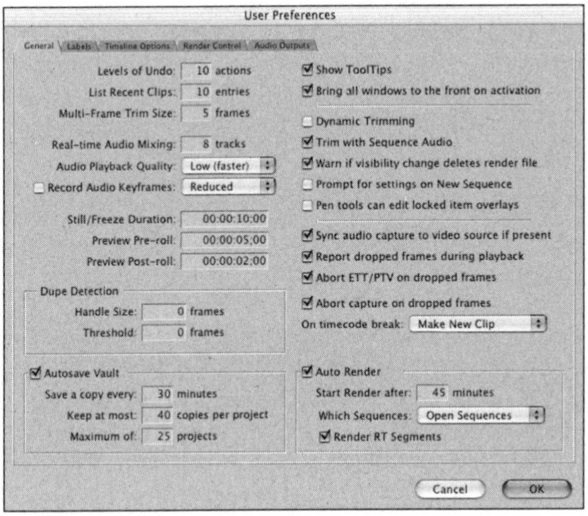

User Preferences

General | Labels | Timeline Options | Render Control | Audio Outputs

Levels of Undo: 10 actions	☑ Show ToolTips
List Recent Clips: 10 entries	☑ Bring all windows to the front on activation
Multi-Frame Trim Size: 5 frames	
	☐ Dynamic Trimming
Real-time Audio Mixing: 8 tracks	☑ Trim with Sequence Audio
Audio Playback Quality: Low (faster)	☑ Warn if visibility change deletes render file
☐ Record Audio Keyframes: Reduced	☐ Prompt for settings on New Sequence
	☐ Pen tools can edit locked item overlays
Still/Freeze Duration: 00:00:10:00	
Preview Pre-roll: 00:00:05;00	☑ Sync audio capture to video source if present
Preview Post-roll: 00:00:02;00	☑ Report dropped frames during playback
	☑ Abort ETT/PTV on dropped frames
Dupe Detection	
Handle Size: 0 frames	☑ Abort capture on dropped frames
Threshold: 0 frames	On timecode break: Make New Clip
☑ Autosave Vault	☑ Auto Render
Save a copy every: 30 minutes	Start Render after: 45 minutes
Keep at most: 40 copies per project	Which Sequences: Open Sequences
Maximum of: 25 projects	☑ Render RT Segments

Cancel   OK

Figure 2-5:
The Autosave Vault on the General tab in the User Preferences dialog box.

Managing projects

If you have experience in using other applications in the OS X operating system, managing projects in Final Cut Pro is pretty standard stuff. Here's a quick rundown of the fundamentals:

✔ **Create a new project:** To create a new project from scratch, choose — you guessed it! — File➪New Project. Final Cut Pro opens an untitled project tab in the Browser window and makes it your active project. I recommend naming and saving the project right away.

✔ **Open a project:** To open a project, use the following options:

  • Final Cut Pro remembers the last several projects you opened. You can quickly open any of them by choosing File➪Open Recent and selecting the project's name from the submenu.

  • You can open any Final Cut Pro project by choosing File➪Open. In the Choose a File dialog box (see Figure 2-6), browse your hard drive (click folders to see their contents, and use the horizontal scroll bar to move backward and forward through open folders) and double-click the project name when you see it. Final Cut Pro opens the project as a new tab in the Browser and makes it active.

  • You can also open a project from the Mac's Finder by double-clicking its icon.

✔ **Close a project:** To close a project you're no longer working on, make the project active in the Browser window (click its tab at the top of the window) and choose File➪Close Project. Before closing the project, Final Cut asks whether you want to save the current version, in case you have made any changes since the last save.

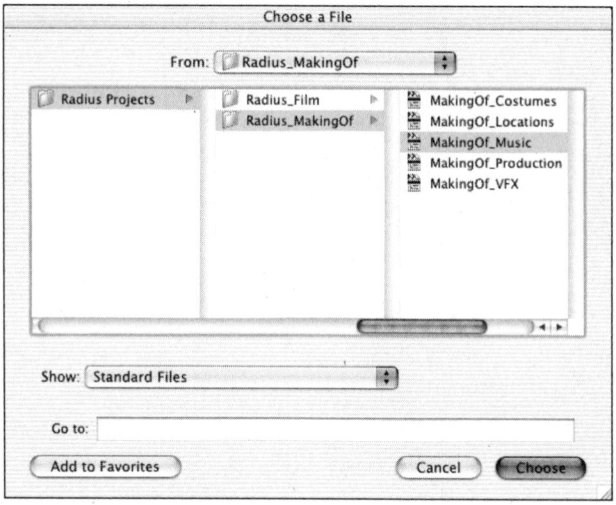

Figure 2-6:
The Choose
a File
dialog box.

> **Restoring a project:** If you want to load an autosaved version of the cur-rent project, choose File⇨Restore Project and select the autosave ver-sion you want by its date and time from the pop-up menu that appears. Final Cut loads up that autosave version as a new project, using its long, unwieldy autosave filename. If you want to continue working with this project, you may want to use the Save As command to give the project a more manageable name.

> **Reverting a project:** Choose File⇨Revert Project to load up the last ver-sion of a project that you manually saved (not the last autosave version). This feature is handy if you have made changes to a project, but decide that you want to go back to the way you had it when you last saved.

Again, you can have multiple projects open at the same time. To work with an open project, just click its tab at the top of the Browser to make it active. You see all the project's clips, bins, and sequences listed in the Browser window, as shown in Figure 2-7. (*Note:* The Effects tab is always a part of the Browser, and doesn't represent an open project.)

When you exit Final Cut Pro with open projects (that is, without closing them first), Final Cut Pro automatically opens those same projects the next time you launch the program. This feature is handy when you're working on the same project, day in and day out, but it can be downright annoying when you're finished with a project and it keeps opening each time you launch the Final Cut software. To put an end to this vicious cycle, you have two choices. Choice #1: just close a project you're finished with before clos-ing Final Cut Pro. After you close the project, it doesn't come back until you open it again. And choice #2: you can turn this entire feature off by choosing Final Cut Pro HD⇨User Preferences and deselecting the option "Open last project on application launch".

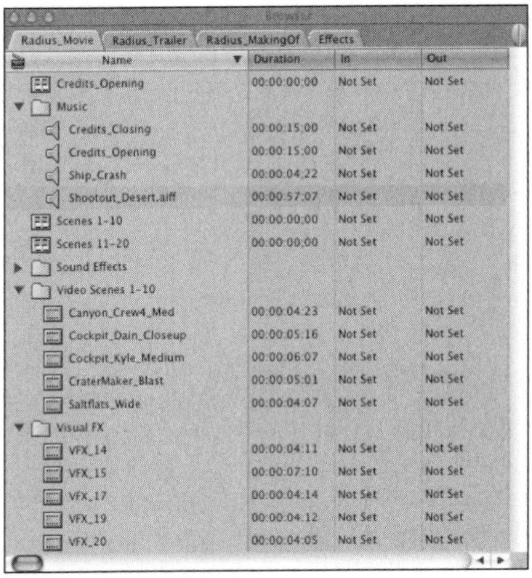

Figure 2-7: The Browser shows three open projects. Click a project tab to make the project active.

Adjusting Your Project and Sequence Settings

After you choose an initial setup for Final Cut Pro (as you did when you first loaded the program — see the section "Choosing an initial setup," earlier in this chapter), you probably never need to tweak that setup again, as long as your hardware setup and video and audio format don't change (and if you don't feel the need to tweak settings, you can skip this section because it's not necessary for getting you started). But, if these things change, the Final Cut Pro settings allow you to quickly make any adjustments you need.

Final Cut Pro offers the following items that you can change:

- **A setting:** A *setting* controls a specific feature — for example, the frame rate of a sequence, the quality of the audio that the sequence uses (32 kHz or 48 kHz, for example), or the frame size for the sequence's video (640 × 480 pixels or 720 × 480 pixels, for example).

- **A preset:** A *preset* is a group of related settings that you can apply quickly and easily, time and time again. Final Cut Pro has four *families,* or kinds, of presets. You can create your own presets within each family or choose from a long list of presets that Apple has already assembled for you. (For more about changing a preset, see the section "Creating new presets," later in this chapter.) The four preset families you can work with are as follows:

- **Sequence preset:** The settings that are contained by a Sequence preset apply to any new sequences you create in your project. (In other words, when you create a new sequence, it conforms to the settings defined in the Final Cut Pro current Sequence preset.) Settings include frame resolution (such as 720×480 pixels), frame rate and audio quality, video field dominance, and more.

- **Capture preset:** This group of settings defines how your video is captured (resolution, frame rate, and compression used, for example). For example, if you're capturing uncompressed video from a high-end DigiBeta deck, Final Cut Pro uses a different Capture preset than if you're capturing DV video from a DV camera.

- **Device Control preset:** These settings define how your video deck or camera is controlled (which protocol is used to control the hardware or how much preroll and postroll are used, for example). If you're not using some exotic video hardware, you don't have to worry about this one. If you are, you should consult the exotic hardware's manual for information on these settings.

- **Video/Audio Playback:** These settings define whether Final Cut Pro sends video and audio to an external TV or other gear that you have hooked up to your system. (***Note:*** Final Cut Pro doesn't technically call them presets, but they work just the same.)

✔ **An Easy Setup:** The last level of settings is the (presumably) familiar Easy Setup, which is just a collection of the four preset families (sequence, capture, device control, and video and audio playback). By choosing an Easy Setup, you don't have to worry about choosing individual presets. As I discuss earlier, Final Cut Pro makes four Easy Setups available to you right away, each featuring slightly different presets. (For example, the sequence preset used by the DV-PAL Easy Setup calls for a video frame size of 720×576 pixels, whereas the sequence preset used by the DV-NTSC Easy Setup uses a frame size of 720×480 pixels.)

You can change the Final Cut Pro individual presets, or you can choose a different Easy Setup (which, in turn, includes different presets). When you change either a preset or an Easy Setup, any projects or sequences you create from that point on use the settings defined by your new choice. However, any existing projects or sequences keep their original settings.

Later, as you become comfortable with Final Cut Pro, you may want to change the settings for an existing sequence. In this case, you *don't* want to change your Sequence preset because doing so affects only new sequences you create. Instead, just open the existing sequence in the Timeline window and then choose Sequence⇨Settings. From the Settings dialog box, you can adjust any sequence settings you want (they're the same settings you find in the Sequence preset). When you click OK, Final Cut Pro applies your changes to only the current active sequence on the Timeline.

Choosing a different Easy Setup

If all you want to do is change your Easy Setup, that's easy. Just choose Final Cut Pro⇨Easy Setup and choose a new option from the dialog box's pop-up menu. Select the Show All check box to see all the Easy Setups available to you.

Changing the Easy Setup doesn't affect settings for sequences you have already created — only new ones.

Choosing a different preset

If you can't find a premade Easy Setup that offers the exact settings you need, you can change one or more of the presets that Final Cut Pro is now using. You can choose from a variety of different presets for each of the preset families I discuss (in addition to any new presets you create). I show you how to create new presets in the next section.

To choose another existing preset, follow these steps:

1. **Choose Final Cut Pro HD⇨Audio/Video Settings from the main menu.**

2. **In the Audio/Video Settings dialog box (as shown in Figure 2-8), make sure that the Summary tab is selected.**

   The Summary tab contains several pop-up menus — one for each type of preset family (sequence, capture, and device control) — as well as menus for video and audio output. Below each pop-up menu is a description of the selected preset.

3. **Use the pop-up menus to choose a new preset.**

4. **Click OK to accept the new preset.**

Creating new presets

You can also create new presets with different settings that you customize by following these steps:

1. **Choose Final Cut Pro HD⇨Audio/Video Settings.**

2. **In the Audio/Video Settings box, click the tab for the kind of preset you want to create.**

   In this example, click the Sequence Presets tab.

3. **In that tab's Presets box, click an existing preset that you want to base your new preset on.**

   Figure 2-9 shows all the presets on the Sequence tab.

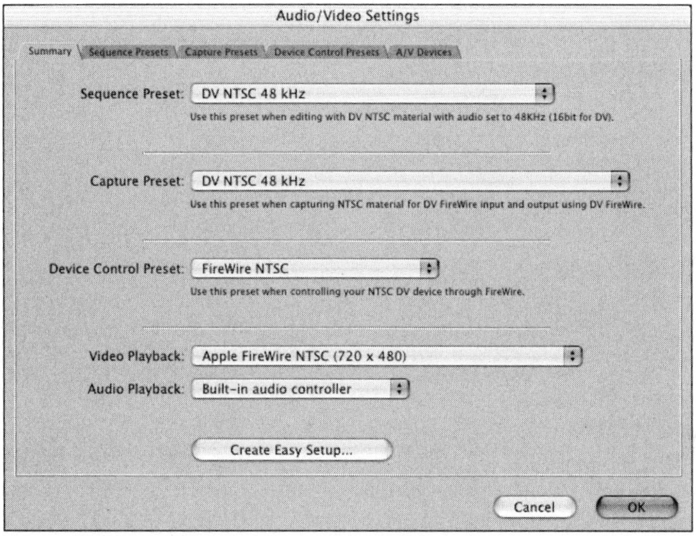

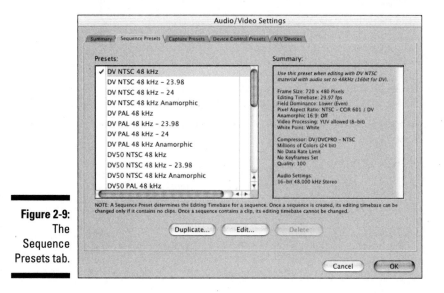

Figure 2-8:
The Summary tab in the Audio/Video Settings dialog box.

Figure 2-9:
The Sequence Presets tab.

When you click an existing preset, Final Cut Pro lists all its settings in the Summary box on the right side of the dialog box. This arrangement helps you see which preset is most like the preset you're about to create, so you have less tweaking to do.

4. Click the Duplicate button.

Final Cut Pro opens the Sequence Preset Editor dialog box, as shown in Figure 2-10.

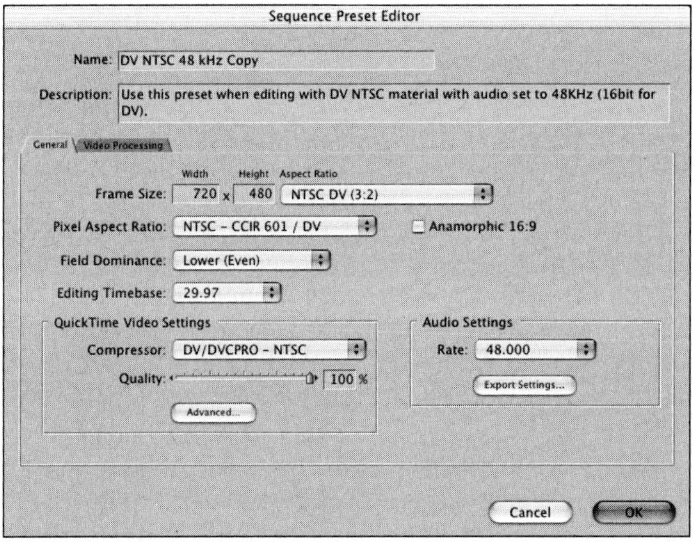

Figure 2-10:
The Sequence Preset Editor dialog box.

5. In the dialog box, type a new name for your custom preset in the Name field and adjust the settings as needed. Then click OK.

6. In the tab's Presets box (refer to Figure 2-9), click to the left of your new preset's name to select it.

That's it! You're done.

Chapter 3

All About HD (High Definition)

So, you want to know what the big fuss is about HD? Well, you've come to the right place because this chapter gives you a broad overview of this exciting new technology and how Final Cut Pro HD works with it.

Of course, the chances are that if you're reading a *For Dummies* book, you don't work much with HD, if at all; it's a professional video format used to shoot broadcast television content, and even theatrical movies, and it still requires some expensive, heavy-duty gear to tackle properly. HD is clearly the wave of the future: More and more HD-compatible television sets are sold into homes; the price of the gear required in order to make and work with HD content — HD cameras, HD videocassette decks, and computer editing systems capable of editing HD — is steadily dropping, and the format is becoming more accessible.

It may take a few years, but one day HD will be something that all video and filmmakers will be working with, so you should know what kind of exciting developments are on the horizon.

Having said that, I should note that this chapter deals with some issues that may be a bit technical for beginning video editors. If you fall into this camp, you may want to return to this chapter later on, after you've gotten your feet wet working with DV video and the basic Final Cut features.

What Is HD?

For starters, HD stands for *high definition*, and it's a video format (or a collection of related formats — more on that in a moment) that offers two major improvements over the everyday, old-school NTSC video (also known as *standard-definition* video) that has been the standard for decades:

✔ Improved image quality

✔ Wide-screen aspect ratio

You can find more information on these topics in this section.

Supersharp image quality

HD video looks much sharper (that means *better*) than standard-definition NTSC video. "Standard-def" video has an effective resolution of only 720 horizontal pixels by 486 vertical pixels, but the best HD format has a resolution of 1920 x 1080 pixels! Many more pixels make up an HD image, and the result is that those HD images look much sharper and more detailed than you're accustomed to (in the same way that still pictures from a 5-megapixel digital camera look sharper than pictures from an old 1-megapixel camera!).

If you already have an HD TV set at home, you know firsthand how good HD television can look. If not, mosey on down to your local consumer electronics store and visit its HD TV section (you can't miss it). The HD TVs are likely to be playing demo videos showing off the beauty of HD — often, nature shows or perhaps sports events — and you can clearly see HD's superior quality. One of the best demonstrations I've seen is an HD shot of a flower — when you can see the individual, near-microscopic hairs on the flower's stem, you know that you're not in Kansas any more.

These sharp, crisp images make HD video a pleasure to watch on a television set in your home (as long as you have an HD-compatible set, of course), but they also make HD feasible for projecting on huge theatrical film screens. If you're into indie films, you've probably come across a film or two that were shot with standard-definition videocameras — for instance, Steven Soderberg's *Full Frontal*, or *28 Days Later*, the zombie flick by Danny Boyle. When the relatively low-resolution images from these cameras (again, roughly 720 × 486 pixels, or even 720 × 576 pixels, if the video was shot in the slightly higher-resolution European PAL format) are blown up on a huge movie screen, you can see jagged edges in the images, and the images have a slightly dull and blurry quality (as though you tried to print a poster-size image from a still picture taken by a 1-megapixel digital camera). The bigger the image is projected, the easier it is to see the imperfections in its image quality.

But, because HD video has so much more detail (remember — as much as 1920 x 1080 pixels), its images hold up much better when projected on the big screen. In fact, these days, many theatrical movies are shooting in HD; for instance, the George Lucas film *Star Wars: Episode II — Attack of the Clones* and the Robert Rodriguez films *Spy Kids* and *Once Upon a Time in Mexico* come to mind.

Of course, if you've seen these movies, you may have noticed something a little different about their "look"; some people notice a difference and prefer it less to movies shot on conventional 35mm film, and other people don't even notice the difference. I confess that theatrical movies shot on 35mm film still look a little sharper and slightly more real than those shot on HD. The difference is often hard to spot, and it's certainly not enough to prevent me from enjoying the overall movie experience (whereas theatrical films shot on standard-definition video clearly have a low-resolution video look and can be jarring).

Thanks to its high image quality, HD video can work for shooting made-for-TV content, like news and sports broadcasts, documentaries, dramas, and sitcoms, and it can also handle films that are meant to play at your local multiplex!

Wide-screen aspect ratio

The second great thing about HD video is that it has a wide-screen aspect ratio (16 units wide by 9 units tall), whereas standard-definition NTSC video has a more squarish ratio (4 units wide by 3 units tall). The result is that HD video feels more "movielike," and many people seem to prefer its wider presentation — for films, certainly, and even for news broadcasts and TV shows like *The Sopranos*. I know I do!

The many flavors of HD

You should think of HD as an overall family of related but different formats. Three different factors make up each format:

- Pixel resolution of the HD video image
- The frame rate used to record and play the HD video (rates such as 24 frames per second or 60 frames per second)
- Whether each frame is captured as a "progressive" frame or an "interlaced" one (I'll explain these terms a bit later in this section).

There are many different HD formats that combine these three factors in different ways, and some HD equipment can work with all these formats, and others can't. Here's a rundown of the three major HD formats you're likely to encounter:

- ✔ **720p:** This HD format features an image resolution of 1280 x 720 pixels and plays video at a rate of 60 frames per second. Thanks to this resolution, 720p offers a considerable increase in sharpness over standard-definition NTSC video, but not as much as HD's higher-end formats do. Why is this lesser format useful? Some HD cameras and other equipment support only 720p because it requires less expensive or advanced hardware to process, yet still offers significant benefits over NTSC video. For instance, many HD broadcasts over cable television use this format because it requires less information to be passed over cable connections or satellite links than higher-resolution formats, and it still makes customers say, "Ahhhh." Another feature of the 720p format is that it uses a progressive scan technology (that's where the *p* comes from), in which each frame of captured video contains a full frame's worth of image information and isn't split into two different fields. (See my description of 1080i, in the next bulleted paragraph, for more information about fields.)

- ✔ **1080i:** This HD format features a supersharp image resolution of 1920 x 1080 pixels, which is as good as it gets for picture resolution. The *i* in this format's name stands for *interlaced.* Rather than capture 30 full, progressive frames of imagery per second (as the 720p format does), it captures 60 *fields* per second, where each field contains only half the visual information of a single frame (one field has even-numbered rows of pixels, and the other field has odd-numbered rows of pixels, so that during playback, they can interlace). But, because fields are played superfast — each one lasts $\frac{1}{60}$ of a second — your eye doesn't really notice that each field isn't quite as detailed as a full frame would normally be. NTSC video uses a similar interlaced technology, and although video purists argue that progressive frames are preferable to interlaced images, the higher resolution of the 1080i format more than makes up for its interlaced quality.

- ✔ **1080 24p:** This format, the "bee's knees" of the HD world, features a 1920 x 1080 pixel resolution, and its video plays at a rate of 24 frames per second rather than at the 30 frames per second of 720p and 1080i. Twenty-four frames per second, of course, is the same frame rate used to shoot and project theatrical movies (many people think that this frame rate looks more "lifelike" and realistic), and that's why 1080 24p is the format of choice for Hollywood filmmakers who choose to shoot on HD rather than on film (the latest George Lucas *Star Wars* film was shot in the 1080 24p format). Also, the *p* in 24p tells you that it's a progressive scan format, so it has no interlaced frames — just pure image bliss.

How Final Cut Works with HD

Final Cut Pro HD offers the most painless and inexpensive way to edit high-quality HD projects. In essence, Final Cut Pro HD makes working with HD as flexible and convenient as working with standard-definition DV video, and that's a huge accomplishment, considering how unwieldy HD video has been to work with.

The way things were

To appreciate Final Cut Pro HD, you should understand how earlier versions of Final Cut worked with HD video (the difference is the same as the difference between night and day). Final Cut has been HD-compatible since Version 3, but that compatibility required you to have some serious hardware. For instance, back then, your Mac needed a third-party capture card (which cost between $2,000 and $4,000) that could connect to HD videotape decks, capture digital video from HD tapes, and then play that HD video smoothly in Final Cut. To store all the digital video, you also needed a RAID (Redundant Array of Independent Disks), which is a collection of very large, very fast hard drives that work as though they're a single huge hard drive. A typical HD-friendly RAID has 3½ terabytes of storage (a terabyte equals roughly 1,000 gigabytes) and costs about $11,000. And, because HD video could consume as much as 9.6 gigabytes per minute, even a big RAID could comfortably store only about five hours of video!

What's more, a true HD system wouldn't be complete without an HD preview monitor — a high-end HD television that's matched to professional standards and lets you see the footage you're editing just as your audience would on an HD set. These types of preview monitors can cost around $20,000!

Finally, even with all this expensive gear, Final Cut could not create real-time previews of many (if any) of the effects you may apply to your HD video. If you wanted to do lots of fancy transitions or montages of moving imagery or color-correction effects, you would have to painstakingly render them to see how they would look, make changes, re-render, make more changes, re-render, and so on.

In other words, using earlier versions of Final Cut Pro to edit HD was an expensive and potentially tedious proposition!

Final Cut Pro HD makes HD easy

Final Cut Pro HD has changed everything about working in HD — as long as you're willing to work with the new HD format, DVCPRO HD, developed by Panasonic. DVCPRO HD is basically regular HD video that has been compressed (like a JPEG picture is compressed, or, more accurately, like DV video is compressed — see Chapter 18 for more information about the basics of compression). That compression is the key: It means that HD video requires much less data to describe than uncompressed HD — for instance, the compressed HD needs only as much as 840 megabytes per minute rather than uncompressed HD, at as much as 9.6 gigabytes per minute — but the compression doesn't appreciably affect the quality of the HD imagery. In other words, you still enjoy super-crisp-looking HD video!

Because DVCPRO HD doesn't require as much data as uncompressed HD, it's easy to manage and offers a number of benefits when you're editing, such as the ones described in this list:

- ✔ **It uses non-RAID disk drives:** Because a smaller amount of data is describing DVCPRO HD video, you don't need to have a RAID hard drive to store the data or play it smoothly. You still need a fast hard drive to work with DVCPRO HD, though — for instance, a 7200 RPM Serial ATA drive that works with Apple G5 desktop computers — but that's a far cry from a RAID, which can run several thousands of dollars. If you want your Mac to store lots of HD video, or if you plan to work on projects that merge lots of different HD video clips so that they have to play at one time (as with a montage or picture-in-picture tricks), a RAID may still be handy, but not necessary.

- ✔ **You see real-time previews of effects:** Because DVCPRO HD video requires less data, thanks to its compression, Final Cut Pro can generate real-time previews of effects such as transitions, color corrections, picture-in-picture effects, and other image manipulations. When Final Cut is running on a fast Mac, like a dual CPU G5 PowerMac, it can offer the same level of real-time effects as though it were working with DV video!

- ✔ **No HD capture card is required:** DVCPRO HD video also lets you skip buying an expensive capture card to capture HD video. You can use a simple FireWire cable to connect a DVCPRO HD videotape deck to your Mac (the same kind of FireWire cable you use to connect your DV camera), and that's all you need!

Thanks to this smaller size, you can use a much more standard Mac, with non-RAID drives, to work with HD and enjoy real-time previews of effects!

Here's a bonus: Final Cut Pro HD lets you use an Apple Cinema Display as an HD preview monitor so that you can watch your HD edits on a true HD screen, and not on the small Final Cut Viewer and Canvas windows. Sure, a 23-inch Cinema Display isn't exactly cheap ($1,999 at the time this book was written), but it's *much* cheaper than buying a professional HD preview monitor, and it gives you much of the same functionality (professionals will still want to use a conventional HD preview monitor for doing ultraprecise color correction, but many projects can live without it, and even if you can't, you can always take your project to a top-tier color-correction specialist right before you're finished). If you want to use a Cinema Display as a preview display for HD, choose View⇨Video Playback⇨Digital Desktop Cinema Preview.

DVCPRO HD has one "gotcha": It doesn't support the 1080 24p flavor of HD. DVCPRO HD can work in both 720p or 1080i, but if you want 1080 24p (for instance, if you ever want to make a movie that could be theatrically distributed, which the 24p format is best qualified for), you have to bring it into Final Cut as uncompressed HD video. You need an HD capture card and fast RAID drives to work with it, and you don't enjoy real-time previews of many effects. On the bright side, Final Cut does support a 24 frames-per-second version of the 720p HD format, so you can use this as a fallback option if 24 frames-per-second playback is very important to you (though you won't get the supercrisp picture resolution of the 1080i 24p format).

Creating DVCPRO HD Video

Panasonic has created a new line of hardware specifically designed to work with video in DVCPRO HD. For instance, the Panasonic VariCam HD Cinema videocamera records DVCPRO HD video directly to special tapes (just as a consumer DV camera records DV video to DV tapes). Likewise, the Panasonic AJ-HD1200A videocassette deck plays and records tapes in the DVCPRO HD format.

Because DVCPRO HD is basically a compression codec (just as DV is a codec used for making standard-definition NTSC video more manageable — see Chapter 18 for more information about codecs), your Mac can encode raw video into the codec. For instance, if you're animating sequences for an HD movie (for instance, a title sequence in LiveType or AfterEffects), you could compress them by using DVCPRO HD compression so that they can easily be edited in Final Cut Pro HD.

Affordable HD Cameras — the Good and the Bad News

There are many different HD cameras available from manufacturers like Panasonic and Sony, but with price tags ranging from about $50,000 on up (in some cases, *wayyyy* up), they're not exactly affordable for many digital filmmakers. Of course, you could always rent a high-end HD camera on a per-project basis, which is what many independent filmmakers end up doing, but a new breed of HD camera is making its way onto the market, and it's much more affordable.

These models are called HDV cameras (think "High Definition Video"), and they offer some good news and some bad news for indie filmmakers who want to get into the HD world for as little money as possible.

More HD basics

Here are some other helpful tidbits about the world of HD video. None of this information is directly related to using Final Cut Pro and HD together, but the information may help you understand the broader issues of HD:

HD TV sets: Just to be clear, to enjoy HD video, you (or your audience) need to have an HD-compatible TV set. If your TV is a few years old, chances are that it's not HD compatible. Likewise, if you paid only a few hundred dollars for your set, it's not likely to be HD compatible because HD still generally costs an arm and a leg (although, a little later, you may be able to get away with paying only an arm *or* a leg, and not both). By the way, even if a TV is HD compatible, it may be able to display video only in HD's lower-end 1280 x 720 image format (see my explanation of the 720p format in the section "The many flavors of HD," earlier in this chapter). This limitation isn't generally a drawback because HD TV broadcasts use this lower-end resolution, but it may become an issue if HD becomes more popular and some broadcasters or DVD publishers start to take advantage of everything that HD has to offer.

HD TV broadcasts: Even if you have an HD set, you can't enjoy HD video unless the set is receiving true HD broadcast signals. The vast majority of TV stations in the United States still broadcast their content as NTSC signals (in standard definition), and although you can watch these shows on an HD set, they don't look any better than they do on an everyday cheap television set. Fortunately, more and more broadcasters are offering their content in HD as well: NBC News, ESPN sports events, the Discovery Channel's nature shows, and some select HBO and Showtime channels, to name a few. (Obviously, most of these stations and events require you to subscribe to a cable or satellite TV service.) The pickings are still a little slim, although more options are on the way.

HD and DVDs: If you love the idea of watching your favorite DVDs on an HD set, remember that there's a catch: Although your DVDs play in all their wide-screen glory, they don't take full advantage of HD's supersharp image quality. That's because DVDs still contain NTSC (standard-definition) video, and although certain technologies built into modern DVD players can make the NTSC imagery look respectably crisp, the results still don't compare to what true HD video can offer. If you really want to watch your movies at their best, you have two options: You can buy an HD VCR (check www.google.com), and then find a few big-ticket movies that are available on HD videotape (although most movies are never released in this format). As for the second option, you can save your pennies and wait for the new kind of HD-DVD player that's heading our way in the next couple of years. Based on a technology named BluRay, which can store as much as 26 gigabytes of data on a DVD (rather than the customary 9 gigabytes), these disks have enough space to offer movies in full HD quality. Of course, the technology won't be available to consumers until at least 2005. *And,* the first BluRay DVD players will be quite expensive. *And,* a competing format to BluRay (similar to Beta versus VHS) is likely, which means that your early-adopter equipment may be made obsolete after a winning format emerges. That's the price you pay for your love of movies, eh?

First, the good news: These cameras — such as the JVC GR-HD1 or upcoming HDV cameras from Sony — cost as little as $2,100 and as high as $5,000, so they're quite affordable (relatively speaking!). And they can shoot video in the 720p HD format, and in some cases, even higher resolutions.

The bad news, however, is that video shot in the HDV format is highly compressed, using an MPEG-2 compression technology similar to the compression used for DVDs (see Chapter 18 for more about compression). This compression technology lets HDV cameras manage all that HD data pretty easily, and record it to regular DV tapes (like the tapes you use for recording standard-definition video from your camcorder today). At the same time, this extreme compression produces an image that is not well-suited for color correction and compositing with other video, so it may not be suitable for your particular projects. Plus, HDV video's unique compression scheme is incompatible with Apple's QuickTime video format, so the video you shoot on an HDV camera can't natively be edited or even played in Final Cut Pro! Instead, you'll have to buy third-party software like the Indie HD Toolkit from Heuris Logic ($199 and up) that lets you convert HDV video into a QuickTime-compatible format, which Final Cut can work with. But this conversion process can lose some of HDV's quality, and it adds a time-consuming step to your editing workflow.

So that's the skinny on HDV cameras and the video they shoot. HDV puts high-definition video in the hands of many, but not without some tradeoffs. It's up to you to decide if those tradeoffs are worth HDV's low price.

Part II
Importing and Organizing Your Media

The 5th Wave   By Rich Tennant

©RICHTENNANT

"Mary-Jo, come here quick! Look at this special effect I learned with the new Final Cut Pro software."

In this part . . .

Part II explains how to capture, import, and organize all the media in your Final Cut projects (video, dialogue, music, sound effects, and still pictures, for example). I show you how to capture media from DV videotape and how to bring media into Final Cut from other sources, such as video or audio files already on your hard drive, songs from a music CD, or graphics from Photoshop.

Finally, I explain how to name, annotate, and organize all these different media clips in the Final Cut Browser window so that you can easily find 'em when you need 'em.

Chapter 4

Capturing Media from Tape

In This Chapter

- ▶ Setting up a camera or deck
- ▶ Understanding timecodes
- ▶ Capturing clips in the Log and Capture window
- ▶ Letting Final Cut Pro find scenes for you
- ▶ Saving captured clips
- ▶ Batch-capturing clips

*F*inal Cut Pro can bring in media from a variety of sources (music CDs, still pictures from a camera, and QuickTime movies that are already on a hard drive), but you probably get most of a project's content by capturing video from MiniDV tapes (from now on, just *DV*) by using a digital video (DV) camera or DV playback deck that's attached to a Mac.

Capturing video requires you to think about a few issues: how to capture the video (Final Cut Pro gives you a few different options), where to store video on your hard drive when it's captured, and how to properly name and describe video clips so that you can easily manage them later on. (This issue is important when you add more media to projects!)

Final Cut Pro generally works well with all DV cameras and decks, but you may run into occasional glitches with a couple of models. I suggest that you visit www.apple.com/finalcutpro/qualification.html and look up the list of DV devices that are qualified by Apple to work with Final Cut Pro. To be sure that your Mac and DV camera or deck work harmoniously, use a device that's listed on that site. However, if you don't use a device listed there, it's probably not the end of the world — the device should still function well in most cases.

Connecting a DV Camera or Deck

Before you can capture video from a DV camera or deck, you need to connect it to the Mac by using a FireWire cable. *FireWire,* also known as IEEE 1394, is an Apple-invented technology that lets you quickly move lots of data (which DV video and audio require) through a thin cable. Most DV cameras and decks have a built-in FireWire port. A common FireWire cable has a 4-pin connector on one end (for the camera or deck) and a 6-pin connector on the other end (for the computer). To get all your gear ready for capture, follow these steps:

1. **Use a FireWire cable to connect a DV camera to the Mac (or deck, but I assume from now on that you have a camera).**

    Mac laptops typically have only one FireWire port. If you're using an external FireWire hard drive with a Mac that is already using the single FireWire port, how do you connect the camera to the Mac? Well, most FireWire hard drives have two FireWire ports on them, so just connect the camera to the open FireWire port on the external hard drive. The camera then works with the Mac through the FireWire hard drive.

2. **Turn the camera on, if you haven't already done so.**

3. **Insert a DV tape.**

4. **Make sure that you have switched the camera to the VTR setting (on some models, it's called VCR or Playback).**

    This setting lets the camera play DV tape, like a VCR plays a tape, rather than record images seen through the camera.

5. **Launch the Final Cut Pro HD application.**

    If your DV device is properly connected, the application should start without any problems. However, if a device isn't connected or isn't recognized as valid, Final Cut Pro asks whether you want to check again for a device or proceed without it.

6. **Choose File⇨Log and Capture in Final Cut Pro (or press ⌘+8).**

    This command brings up the Final Cut Pro Log and Capture window, which I describe in a moment. In the lower-left portion of the window, check the VTR status area to make sure that you have good communication with the device, as follows:

    • When you see the message VTR OK in the status area, all is well, and you're ready to proceed.

    • When you see the message No Communication in the status area, the camera is either turned off or not connected to your Mac via a FireWire cable. Another possibility for this message is that you have a piece of faulty equipment, such as a bad cable or FireWire port.

Understanding Timecode

A *timecode* is a series of sequential numbers that describes your exact location in a piece of video. As an editor, you can't escape timecodes, which tell you where you're located in a clip, how long a shot lasts, and where to start or stop recording.

Timecodes are made up of four sets of double-digit numbers that are separated by colons and semicolons (like 00:12:23;07). From left to right, the numbers indicate hours, minutes, seconds, and finally, frames. Frames are always last (after the semicolon), and there are 30 frames in a second, so frames act as a measurement of time as well. If you were speaking in timecode, you could say "The shot that I want to capture on my DV tape starts at 00:05:10;04," which means that the shot starts at 5 minutes, 10 seconds, and 4 frames into your tape.

You see timecode values all over Final Cut Pro. For instance, the Viewer window uses a timecode to note the duration of a shot. On the Timeline, you can see timecode values displayed across the Timeline ruler, and the Canvas window reports the entire length of your movie as timecode. Additionally, the Final Cut Pro Log and Capture window displays the timecode that it reads off your DV tapes (each frame of video that's recorded to DV tape has a timecode stamp), and when you set In and Out points to mark video for capturing, Final Cut Pro records these marks as timecode values, too.

Capturing in the Log and Capture Window

Capturing clips means that you take digital video data from a DV tape and bring it into a Mac as digital QuickTime files. *Logging* is the process of noting those portions of a tape (specified with timecode) that should be marked for capture at a later time. (These are referred to as *offline* clips.) The main hub of the video-capturing universe is the Final Cut Pro Log and Capture window, as shown in Figure 4-1, which you can access by choosing File⇨ Log and Capture from the main menu.

The Log and Capture window lets you perform the following three basic steps in the capturing process:

1. **Navigate through a DV tape until you find the piece of video you want to capture.**

2. **Describe and log this video by giving it In and Out points, naming it, and writing any other useful, descriptive comments about it (such as the name of the DV tape you're capturing it from).**

Duration of selected shot   Current timecode

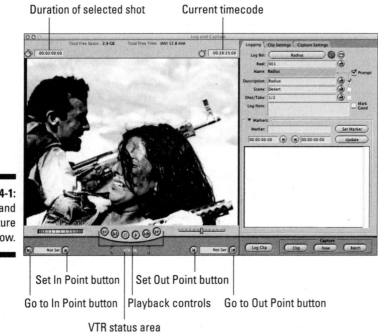

Figure 4-1:
The Log and
Capture
window.

Set In Point button | Set Out Point button

Go to In Point button | Playback controls   Go to Out Point button

VTR status area

3. **Capture the video by saving it to the hard drive as a QuickTime digital file and also adding it to the Browser window of a project as a media clip, which you can then edit on the Timeline.**

This section outlines these three steps.

Navigating through a DV tape

Use the Log and Capture window's playback controls (as shown in Figure 4-2) to move through a tape and find the piece of video you want to capture. While you do this, you can see the video playing in the Preview pane.

Fast Forward

Figure 4-2:
These
controls
determine
the play-
back of
DV tape.

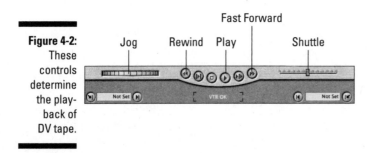

Jog   Rewind Play   Shuttle

You have the following controls available so that you can either move quickly through the tape or proceed frame by frame (for high-precision work):

✔ **Play, Stop, Fast Forward, and Rewind buttons:** Clicking the Play button begins your DV tape immediately in the Preview pane of the Log and Capture window, and clicking Stop . . . well, you can imagine what that does. To move to another part of the DV tape quickly, use the Fast Forward and Rewind buttons. Unfortunately, you can't preview the video while the tape speeds by, but you can watch the Log and Capture window's Current Timecode box to see where you are now on the tape.

✔ **J, K, and L keys:** Although using shortcut keys is a matter of preference, I find that the best way to quickly and precisely navigate through a tape is by pressing J, K, and L on the keyboard, as follows:

  • Pressing J plays the tape in reverse.

  • Pressing K pauses playback.

  • Pressing L plays the tape forward.

Even better, pressing the L or J key repeatedly increases the speed of the forward or backward motion while showing you the video in the Preview pane. Try it: Press either key once, and then again, and then again — and watch your video fly by superfast. This approach lets you see the video moving smoothly as it zips by, as opposed to using the window's Fast Forward and Rewind buttons, which move through the tape quickly but don't show your video in the process.

✔ **Arrow keys:** Occasionally, you may want to move through a tape frame by frame. Press ← on the keyboard to move back one frame and → to move forward one frame.

✔ **Jog and Shuttle (refer to Figure 4-2):** Few people prefer to use these controls rather than use keyboard commands (J, K, and L and the arrow keys). However, you can drag the Shuttle control to the left and right to move back and forward, respectively, through a tape at different speeds. (The farther from center you drag the control, the faster you go.) You can move the Jog wheel to the left or right to slowly roll backward or forward as little as one frame at a time.

✔ **Current Timecode field:** The Current Timecode field, in the upper-center portion of the Log and Capture window, always shows the timecode of the frame that appears in the Log and Capture window. By entering a timecode in the Current Timecode field, you tell Final Cut Pro to go to that timecode location. This field comes in handy when other people (such as your producer or a client) screen source tapes in advance and make notes about shots that they like on the tapes.

Describing and capturing video — the long way

When you find a clip of video you want to capture, you need to give Final Cut Pro some details about it before capturing it. For instance, you need to give the clip a name, and you need to tell Final Cut Pro at what point on the tape to start capturing the video to the hard drive and at what point to stop (by setting what Final Cut Pro calls *In* and *Out points*). This information is also important for logging clips that you want to capture later.

Follow these steps to capture a clip the long way and provide important logging information:

1. **Move to the frame on a DV tape where you want to begin capturing video, and then press I to mark an In point.**

   The timecode for that first frame appears in the Log and Capture window's In Point Timecode field (refer to Figure 4-2).

2. **Move to the last frame you want to capture on the DV tape, and then press O to mark an Out point.**

   The timecode for this last frame appears in the Out Point Timecode field. Just so you know: Final Cut Pro doesn't care whether you mark the Out point before you mark the In point.

3. **Type the reel name in the Log and Capture window's Reel field, as shown in Figure 4-3.**

New Bin button

Up button

Figure 4-3: Describe the captured clips in these fields in the Log and Capture window.

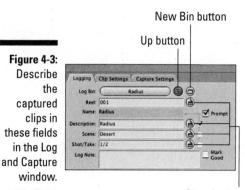

Slate buttons

Reel names are nothing more than the tape names you may have created for DV tapes. Although entering this information isn't mandatory, noting the tape that your video was captured from makes going back to that source tape easier in case you ever need to recapture media from it. Together with the clip information in the next step, this step is the most important part of the logging process and should not be underestimated.

4. **Fill in the fields that describe important stuff about a clip (refer to Figure 4-3).**

   Final Cut Pro gives you lots of information to record about a clip — for instance, a description of the clip, scene, shot or take data, and general notes (such as John blinks a lot or slightly shaky camera).

   You can click the Slate button next to each field to increase (by one) the current value shown in that field. For instance, when a 2 is in the Scene field, clicking the field's Slate button changes that value to a 3, saving you time from keying in a number yourself. Also, when you click the Slate button in the Scene field, Final Cut Pro is smart enough to not only increase the current scene number by 1 but also reset the current shot or take number to 1.

   If you really like a particular shot, select the Mark Good check box. After you have captured all your clips, Final Cut Pro can quickly search out the most promising shots you marked in this way. (See Chapter 6 for more information.)

5. **Type a name for the clip, and click OK.**

   By default, Final Cut Pro generates a name for the clip based on information you enter in the Log and Capture window's Description, Scene, and Shot/Take fields (if you have selected the check box to the right of each of these fields — refer to Figure 4-3 again). For instance, when you type **Sunrise** in the Description field and **Scene54** in the Scene field, Final Cut Pro automatically names the captured clip Sunrise_Scene54 (again, as long as the Description and Scene fields have check marks next to them). If you don't want the clip's name to use one or all of these fields, just select the field's check box to toggle the field off. However, even when you have a field's check box turned off, Final Cut Pro records any info you enter in the field with the clip. You can search to find the clip by its scene or description, but the information isn't added to the clip's name.

   When you don't want the clip's name to include *any* of the Log and Capture window's fields, toggle each field's check box off and toggle the Prompt check box so that it's enabled. When you capture the clip, Final Cut Pro opens a new dialog box and lets you type a name and any additional comments for the clip.

   When you don't select the Prompt check box or any other fields, Final Cut Pro names the clip something like Untitled 0001, and you don't want that! Make sure that you come up with a good name.

6. **Click the Clip button in the lower-right corner of the Log and Capture window to capture the clip immediately, or click the Log Clip button to capture the clip later as part of a batch.**

   If you have chosen the Capture Clip option, Final Cut Pro cues the camera to the In point you set and captures the clip from the DV tape until it reaches the Out point you set. (You can abort the capture any time by pressing Esc.) The clip then appears in the Browser window under the name you gave it. Final Cut Pro also stores the clip as a QuickTime file on the hard drive, using that same name (see the section "Locating captured clips," later in this chapter, for information on controlling exactly where Final Cut Pro saves those QuickTime files.) If you have chosen Log Clip, the new clip appears in the Browser window as an offline file that can be captured as part of a batch of clips (see the sections "Logging clips" and "Batch-Capturing Clips," both later in this chapter, for more information). If you're wondering what the Capture Now button does, refer to the "Capturing the video — the short way" section, later in this chapter, for more information on this feature, which lets you bypass the detailed logging process.

By default, Final Cut Pro aborts a capture if it encounters a break in your DV tape's timecode. A *break* means that the tape's timecode starts over at 00:00:00;00 (in most cases) or otherwise skips sequential numbers. A break usually occurs because you turned your camera off and then on again while recording footage. These breaks can have some bad side effects if you ever plan to recapture the clip you're capturing now, so see the section "Capturing over Timecode Breaks" later in this chapter, to fully understand the consequences. If you don't want to include clips with these breaks in your project, choose Final Cut Pro⇨User Preferences, and select the Abort Capture option from the On Timecode Break drop-down menu.

Logging clips

Logging is a common practice among video editors. The process basically involves noting the shots (or *clips,* as they're called in Final Cut Pro) and their locations (in timecodes) on the tape. Logging is helpful because it gives you a chance to review and organize what you have and figure out what shots you may still need to get. It also helps you save space on your hard drives because you capture only the clips you need for your project (as opposed to capturing an entire tape at once).

In Final Cut Pro, the act of logging entails using the Log and Capture window. As you scroll through your tape, you use In and Out points to mark the beginning and ending timecodes for each clip, and you use the Logging tab to record information about the clip. (You can also establish a number of settings on the other tabs, which I discuss later in this chapter.) When you're done tinkering with your clip, you save it. Note that you don't *capture* the clip yet.

Just save it in the Browser, where this *logged* but uncaptured clip appears with a red slash across it, as shown in Figure 4-4. The uncaptured clips and the information in the Browser about them serve as your log, much like the ones that were handwritten before the days of computer-based editing. Later, you can select this logged shot and tell Final Cut Pro to capture it for you.

A logged or "offline" clip has a slash through it.

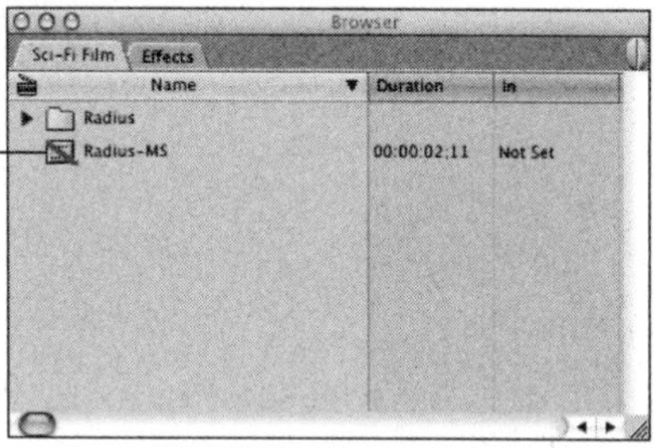

Figure 4-4:
You can capture this logged clip later.

You aren't required to log before you capture. After you log each shot, you can capture it in Final Cut Pro. I recommend first carefully logging tapes and then capturing them later. Many editors scoff at this approach because it seems time-consuming to them, but I argue that this method saves time and energy later in the edit. If you log first, you tend to be much more careful about the amounts of material you capture. Editors who capture on the fly often capture a whole lot more than they need. And, even at the comparatively lean data rates of DV, you need 1 GB of hard drive space for every 4½ minutes of video.

You can log clips by following the steps described in the preceding section while continuing to add more clips from the same tape by either pressing the Log Clip button as described or repeating the steps with multiple tapes. As long as you remember to enter the appropriate reel and name information, you can easily batch-capture these clips later.

Changing your logging bin

When you capture a clip, Final Cut Pro adds it to the Browser window. However, you may want your captured clips to go directly into a bin in the Browser. Putting clips in a bin keeps you from having a bunch of captured clips cluttering up the Browser.

You can create a new bin in the Browser directly from the Log and Capture window. Just click the New Bin button (refer to Figure 4-3), and Final Cut Pro creates a new bin in the Browser (see Figure 4-5). This new bin is designated as the Logging Bin, so that any new clips you capture go there automatically.

The Browser displays a Logging Bin icon to the left of this new bin, but you may want to rename the bin to be more descriptive. (See Chapter 6 for more on working with bins.) To toggle off this designation (so that captured clips go directly into the main Browser and not into a bin), click the Up button in the Log and Capture window.

A small slate icon indicates the current Logging Bin in your Browser.

Figure 4-5:
A logging
bin.

You can turn any existing Browser bin into your logging bin. In the Browser window, press and hold Control, click the bin that you mean to use as the logging bin, and then choose Set Capture Bin from the pop-up menu that appears.

Capturing the video — the short way

Capturing a video clip by using the steps I describe in the preceding section can sometimes get tedious because you have to navigate through the DV tape, set In and Out points for each clip, and then wait while the camera again returns to those points to capture each clip to the hard drive. Although this process works fine when you're capturing a couple of clips at a time, it can be inefficient when you have lots of capturing to do. Instead, you can use the Final Cut Pro Capture Now feature, which captures whatever happens to be playing on the camera at the moment and spares you from setting In and Out points or even naming the clip.

Capture video quickly and easily by following these steps:

1. **Begin playing the tape in the Log and Capture window.**

   You can press L to start playing the tape forward or just click the window's Play button.

2. **Click the Now button in the Log and Capture window when you want to start capturing the video that's playing.**

   Click the Now button a few seconds before you want the capture to begin, in case the Mac has to "wake up" the hard drive. Either way, Final Cut Pro starts capturing the video that's playing through the camera.

3. **Press Esc to stop the capture.**

   Final Cut Pro automatically names the captured clip something generic like Untitled001, adds the clip to the Browser window, and saves it as a QuickTime file on the hard drive.

This Capture Now process is very quick and painless, but the only drawback is that you get a bunch of clips with not-very-useful names, such as Untitled 0001. Of course, you can quickly change the clip's name in the Browser window after it's captured. (See Chapter 6 for more information about renaming clips in the Browser.) However, the QuickTime media file that's saved to the hard drive keeps its original, generic name, and that can lead to some confusion if you want to look at the media files from the Mac desktop.

If this naming issue doesn't bother you, you're all set. However, Final Cut Pro offers a middle ground that lets you name a clip quickly, before it begins to capture any video, so that your clip ends up in the Browser and on your hard drive with a more useful name.

Follow these steps to quickly capture clips and provide them with specific names:

1. **Before playing the tape, name the clip to be captured by typing some descriptive information in the Log and Capture window fields.**

   See Step 5 in the section "Describing and capturing video — the long way," earlier in this chapter, for a description of how these fields work. Make sure that Final Cut Pro automatically incorporates your entries into the Log and Capture window's Name field by checking the box to the right of each field you want to include. You can also enter the clip's reel name here, but be aware that Final Cut Pro uses any information you enter in the window's other fields (Scene, Shot/Take, and Description, for example) only to build the clips. When captured, the clip doesn't retain any of this additional information (again, like Scene, Shot/Take, and so on); it retains only the name itself that you've created. (*Note:* If you want to capture a clip with all this information saved along with it, you can't use the Capture Now approach. Read on.)

2. **Do a Capture Now, as you normally would (refer to the preceding set of steps).**

   Final Cut Pro captures the clip, using the name that was generated in the Log and Capture window's Name field.

Locating captured clips

When you capture clips from DV tape, Final Cut Pro saves them to what-ever hard drive you set as the scratch disk (the hard drives where audio and video media are stored) — you do this for the first time when you first launch Final Cut Pro, after you install the application. Additionally, Final Cut Pro puts the files in specific folders on that hard drive. To determine where those folders are located (and to change their location, if you want), choose Final Cut Pro HD⇨System Settings and then click the Scratch Disks tab, as shown in Figure 4-6.

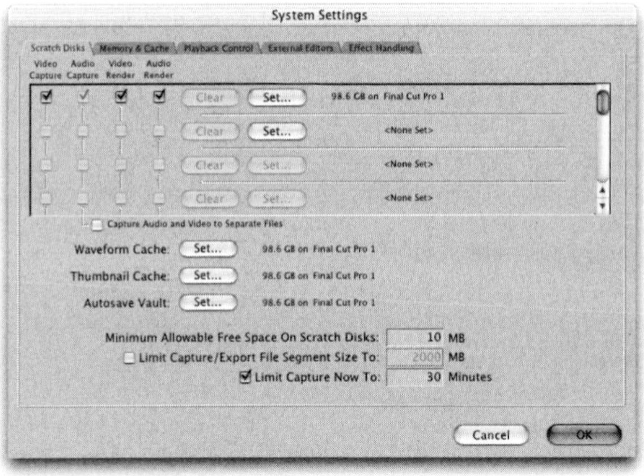

Figure 4-6: The Scratch Disks tab, found in the System Settings dialog box.

Under the Scratch Disks tab, you should see a pathname that tells you the folder in which Final Cut Pro saves the video and audio for your projects. In that folder, Final Cut Pro creates another folder, named `Capture Scratch`, as shown in Figure 4-7. Within that folder, the program creates another folder using the same project name you used in capturing the video. (For instance, if you name the project `Radius_TheMovie`, the folder's name is `Radius_TheMovie` as well.) And, this folder is (finally!) where you can find the cap-tured QuickTime files.

You can change the folder — or even the hard drive where the files are cap-tured — by doing the following:

1. **Click the uppermost Set button in the Scratch Disks tab (refer to Figure 4-6).**

   The Choose a Folder dialog box appears, and you can navigate to any folder on your hard drive (or drives).

2. **Find the folder you want to capture to, and click it once to select it.**

3. **Click the Choose button.**

   Final Cut Pro updates the Scratch Disks tab to show you this new folder as the capture destination.

You can set up multiple scratch disk folders by clicking the other Set buttons on the Scratch Disks tab. However, Final Cut Pro captures only to the disk or folder that has a check mark in the Video Capture or Audio Capture check box, to the left of the tab. I like to set up multiple scratch disks and switch between them, depending on the project I'm working on.

Dropping frames during capture?

When you capture clips, Final Cut Pro may interrupt the capture process to tell you that it's *dropping frames* while capturing, which means that the hard disk isn't recording all the frames of video that are flowing from your camera in real time. Captured clips that are missing some of their frames play with slight stutters or pops, so Final Cut Pro warns you ahead of time, thankfully, that it's happening. If you're dropping frames during capture, consider these culprits:

✔ **The hard drive isn't fast enough.** Lots of factors determine how fast a hard drive can write data, but a major one is its rotational speed — that is, how fast the drive's physical magnetic disk spins. A drive with a 4200 rpm rotational speed (particularly ones in older Macs or laptops) can suffer from dropped frames, but drives with 5400 rpm, and especially 7200 rpm, ratings should be safe.

✔ **The hard drive is fragmented.** Hard drives write data to the surface of a spinning magnetic disk. Ideally, when writing a video file, that spinning disk has enough empty space to record the file from start to finish in the same physical place. As you use a hard drive more (writing files to it and deleting

files from it), the disk's surface becomes a patchwork of filled and empty areas of different sizes. And, when the hard drive can't write a video file from start to finish in one spot, the drive writes parts of it in different places on the disk's surface (wherever the disk has empty space), which means that the hard drive's *heads* (which read and write the data) have to move around the disk, back and forth, to write the file. All this moving around takes extra time and sometimes slows the drive so that it can't record the video frames fast enough — resulting in dropped frames. The solution is to defragment the disk with a third-party utility, such as Norton Utilities, which can cleverly rearrange all the data on the drive so that the drive can keep each file's data together. The result is a faster drive!

✔ **The hard drive is too full.** If a drive has only about 10 percent free space, it can lose enough speed to start dropping frames. The solution: Delete some files that you no longer need. (You may want to back up these files to a CD, DVD, or some other media beforehand.)

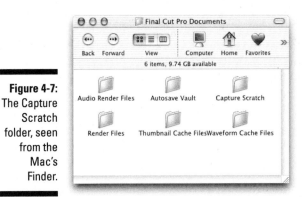

Figure 4-7:
The Capture
Scratch
folder, seen
from the
Mac's
Finder.

Letting Final Cut Pro Find Scenes for You

Final Cut Pro has a feature that can save you loads of time and free you from the burden of capturing many clips — one after the other — from the same DV tape. The feature is DV Start/Stop Detection, and it detects each instance on a DV tape where you or your cameraperson stopped and then started recording the action again. Final Cut Pro treats each Start/Stop instance as a separate unique scene and quickly turns each scene into a separate clip in the Browser window for easy organization. By using this feature, you can save yourself from manually capturing one clip after another on the DV tape.

To take advantage of the DV Start/Stop Detect feature, follow these steps:

1. **Capture the entire length of the tape, following the steps I present earlier in this chapter (such as in the section "Capturing the video — the short way").**

   For example, if you have a half-hour tape, capture it all at one time. You can capture this media by using a variety of techniques, but choosing Capture Now is probably quickest.

2. **After the clip appears in the Browser, select the clip and choose Mark⇨ DV Start/Stop Detect from the main menu.**

   Final Cut Pro scans the clip and marks all locations where you pressed the Record/Pause button on the camera during the shooting. Small markers appear wherever you paused the camera, as shown in Figure 4-8.

You can go even further and create subclips from these markers. *Subclips* are pieces of a long clip that have been divided into smaller clips. To create subclips, follow these steps:

1. **In the Browser, select all the markers within your clip.**

   You can hold down ⌘ while clicking each marker to select them individually, or you can use your mouse to highlight all the markers and select them as a group.

2. **Choose Modify⇨Make Subclip.**

   All the material between the markers appears as subclips in the Browser (no longer under the original clip they came from). The subclip icons look just like the clip icons in the Browser but have jagged edges (as though they were ripped from a longer clip).

At this point, you may want to rename some of the subclips to better reflect what they contain. (See Chapter 6 for more information.)

Select the markers, and create subclips for your scenes.

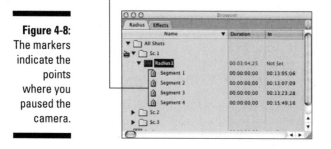

Figure 4-8:
The markers indicate the points where you paused the camera.

Capturing over Timecode Breaks

Capturing video clips can become a real mess if the DV tapes you're capturing media from have timecode breaks in them. A *timecode break* occurs when the timecode restarts at any point on your tape — basically, returning to 00:00:00;00 (in most cases). Timecode breaks usually happen when you're recording video with your DV camera (and consequently laying down timecode on the DV tape as well). These breaks usually occur when you turn the camera off, turn it on again sometime later, and then start recording more video — thereby resetting the timecode with a new round of footage you're recording. (***Note:*** Pausing or stopping your recording doesn't reset the timecode, so pausing when you can is better than turning your camera off.)

How do timecode breaks affect your attempts to recapture an entire project? When you recapture your clips, a video editing application looks at each tape you originally captured media from and notes all the clips that it should recapture by their timecode values (for example, capturing a clip starting at 2 minutes on the tape and then another at 5 minutes). However, a tape with timecode breaks may have several instances of video with the same timecode (for example, two instances of 5 minutes, or 00:05:00;00). So, how does most video editing software know which instance to capture? It doesn't! Instead, it just finds the nearest 5-minute mark on the tape and starts capturing from that point. Unfortunately, the software may be capturing video from the wrong segment of your tape, giving you the wrong clip of video as a result.

Fortunately, the newest version of Final Cut Pro knows how to deal with timecode breaks. In older versions of Final Cut Pro, a clip of video that was captured with timecode breaks would display an error and require you to recapture footage or repair your tapes before recapturing. But, in Final Cut Pro HD, you can now capture and deal properly with tapes with timecode breaks by choosing from a few different options. In the User Preferences window (choose Final Cut Pro HD⇨User Preferences from the main menu to get there), select from three different options for dealing with timecode breaks. Choose one of these options from the On Timecode Break drop-down menu: Make New Clip, Abort Capture, or Warn After Capture (see Figure 4-9).

Figure 4-9:
Final Cut Pro
HD lets you
capture
over
timecode
breaks and
work with
clips by
using three
different
options.

These options are described as follows:

✔ Make New Clip is best for capturing a tape in one capture session (where you can grab a latte down the street while Final Cut captures a full 60-minute tape). This option creates a new clip beginning with its own timecode, starting from where the break occurs, and it's generally the best option to work with because it names clips sequentially, without having to involve you in the process.

✔ Abort Capture keeps a clip intact up to the point where a break occurs and stops further capture at that point, alerting you to a problem with the tape.

✔ Warn After Capture lets you know that timecode breaks are present in your media while continuing to capture the footage.

Of these three options, Make New Clip is the best choice for most projects because it can capture and name clips (Final Cut Pro names all these clips sequentially) without requiring you to take special measures. However, you should be aware that you may have difficulty recapturing video later because of the way the new clip's timecode is created.

Batch-Capturing Clips

One of the best Final Cut Pro features for editors who work with large projects and lots of tapes is its ability to batch-capture clips. *Batch-capturing* is an automated process you use for capturing logged clips or offline footage in a single operation, without needing to manually rewind, fast forward, or play your video. The only thing you need to do, apart from starting the capturing process, is to insert new tapes as Final Cut Pro prompts you to do so. After you have logged enough clips, follow these steps to do a batch capture:

Before starting the batch-capturing process, you must first have in the Browser window some offline clips that are logged and ready to go:

1. **From the Browser window, select any offline clips that you want to import (clips that are logged but not captured).**

   You can select individual clips by clicking them or by Control-clicking several clips to select multiple clips.

2. **Choose File⇨Batch Capture, or click the Capture Batch button in the Log and Capture window.**

   Press Control+C to easily activate the Batch Capture function. Final Cut Pro opens the Batch Capture dialog box, as shown in Figure 4-10.

3. **In the Batch Capture dialog box that appears, choose All Selected Items (that are in the logging bin) from the Capture drop-down menu.**

4. **Click the OK button in the Batch Capture dialog box to accept the default options, which are based on your clip settings.**

5. **Insert the reel from which you want to batch-capture clips into your DV camera.**

   Follow the prompts to insert and accept new reels (tapes) as they are needed.

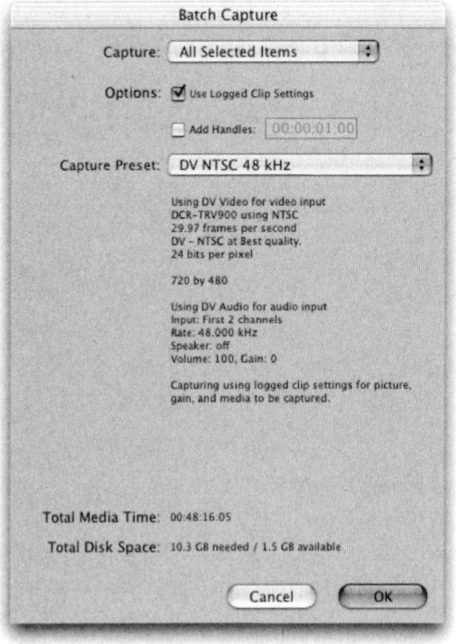

Figure 4-10:
The Batch
Capture
feature
enables you
to capture
several clips
at one time.

The batch-capturing process is used frequently for larger projects, particularly feature films or documentary work. Understanding the benefits of a batch capture helps you to better appreciate the importance of logging your footage, even if you're working from a single tape. For more information on capturing offline media, see Chapter 6.

Chapter 5

Importing Media That's Already on Your Mac

Most likely, plenty of the media you use in Final Cut Pro doesn't have to be captured from videotape; you probably already have the media in digital form on your hard drive. This media may consist of a sound effects file in the AIFF format, an MP3 song from your favorite album, still picture files from a digital camera, or a video clip that's already digitized into the QuickTime format. And, if the media is already on your Mac, you can bring it into Final Cut Pro — that is, *import* it — with little trouble. That's what this chapter is all about: I tackle all the ways that you can import media into your projects, and I look at some tools that can help you convert media from one digital format to another so that it works best with Final Cut Pro.

Your Media Files Are Welcome Here

What kinds of media can you use with Final Cut Pro? The good news is you can use plenty, although you should know about a couple of notable exceptions to avoid any unpleasant surprises.

As far as video is concerned, you can import any video files in the QuickTime file format (for instance, DV video or HD video, and other types). Because you're using a Mac, any digital video files you have on hand are probably in QuickTime anyway: That file format is the preferred "homegrown" format for multimedia on the Mac.

On the flip side, Final Cut Pro doesn't work with video in other file formats, such as RealVideo or the Microsoft Windows Media Format — both are popular on PC machines. If you have a video file in these formats, try searching the Internet for a utility program that can export the video's individual frames as Targa images, and then reimport those images into Final Cut Pro.

For importing still pictures, Final Cut Pro isn't very discerning. You can import pictures in just about every file format known to Macs and PCs. As for sound and music, Final Cut Pro welcomes all major formats: AIFF, WAV, and almost any other audio format that the QuickTime architecture supports. (QuickTime carries not just video but also audio.) These formats are popular on both the Mac and PC, so you can work with just about any audio you can dig up.

Unfortunately, Final Cut doesn't work well with MP3 music files. A favorite in the music world, MP3 compresses music into a very small file so that it can be easily stored and traded. Unfortunately, Final Cut Pro plays MP3 files with weird distortion that your audience isn't likely to appreciate. But, all is not lost. You can solve the distortion problem with some easy steps, which I discuss in the section "Converting MP3 (and Other Kinds of Audio) with QuickTime Pro," later in this chapter. Similarly, Final Cut can't import M4P music files downloaded from the hot Apple iTunes Music Store (which are also called AAC files, due to the AAC compression they use). And, unlike with MP3 files, you can't convert these M4P files to a more Final Cut-friendly format.

Some Media May Need Rendering

Although Final Cut Pro can import any video or audio that's in the QuickTime format, you may have to render those media clips before playing them on the Timeline. *Rendering* isn't the end of the world — it's just a process where Final Cut Pro has to calculate how a media clip should look or sound before you can play it in your movie. (Admittedly, rendering is a hassle if you have many media files to render.)

Final Cut Pro is very clear about when you need to render your media files: When you play them on the Timeline, you hear beeps for audio that needs to be rendered, and the Canvas window shows the message Unrendered for any video clips that need to be rendered. (At the top of the Timeline, above all the tracks, Final Cut Pro also draws a thin, red horizontal line over any clips that need rendering.)

What determines why you must render some media and not other media? One factor is the compression technology that's used to save the media. Any compressed audio (for instance, an AIFF file that has been compressed with the IMA or MACE compressor) has to be rendered before playing. Similarly, if a video clip has been compressed with a different technology than your current Timeline sequence is set to work with, you probably have to render that clip (for instance, if your Timeline sequence is set to work with DV-compressed video — as this book assumes — and you import a video clip that uses Sorenson 3 compression). Other factors can affect whether clips need to be rendered before playing them. See Bonus Chapter 3 on this book's companion Web site for more information on this topic.

Importing Your Media into Final Cut Pro

Okay, so you're ready to import some media files. You can import files individually, or you can bring in an entire folder of files at one time. Regardless of your approach, your goal is the same: Get those media files into the Final Cut Pro Browser window (see Figure 5-1), which acts as the central repository for all the media in your project. When you bring a media file into the Browser, the file becomes a *clip,* and after it's in the Browser, it's ready to be worked with. That is, you can watch or listen to it, make a variety of adjustments to it, and ultimately move it to the Timeline for editing into your movie. You know that a file has been imported successfully because a small clip icon appears in the Browser window, with your media file's name next to it. (Check out Chapter 6 for a full rundown on the Browser and tips for managing all the clips in it.)

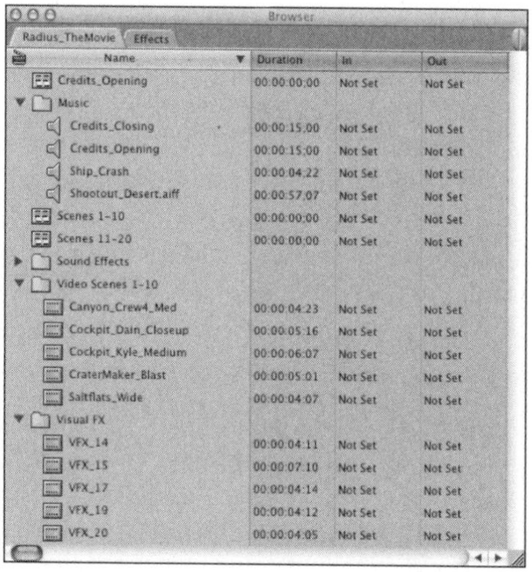

Figure 5-1:
Before you can begin working with your clips, you must import them into the Browser.

If you don't see the Browser window, you can display it by choosing Window⇨Browser, or you can toggle it on and off by pressing ⌘+4.

Sometimes, you may want to import media that's not on your hard drive. You may want to import media from a CD, a DVD-R disc (which is like a super-charged CD), a Zip disk, or even another computer connected through a network. If this is the case, first copy that media to your own hard drive (an internal or external drive works fine), and then import the media from the hard drive. This method guarantees that Final Cut Pro always has your media available and can access it quickly.

Importing one or more files at a time

To import a single file or group of individual files (but not a folder), follow these steps:

1. **Select the Browser window to make it active.**

   When you have another window selected, Final Cut Pro may not let you import files. If the Browser isn't active, you can also select it by pressing ⌘+4.

2. **To import your files directly to an existing bin in the Browser window, double-click that bin so that it opens in a new window.**

   Remember that a bin is the Final Cut Pro version of a folder. If a bin window isn't open and active, Final Cut Pro imports your files into the top level of the Browser.

3. **Choose File⇨Import⇨Files from the menu bar, or press ⌘+I.**

   The Choose a File dialog box appears, as shown in Figure 5-2.

4. **Use the Choose a File dialog box to navigate through your hard drive folders until you see the media file you want.**

   The dialog box is divided into columns. When you click a drive or folder name in the left column, the column to its right shows the drive or folder contents. Just keep clicking folders until you see the file you're looking for. If you accidentally choose the wrong folder, move the dialog box's scroll bar back a bit until you see the previous levels of folders.

   You can speed your file search by telling Final Cut Pro to show you only movies, sound clips, or still pictures. Just select your preference from the Show pop-up menu at the bottom of the dialog box.

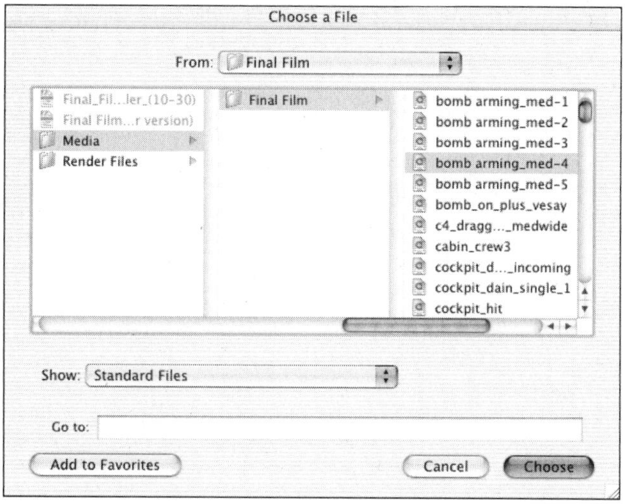

Figure 5-2:
Navigate
through the
Choose a
File dialog
box to find
the media
you want to
import.

Choose a File

From: Final Film

Final_Fil...ler_(10-30)   Final Film   bomb arming_med-1
Final Film...r version)   bomb arming_med-2
Media   bomb arming_med-3
Render Files   bomb arming_med-4
                                            bomb arming_med-5
                                            bomb_on_plus_vesay
                                            c4_dragg..._medwide
                                            cabin_crew3
                                            cockpit_d..._incoming
                                            cockpit_dain_single_1
                                            cockpit_hit

Show: Standard Files

Go to:

Add to Favorites   Cancel   Choose

5. **Select the media files you want, and then click the Choose button to add the media to the Browser window.**

   To select a continuous range of files for importing, click the first and the last files of the range while holding down the Shift key (called *Shift-clicking*). Or, you can select multiple files, regardless of their order in the file list, by holding down ⌘ while clicking each one of them.

   Either way, Final Cut Pro adds your media files as new clips in the Browser window (refer to Figure 5-1), where they're ready to rumble.

Just because a file's name is grayed out in the Choose a File dialog box doesn't mean that it can't be imported. The key to selecting a valid file for importing is the icon for the file. If the file's icon isn't grayed out, you can import the file.

If you often import files from the same folder, you can make that folder a Favorite by highlighting its name in the Choose a File dialog box and then clicking the Add to Favorites button at the bottom of the dialog box. From now on, you can access that folder quickly by opening the From drop-down list at the top of the dialog box and selecting your folder name from Favorite Places. You no longer have to navigate all the way through your hard drive!

Importing a folder full of files (or other folders)

To import lots of media files into Final Cut Pro at one time, use your Mac's Finder to drag all your files into a single folder (you can even place folders within folders), return to Final Cut Pro, and follow these simple steps:

1. **Make sure that the Browser window is active.**

2. **Choose File⇨Import⇨Folder.**

   The Choose a Folder dialog box appears, as shown in Figure 5-3.

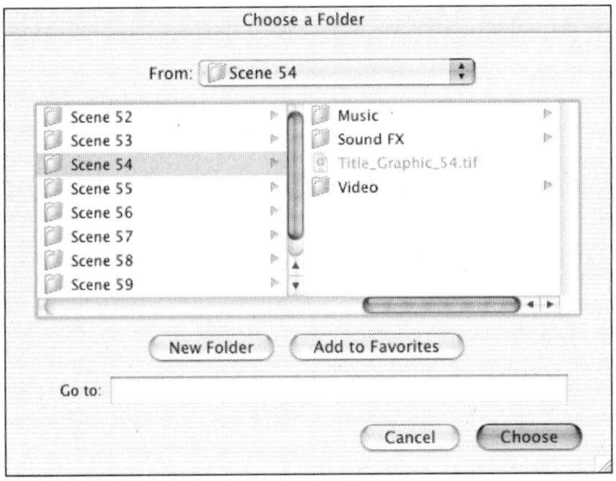

Figure 5-3: Importing the Scene 54 folder moves all the files and folders inside this folder to the Browser.

> Choose a Folder
>
> From: 📁 Scene 54 ▼
>
> | | | |
> |---|---|---|
> | 📁 Scene 52 ▶ | 📁 Music | ▶ |
> | 📁 Scene 53 ▶ | 📁 Sound FX | ▶ |
> | 📁 Scene 54 ▶ | 📄 Title_Graphic_54.tif | |
> | 📁 Scene 55 ▶ | 📁 Video | ▶ |
> | 📁 Scene 56 ▶ | | |
> | 📁 Scene 57 ▶ | | |
> | 📁 Scene 58 ▶ | | |
> | 📁 Scene 59 ▼ | | |
>
> (New Folder) (Add to Favorites)
>
> Go to: [   ]
>
> (Cancel) (Choose)

3. **Select the folder you want to import, and click the Choose button.**

   Final Cut Pro adds your folder to the Browser, making it a bin. When the folder you imported contains other folders inside it, you see that those folders have become bins within the master bin.

   Navigating this dialog box is just like navigating the Choose a File dialog box. Refer to the preceding section, "Importing one or more files at a time," if you aren't sure how to navigate this dialog box.

Importing whole folders rather than individual files not only saves you time but also has a nice side effect: It encourages you to keep your media files organized in folders that make sense. For instance, maybe you keep all your video clips in a Video folder and your music in its own folder. The point is that you work much faster when you corral your media into folders rather than leave random files strewn throughout your hard drive.

Importing files by dragging them from the Finder

A quick way to import media files and folders is by dragging their icons directly from your Mac Finder to the Final Cut Pro Browser window. But, why do this when you can just use the Final Cut Pro Import File or Import Folder options? Because you may instinctively know how to find a file more quickly by navigating to it via the Finder rather than by using a navigation dialog box. Follow these steps to import files and folders via the Finder:

1. **From Final Cut Pro, click the Finder icon in the OS X Dock (see Figure 5-4).**

   The Finder becomes active, but if you don't have any open windows in the Finder, you may not notice the change because the Final Cut Pro windows remain visible in the background. If the Finder *does* have open windows, they pop up immediately, making it very clear that you have switched from Final Cut to the Finder.

2. **In the Finder, find the files or folders that you want to import into Final Cut Pro.**

   If you don't have a Finder window open, choose File⇨New Finder Window. Then, use the window to navigate to your files or folders.

3. **Click and drag the files from the Finder window to the Browser window.**

   You may have to move the Finder window so that it doesn't cover the Browser. When you drag your files to the Browser, they become clips. When you drag a folder, it becomes a bin with the files or clips inside.

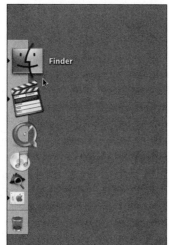

Figure 5-4:
The Finder icon and the Final Cut Pro HD icon on the Dock.

Importing music tracks directly from a CD

Final Cut Pro can also import music tracks from all your audio CDs. The best way to import CD tracks is to first copy the CD tracks to your hard drive and then import the tracks into Final Cut Pro as you would any media file. Follow these easy steps to import a music track from an audio CD:

1. **Place a CD in your Mac's CD drive.**

2. **From the Mac Finder, double-click the CD icon so that you can see its contents (as shown in Figure 5-5).**

   You can go to the Finder by clicking its icon in the OS X Dock (refer to Figure 5-4).

Figure 5-5:
A window
in the Finder
shows the
tracks of an
audio CD.

3. **Copy the CD track (or tracks) that you want to import to your hard drive.**

   The Finder lists the CD tracks as files. Just click and drag to your hard drive (or, preferably, to a folder on your hard drive) the files you want. You can also copy the files to your Mac's desktop. While in the Finder, you may want to rename your copied tracks so that they're more descriptive, but you can also do this within Final Cut Pro.

4. **Go back to Final Cut Pro, and import the tracks as you normally would.**

   You can jump back to Final Cut Pro by clicking its icon in the Dock. When you import a track file, you see it listed in the Browser window as an audio clip.

Importing Photoshop files (layers and all)

You already know that you can import all sorts of still-picture formats into Final Cut Pro, but if you have created graphics in Photoshop that use its Layers feature (for instance, an elaborate logo made up of overlapping images and effects), you're in luck: Final Cut Pro can preserve those Photoshop layers so that you can animate and otherwise manipulate them individually.

When you import a Photoshop PSD file, Final Cut Pro imports the file, not as a single image clip but, rather, as an entire Timeline sequence. (A *sequence* is the Final Cut Pro way of organizing a group of clips; see Chapters 2 and 7 for a full explanation.) In the sequence, Final Cut Pro places each Photoshop layer on its own video track (track V1, track V2, and so on). Final Cut Pro also preserves the order of your Photoshop file layers by assigning the background layer to the sequence's first video track (V1) and ordering every other layer as you did in your Photoshop file. For instance, your fifth layer, including the background, would be on the V5 track.

Final Cut Pro also interprets many of the settings you gave your layers in Photoshop — for instance, opacity settings, modes, and visibility. (See Chapters 14, 15, and 16 for more on effects and compositing.) On the other hand, Final Cut Pro tosses out any layer masks you created, and if you're using some weird compositing modes that Final Cut Pro can't understand, it ignores those layers.

In general, though, you can successfully import some pretty sophisticated Photoshop masterpieces into Final Cut Pro and, with a little tweaking, get them ready to take the stage in your movie.

A few words about still pictures

When you work with DV video in Final Cut Pro, each video frame is sized at a resolution of 720 horizontal pixels × 480 vertical pixels. (This is true of all standard, NTSC-based DV video.) But, when you import a still image into Final Cut Pro, the image probably doesn't match that standard video resolution. A still picture could be 640 × 480 pixels, 1280 × 960 pixels, or 2560 × 1920 pixels — all depending on how it was taken, scanned, or otherwise edited before it ended up in Final Cut Pro. The result? When you import that image into your movie, it's either too small or too large to fit the video frame. A black border appears around an image that's too small. If the image is too large, you don't see the whole image, which makes it look cropped.

Sometimes, that's a good thing. For instance, if you bring in an oversized high-resolution picture (a high-resolution scan of an old map, for example), you can use the Final Cut Pro animation features to slowly pan or scale it through your 720 × 480 video frame. (You see this effect used frequently in documentaries, like those historical masterpieces done by Ken Burns.) On the other hand, sometimes you simply want your still pictures to fill the screen — nothing more, nothing less.

Fortunately, Final Cut Pro gives you full flexibility to handle your still pictures. You can bring them in with the intention of showing just parts of them, or you can resize them to fit the frame of your movie. I cover the "how-to" of scaling images to different sizes and moving them around (à la Ken Burns) in Chapter 15.

When you import a Photoshop file with layers, Final Cut Pro doesn't make a copy of that image; it just references the original Photoshop file on your hard drive. If you go back to Photoshop and change the artwork, you see the changes reflected in your Final Cut Pro sequence. That's pretty cool, but if your changes include adding or deleting layers in your Photoshop file, you're likely to confuse Final Cut Pro. If you want to add or delete layers in a Photoshop file that you have already imported into Final Cut Pro, I recommend importing the file again rather than working with the earlier version.

Converting MP3 (and Other Kinds of Audio) with QuickTime Pro

One of the most popular file formats for audio is now MP3, which compresses audio into small file sizes while keeping high sound quality. (That's why MP3 files are so popular on the Internet — they don't take long to download, but they still sound pretty good.) At some point, you may want to use an MP3 file in your movie. For example, a composer may e-mail you the latest version of a movie's musical score as an MP3 file so that you can quickly try it out. However, it turns out that MP3 files and Final Cut Pro don't work well together, thanks largely to MP3's extreme compression. (Final Cut Pro needs to render MP3 files before playing them, and even then the files sound warbled.)

Your best bet is to convert an MP3 file (or any compressed audio format) to a friendlier file format by using QuickTime Pro (see Figure 5-6). This advanced add-on to the QuickTime 6 software is built into every Mac. Apple usually charges about $30 for QuickTime Pro, but you probably already have it on your Mac because it's included with the Final Cut Pro 4 software. By the way, QuickTime Pro has some other cool features. You can do simple video editing by using Cut and Paste commands, and even add multiple audio tracks. For now, I talk about how to use QuickTime Pro to convert media from one audio format to another.

To use the QuickTime Pro features, you have to "unlock" them with a special access code. You probably did this when you installed Final Cut Pro, but if you're unsure, you can check to see whether QuickTime Pro is activated on your Mac by opening the QuickTime Player application. (Look for an icon in the OS X Dock, or check your Applications folder.) After you open the application, choose QuickTime Player➪Preferences➪Registration and see whether the QuickTime Key setting says Pro Player Edition. If you see it, you're all set. If you don't see this message, you haven't activated QuickTime Pro yet.

In the materials that came in your Final Cut Pro box, look for a sheet of paper that lists the special *key code* for unlocking the Pro edition and then follow the written steps for doing so. If you can't find the code, surf over to www.apple.com/quicktime. Look for the Get QuickTime Pro option, and get your credit card warmed up.

Figure 5-6:
QuickTime
Pro is a
collection of
advanced
features
that are built
into the
QuickTime 6
player
software,
shown here.

Follow these steps to use QuickTime Pro to convert compressed audio formats (like MP3 or MP4) to a Final Cut Pro–friendly format (like AIFF):

1. **Open the QuickTime Player application.**

   An icon for the QuickTime Player is probably already in the OS X Dock. Click the icon, or find the program in your OS X Applications folder.

2. **Choose File➪Import.**

3. **In the Open dialog box (as shown in Figure 5-7), navigate through your hard drive until you find the MP3 or other audio file you want to convert.**

   Click a folder in the dialog box, and you see its contents in the column to its immediate right. Keep opening folders until you find your file.

4. **Select the file you want, and click the Open button.**

   The QuickTime Player opens your MP3 file in a new window with the familiar QuickTime Play, Rewind, and Fast Forward controls at the bottom of the window. Make sure to keep this window active. Don't click or open any other windows before the next step.

5. **Choose File➪Export.**

   This step opens the Save Exported File As dialog box, where you can name your newly converted file, set other options, and ultimately save the file. And, remember: You can't export a music file downloaded from the Apple iTunes Music Store. These files have unique copy protection that prevents you from exporting the music to another format.

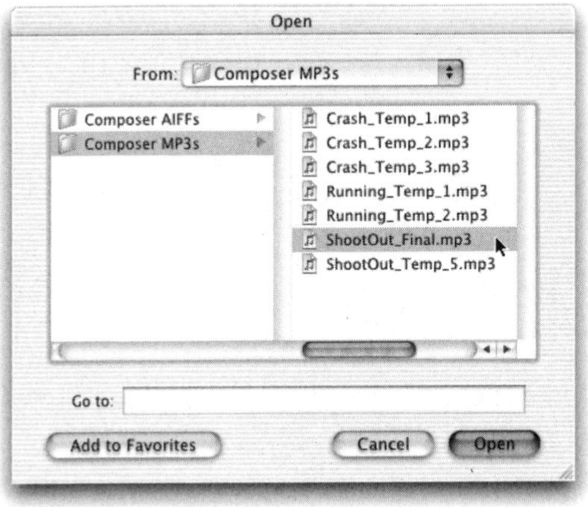

Figure 5-7:
The Open
dialog box.

6. **From the Export drop-down menu at the bottom of the dialog box, choose Sound to AIFF, as shown in Figure 5-8.**

   This drop-down menu lets you choose the format for your new sound file. Although you have other options, such as Sound to WAV, AIFF files are more popular on Macs, so stay with that format.

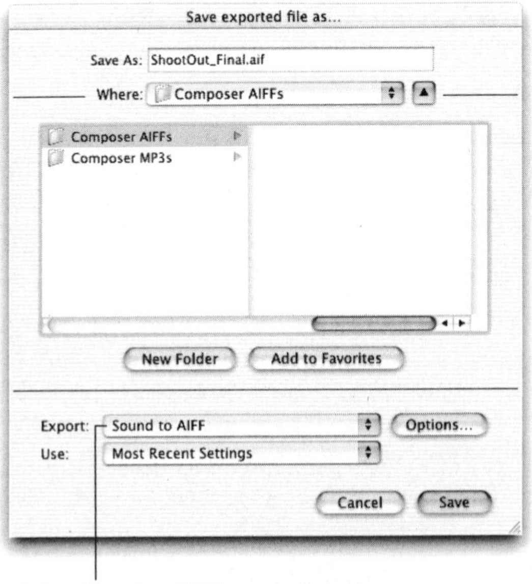

Figure 5-8:
The Save
Exported
File As
dialog box,
with Sound
to AIFF
selected.

Select Sound to AIFF from the Export menu.

7. **Click the Options button.**

   This step brings up another dialog box, as shown in Figure 5-9, with a handful of techie-looking settings.

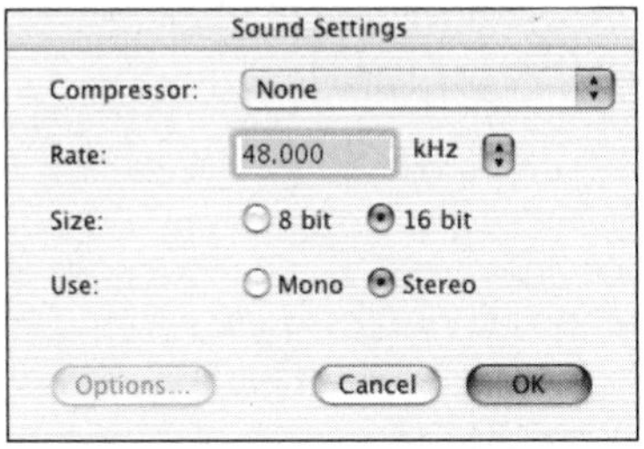

Figure 5-9:
The Sound
Settings
dialog box.

8. **In the Sound Settings box, choose the settings that define the quality of your new AIFF file and then click the OK button.**

   These different settings affect your new AIFF file's size. Smaller sizes are easier to handle on crowded hard drives and can be sent over the Internet more quickly, but smaller sizes also compromise your sound's quality. It's up to you, but I recommend staying with the highest settings, as follows:

   • **Set the Compressor to None.**

      Selecting this setting means that QuickTime doesn't compress your sound.

   • **Choose 48.000 as the rate.**

      This setting preserves good sound fidelity and best compatibility with media that's in the DV codec. Choosing lower rates squeezes your music into a smaller file size, but leads to lower quality.

   • **Choose 16 bit as the size.**

   • **Choose Stereo (if your original audio file is in stereo, that is).**

      Just so you know, choosing Mono cuts your file size roughly in half because separate sound data no longer exists for two stereo speakers (left and right).

9. **From the Save Exported File As dialog box, name your new AIFF file, navigate to the folder you want to save it to, and click Save.**

Congratulations! QuickTime leaves your original MP3 or other audio file untouched. But you now have a copy of it in a file format that Final Cut Pro can import and play without a hitch.

When you convert an MP3 (or other compressed audio) file to the AIFF format, the AIFF version doesn't improve on the MP3's sound quality, even if you keep your AIFF sound settings as high as possible. Why not? The MP3 source is already compressed, and the AIFF file that QuickTime Pro spawns can't magically recover data that was lost during the MP3's original compression. You may say "That's fine by me. The MP3 file sounded great anyway!" But, here's the catch: Although the sound of an MP3 file holds up on your Mac's built-in speakers or an average television or headphone set, when you compare MP3 to uncompressed sound on a good sound system, the MP3 rendition is noticeably inferior. I say this only to warn you about converting MP3 sound to an AIFF format and then using it in your finished Final Cut Pro movies. MP3-based sound is great placeholder material, but, for best results, you may want to use uncompressed sound in your finished Final Cut Pro movies.

Chapter 6

Organizing Your Media

. . . .

In This Chapter

▶ Understanding Browser bins and icons

▶ Working with clips — viewing, copying, deleting

▶ Using the columns in the Browser

▶ Searching for clips

▶ Bringing offline clips back online

. . . .

As you edit your movies — especially long ones — keeping all the media clips and Timeline sequences for your project well organized is very important. Because a project may use hundreds of clips and dozens of sequences, working with all this stuff can be a nightmare if you don't have a good system for keeping track of it. Fortunately, Final Cut Pro gives you plenty of tools to run a tight ship.

Working in the Browser

When you capture or import media clips or when you create new Timeline sequences, Final Cut Pro HD places all these elements into its Browser window, as shown in Figure 6-1. The Browser is like the central repository for all the stuff your project uses, just as your hard drive is the central repository for all the data your Mac uses. In fact, the Browser works much like your hard drive. A hard drive is full of many different files, stored in many different folders, just as the Browser can be filled with many different media clips and sequences of clips, stored in many different *bins,* which act just like folders within the Browser.

Chances are, you can see the Browser on your screen at all times, but if it ever gets covered up by another window, you can call it forward by choosing Window⇨Browser from the main menu or by pressing ⌘+4.

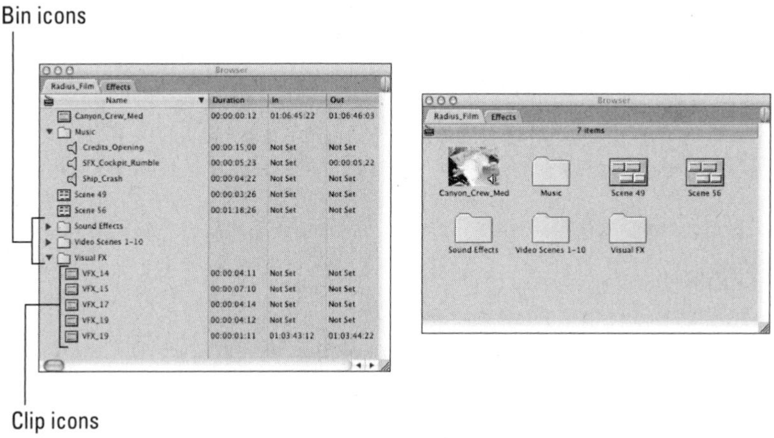

Bin icons

Figure 6-1:
The
Browser
window can
show its
contents in
both Large
Icon view
and List
view.

Clip icons

Besides letting you organize clips and sequences (preferably into bins), the Browser gives you easy access to the following:

- ✓ **Helpful clip info:** The Browser can show you a great deal of information about your media clips via its data columns, which are arranged horizontally across the window. (You can use the Browser's horizontal scroll bar to see more columns — you find lots of 'em!) To help you scan for media clips quickly, you can list the contents of the Browser by the information in any of these columns. For instance, you can see clips in alphabetical order, from longest to shortest, by their data rate or their source tape, for example. (I show how to do this in the section "Using Browser Columns," later in this chapter.)

- ✓ **Other open projects:** You would expect the Browser to show all the media and sequences that are available in your current project, but the fun doesn't stop there. You can have multiple projects open at the same time, in which case each open project gets its own tab in the Browser. (The tab displays its project's name.) You can click a tab to see its project media and sequences within the Browser, or you can drag each tab outside the Browser to open the project in a new Browser window. To close a project, Control+click its tab — hold down Control as you click — and choose Close Tab from the pop-up menu that appears.

- ✓ **Effects, transitions, and more:** Speaking of tabs, the Browser also features a tab named Effects. Clicking this tab shows you all the transitions, video filters, audio filters, and generators that are available in Final Cut Pro. From this tab, you can easily select an effect and apply it to your media — I show you how in later chapters. The thing to keep in mind, though, is that the Browser lists them all in one convenient place.

Using bins

Keeping your media clips and sequence files organized into bins should always be a priority as you work. Take the time to set up bins in advance for items such as video clips, music, and sound effects — or you can organize bins according to scenes in your movie. Some key tips for working with bins are as follows:

- ✓ **Making new bins:** To make a new bin in your Browser, choose File⇨ New⇨Bin from the main menu or press ⌘+B. You see a new bin appear in your Browser, with its name highlighted for renaming. Click in the Name field of the bin, and give it a new name.

- ✓ **Adding items to bins:** Adding items (like clips or sequences) to bins is like adding files to your folders in the Mac OS. Simply drag any item into your bin to add that item to that bin. You can also drag a bin into another bin.

- ✓ **Opening bins:** You can double-click a bin to open it in its own Browser-like window. Or, if the Browser is set to display its contents in its default List view (more on the Browser's views in a moment), notice how each bin has a small triangle next to it. (Apple calls it the *disclosure triangle.*) To open your bin, click the triangle so that it points down and reveals the contents of your bin. Click the triangle again to hide the bin's contents.

Viewing clips as icons or in lists

Final Cut Pro can show the Browser's contents in a number of different views, as shown in Figure 6-2.

To select your viewing preference, choose View⇨Browser Items from the main menu and choose from one of the following four views in the submenu:

- ✓ **List:** List view is the most efficient and shows you the most information about all the clips and sequences. The only drawback is that you have no way of quickly seeing the contents of a media clip because you see only its name (this makes a good case for naming clips with descriptive names). If you like the idea of seeing a visual representation of the contents of your clips, consider using an icon view.

- ✓ **Small Icons:** Small Icon view displays small icons for clips and other items in the Browser. In practice, I don't find this view helpful because the icons are too small to be seen clearly.

> ✔ **Medium Icons:** Medium Icon view displays a slightly larger view of the icons. The icons show the first frame of each video clip (this frame is called a *poster* frame) and are fairly large and easy to see.
>
> ✔ **Large Icons:** Large Icon view shows you the largest icons of any of the views.

If the Browser is in Medium or Large Icon view, Final Cut lets you quickly view all the frames of any clip directly from the Browser, saving you from opening the clip in the Viewer window, just to see its contents. First, select the Scrub Video tool from the Final Cut Pro Tool palette. (The Scrub Video tool looks like a hand with two small arrows — it's hidden behind the Tool palette's Zoom tool, so click and hold the Zoom tool to reveal the Scrub Video tool, as shown in Figure 6-3.) Next, click the Scrub Video tool on any video clip icon in the Browser and drag the mouse left or right to play through (or "scrub") the video of that clip.

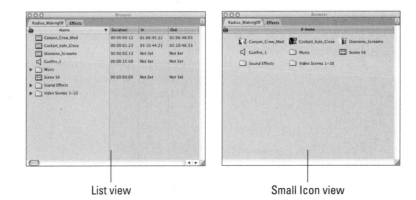

List view   Small Icon view

Figure 6-2:
The four
Browser
views.

Medium Icon view   Large Icon view

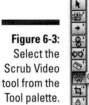

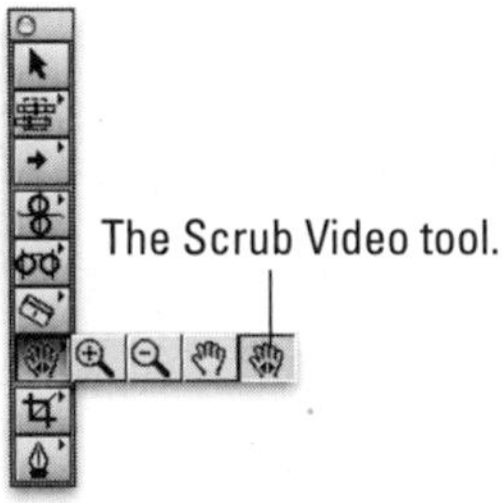

Figure 6-3:
Select the
Scrub Video
tool from the
Tool palette.

The Scrub Video tool.

When you set the Browser to an icon view, you may find that your icons
are messily strewn across the Browser rather than neatly aligned with one
another. To bring some order to this mess, choose View⇨Arrange to make
the Browser tidy up the icons in a more organized fashion.

Figuring Out the Browser Icons

Each type of item in the Browser has its own icon to help you quickly figure
out what kind of clip or other element you're looking at. Table 6-1 shows the
icons in the Browser window and indicates what they stand for. The chapters
listed in the table indicate where you can turn to find more information.

Table 6-1	Icons in the Browser Window	
Icon	*Item*	*To Find Out More, See This Chapter*
	Bin	1
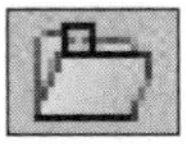	Open bin	6
	Locked bin	6
	Marker	9
	Video/audio clip	7 and 10

(continued)

Table 6-1 *(continued)*

Icon	Item	To Find Out More, See This Chapter
	Subclip	6
	Audio clip	10
	Offline clip	4 and 6
	Sequence	2 and 7
	Graphic/still	5
	Video filter	14
	Video transition	12
	Audio filter	10
	Audio transition	10
	Generator	13

Using Browser Columns

When the Browser is in List view (choose View➪Browser Items➪List from the main menu), it sports a long list of columns that give you all sorts of facts and figures about your media clips and Timeline sequences (see Figure 6-4).

Although this information may not be useful to you every day, it can often come in handy.

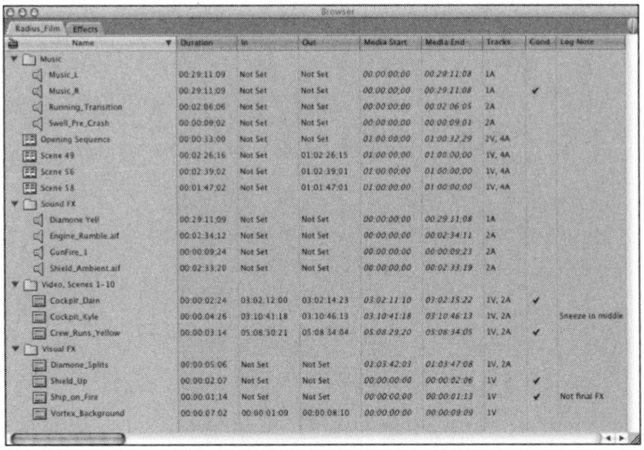

Figure 6-4:
These
Browser
columns
give you
useful (and
some not-
so-useful)
information
about your
clip.

Understanding the column headings

The Browser boasts 33 different column headings that you can display or hide. You may not need many of them in your project, but most editors prefer to see lots of information about their media in the Browser.

The column headings you probably use the most are as follows:

- **Name:** The Name column is always the first column in the Browser window. The name of your clip is the name you typed when you captured it from tape using the Log and Capture window or the name of the file you imported from your hard drive.

- **Reel:** This column shows the clip's reel name as you entered it in the Log and Capture window. The reel name is the name of the tape from which the clip was captured.

- **Capture:** You can see the current capture status of your clip in this column. The indicators that appear in this column are Not Yet, OK (which means that the clip has been captured), Aborted, and Queued. Another indicator that appears in this column is Error, indicating that your clip dropped frames during the capture process.

- **Data Rate:** This column indicates the data rate of your captured clip. For DV clips, the data rate is always 3.6 MB (megabytes) per second.

✔ **Size:** This column shows the size of your clip in megabytes (MB) as it exists on the drive. Using this column, you can identify unnecessary clips that take up large amounts of hard drive space. *Note:* The Browser normally hides the Size column. To reveal it, see the section "Working with column headings," later in this chapter.

✔ **Source:** Each clip you see in the Browser is a media file that is stored somewhere on your hard drive. This column lets you see the path of the media file on your drive. In short, to find out where you stored a file on your drive, look in this column. *Note:* The Browser normally hides this column too because it can be very wide. To reveal the column, see the section "Working with column headings," later in this chapter.

✔ **In:** This column indicates the timecode of an In point. This point may not necessarily be the start of your clip. If you move the In point for the clip, the timecode changes here to reflect that move.

✔ **Out:** This column shows the timecode of an Out point. Again, this point isn't necessarily the end of your clip because you may have set an Out point before the clip ends.

✔ **Duration:** This column gives you a timecode value that indicates how long your clip lasts (in hours, minutes, seconds, and frames), between any In and Out points you've set in the clip.

Sorting clips by column

The Sort feature is one of the more helpful functions of the Browser. You can sort the clips and sequences in the Browser by any of the Browser's many columns — for instance, by clip name, the clip's reel name, the clip's duration, or the compression code the clip uses.

To sort by a particular column's contents, just click the heading (that is, the name) of that column at the top of the Browser window. When you click a column, you see a small green arrow that points down (indicating a sort), and your clips sort themselves in alphabetical order (or from largest to smallest).

To reverse-sort (for instance, to sort clip names from Z to A rather than from A to Z), click the column heading again so that the small green arrow points up.

Working with column headings

With so many different column headings, you may want to organize them in some logical fashion. You can display or hide any column, rearrange the order of columns, and change column widths to match your needs. Use the following tips to whip your Browser's columns into shape:

✔ **Display a column:** To display a column that's not visible, Control+click any column heading and choose a heading from the pop-up menu that appears.

✔ **Hide a column:** To hide any column, Control+click the column heading you want to hide and choose Hide Column from the pop-up menu that appears.

✔ **Rearrange columns:** To rearrange the order of the columns, you can click and drag any column heading to move it to the left or right.

✔ **Change column width:** Many times, you may find that the width of a certain column is too narrow. (For instance, if you use media clips with very long names, the full names may not fit in the Names column.) Just click the line between two column headings, and drag left or right to change the width of a column.

✔ **Save column layout:** After you have customized the Browser's column layout, you can save it for later use. Saving is especially helpful if several people are using the same Final Cut Pro workstation, and each has his or her own tastes. To save a layout, Control+click any column heading and choose Save Column Layout from the pop-up menu that appears. Name and save your layout in a folder that you can find later.

✔ **Restore column layout:** To restore a column layout, Control+click any column heading and choose Restore Column Layout from the pop-up menu that appears. Use the Choose a File dialog box to select a column layout you saved earlier.

Changing names and settings in a column

All the columns in the Browser show you information about the clips or sequences in the Browser. You can change many of these column settings by using one of the following on-screen elements:

✔ **Browser item names:** You can rename any bin, clip, subclip, sequence, or marker in the Browser by selecting the clip, clicking it again (two single clicks, not a fast double-click), and typing a new name.

✔ **Check marks:** Some fields in the columns display check marks. By changing the check marks, you can change the clip's settings. For example, in the Good column, you can change a clip's Good status by clicking the check mark that appears in the field. (The Good setting is a carryover from the Capture window and indicates that you thought a clip was especially good when you captured it.)

✔ **Fields in the Browser:** You can usually modify data fields in the Browser (such as information in columns like Reel, Log Notes, Scene, and Take) by single-clicking the fields twice (not a double-click, but, rather, two single clicks) and typing new information, such as a new reel name. *Note:* Depending on the fields, you may need just a single click.

 ✔ **Pop-up menus:** You can change a clip's settings in other Browser fields by Control+clicking the field and selecting a new setting for the clip from the pop-up menu that appears. For instance, you can change a clip's composite mode, its alpha channel settings, or its reel name by using a pop-up menu.

You can also change a clip's name and settings from one convenient dialog box. Select the clip in the Browser, choose Edit⇨Item Properties, and choose one of the three submenu options. Choosing the Logging submenu, for instance, lets you edit all the clip's logging information, such as its name, reel name, and comments.

Making Copies of Clips

Sometimes, you want to make a copy of a clip in the Browser — for instance, maybe a long clip has media that suits two different purposes in your story, and you want to create two versions of the clip, by giving each one a unique name to reflect the content that's important about each one. Another reason you may copy a clip is to keep the same clip in multiple bins — for instance, you may organize media into Scenes bins, and also in bins that follow some other criteria (subject matter, perhaps). By making a copy of a clip, you can keep the same clip in different bins.

You can make a copy of a clip in two ways. The difference between each approach determines whether the copied clips are linked. This has to do with the fact that when you first capture or import a clip into the Browser, it's treated as a so-called master clip. When you copy a master clip, you can make the copy an affiliate clip or a new master clip altogether, as described in this list:

 ✔ **Make the copy an affiliate clip.** Select the master clip you want to copy in the Browser, and choose Edit⇨Duplicate. Final Cut creates a new copy of the clip in the Browser window, using exactly the same name as the original clip. This clip is now an affiliate of the master clip. If you ever change the name of either the affiliate or the master clip (or either clip's reel name, online/offline status, or timecode information), its copy is also updated to reflect this change. It's as though the master and affiliate clips are mirror images of each other.

 ✔ **Make the copy a new master clip.** Select the master clip you want to copy in the Browser, and choose Modify⇨Duplicate As New Master Clip. Final Cut creates a new copy of the clip in the Browser window, using exactly the same name as the original clip, but with no link to the original. You can change the copied clip's name, without that change affecting the original master clip.

A form of a copied clip is the subclip. The *subclip* is just a smaller portion of another clip in the Browser. For instance, if Clip A features a minute of footage and you want to work with only its last 30 seconds, you can create a subclip of A, which features only that part of Clip A. To create a subclip, open a master clip in the Viewer and set In and Out points that contain the frames you're interested in. (See Chapter 7 for more about setting these points in the Viewer.) Then, simply choose Modify➪Make Subclip. Final Cut places in the Browser a new subclip containing the frames you're interested in. This clip is treated as a new master clip — you can rename it without affecting the name of the clip the subclip came from.

Adding Transitions and Effects to the Favorites Bin

The Browser window features a special tab just for Final Cut Pro's Effects (see Figure 6-5). Click this tab, and you can find all the effects that Final Cut Pro offers, such as transitions, video and audio filters, and generators. I explain how to apply these effects in later chapters, but what's good to note now is that the Browser's Effects tab includes a Favorites bin, where you can store transitions and effects you plan to use again. By placing these items in the Favorites bin, you make it easier to find 'em quickly rather than dig through all the effects listed on the Effects tab itself (most of which you rarely, if ever, use).

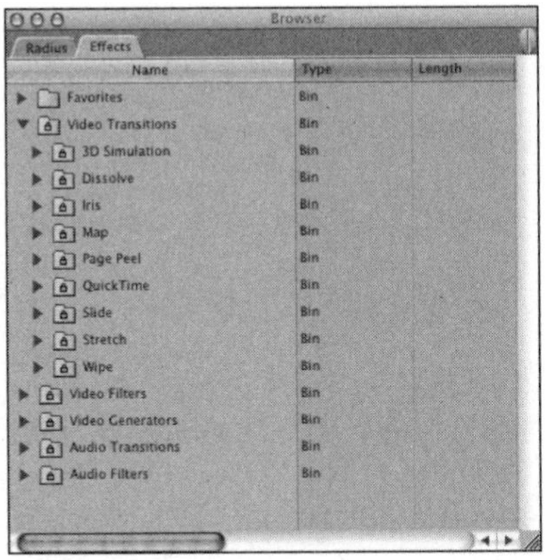

Figure 6-5:
Click the
Browser's
Effects tab
to see all
the Final Cut
Pro filters,
transitions,
and
generators.

Making an effect a Favorite is easy. From the Browser's Effects tab, just select an effect and drag it to the Favorites bin. Final Cut Pro responds by placing a copy of that effect in the Favorites bin. From now on, you can drag this transition or effect from the Favorites bin and add it to your clips. These effects in the Favorites bin are also available to you when you choose Effects➪Favorites.

Finding Clips Fast

On a large project, the Browser can quickly become a mess, strewn with media clips and cluttered with bins within bins. If you ever find your Browser in this state of disarray, finding a particular media clip or Timeline sequence in all this chaos can become pretty time-consuming. Thankfully, Final Cut Pro includes an awesome search function to help find the proverbial needle in a haystack.

Searching by clip name

The most basic search is to look for a clip or sequence by name. (Of course, you have to remember the name of the item you're looking for.)

To do a basic name search, follow these steps:

1. **Make sure that the Browser window is selected.**

   If the Timeline or Canvas window is selected instead, Final Cut Pro searches for clips only in the Timeline's active sequence. You want to search the entire contents of your project, though, so make sure that the Browser is selected.

2. **Choose Edit⇨Find, or press ⌘+F.**

   The Find dialog box appears, as shown in Figure 6-6.

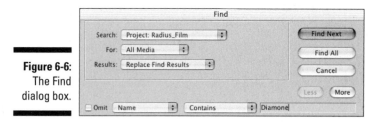

Figure 6-6:
The Find
dialog box.

3. **From the Find dialog box's Search pop-up menu, select the name of your project.**

   Or, you can also choose to search through all open projects in the Browser, but it usually makes sense to search only the active project.

4. **From the For pop-up menu, choose All Media.**

   Or, you can choose to search for only media that's already being used in a Timeline sequence, or media that hasn't been used yet.

5. **From the Results pop-up menu, choose Replace Find Results.**

   Choosing this option replaces the results of a previous search. Choosing Add to Find Results simply adds the results of your upcoming search to the results of your last search.

6. **From the two pop-up menus at the bottom of the Find window, choose Name in the left one and choose Contains in the right one.**

7. **In the lower-right field of the Find dialog box, type the name of the clip you want to search for, and then click Find Next.**

   You can type part of the name or the whole name in the Name field. The Find dialog box closes, and the first clip in the Browser that matches the name is highlighted.

8. **Choose Edit⇨Find Next or press ⌘+G to find the next clip based on the name you entered.**

Rather than search for clips one at a time (by using Find Next), you can search in one fell swoop for all clips that meet your criteria. When you're ready to start your search from the Find dialog box, just click the Find All button rather than the Find Next button. Final Cut Pro responds by opening a Find Results window (see Figure 6-7) that contains *all* the clips it found that match your criteria.

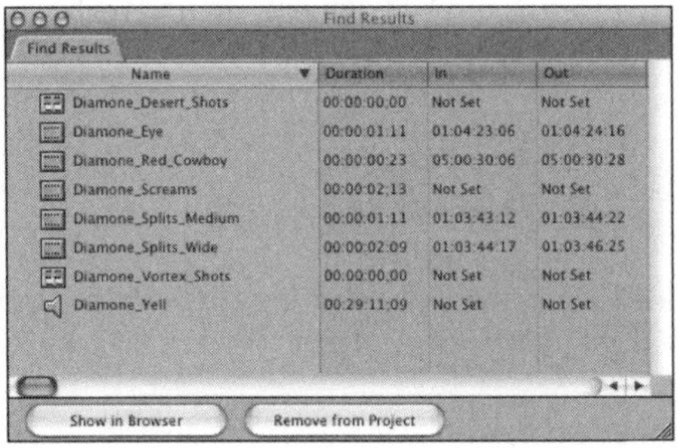

	Name	▼	Duration	In	Out
	Diamone_Desert_Shots		00:00:00:00	Not Set	Not Set
	Diamone_Eye		00:00:01:11	01:04:23:06	01:04:24:16
	Diamone_Red_Cowboy		00:00:00:23	05:00:30:06	05:00:30:28
	Diamone_Screams		00:00:02:13	Not Set	Not Set
	Diamone_Splits_Medium		00:00:01:11	01:03:43:12	01:03:44:22
	Diamone_Splits_Wide		00:00:02:09	01:03:44:17	01:03:46:25
	Diamone_Vortex_Shots		00:00:00:00	Not Set	Not Set
	Diamone_Yell		00:29:11:09	Not Set	Not Set

Figure 6-7:
The Find
Results
window.

Show in Browser   Remove from Project

More-powerful searches

You can use the Find dialog box to search for clips by lots of other criteria — for instance, by scene, reel name, label, or descriptive comments you may have entered for the clip when you logged it during the capture process (refer to Chapter 4). You can also search by multiple criteria at the same time. A creative mix and match of the options that are available in the Find dialog box can turn up just about any item.

Use the steps I used to search for clips by name, and mix in the following different options to customize your search:

- ✔ **To add criteria:** Click the Find box's More button (refer to Figure 6-6) to get additional criteria that you can use for your search. For example, you may want to search for clip names *and* log notes.

- ✔ **To remove criteria:** Click the Find box's Less button to remove criteria from your search. This button is available only when you have enabled multiple criteria.

- ✔ **To omit criteria:** Select the Omit check box in the lower-left corner of the Find box to omit particular criteria. For example, you may want to omit any clip with the word *car* in its name.

- ✔ **To choose a Browser column to search:** Click the Column pop-up menu (next to the Omit check box), and select the Browser column you want to search in (in my earlier example, I chose to search in the Name column). For instance, if you're searching for any clips from Reel 5, you would select the Reel column.

- ✔ **To further refine your search:** The Contains pop-up menu, which is to the left of the Column pop-up menu, lets you narrow your search further. Your options are Starts With, Contains, Equals, Ends With, Less Than, and Greater Than.

- ✔ **Text field:** Type the text you want to search for in the text field in the lower-right corner.

Dealing with Offline Media

At some point in your Final Cut Pro travels, you may find that some of your project's media has gone *offline* — in other words, Final Cut can no longer find the media your movie depends on.

Remember that any clip you import or capture into the Browser is simply just a pointer to a digital media file located somewhere on your hard drive (such as a QuickTime movie, a TIFF image from Photoshop, or an AIFF music file). Final Cut Pro usually knows where to find all your project's media files — it knows each file's name, which hard drive it's on, and which folder it resides in.

But, things can go awry if you alter your digital media files in such a way that Final Cut can't find them. For example, you may import a media file into the Browser (where it's represented as a clip) and later go to your Mac's Finder and rename the media file, move it to a different folder, or delete it altogether (or, you may have forgotten to turn on an external hard drive where the media is stored). In this case, you're in trouble: Final Cut can't play your clip because it can no longer find its associated media file. Tragically, your clip has gone from being *online* (a happy and productive member of your fine movie) to *offline* (lost and presumed dead).

Final Cut Pro continually checks your hard drive to make sure that the media for your project is online. If the software finds that any media is missing in action, the software alerts you via the dialog box you see in Figure 6-8. Also, your Browser draws a slash through each offline clip's icon, as shown in Figure 6-9, and Final Cut Pro displays the message Media Offline when you play the clip in the Viewer or from the Timeline.

When Final Cut reports that a clip is offline, you have a couple of options for bringing it back to life, as the rest of this section discusses.

Pathname to missing files   Missing media files

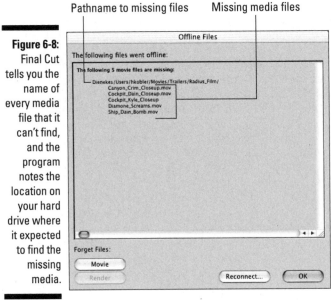

Figure 6-8:
Final Cut tells you the name of every media file that it can't find, and the program notes the location on your hard drive where it expected to find the missing media.

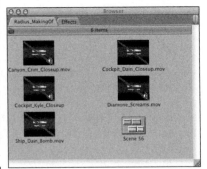

Figure 6-9:
The Browser shows that a clip is offline by placing a slash through its icon.

Recapturing deleted clips

If you deleted media clips from your hard drive, Job 1 is getting those media files back on your drive so that Final Cut Pro can find them. If the media didn't come from videotape (for instance, the missing item is a still picture taken by a digital camera or an AIFF music file from a CD), you have to track down those original files and copy them back to your hard drive. After they're back on your drive, use the steps listed in the next section, "Reconnecting an offline clip."

If the missing media was initially captured from videotape, you can use the Final Cut Pro Batch Capture command to recapture it from tape. This process can go one of two ways: the easy way or the hard way. It goes the easy way if, when you're capturing your clips the first time, you typed some key information about each clip, such as the reel name of the videotape that the clip was taken from and the timecode location of the clip on that particular tape. If you recorded this info when you captured your now-offline clip (refer to Chapter 4 to find out how to log this information), Final Cut Pro simply prompts you to insert a particular tape into your videocamera or deck (for instance, Tape 5) and then automatically moves to the clip's timecode location on the tape and captures the clip for you, bringing it back online.

On the other hand, if you didn't record this key information when you originally captured your clips from tape, Final Cut Pro has no way to know how to find your clips itself, and you have to do all the heavy lifting. For starters, you have to figure out the particular tape that your clip's media came from. (I hope that you don't have a shoebox full of poorly labeled tapes; if so, good luck!) Then, you have to manually review the tape, find your media, and capture it, as though it's from scratch.

Reconnecting an offline clip

If a clip has gone offline and you know that its media file is still on your hard drive, you can reconnect the clip with its media in one of the following ways:

- ✔ When Final Cut Pro displays a dialog box warning you that clips in your project have gone offline (refer to Figure 6-8), click the Reconnect button in the dialog box.
- ✔ Select any offline clips in the Browser (these clips display slashes through their icons), and then choose File➪Reconnect Media.

Either way, Final Cut Pro responds with the Reconnect Options dialog box, which asks what kind of clips you want to reconnect, as shown in Figure 6-10. Make sure to check Offline (it should be checked already), and don't worry about checking any other options. Click OK.

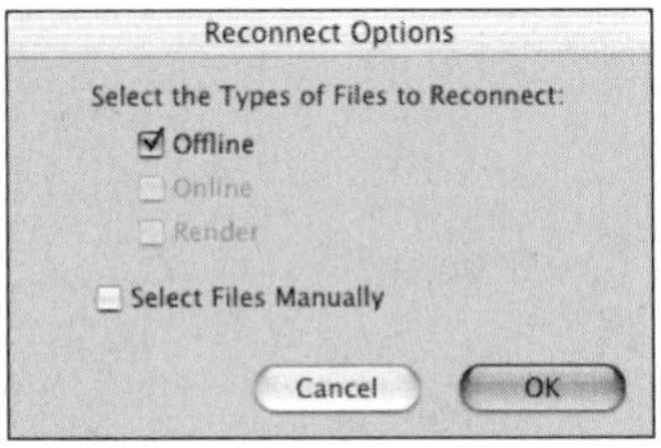

Figure 6-10: Check the media types that you want to reconnect.

In response to your input in the Reconnect Options dialog box, Final Cut Pro opens the Reconnect dialog box, as shown in Figure 6-11. This dialog box lets you navigate through your hard drive's folders and files so that you can show Final Cut Pro where each piece of offline media is located on your hard drive.

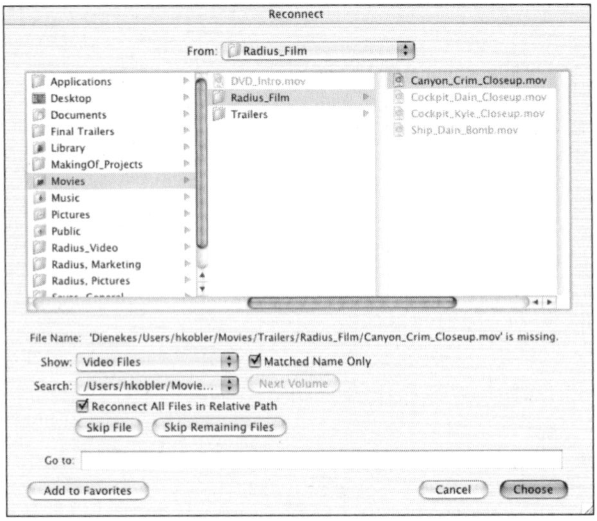

Figure 6-11: The Reconnect dialog box.

In the File Name field of the Reconnect dialog box, Final Cut Pro prompts you for the media file that it's looking for. Use the dialog box's file selector to browse to the file on your hard drive, select it, and click the Choose button to reconnect it and bring it online again.

If you have multiple offline files, Final Cut Pro prompts you to find each file, one after another. To skip finding a file (maybe this particular file is no longer on your drive), just click the Skip File button.

After you reconnect a file in a particular folder on your hard drive, Final Cut Pro can automatically reconnect any other offline files that happen to be in that folder, saving you from having to handle each file manually. To take advantage of this feature, make sure that you have checked the Reconnect All Files in Relative Path option in the Reconnect dialog box.

If your clips have gone offline because you renamed their media files on your hard drive, make sure to uncheck the Match Name Only option in the Reconnect dialog box. This action lets you associate an offline clip with *any* media file on your drive, not just a file that matches the clip's original name. Just make sure that you're reconnecting a clip to the right media file — otherwise, when you use that clip in the future, it doesn't play the media you expected!

Part III
Editing Your Media

The 5th Wave   By Rich Tennant

THE LEVINES EDIT THEIR AFRICAN SAFARI VIDEO

"Do you think the 'Hidden Rhino' clip should come before or after the 'Waving Hello' video clip?"

In this part . . .

I start off Part III with the basics of editing video and audio: how to move clips to the Final Cut Timeline window and then how to resize them, cut them up, or move them in time. I round out your new skills by giving you finer control over the Final Cut Timeline. I also tackle the Final Cut advanced editing features, which you don't *need* to know, but which will make your editing work much easier in the long run.

Chapter 7

Editing Basics

. . . .

. . . .

*E*diting is a unique form of magic. You begin the process with hordes of raw video, audio, and still pictures that, taken on their own, mean nothing. But, through editing, you weave all those disparate parts into a new whole — something with its own identity and the power to entertain, inform, provoke, gall — take your pick.

The process of editing may seem complex and mysterious to the uninitiated (again, like magic), but that's just an illusion. In fact, after you begin to explore the Final Cut Pro editing tools and methods, you realize that they're all straightforward and even — dare I say? — *simple.*

Understanding the Editing Process

At the center of all your editing work is the Final Cut Pro Timeline window, where you visually arrange all your video clips, audio clips, and still pictures in time. The following other major windows also play a big part in editing:

✔ **The Browser:** As shown in Figure 7-1, the Browser is where you store and organize all the media clips you have imported into your project before you move them to the Timeline.

✔ **The Viewer:** The Viewer window is where you watch (or listen to) clips before you move them to the Timeline (double-click a clip in the Browser to open it in the Viewer).

✔ **The Canvas:** The Canvas window plays any clips you have arranged in the Timeline window. In other words, it's the window you use to preview your movie in progress.

✔ **The Tool palette:** Although the Tool palette isn't technically a window, it contains the editing tools for cutting, moving, and resizing clips, among other things.

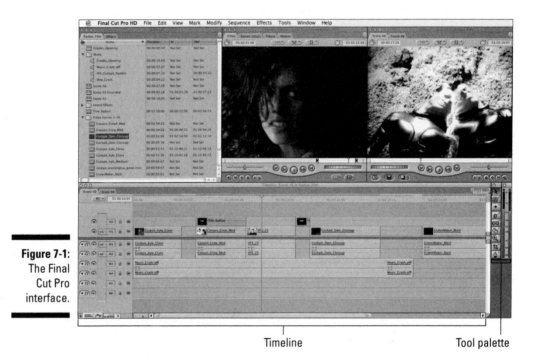

Figure 7-1:
The Final
Cut Pro
interface.

Timeline   Tool palette

As you edit, you continually move back and forth between the Final Cut Pro windows. The overall process goes something like this:

1. Find a clip using the Browser.

2. Preview the clip in the Viewer to see whether you like it.

3. Add the clip to the Timeline, making it part of your movie.

4. Watch your movie in the Canvas to see how your new clip fits in with all the other clips.

5. To tweak how your clip works with the rest of the movie, use the appropriate tool from the Tool palette to resize, split, or rearrange the clip on the Timeline.

6. Check out your movie again in the Canvas window to see how your edits look.

7. Move on to the next shot or scene, and repeat the process.

If this process sounds a bit daunting, don't worry. Editing in Final Cut Pro is like learning to drive a car with a stick shift: You wonder how you can possibly steer the car, press the gas or brake pedal, and shift gears at the same time (not to mention tune the radio, chat on the phone, and decipher those directions you scrawled on a napkin). But, sure enough, before you know it, the process is second nature. So it goes with Final Cut Pro.

Getting to know the Timeline

The Final Cut Pro Timeline, as shown in Figure 7-2, lets you arrange all your video and audio clips so that they tell the story you want to tell. To understand how the Timeline works, think of it as a page of sheet music, but, rather than place musical notes of different lengths of time (quarter notes, half notes, and whole notes), one after another, you place video and audio clips of different lengths of time, one after another. And, when you want to see how your clips are played together, you can watch your movie in progress in the Canvas window.

Sequence tabs   Playhead   Timeline ruler

Figure 7-2:
The
Timeline.

Audio tracks

Video tracks

This section points out the key features of the Timeline.

The Timeline ruler

The *Timeline ruler* stretches across the top of the Timeline and looks like a conventional ruler (refer to Figure 7-2), except that it marks increments in time (4 seconds or 8 seconds, for example), not distance. When you place a media clip on the Timeline, the clip plays at the point where you have placed it on the Timeline ruler. For instance, if the clip starts at the 4-second mark on the ruler, the clip plays 4 seconds into your movie.

The ruler markers show hours, minutes, seconds, and, finally, frames of video; these values are known as the *timecode*. A timecode measurement that reads 01:02:40;04 means that you're in the first hour, second minute, 40th second, and fourth frame of your story.

The playhead

The *playhead* (refer to Figure 7-2) is like a record needle on an old LP record player: The music plays wherever the needle is, and your movie plays wherever the playhead is on your Timeline. In the Timeline ruler area, click the location where you want the playhead to start playing. The playhead automatically jumps to that point, and you see the video frame that happens to be under the playhead in the Canvas window. To begin viewing your movie from that point, click the Play button in the Canvas window.

Timeline tracks

The Timeline is divided into horizontal rows called *tracks*. You use tracks to play two or more clips at the same time by placing the clips on different tracks, stacked on top of each other (refer to Figure 7-2). For instance, if you want your movie to feature dialogue and background music playing together, place the dialogue clip on one track and the music directly below it on a different track.

Timeline tracks come in two flavors — video and audio — so you put your video clips on video tracks and your audio clips on audio tracks. You can have as many as 99 tracks of each one, but for most purposes, you need only a handful of them. Video tracks are numbered V1, V2, and so on, and audio tracks are A1, A2, and so on.

Sequence tabs

You may recall that a *sequence* is a collection of clips you have organized on the Timeline. (You typically use sequences to break a movie into smaller, more manageable parts — for instance, you can create each of your movie scenes in its own sequence.) You can open your project sequences by double-clicking them in the Browser window, and every open sequence is represented by a tab in the upper-left corner of the Timeline window. You can work with each sequence by clicking its tab. (See Chapters 6 and 8 for more about how to create and manage sequences.)

Playing back video: The Viewer and Canvas windows

Before you get into the thick of editing, consider the one thing you do in Final Cut Pro more than anything else: Play back video by using either the Viewer or Canvas window.

The Viewer window plays a single media clip so that you can check it out, see what you like about it, and possibly make edits to it. You open a clip in the Viewer by double-clicking the clip from either the Browser window or the Timeline, if you have already moved the clip there.

Although the Viewer lets you play a single clip, the Canvas window plays the sequence of clips you have assembled in the Timeline window. In other words, you use the Canvas, as shown in Figure 7-3, to watch your movie in progress so that you can judge how all your edited clips work together.

Timecode duration

Zoom   Current timecode

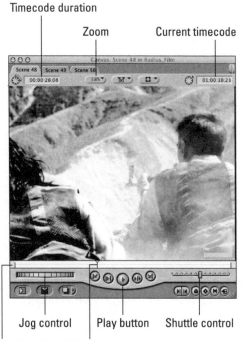

Figure 7-3:
The Canvas
window.

Jog control   Play button   Shuttle control

Scrubber bar   Playhead

So, the Viewer and Canvas windows perform different functions, but they work similarly in that they both offer essentially the same playback options: You can play video and audio forward and in reverse at normal speeds, speed through the video and audio with fast forward and rewind, move slowly, or jump to any point with a single mouse click. Some of the controls that work in both the Viewer and the Canvas are as follows:

✔ **Play button:** Click it to play, and click it again to pause.

✔ **Scrubber bar and playhead:** The scrubber bar runs horizontally across the Viewer and Canvas windows, right under your video. The length of the scrubber bar represents the length of your clip (Viewer) or movie

(Canvas), and you can position the scrubber playhead anywhere on the bar by clicking your mouse button at the desired location. The window shows the frame of video that is at the playhead position. By the way, notice that the Canvas and Timeline playheads mirror each other: When you position the playhead in the Canvas scrubber, the playhead on the Timeline jumps to the same position.

✔ **Jog control:** Click and drag the Jog control to the left or right to slowly roll the Viewer or Canvas playhead forward or backward, as little as a frame at a time. (You can also move the playhead frame by frame with the left- and right-arrow keys.)

✔ **Shuttle control:** Click and drag the shuttle control left or right to rewind or fast forward. The farther you drag the shuttle head from its middle point, the faster your playback.

As intuitive as these play controls are, they do have a downside. As you play your clips repeatedly and scrutinize each frame or edit, you may get tired of continually clicking buttons in the Viewer or Canvas. Instead, place your fingers on the keyboard and try out the following keys:

✔ **J:** Play backward (in reverse, like rewinding)

✔ **K:** Stop

✔ **L:** Play forward

Keeping your fingers on these keys gives you lightning-quick control over clip playback. Plus, you can use the same keys, rather than use the Shuttle control, to quickly go into fast-forward or fast-rewind modes. For instance, to fast forward, just press L twice. Press L a third or fourth time for even faster fast forwarding.

If the Viewer or Canvas windows don't play your video smoothly (in other words, if the video appears to "stutter"), click the Zoom icon at the top of either window (refer to Figure 7-3) and choose Fit to Window from the Zoom pop-up menu that appears. This action scales your video to match the size of your window and allows it to play without jerkiness.

Looking at timecode data in the Viewer and Canvas

Both the Viewer and Canvas windows give you the following handy timecode information about the clip or Timeline sequence you're working on:

✔ **Timecode Duration:** The Timecode Duration field (refer to Figure 7-3) tells you how long your clip or your entire Timeline sequence is. The Viewer window reports the length of the clip, and the Canvas reports the length of the current active sequence, measured at the last frame of the last clip of your Timeline sequence. If you have selected a segment of a clip or sequence by using In and Out points in the Viewer or Canvas — more on these points in a moment — this field shows the length of any media that falls within those points.

✔ **Current Timecode:** The Current Timecode field tells you the timecode of any frame that the Viewer or Canvas playhead happens to be on. See for yourself: Click inside the scrubber bar of either window to move the playhead from place to place, and watch the Current Timecode value change.

Again, a timecode measures hours, minutes, seconds, and frames, so the timecode value 01:04:40;26 means that you're in the first hour, fourth minute, 40th second, and 26th frame of a clip or Timeline sequence.

Moving Clips to the Timeline

When you're editing, you spend lots of time moving media clips from the Final Cut Pro Browser window to the Timeline (more specifically, to a video or audio track on the Timeline) as you weave the clips into your story. Final Cut Pro gives you several options for accomplishing this. This section begins with the easiest, most intuitive approach and ends with the quickest, most flexible method.

Inserting and overwriting

When you add a clip to a track on the Timeline, you're making an *edit.* The two edits you're most likely to make in Final Cut Pro are *insert edits* and *overwrite edits.* The difference between these two edits is described as follows:

✔ **Insert:** With an insert edit, Final Cut Pro creates new room on the Timeline track for your clip so that it doesn't copy over other clips that are already there. (In other words, this edit works and plays well with others.)

✔ **Overwrite:** When you do an overwrite edit, Final Cut Pro adds your clip to the Timeline. If the new clip is long enough to run into other clips that are already on that track, however, the new clip erases the existing ones (a decidedly selfish kind of edit).

Figure 7-4 shows the original arrangement of Clips A, B, and C and then shows what happens when Clip D is added after Clip A via both an insert edit and an overwrite edit.

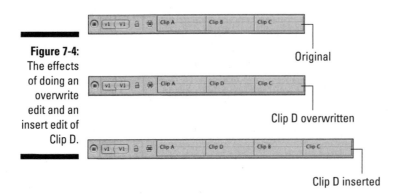

Figure 7-4:
The effects
of doing an
overwrite
edit and an
insert edit of
Clip D.

Original

Clip D overwritten

Clip D inserted

Which type of edit should you use? The answer depends on what you're trying to do. To add a clip to a bunch of other clips, use an insert edit. If you don't like how a certain clip is working on the Timeline and want to see how a new one does in its place, an overwrite edit probably would work better. The important thing is that you don't "overthink" or fret about these options. You develop a natural feel for this kind of thing soon enough.

In any case, the easiest, most intuitive way to do either edit is as follows:

1. **Position the Timeline playhead at the time you want to add your new clip.**

   Final Cut Pro places your clip at the playhead's location on the Timeline. Click within the Timeline's ruler to position the playhead at that point. (To fine-tune the playhead's position, you can move it frame by frame with your left- and right-arrow keys or move it clip by clip with the up- and down-arrow keys.) The Canvas window shows the current frame that the playhead is on — if a frame is there, as opposed to empty space.

2. **Drag your clip from the Browser window to the Canvas window.**

   Yes, drag it to the Canvas, not to the Timeline. As you drag, a number of buttons pop up over the Canvas window. These buttons are called *sections,* and as a group, they make up the Canvas's Edit Overlay feature. This overlay gives you several choices for the kind of edit you want to make, as shown in Figure 7-5. Don't release the mouse button yet!

3. **Move the mouse pointer over either Insert or Overwrite, and then release the mouse button.**

   Final Cut Pro either inserts or overwrites your clip to the Timeline. If your clip includes both video and audio tracks, the video portion appears on the Timeline video track and the audio elements are found on the Timeline's audio tracks. (Mono audio uses only one track, and audio that's captured in stereo uses two — see Chapter 10 for more information on audio.)

Overlay

Figure 7-5:
Drag a clip
to the
Canvas
window,
and the Edit
Overlay
feature
appears.

Choosing the right track on the Timeline

If your Timeline has lots of tracks, you need a way to tell Final Cut Pro which track gets the clip you're inserting or overwriting to the Timeline. For instance, if you have multiple audio tracks for stereo dialogue, sound effects, and music, you don't want to insert a clip of music on a track you're using for dialogue clips. To control which track gets the clip you're editing, you set a *destination track*. By default, Final Cut Pro sets your V1 video track and the A1 and A2 audio tracks as destination tracks (see Figure 7-6), but you can set as destination tracks any other tracks you have created. I show you how to do that in Chapter 8 and how to add more tracks to the Timeline (and delete others) because these two functions work hand in hand.

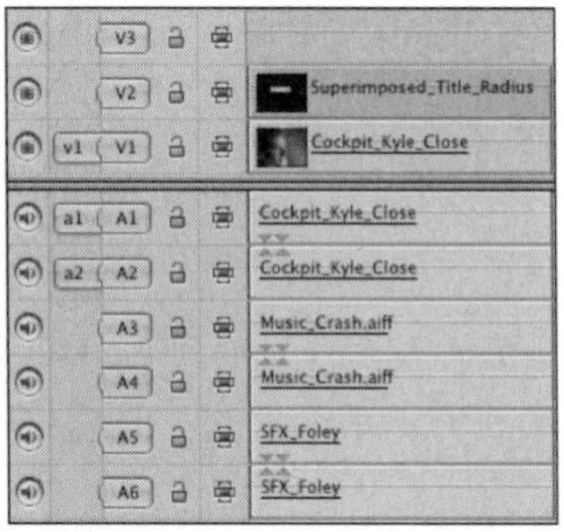

Figure 7-6:
By default,
Track V1
is your
destination
video track,
and Tracks
A1 and A2
are your
destination
audio
tracks.

Using a shortcut to insert and overwrite

When you're comfortable doing insert and overwrite edits by dragging clips from the Browser to the Canvas, you may want to try out an even more direct approach, which I discuss in this section.

Select a clip in the Browser window, and drag the clip to any point (regardless of the playhead position) and to any track on the Timeline. As you drag your clip to its track (video or audio), notice that the upper third of the track has a horizontal line running through it. (See Figure 7-7; this line is easy to miss.)

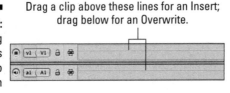

Figure 7-7:
Dragging clips directly to tracks on the Timeline.

Drag a clip above these lines for an Insert;
drag below for an Overwrite.

Your mouse pointer's position relative to this line determines whether you insert or overwrite the clip to the Timeline, as follows:

- ✔ **Insert:** When you drag your clip above the line, Final Cut Pro assumes that you want to *insert* your clip on the Timeline. Your mouse pointer becomes an arrow pointing to the right and signals an insert edit.

- ✔ **Overwrite:** When you drag your clip below the line, Final Cut Pro assumes that you want to make an *overwrite* edit. Your mouse pointer becomes an arrow pointing down when an overwrite edit is in the cards.

If your Timeline is set to display tracks in Reduced view, you can't see or use this helpful line. Any clip you drag to the Timeline is overwritten. To do an insert edit, hold down Option when you drag the clip to the Timeline and then release the mouse button.

Setting a clip's In and Out points in the Viewer

When you're moving clips to the Timeline, you can move either the entire clip or just a part of it. At first, you may feel more comfortable dragging entire clips to the Timeline and then trimming them after they are there. But, in many cases, you should look at the clip ahead of time, identify only the part you're interested in (by setting In and Out points), and then move the trimmed clip to the Timeline. This method minimizes clutter on the Timeline. To set In and Out points, follow these steps:

1. **Find the clip in the Browser window, and double-click the clip to open it in the Viewer.**

2. **Within the clip, find the first frame that you want to move to the Timeline.**

   To find the frame, click in the Viewer scrubber bar (see Figure 7-8) to move the playhead until it's on the frame you want. The frame that's displayed in the Viewer window corresponds to the frame that the playhead is on. If you're working with an audio clip, you can use the audio waveform that's displayed as a guide. The higher a waveform, the louder the audio.

Figure 7-8:
The Viewer window with In and Out points set.

Mark In button   Mark Out button   In and Out points

Scrubber bar

3. **To set an In point, click the Mark In button in the Viewer or press I.**

   You see an In point symbol, which looks like a triangle pointing to the right, appear at the playhead position on the Viewer's scrubber bar (refer to Figure 7-8) and also in the upper-left corner of the frame you have marked. (This symbol makes it easy to find marked frames.)

4. **Mark an Out point at the last frame that you want to move to the Timeline.**

   Follow the same procedure as described in Steps 2 and 3, and click the Mark Out button in the Viewer window (or press O).

Congratulations! You have now marked a range of frames within a larger clip. When you move this clip to the Timeline (using any of the steps that I cover), Final Cut Pro moves only the frames that fall within the In and Out points you set.

To move existing In or Out points that you have set for a clip in the Viewer, drag the In/Out symbol on the Viewer's scrubber bar to a new location. You can also clear In and Out points by choosing that option from the Mark menu or by pressing Option+X.

Recycling a clip by changing its In and Out points

In the thick of editing, you may want to use a clip again and set different In and Out points for each instance of use. For example, you may have a clip whose early frames are great at the beginning of a scene, but whose later frames work nicely toward the end of the scene. When you want to use different parts of the same clip, you open it in the Viewer, set In and Out points for the first part of the clip, and move those frames to the Timeline. Next, to use a different range of frames from the same clip, go back to the Browser, open that clip again in the Viewer window, set different In and Out points, and move the clip again to the Timeline. Voilà! You now have two different clips on the Timeline, each one taken from the same master clip in your Browser (refer to Chapter 6 for more about master clips).

If your Browser is cluttered with tons of clips, you may have difficulty finding the instance of a clip you have already edited to the Timeline. If that's the case, you can select the edited clip on the Timeline and then choose View⇨ Reveal Master Clip. Final Cut responds by selecting your master clip in the Browser window and saving you from tracking it down yourself.

Selecting Clips on the Timeline

After you move your clips to the Timeline, you usually have to select them before you can edit them in various ways (for instance, move or delete them). Doing so isn't rocket science: Select a clip on the Timeline by using the Selection tool, the arrow-shaped tool at the top of the Tool palette (choose Window⇨Tool Palette if you can't find it).

To select a single clip on the Timeline, make sure that you're using the Selection tool and click the clip.

If you select a clip or clips but then decide not to do anything with them, deselect them. To deselect a clip, try clicking in the Timeline window but outside of a track (as long as you don't have an All Tracks selection tool active). Or, you can use the Final Cut Pro Deselect All command by either choosing Edit⇨Deselect All or pressing ⌘+Shift+A.

Sometimes, you may want to select a number of clips at one time or a range of frames within one clip or a group of clips. Table 7-1 outlines some handy tools that Final Cut Pro offers for selecting multiple clips or ranges of frames. You can select these tools by clicking their icons on the Final Cut Pro Tool palette. In some cases, the tool is hidden behind another tool, so you have to click and hold your mouse button on the visible tool to see the related tools hidden behind it.

Table 7-1	Tools for Selecting Clips and Frames on the Timeline	
Button	*Tool*	*What It Does*
↖	Selection	You use this tool the most. To select multiple, continuous clips, click the first clip and then hold down Shift while clicking the last clip. Final Cut Pro selects all clips in between. To select multiple clips with a selection marquee, click your mouse over an empty spot on your Timeline tracks (as long as no clip is there) and drag your mouse to select multiple clips. To select multiple but noncontiguous clips (those that aren't together), hold down ⌘ while clicking each clip. You can quickly invoke the Selection tool by pressing A.
⊞	Group Selection	This tool selects a range of whole clips by dragging a selection marquee across any clips you want. You can also hold down Shift to select multiple groups of clips with this tool. When your clips are linked (the way that audio clips are usually linked to their corresponding video), this tool selects those linked clips too, even if your selection marquee doesn't touch the linked clips. However, you can also make these kinds of group selections with the standard Selection tool, so you may want to skip using this tool in favor of the more versatile Selection tool.

(continued)

Table 7-1 *(continued)*

Button	Tool	What It Does
	Range Selection	This tool selects a range of frames — anything that falls within the tool's selection marquee.
	Select Track Forward	This handy tool selects any clip you click as well as every clip on that track that follows the selected clip (that is, to the right of the clip you click). This tool is a godsend when you want to move a string of clips forward and backward in time. The tool also has some siblings: the Select Track Backward tool (which selects all clips to the left of your selection) and the Select Track tool (which selects the entire track).
	Select All Tracks Forward	This tool works just like the Select Track Forward tool, but when you click a clip, you select both the clip and every clip that follows it — on not one but all tracks. This option is useful when you want to select not only clips on your video track, for instance, but also all your audio tracks at the same time (to move or delete video and audio together). Final Cut Pro also provides a variation of this tool that selects all clips on all tracks behind (backward from) the selection point.

 After you select clips with any of the tools listed in Table 7-1, you can quickly move the entire group of clips by clicking inside one of the highlighted clips and then dragging the group.

Moving a Clip That's Already on the Timeline

After you have a clip on the Timeline, you can click and drag it to another point on the Timeline, or to another track. (For instance, you can move an audio clip from Track A1 to A2.) To move the clip, you have to select it first using any of the selection tools I cover earlier in this chapter. However, you usually work with single clips at a time, so the best way to select a clip is to use the Final Cut Pro standard Selection tool (the arrow at the top of the Tool palette). Using this tool also gives you the most options for handling your clip when you move it. For instance, you can overwrite the clip in its new location, swap it (more on this in a moment), or create a copy of it as you insert or overwrite it.

Overwriting a moved clip

When you move your clip to its new location, the clip fills as much space on the Timeline as it needs, erases any clips that are already there, and leaves an empty gap on the Timeline where it originally was, as shown in Figure 7-9. To do an overwrite edit, use the Selection tool to click and drag your clip to the desired point on the Timeline. As you can see from practice, overwrites aren't always the most helpful of edits, partly because you usually don't want to leave an empty gap on your Timeline when you move a clip from one place to another.

Figure 7-9:
Clip C moves into Clip B's position, overwriting Clip B.

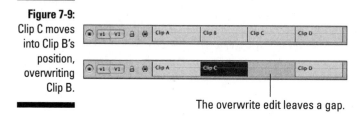

The overwrite edit leaves a gap.

Swapping a moved clip

A *swap edit* is done when Final Cut moves a clip, but, rather than overwrite it, the program inserts the clip at its new location (meaning that it creates new space on the Timeline so that it doesn't overwrite existing clips) *and* closes the gap that your moved clip left behind in its original spot. Suppose that you have arranged Clips A, B, C, and D on the Timeline one after another, but you later decide that Clip C should come before Clip B. Simply drag Clip C in front of Clip B, as shown in Figure 7-10, and you have a seamless sequence of clips — A, C, B, and D — and no empty space where Clip C was.

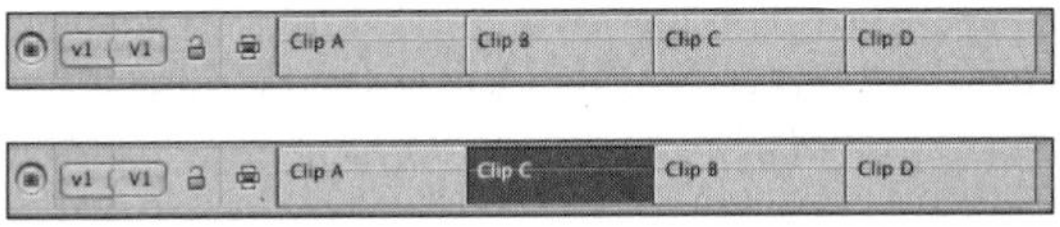

Figure 7-10:
A swap edit, as Clip C moves into Clip B's position and Clip B takes Clip C's position.

Follow these steps to do a swap edit:

1. **Use the Selection tool to select the clip on the Timeline.**

2. **Drag the clip to its new spot.**

3. **Before releasing the mouse button, press and hold down Option.**

   When you press Option, your mouse pointer becomes a curved arrow pointing downward, indicating that you're about to make a swap edit.

4. **Release your mouse button to complete the swap.**

Inserting or overwriting a copied clip

You can also move a copy of a clip anywhere on the Timeline, either inserting it or overwriting it. Although this function is a bit more obscure, it comes in handy from time to time. Try these steps:

1. **Use the Selection tool to select the clip, and then release the mouse button.**

2. **Press and hold down Option.**

   Notice that your mouse's Selection tool arrow displays a plus (+) sign. This sign tells you that you're making a copy.

3. **While holding Option, drag the clip copy to its new location.**

   The mouse pointer becomes an insert symbol (an arrow pointing to the right).

4. Insert or overwrite the clip's copy.

To insert the clip copy, continue holding Option while you release the mouse button. To overwrite the clip rather than insert it, release Option before releasing the mouse button.

You can also move clips by using the time-honored, no-frills Cut, Copy, and Paste commands. Select a clip or clips, and choose Edit⇨Cut or Edit⇨Copy (or press ⌘+X or ⌘+C, respectively). Position the Timeline playhead where you want to paste the clips, and then choose Edit⇨Paste to overwrite the clips at that point or choose Edit⇨Paste Insert to insert them. Final Cut Pro then pastes the clips to the track you have designated as your destination track.

Speeding Editing with Snapping

Snapping makes aligning clips on the Timeline easy because it causes clips to magnetically stick to each other and to other important elements on the Timeline (such as the Timeline playhead, Timeline In and Out points, or markers you have placed). Go ahead and try this feature: When you move a couple of clips to the Timeline, drag one toward the other. When the clips get close, they automatically snap together.

You can turn snapping on or off in Final Cut Pro, but you want to have it on for most editing work. It's on by default, but you can verify that by making sure that Snapping is checked on the View menu. On rare occasions when you want to make precise edits and snapping interferes, you can turn off snapping by choosing View⇨Snapping. Better yet, get used to using the keyboard shortcut for snapping: Press N to toggle it on and off.

Resizing Clips That Are Already on the Timeline

After you place your clips on the Timeline, you devote most of your editing energy to resizing those clips — that is, trimming frames from one clip or adding frames to another. You can do these edits in one of the following ways:

✔ On the Timeline, drag the edges of a clip inward or outward to trim or extend it.

✔ Open the clip in the Viewer window, and set new In and Out points for the clip. This action automatically resizes the clip on the Timeline.

Which tack should you take? When you open a clip in the Viewer, you can play through the entire clip, back and forth, until you have found the right frame to extend or trim the clip to. It's the easiest way to gauge the clip you're working with. On the other hand, you can't beat the speed of resizing clips directly on the Timeline. In the end, give both methods a try, and you soon develop a natural feel for when each works best.

Resizing clips directly on the Timeline

To resize clips as quickly as possible, do it directly on the Timeline. Follow these steps:

1. **Choose the Selection tool from the Tool palette.**

   The Selection tool may already be selected, but you can also press A, just in case.

2. **Move the Selection tool to the left or right edge of a clip on the Timeline.**

   When the mouse pointer is over either edge of the clip, the pointer becomes a Resize symbol, as shown in Figure 7-11.

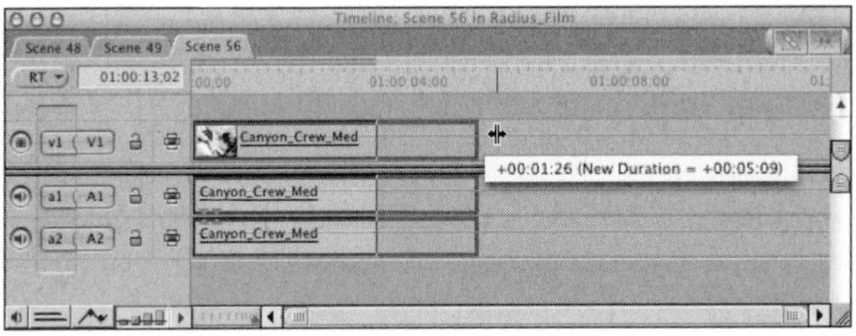

Figure 7-11: Dragging a clip on the Timeline.

3. **Drag the edges of the clip in or out to resize it.**

   Dragging inward (toward the center of the clip) trims, or shortens, the clip, and dragging outward extends it (but only if the clip has unseen frames that you didn't already edit on the Timeline). As you drag the clip's edge, keep an eye on the Canvas window. It shows which frame is at the clip's edge. (This feature helps you decide when to stop resizing the clip.) Also, a pop-up number appears on the Timeline to show you how many frames you're trimming or extending the clip to.

When you're trimming (shortening) a clip on the Timeline, you can use the Final Cut Pro Snapping feature to precisely drag the clip edge to a new frame you're trimming to. Try the following steps:

1. **Make sure that the Snapping feature is turned on.**

   On the View menu, Snapping is checked if it's on. You can toggle it on and off by pressing N.

2. **Position the Timeline playhead at the frame you want to trim your clip to.**

   You may want to play the clip a couple of times to look for the best place to trim it to. To position the playhead precisely on that frame, move it frame by frame with your keyboard's left- and right-arrow keys. Or, use the up- and down-arrow keys to move to the edge of the nearest clip.

3. **Drag either the beginning or ending edge of the clip toward the playhead.**

   Final Cut Pro quickly snaps the edge to the playhead (and therefore the frame you want to trim to).

When you resize a clip by dragging its edges, you may find that you can't move the clip edge to the exact frame you want. (Even if you drag the mouse a tiny bit, the clip's edge can jump several frames at a time.) To fix this problem, zoom in your view of the Timeline, and your mouse movements then have greater precision. You can zoom quickest by pressing ⌘++ (the ⌘ key and the plus key) or by using the Zoom In tool on the Tool palette, as shown in Figure 7-12. With the Zoom tool selected, click anywhere on the Timeline. To zoom in further, keep pressing ⌘++ or keep clicking the Timeline with the Zoom tool. To zoom out, press ⌘+– (⌘ and the minus key) or use the Zoom Out tool on the Tool palette.

Track forward

Zoom In tool

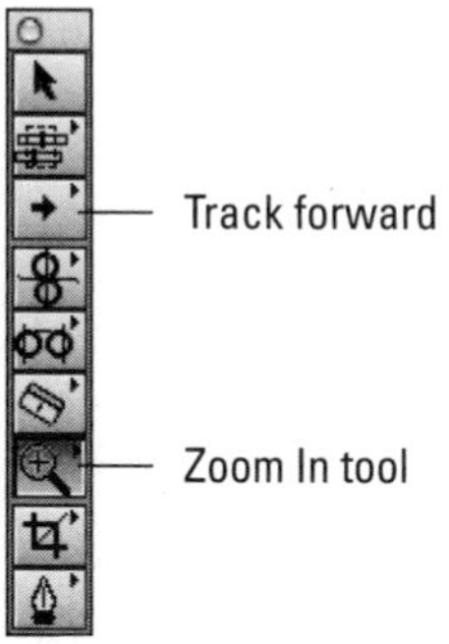

Figure 7-12:
The Zoom In
tool on the
Tool palette.

Resizing clips in the Viewer window

Using the Viewer window to resize clips that are already on the Timeline isn't as quick as resizing clips directly on the Timeline, but it's the way to go when you want to do a precise edit. Follow these steps to resize your clips:

1. **Make sure that the Selection tool on the Tool palette is active.**

2. **On the Timeline, double-click the clip you want to resize.**

   Final Cut Pro opens the clip in the Viewer window (see Figure 7-13). You can see the entire clip as well as any In and Out points you may have set for it earlier (represented by In and Out symbols on the Viewer's scrubber bar).

Figure 7-13:
Set In and Out points in the Viewer window to precisely resize a clip.

Mark In button   Mark Out button

3. **Mark any new In and Out points to trim or extend the clip.**

   To change the clip's first frame (that is, the first frame to appear on the Timeline), set an In point at the frame where you want the clip to start. To set a new In point, position the Viewer's playhead on that frame and press I, or click the Viewer's Mark In button.

   To adjust the last frame of the clip to appear on the Timeline, set an Out point at the desired frame. (Position the Viewer's playhead and press O, or just click the Mark Out button.)

   As you mark a new In or Out point, Final Cut Pro automatically adjusts the size of your clip on the Timeline, making it longer or shorter (with a few exceptions, which I cover in a moment).

Understanding the limitations of resizing clips

Just when you think that you have mastered the fine art of resizing clips, I have some bad news: The steps I outline in the preceding section have some annoying limitations. The biggest roadblocks are as follows (see Figure 7-14):

✔ **Blocking extended clips:** Final Cut Pro doesn't let you extend a clip if another clip is right next to it, without a gap. In other words, if you have Clips A, B, and C arranged side by side and want to extend either edge of Clip B, you can't do it. Clips A and C effectively block it, refusing to move over on the Timeline to make room for the extended frames of Clip B.

✔ **Unwanted gaps on the Timeline:** If you trim a clip that's next to other clips, your trim creates a gap on the Timeline. In other words, if you have Clips A, B, C, and D next to each other, and you decide to trim frames from the end of Clip B, Clips C and D don't automatically move over to fill the space that's left by trimming Clip B. Your Timeline looks like this: Clip A, trimmed Clip B, empty space, Clip C, Clip D.

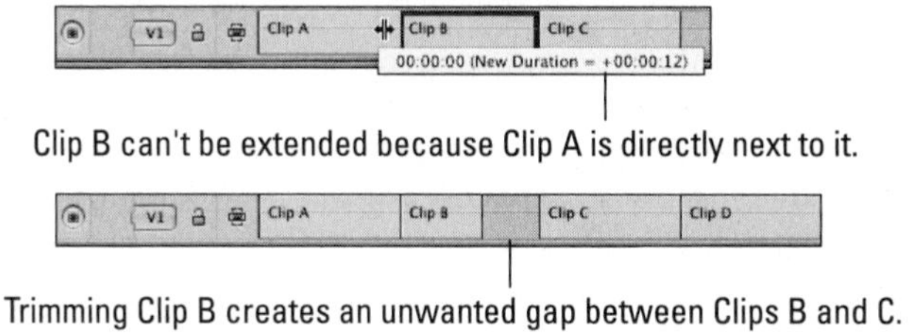

Figure 7-14:
You can run into limitations when you're resizing clips.

Clip B can't be extended because Clip A is directly next to it.

Trimming Clip B creates an unwanted gap between Clips B and C.

Now, here's the good news! You can use some of the other Final Cut Pro tools, described as follows, to solve these two headaches:

✔ Two handy options are the Select Track Forward tool and the Select All Tracks Forward tool (refer to Figure 7-12), which let you quickly select a group of clips on one or all tracks and move the clips either forward or backward on the Timeline, in one fell swoop. With either tool, you can quickly create room for a clip you want to extend or close gaps that were left by a clip you just trimmed.

✔ If you trimmed a clip that's next to other clips, and you now have an empty gap on the Timeline, you can quickly close that gap by positioning the Timeline's playhead in the empty, lifeless void and choosing Sequence⇨Close Gap (but pressing Control+G is a much faster alternative).

The quickest and most efficient (that is, the best) way to deal with resizing clips is to use the Final Cut Pro advanced editing tools, which are on the Tool palette. These tools — Roll Edit, Ripple Edit, Slip Item, and Slide Item — let you extend and trim clips in all sorts of ways, while Final Cut Pro seamlessly adjusts all the other clips on the Timeline.

So, now you're probably wondering "Why didn't he mention these tools in the first place?" Here's the answer: The tools can be a bit overwhelming to new editors and are harder to appreciate if you haven't worked without them first. Try resizing your clips by using the steps I explain in this section, and when you think that you're ready, head on over to Chapter 9 to tackle the Final Cut Pro advanced tools in all their glory.

Cutting a Clip in Two

After you have moved a clip to the Timeline, you may want to cut it into smaller pieces, for one or more of the following reasons:

- ✔ To use the clip's early frames at one spot in your Timeline sequence and then move its later frames to another point
- ✔ To cut off and then delete extra frames you don't need
- ✔ To insert a third clip between the two freshly cut parts

Final Cut Pro lets you cut clips in two different ways: You can cut a single clip on one track of the Timeline, or your cut can carry through all tracks on the Timeline, splitting any clips that are carried on those tracks, as shown in Figure 7-15.

The type of cut you choose depends on what's going on in your movie. Suppose that you're working on a sequence that uses three tracks on the Timeline: one video track, one audio track for dialogue, and another audio track for background music. Suppose that your video track features a stock analyst talking about stocks and bonds, but while the analyst is blabbering, you decide to quickly cut to a new video clip of the New York Stock Exchange. All the while, the analyst's dialogue and your background music continue to play, uninterrupted, over this new shot. To insert the clip of the stock exchange, you would make a cut in the video clip featuring your analyst, but not the dialogue or music tracks, because you want the dialogue and music tracks to continue playing, even over the new shot of the stock exchange.

Figure 7-15:
Clicking the
Razor Blade
tool on a
clip cuts
only that
particular
clip (as well
as any clips
that are
linked to it,
such as
audio). The
Razor Blade
All tool cuts
through clips
on all the
Timeline's
tracks.

Razor Blade tool   Razor Blade All tool

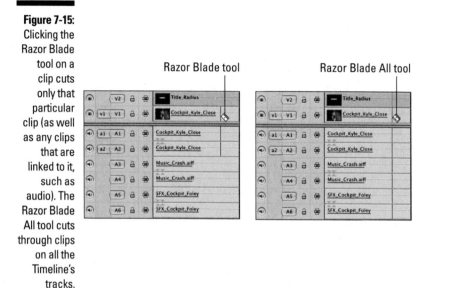

Figure 7-15:
Clicking the Razor Blade tool on a clip cuts only that particular clip (as well as any clips that are linked to it, such as audio). The Razor Blade All tool cuts through clips on all the Timeline's tracks.

Alternatively, suppose that your stock analyst's discussion is getting a little dry, so you decide to cut away to an entirely different scene — perhaps an establishing shot of some glistening corporate campus, with a new voice-over in your dialogue track and new background music, too. To cut from the stock-analyst segment to this new scene, you want to cut the stock analyst clips on all your tracks because you want the video, dialogue, and music clips all to end at the same point.

To cut clips on one or multiple tracks, follow these steps:

1. **Move the Timeline playhead to the frame where you want to make a cut.**

   Click in the Timeline ruler to move the playhead to that point, or use your keyboard arrow keys to move frame by frame for extra precision. Keep an eye on the Canvas window — it shows the frame that the playhead is on.

2. **Select the Razor Blade tool or the Razor Blade All tool from the Tool palette (as shown in Figure 7-16).**

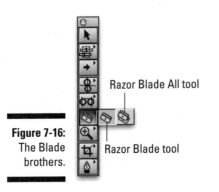

Razor Blade All tool

Figure 7-16:
The Blade
brothers.

Razor Blade tool

To cut a clip on only one Timeline track, select the Razor Blade tool (or press B).

To cut clips on all the Timeline tracks, use the Razor Blade All tool. It's hidden beneath the Razor Blade tool on the Tool palette. Just click and hold down the mouse button with the pointer over the Razor Blade icon, and the Razor Blade All tool pops up. Or, you can press B twice.

 3. **Click the clip you want to cut.**

    After you have selected a blade tool, the mouse pointer changes to a blade symbol. Line up the blade with the Timeline playhead so that you cut the frame you selected in Step 1. When you have the Snapping feature turned on, Final Cut Pro automatically snaps the blade to the playhead so that you can quickly line up the two. (Turn snapping on and off from the View menu, or press N.)

The Razor Blade tool not only cuts the clip you click, but also any clips that are linked to that clip (for instance, clicking the blade on a video clip also cuts its two tracks of stereo audio). If you don't want the razor blade to affect even linked clips, just hold down the Option key while you make a cut.

What happens if the Timeline sports many tracks and you want to make a cut through some of those tracks but not all of them? It's easy: Use the Razor Blade All tool; but, before cutting, lock any tracks that you don't want your cut to affect. To lock a track, click the small lock icon to the left of each track. By locking a track, you protect any clips that are on it from being cut, moved, or otherwise changed.

Deleting Clips from the Timeline

You can delete an unwanted clip so that it doesn't play in your movie or clutter the Timeline. (**Remember:** Even when you delete a clip from the Timeline, it stays in the Browser window so that you can use it again.) Final Cut Pro offers two ways to delete a clip: a lift edit and a ripple delete.

Using lift edits and ripple deletes

A *lift edit* is your no-frills, garden-variety delete. You select a clip and then delete it, leaving an empty gap on the Timeline, which plays as a black void in your movie. This kind of deletion may be okay, but if other clips follow the deleted clip on the Timeline, you probably want to move all those clips to the left so that they fill in the empty gap that was left by your now-departed clip (that's more work for you). That approach shows the beauty of using the ripple delete alternative. A *ripple delete* removes your clip from the Timeline and automatically moves all the following clips to the left so that they close the gap that was left by the deleted clip, as shown in Figure 7-17.

Figure 7-17:
This
sequence
of clips
changes
when you
delete Clip B
via a lift edit
or ripple
delete.

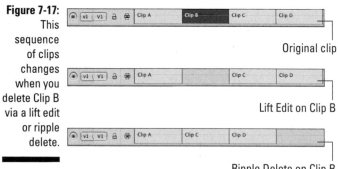

Original clip

Lift Edit on Clip B

Ripple Delete on Clip B

The ripple delete also has its own weakness: It can change how clips in different tracks are synced, leading to problems. Suppose that you're editing a music video and you just spent endless hours timing your video cuts to beats in the music track. Suppose that you also decide that you don't like a video clip in the middle of your sequence, and you use a ripple delete on it. All the video clips that are to the right of your deleted clip now shift left (to close the gap on the Timeline) and, unfortunately, fall out of sync with your music because you didn't delete anything from the music track. To dodge this headache, in this case, I recommend that you skip using a ripple delete. Instead, do a lift edit, and find a new video clip to fill in the gap left by the deleted one; that way, your video and music stay in sync.

You probably use the ripple delete most in your work, but the following steps outline how to do either a lift edit or a ripple delete:

1. **Select on the Timeline the clip or clips you want to delete.**

   You can select a single clip by clicking it with the Selection tool or select a group by using the tactics I discuss in the section "Selecting Clips on the Timeline," earlier in this chapter.

2. **Press Delete to do a lift edit or press Shift+Delete to do a ripple delete.**

Deleting a range of frames on multiple tracks

You can delete a range of frames that are within a single clip, or within a sequence of clips, by setting In and Out points on the Timeline. (Any frames that fall within those points get the ax.) As you get comfortable with Final Cut Pro, you probably will favor this tactic because it's so direct. To delete a range of frames from the Timeline, follow these steps:

1. **Move the Timeline playhead to the first frame of the range of clips you want to delete.**

   The Canvas window shows the frame that the playhead is on.

2. **Mark your In point by pressing I or by clicking the Mark In button in the Canvas window (see Figure 7-18).**

   An In point (a triangle pointing to the right) appears on the Timeline's ruler and on the Canvas window's scrubber bar (both display any In and Out points you have set in your movie).

Figure 7-18:
Any frames that lie between the In and Out points on the Timeline are deleted, through all tracks (video, dialogue, and music, for example).

Mark In button   Mark Out button

3. **Move the Timeline playhead to the last frame of the range you want to delete, and mark an Out point there.**

   You can click Mark Out in the Canvas window (refer to Figure 7-18), choose Mark Out from the Mark menu, or press O. Train yourself to use the keyboard shortcut, if you can.

4. **Do a lift edit or ripple delete by pressing Delete or Shift+Delete, respectively.**

   Final Cut Pro now cuts all the frames that fall within your In and Out points on all tracks of the Timeline.

Chapter 8

Getting to Know the Timeline

*I*f you have read Chapter 6, you have already digested quite a bit — namely, all the skills you need in order to edit a video from start to finish. In this chapter, you nibble on smaller fare — the kind of things that can help you work more smoothly with the Final Cut Pro HD Timeline, which is where most of your blood, sweat, and tears spill out while you edit.

Investigating Timeline Tracks

One of the most important things you can do with the Timeline is to take control of your tracks. (Do you remember Timeline tracks? If not, see Chapter 6 or check out Figure 8-1.) You may want to turn off certain tracks so that Final Cut Pro doesn't play any of the clips on them — for instance, turn off your music tracks to better hear dialogue. Or, you may want to lock a track so that no clips on it can be accidentally resized or moved. Finally, you may want to ensure that when you move new clips from the Browser to the Timeline, the clips go directly to the tracks you want (for instance, you may want to put audio clips on tracks A3 and A4, instead of A1 and A2). The Timeline lets you do all this and more.

Video tracks

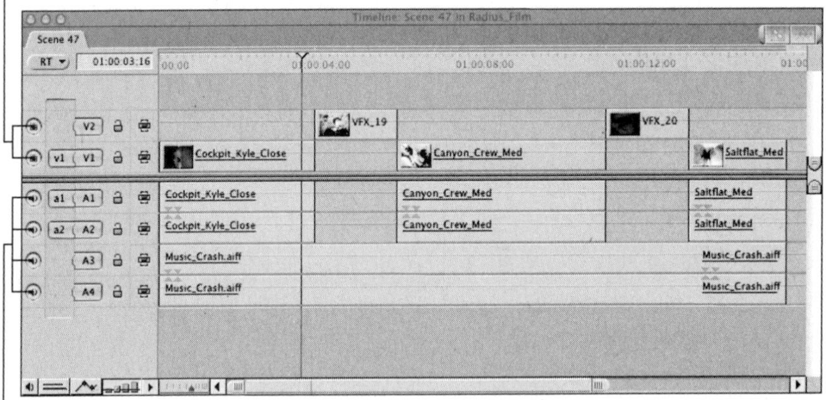

Figure 8-1:
Using tracks
helps you
organize
different
kinds of
clips on the
Timeline.

Audio tracks

Locking tracks so that they can't be changed

When you *lock* a track on the Timeline, you prevent any clips on that track from being resized, moved, deleted, or changed. Why would you want to freeze a track this way in the course of your editing? You would want to for any number of reasons, all of which involve making changes to clips that are on some of the tracks in your movie, but not on all of them. Suppose that your movie sports a number of tracks (a video track and audio tracks for dialogue, sound effects, and music) and you want to cut the video, dialogue, and sound effects of a series of shots and leave the music tracks untouched. (See Figure 8-2 for the before and after views.)

In this case, you need to lock the music tracks first and then make your cut to the rest of the Timeline tracks. (See Chapter 6 for options on the best way to make the cuts.) The result? Final Cut Pro cuts through the clips on all your tracks except the music tracks because these music tracks are locked!

To lock a track, just click the Lock Track control for that particular track. (The Lock Track control is represented by a small padlock icon to the left of each track, as shown in Figure 8-3.) Final Cut Pro draws diagonal lines through the entire length of the track to let you know that that track is now off limits.

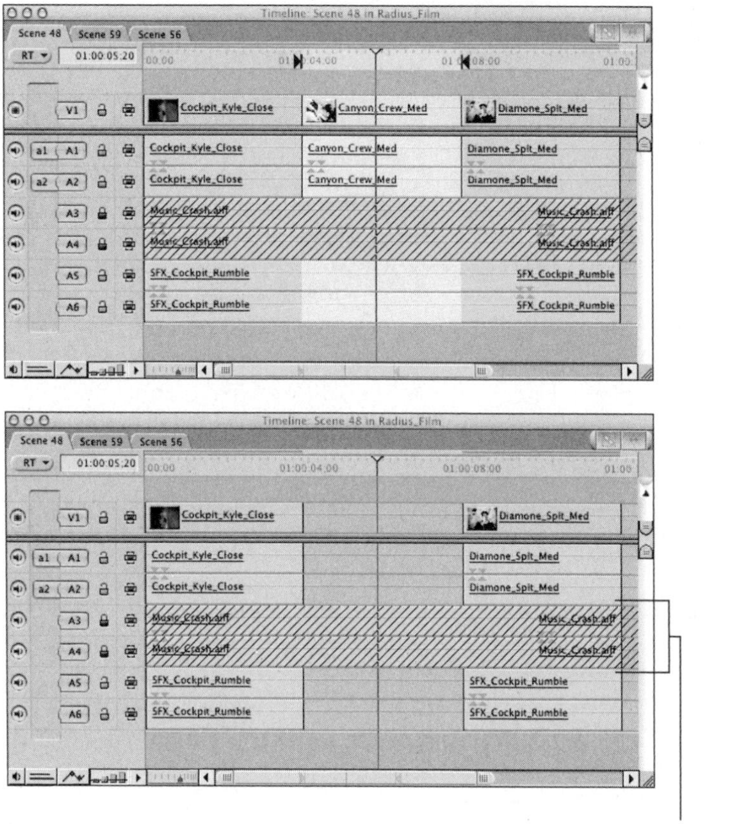

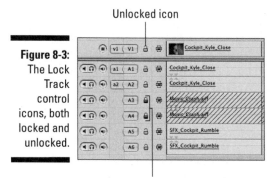

Figure 8-2:
Before and after cutting: All tracks except the protected ones are cut.

The protected tracks are uncut.

Unlocked icon

Figure 8-3:
The Lock Track control icons, both locked and unlocked.

Locked icons

To unlock a track, just click the Lock Track icon again, and your locked track becomes fully editable.

Muting and soloing audio tracks

If your movie uses lots of audio tracks, you may want to play only some of the tracks, and not others. For instance, you may want to watch your movie while carefully listening to its dialogue track, without hearing all the tracks that carry sound effects and music. In this case, you would *solo* your dialogue track so that you hear only its audio. On the other hand, to hear how your sound effects and music tracks work together, you could mute your dialogue track so that you're not distracted by it.

To easily mute or solo tracks, you need to set your Timeline to display its audio controls. To toggle these controls on and off, just click the Audio Controls button in the far lower-left corner of the Timeline (see Figure 8-4). Turning audio controls on displays mute and solo controls for each of your Timeline tracks. To mute an audio track so that its clips don't play, click the Mute control for that track (the Speaker icon on the far left side of that track), as shown in Figure 8-4. All other (unmuted) tracks play as they normally would. When you're ready to bring the muted track back to normal, just click that icon again.

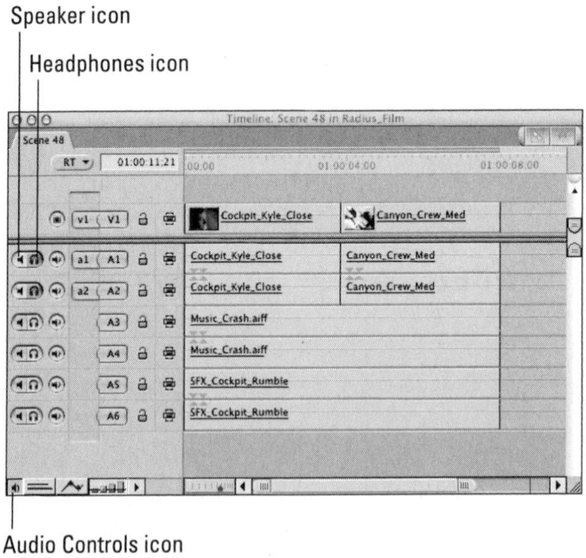

Speaker icon

Headphones icon

Figure 8-4: Click an audio track's Speaker icon to mute that track (or to unmute it). Click its Headphones icon to solo the track.

Audio Controls icon

To toggle a single track so that it plays or doesn't play solo, click the Solo control for that track — it's represented by the Headphones icon next to the Mute control you see in Figure 8-4. A track in Solo mode plays all by its lonesome — all other tracks are silent, as though you had clicked the Mute control for them.

Hiding video tracks so that they don't play

Just as you can mute and solo audio tracks, you can choose to hide a video track so that its clips don't play in your sequence. You can hide tracks if you're compositing multiple video clips together (with each clip on different tracks) and want to temporarily see the clips of certain tracks. To hide a video track, just click that track's Visibility control (the green icon on the far left side of the track), as shown in Figure 8-5. When you're ready to bring the track back to normal, just click that icon again.

Track Visibility icon

Figure 8-5:
This movie's
second
video track
(V2) has
been
hidden.

Setting up destination tracks on the Timeline

Final Cut Pro lets you designate certain tracks on the Timeline as *destination* tracks. By doing this, you're telling Final Cut Pro that these tracks are the main ones you're focusing on and that various edits you make to the Timeline should affect those tracks rather than any others.

In the following instances, Final Cut Pro focuses on the destination tracks you have selected:

✔ When you edit (that is, move) video and audio clips from the Viewer or Browser to the Timeline, the clips go to your destination tracks. The only exception is when you manually drag a clip directly to the Timeline; in this case, the clip appears on the track you have dragged it to.

✔ When you copy and paste clips on the Timeline, the pasted clips appear on your destination tracks.

✔ When you want to mark clips or add keyframes to them, Final Cut Pro works with clips on your destination tracks.

Of course, you don't have to worry about setting destination tracks every time you make an edit. By default, Final Cut Pro sets the Timeline's V1 track as the destination track for video and its A1 and A2 tracks for stereo audio destinations. But, occasionally, you may want to change your destination tracks; for instance, to edit sound-effects clips to the Timeline's A3 and A4 audio tracks, in case you're already using the A1 and A2 tracks for dialogue clips.

The trick to setting destination tracks is to understand that you're telling Final Cut Pro which tracks on the Timeline will be destinations for the video and audio elements of a clip you're about to edit on the Timeline. If that sounds a bit confusing, bear with me. Consider a DV video clip that you're looking at in the Viewer window, before you edit it to the Timeline (see the left side of Figure 8-6). That clip probably has a video element (call it V1), which you can see by selecting the Viewer's Video tab, and it probably has two channels of stereo audio (A1 and A2), which you can see by clicking the Viewer's audio tab (or tabs). Before editing that clip to the Timeline, Final Cut Pro has to know which Timeline track should get the clip's video channel (V1) and which tracks should get the clip's audio channels (A1 and A2).

Video tab

Audio tab

Source controls

Destination controls

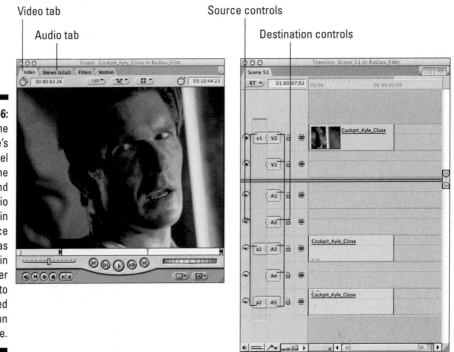

Figure 8-6:
Use the Timeline's Patch panel to match the video and audio elements in the source clip (as shown in the Viewer window) to the desired tracks on the Timeline.

Still with me? Great. The way to tell Final Cut Pro where the source clip's V1, A1, and A2 elements should go is like playing connect-the-dots. Look at the Timeline's Patch panel (on the right in Figure 8-6), and you see the Source controls for each of your current source clip's video and audio elements (again, the source clip is in the Viewer — in this case, V1, A1, and A2 are the video and audio elements carried by the source clip — refer to Figure 8-6). Now, you simply want to connect these Source controls to the Destination controls of the track you want your source clip's video and audio elements to go to.

For instance, in Figure 8-6, I have connected the V1 Source control to the Timeline's V2 track. When I move my source clip from the Viewer window to the Timeline, therefore, the source clip's video (represented by the V1 Source control) ends up on the Timeline's V2 track. As for audio, I have connected the A1 Source control to the Timeline's A3 track, and the A2 Source control to the Timeline's A5 track. The source clip's first audio channel is then edited on the Timeline's A3 track, and its second audio channel goes to the Timeline's A5 track.

How to set a destination track

You can set destination tracks in the following ways:

- ✔ **The easy way:** Click the Source control, and drag it to the Destination control of the track you want to connect it to. Make sure that the Source and Destination controls are really connected.

- ✔ **The quick way:** Control+click any Source control, and choose its Destination control from the pop-up menu that appears. Or, Control+click any Destination control and, from the pop-up menu that appears, select the Source control you want to connect it to.

- ✔ **The other way:** Click any track's Destination control, and the nearest Source control jumps to that track and makes a connection. This feature is usually helpful, but you sometimes find that the nearest Source control isn't the one you want your Destination control connecting to. Oh, well — that's life.

Having no destination tracks

Sometimes, it's helpful to turn off certain destination tracks before editing a clip to the Timeline. This way, only certain elements of a source clip are moved to the Timeline. Suppose that you want to add a clip of video to the Timeline, but that clip also has two channels of audio built in (typical of DV video) and you don't want the audio to be added. Your wish is Final Cut Pro's command: To edit the clip's video to the Timeline without its audio, break the connection between the A1 and A2 Source controls on the Timeline so that they're not connected to the Destination controls of any Timeline track. When you edit your clip to the Timeline, only the video makes the journey.

To disconnect a Destination track from a Source control, click either the Source control or the track's Destination control, and you see the two controls move apart, indicating that the connection has been broken (see Figure 8-7).

Disconnecting Audio Source and Destination controls.

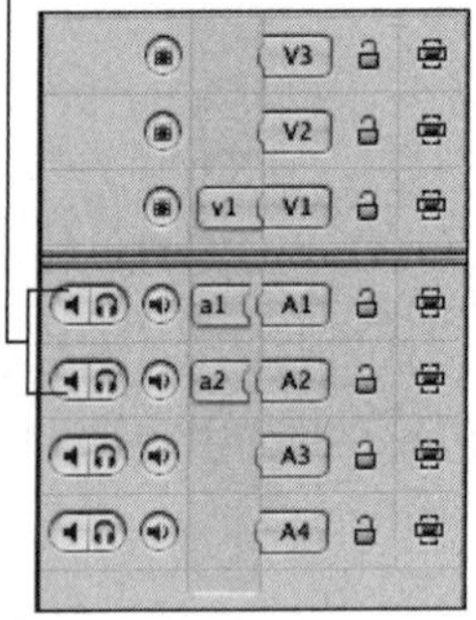

Figure 8-7:
Audio
Source and
Destination
controls
have been
discon-
nected, so
no audio is
added to the
Timeline.

Adding and deleting tracks from the Timeline

Adding and deleting tracks while you build sequences of clips on the Timeline is natural. For example, you may want to add a video track to carry visual effects or titles for your movie or add a slew of audio tracks to hold different versions of your composer's musical score. (Having each version on the Timeline enables you to easily compare one revision with another.) At the same time, you may find reasons to toss out other tracks — maybe you decide not to use the clips on a track or two. Or, you find that you have so many tracks that you can't keep them straight, so you decide to consolidate their clips to a more manageable number.

Adding a single track

To add a track to the Timeline quickly, I recommend one of the following options:

✔ Drag any clip (that is, a clip that's either already on the Timeline or that's now in the Browser window) to the unused area above the last video track on the Timeline (for video clips) or below the last audio track (for audio clips). When you release the mouse button, Final Cut Pro creates a new track on the Timeline and puts your dragged clip right in it. (Check out Figure 8-8.)

Figure 8-8:
To add a video track, drag the clip to the unused area of the Timeline, above the last video track.

✔ Hold down Control and click anywhere in the track header, as shown in Figure 8-9. Then choose Add Track from the pop-up menu that appears. Final Cut Pro adds a track directly below the header you clicked.

Figure 8-9:
Control+ click within a track heading to see this pop-up menu.

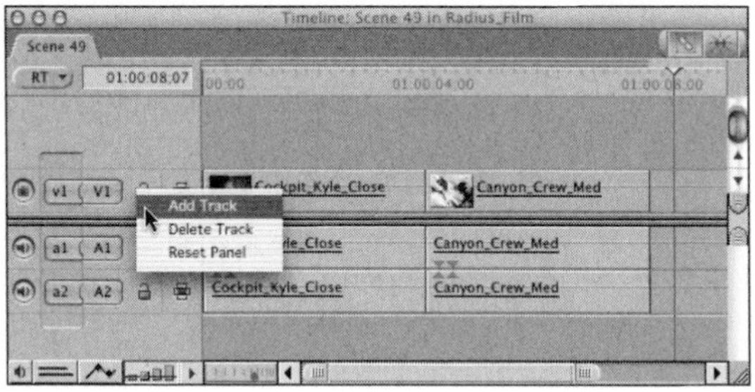

Adding multiple tracks

To add multiple tracks to the Timeline in one fell swoop, make sure that the Timeline window is active and then follow these steps:

1. **Choose Sequence⇨Insert Tracks from the main menu.**

2. **In the Insert Tracks dialog box, as shown in Figure 8-10, type the number of video or audio tracks to add.**

   For example, to add video tracks but not audio tracks, deselect the check box next to Audio Tracks (or just leave the number of audio tracks at 0).

Insert Tracks

☑ Insert [1] Video Tracks:

   ○ Before Base Track
   ● After Last Track

☑ Insert [8] Audio Tracks:

   ● Before Base Track
   ○ After Last Track

(Cancel) (OK)

Figure 8-10:
The Insert
Tracks
dialog box.

3. **Choose where you want to insert your tracks on the Timeline.**

   You have the following options:

   • **Before Base Track:** This option inserts your new tracks before the first video or audio track on the Timeline (that's your *base* track, which is called V1 for video and A1 for audio) and renumbers any existing tracks to make room for the new ones. Suppose that you already have two audio tracks (A1 and A2) on the Timeline and you add another two before the base track. Your two new tracks become A1 and A2, and the original audio tracks become A3 and A4.

   • **After Last Track:** This option is straightforward: Final Cut Pro slips your new tracks behind the last video or audio track that's on the Timeline.

4. **Click OK to insert the tracks.**

You may find that you use lots of audio tracks in your sequence to carry simultaneous dialogue clips, sound effects, or music, for example. Although Final Cut Pro lets you add as many as 99 audio tracks to the Timeline, it can't play all 99 tracks at the same time. Playing a clip of audio is no easy feat for your Mac, and when you ask it to play more than several at one time, it cracks under the pressure. (Truthfully, it plays a repeating beep in place of the lush audio you expect — no harm done, but you can't hear your audio.) The good news is that if you render your tracks first, you can play all those audio tracks together. When you render your audio, Final Cut Pro merges all your audio tracks into a single audio clip, which it can play without breaking a sweat, and it does all this hocus-pocus behind the scenes without your having to worry about it. To render audio tracks, choose Sequence➪Render Only➪Mixdown. See Bonus Chapter 1 on this book's CD for more about rendering.

Deleting a single track

The easiest way to delete a single track is to hold down Control and click anywhere in that track's header (not on its track number; refer to Figure 8-9). Then choose Delete Track from the pop-up menu that appears. Final Cut Pro tosses out that track (along with any clips that are on it) and renumbers all the tracks that are after it.

Deleting multiple tracks

To give a group of tracks the old heave-ho, make sure that the Timeline window is active and then follow these steps:

1. **Choose Sequence⇨Delete Tracks from the main menu.**

2. **In the Delete Tracks dialog box, as shown in Figure 8-11, select the appropriate Video Tracks and Audio Tracks check boxes.**

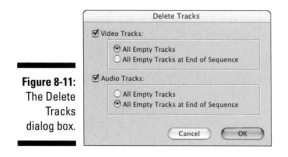

Figure 8-11:
The Delete
Tracks
dialog box.

3. **In the Audio Tracks and Video Tracks check boxes, choose from the following options:**

    • **All Empty Tracks:** Selecting this option deletes all tracks that have no clips on them. (Perhaps you used these tracks as temporary staging areas to assemble clips before moving them to your main tracks and you no longer need these tracks.)

    • **All Empty Tracks at End of Sequence:** This one's a bit more obscure. Select it to delete any empty video tracks that are above and any audio tracks that are below the outermost tracks that have clips on them. Say what? Suppose that you have six audio tracks and Tracks A3, A5, and A6 are empty. Choosing this option deletes Tracks A5 and A6 but not Track A3 because Track A3 is followed by Track A4, which has clips on it.

4. **Click OK to complete the deletion.**

Customizing Your View of the Timeline

You can customize your view of the Timeline so that it shows you tracks and clips in any way that suits your work style. For example, if you're editing on a small monitor or laptop screen, you may want to show your Timeline tracks in Reduced view so that more tracks fit on-screen at one time. Or, suppose that you're trying to sync the big, heavy beats of a music piece to your video clip. To make this process easier, the Timeline can display your music clip as a visual waveform so that you can literally see where the big beats happen in the music and sync them with video more easily.

Making Timeline tracks big and small

You can display your tracks at four predetermined sizes: Reduced, Small, Medium, and Large. (See the difference in Figure 8-12.) The bigger your tracks, the easier it is to see the clips on them, along with any information displayed within the clips (such as opacity and volume keyframes — more on these in a moment). On the other hand, if you display smaller tracks, you can see more of them on the Timeline at one time (without scrolling up and down), which is handy.

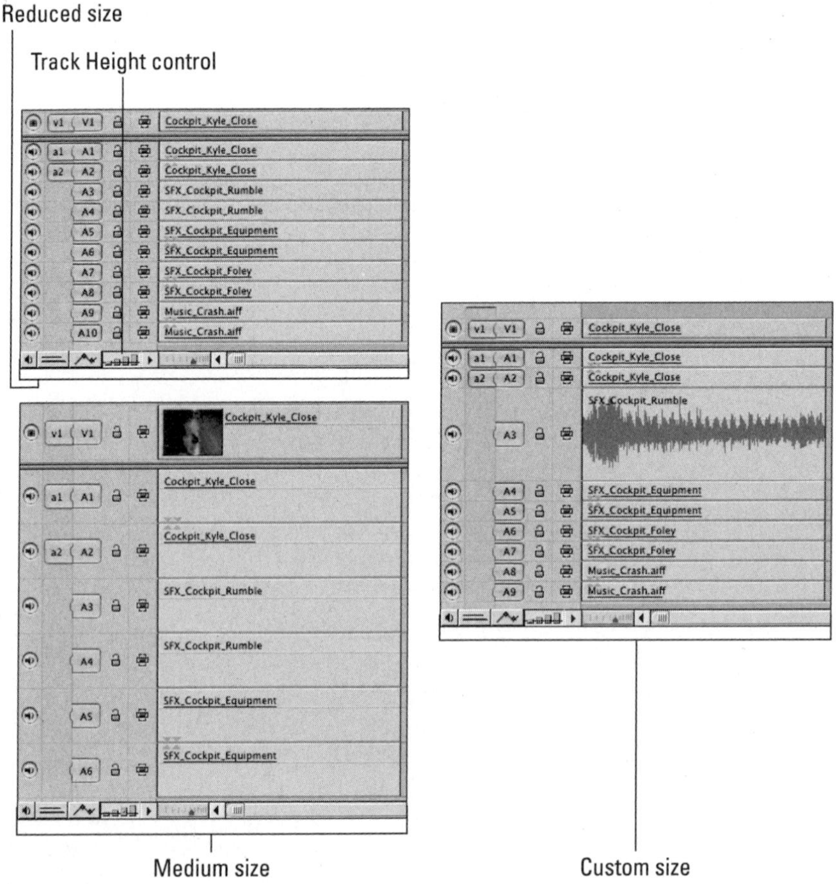

Reduced size

Track Height control

Figure 8-12:
Reduced-
versus
medium-size
tracks, plus
an example
of custom
track sizing.

Medium size

Custom size

The easiest way to resize tracks is to simply click one of the four vertical bars within the Timeline's Track Height control. (Refer to Figure 8-12 — the smaller the bar, the smaller the track size.) Or, if you're into keyboard shortcuts, you can press Shift+T to cycle the Timeline through each successive track height option.

Changing a single track's size

Final Cut Pro lets you set the size of a single track, independently of the size settings for all the other tracks. This feature is useful because sometimes you want to display one track in a jumbo size and keep the others small (refer to Figure 8-12). Here's an example: You can display a music track as a huge audio waveform so that you can more easily see the music's big beats or hits (waveforms are easier to read when they're large) and leave the other tracks at a smaller size because you don't have to study these other tracks as closely.

To set a single track's size, position your mouse in the Track patch panel, over a track's light-gray frame. When your mouse pointer changes to a resizing symbol, click and drag to set that track's new height. It's that easy!

Saving and loading custom track layouts

You can set up your tracks using lots of custom sizes (some big, some small, and some in between). In this case, you can save your tweaked track layout to disk so that you can easily reapply the layout to another Timeline sequence, without having to manually resize your tracks each time.

To save a track layout, click the arrow to the right of the Track Height control on the Timeline and choose Save Track Layout from the pop-up menu that appears. A Save dialog box appears, where you can type a name for your custom track layout and save it in the Custom Track Layouts folder, which is in your Final Cut Pro Documents folder.

To load a track layout you have already saved, click the arrow to the right of the Track Height control on the Timeline and choose the track layout's name from the pop-up menu that appears. (Final Cut Pro remembers all the custom layouts you create.) And, if you happen to modify a saved track layout and then want to return to your original layout, choose Restore Track Layout from the same pop-up menu and then use the Open dialog box to select the saved layout you want to restore.

Customizing other Timeline stuff

You can customize other aspects of your current Timeline sequence. To do so, make sure that either the Timeline or Canvas window is selected, choose Sequence⇨Settings from the main menu, and click the Timeline Options tab.

You see a bunch of options displayed in the Sequence Settings dialog box (see Figure 8-13), including the same options I explain in the preceding section for changing track size. The following rundown describes some the more useful options that I haven't covered elsewhere in this chapter:

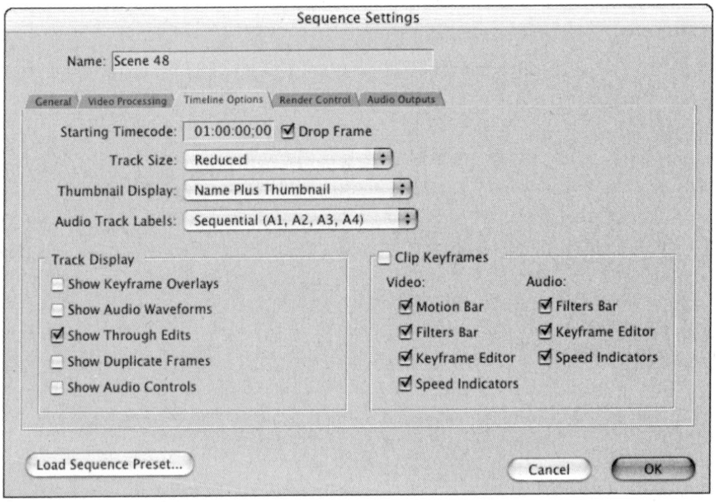

Figure 8-13:
Timeline options as they appear in the Sequence Settings dialog box.

- ✔ **Starting Timecode:** In rare cases, you may want to change the starting timecode value for your sequence so that, rather than starting at 01:00:00;00, the sequence starts at, for example, 03:24:43;00. (Maybe you're planning to merge the current sequence into an existing recorded tape and want to get the sequence's timecode in sync with the tape's.) Just type the new timecode starting value into this box, and you see that new starting point displayed on the Timeline's ruler.

- ✔ **Thumbnail Display:** This option lets you decide how video clips are displayed on their tracks. (Compare these views in Figure 8-14.)

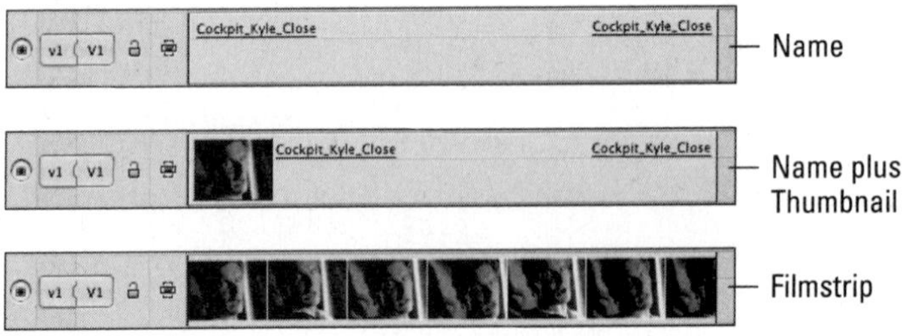

Figure 8-14:
A composite picture showing the three thumbnail display options.

You can choose from the following modes:

- **Name:** Shows only a no-frills clip name.

- **Name Plus Thumbnail:** Shows a clip name and a thumbnail image of its first frame.

- **Filmstrip:** Shows thumbnails for as many frames as can fit in the current zoom level of the Timeline.

I like Name Plus Thumbnail the best. (Seeing the first frame of a clip helps keep me oriented.) Filmstrip, on the other hand, feels quite disorienting.

✔ **Audio Track Labels:** When you capture audio, you usually capture it in stereo — that is, each clip you capture consists of two clips: one for the audio's left channel and one for the audio's right channel. When you move stereo audio to the Timeline, Final Cut Pro normally places each channel's clip on its own track, and the tracks are numbered sequentially (for instance, A1, A2, and so on). But, when you set your audio track labels as Paired, Final Cut Pro labels each audio track to reflect the fact that the two tracks are related (that is, they're stereo pairs). Rather than number the tracks for an audio clip's left and right channels as A1 and A2, Final Cut Pro labels the two tracks A1a and A1b, as shown in Figure 8-15. This approach makes it easy to keep track of which audio tracks are related stereo pairs.

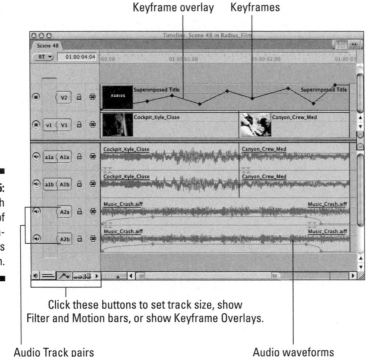

Keyframe overlay   Keyframes

Figure 8-15:
Tracks with
a variety of
customiza-
tion options
turned on.

Click these buttons to set track size, show
Filter and Motion bars, or show Keyframe Overlays.

Audio Track pairs   Audio waveforms

✔ **Show Keyframe Overlays:** Selecting this option draws a horizontal line through any clips on your Timeline. This horizontal line represents opacity levels for video clips and volume levels for audio clips. What's useful about this option is that you can click and drag these lines up and down to adjust your levels right on the Timeline without having to open another settings window. You can also set keyframes here. This option lets you change a clip's opacity or volume level over time: Press Option, and click anywhere on the Levels line. (You can also remove keyframes by Option+clicking them.) For more about keyframes, check out Chapters 9 and 13.

✔ **Show Audio Waveforms:** Select this check box, and any audio clips that are on your Timeline display their waveforms, which use vertical lines to show the loud and soft areas of an audio clip. (The higher the wave-form's vertical lines, the louder the audio. Refer to the audio levels shown in Figure 8-15.) This option is handy for syncing your video clips to events in dialogue, sound effects, and music.

✔ **Show Through Edits:** Final Cut Pro normally uses two red triangles to show through edits on the Timeline. A *through edit* takes place when the adjacent frames of two clips are continuous frames, as though they're part of the same clip. For example, if you use the Razor Blade tool to cut one clip into two parts, that cut would be a through edit because the first frame of the second clip is just a continuation of the last frame of the first clip. If these markers bug you for any reason, you can turn them off right here.

✔ **Clip Keyframes:** Check this box, and Final Cut Pro makes all your Timeline tracks larger to display keyframes for a wide variety of effects you have applied to your clips (see Figure 8-16).

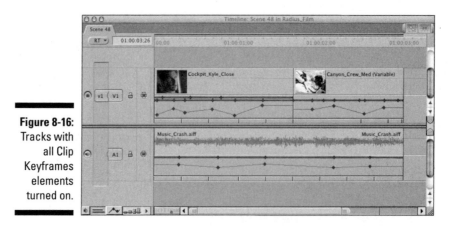

Figure 8-16: Tracks with all Clip Keyframes elements turned on.

You can toggle each type of keyframe family that the Timeline displays by checking the following boxes, for both video and audio clips:

- **Motion Bar:** Displays a thin blue bar across any video clip you have applied motion settings to. (I cover motion settings in Chapter 15.) Here's an even better option: If you have set keyframes for motion settings, those keyframes appear on the bar as well (a small diamond indicates keyframes). You can even click and drag these keyframes to new places in time within your clips, right on the Timeline.

- **Filters Bar:** Displays a thin green bar across any clip you have applied a filter to. This option also shows any keyframes you have set within filtered clips. As with the Motion bar, you can also click and reposition any keyframes that appear on the Filters bar.

- **Keyframe Editor:** Creates a region within a track that displays a keyframe graph for motion and filter keyframes you have applied to a clip; you can create new keyframes right on this graph and edit the settings of existing ones. The keyframe editor can display the keyframes for only one motion or filter setting at a time. (For instance, it can display keyframes for a clip's scale setting or keyframes for its brightness settings but not both kinds of keyframes at one time.) Still, this helpful feature lets you tweak and perfect keyframes without leaving the Timeline. See Chapters 14 and 15 for more about setting keyframes on the Timeline.

- **Speed Indicators:** Displays small indicators that show you the variable speed at which your clip is playing, at a given point in the clip. (Remember that Final Cut Pro can vary the speed at which a clip plays rather than play it at a constant speed throughout the clip.) See Chapter 9 for more about reading these indicators.

By the way, you can quickly customize these aspects of the Timeline without visiting the Sequence Settings dialog box. (I just thought that you should start with the Sequence Settings dialog box, but you may opt for these quicker Timeline shortcuts in practice.) You can click buttons directly on the Timeline to set the track size, display keyframe overlays, and display clip keyframe information (refer to Figure 8-15).

When you customize the Timeline by choosing Sequence⇨Settings, as I have here, you're changing the settings for only the particular sequence that's active on the Timeline. To create more-permanent settings that apply to each sequence you create in every new project, don't choose Sequence⇨Settings to make your Timeline adjustments. Instead, choose Final Cut Pro⇨User Preferences and then select the Timeline Options tab. This tab makes the same options available to you, except that these options now apply to any new sequence you create from now on.

Navigating the Timeline

When you're editing, you continually move the Timeline playhead from one place to another. (Remember that the playhead is like a record needle on your video — refer to Chapter 6 for more on the playhead.) Sometimes, you may move the playhead through a clip in search of the perfect frame to trim the clip to or to make a cut on. Or, you may move the playhead to some edit point on the Timeline (where a clip ends or begins or where two clips come together) so that you can adjust the edit in some way.

Final Cut Pro offers a bunch of useful tools for moving the Timeline playhead wherever you want. I touch on some of these tools in Chapter 6, but now I discuss them in one place so that you can see all your options.

Moving the playhead anywhere on the Timeline

To move the playhead instantly to any spot on the Timeline, use one of the following methods:

- **Use the Timeline ruler:** You can click anywhere on the Timeline ruler, as shown in Figure 8-17, to move the playhead to that point on the Timeline.

- **Go to timecode:** You can also move the playhead directly to any timecode value on the Timeline (refer to Figure 8-17). Just type the value into the Current Timecode dialog box, which you can find in either the Canvas or Timeline window. (Make sure that you don't have a clip selected, or else Final Cut Pro moves that clip rather than the playhead.)

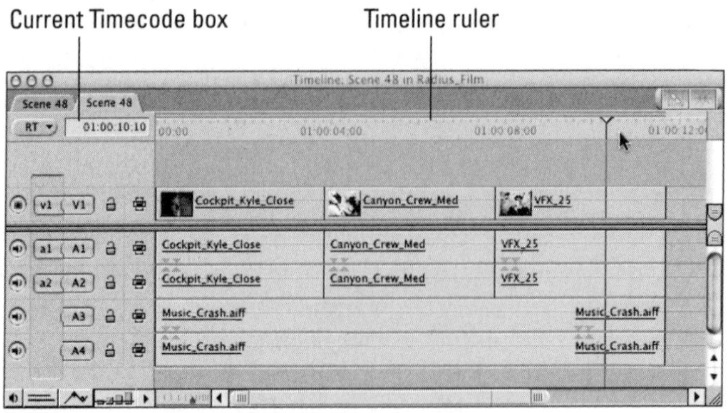

Current Timecode box   Timeline ruler

Figure 8-17:
The Timeline ruler.

Moving the playhead linearly through the Timeline

In Chapter 6, I show you the easiest way to move the playhead linearly through the Timeline. The following list gives you *all* your options — some are quicker and more convenient than others, depending on your personal work style (check out Figure 8-18 to see some of these options):

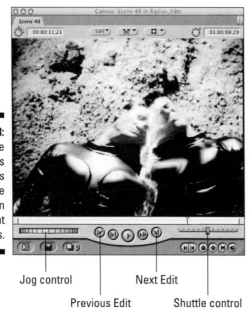

Figure 8-18:
These Canvas controls move the playhead in different ways.

Jog control

Previous Edit

Next Edit

Shuttle control

✔ **By lots of frames:** Use the following methods to move the playhead across continuous frames:

- **Shuttle control:** To move the playhead back and forward at a variety of preset speeds, try using the Canvas window's Shuttle control. You can click and drag this control all the way to the left or right for quick rewinds and fast forwards, or you can set the control closer to its midpoint to move the playhead slowly through your clips.

- **Keyboard shortcuts:** I find that the quickest way to move the playhead is by pressing the letters J, K, and L. Press J to move the playhead back, K to stop it, and L to move it forward. Repeatedly press J or L to move the playhead faster.

- **Click and drag:** To move the playhead along the Timeline in a hurry (often while scrolling a long sequence through the Timeline), click the playhead on the Timeline ruler and quickly drag the playhead to the left or right.

- **Hand tool:** Select the Hand tool from the Tool palette, click anywhere on a Timeline track, and drag left or right to scroll your view of the Timeline (or drag up and down to see tracks that are out of view). *Note:* Using the Hand tool doesn't move the playhead per se, but it shifts your view of the Timeline. You can place the playhead in a new spot by clicking the Timeline's ruler.

✔ **Frame by frame:** You have the following options to move the playhead frame by frame when you want to be precise:

- **The Jog control:** Use the Canvas window's Jog control, which lets you slowly drag your mouse back and forth across the control to move the playhead frame by frame.

- **Arrow keys:** My preferred choice is to use the arrow keys: Press ← to move the playhead back in time by one frame, and press → to move the playhead forward by one frame.

✔ **Edit by edit:** Rather than move the playhead to the next frame, you can move it to the next *edit point* — the beginning or end of a clip — as well as to any In and Out points you have set on the Timeline. This option is handy for quickly moving across a number of clips, and I find that it's easiest to use the keyboard. Press the apostrophe key (') to jump your playhead to the next edit, and press the semicolon key (;) to go to the preceding edit. Or, you can always click the Next Edit or Previous Edit buttons in the Canvas, respectively, but you lose the speed of the keyboard when you use these buttons.

✔ **Marker by marker:** If you have set markers on the Timeline, you can move your playhead to the preceding marker by pressing Shift+↓, or forward to the next marker by pressing Shift+↑. I discuss markers in more detail in Chapter 9.

✔ **Beginning and end:** To quickly jump the playhead to the beginning of your Timeline sequence, press Home. To jump to the sequence's end, press End!

Zooming In and Out of the Timeline

Final Cut Pro lets you zoom in on your Timeline. This feature shows you a smaller sample of time in your sequence and makes your clips larger so that you can resize, move, cut, or otherwise edit the clips with frame-by-frame precision. You can also zoom out of the Timeline to make clips appear smaller and to give you a bird's-eye view of your entire sequence. See Figure 8-19 for a quick comparison.

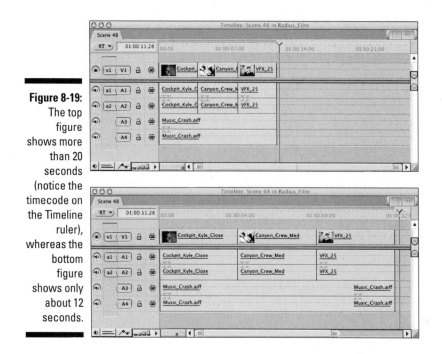

Figure 8-19:
The top figure shows more than 20 seconds (notice the timecode on the Timeline ruler), whereas the bottom figure shows only about 12 seconds.

In Chapter 7, I discuss the easiest way to use the Zoom feature to view the Timeline. You use the Zoom In and Zoom Out tools on the Tool palette, as shown in Figure 8-20. After you select either tool, you can click it repeatedly on the Timeline to zoom in or out. (Holding down Option also toggles the zoom between in and out.)

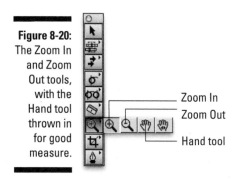

Figure 8-20:
The Zoom In and Zoom Out tools, with the Hand tool thrown in for good measure.

Zoom In

Zoom Out

Hand tool

When you're in the thick of editing, choosing a separate tool just to zoom in or out on the Timeline is often a hassle. Instead, you want to do this task seamlessly, and Final Cut Pro offers the following approaches:

✔ **The Zoom control:** The Zoom control (see Figure 8-21) is straightforward. Click to the left of the control to zoom in and see more detail on the Timeline. (Any clips you see on the Timeline stay centered while you zoom in.) Click to the right, and you zoom out; you see less detail but more clips in your sequence. You can also click and drag the control.

✔ **Keyboard shortcuts:** To zoom in one level, press ⌘++. (Yes, that's the Command key and the plus sign.) Press this key combination repeatedly to keep zooming in. To zoom out, press ⌘+– (minus sign).

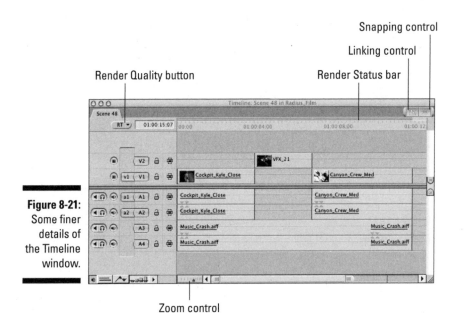

Figure 8-21:
Some finer
details of
the Timeline
window.

Zoom control

Some Timeline Details

By now, you may know more about the Final Cut Pro Timeline than you ever wanted to know. But, since you've come this far, I may as well show you a few other icons and buttons that may come in handy (check out Figure 8-21 to follow along):

✔ **Render Status bar:** This bar shows the render status of any clips on the Timeline. (See Bonus Chapter 1 on this book's companion Web site for more on rendering.) When you need to render a clip on the Timeline before playing it, you see a red line on this status bar, drawn right over the needy clip. When you have already rendered a clip, the Render status bar replaces the red line with a blue one. A green line means that you don't have to render the clip to play a real-time preview, although you need to render the clip before recording your program to tape or displaying it on a TV. Notice that Final Cut Pro divides the Render status bar into two parts: The top line shows the status for video clips, and the bottom line is for audio.

✔ **Render Quality button:** You can change the Final Cut Pro rendering mode by clicking this button and choosing options from the pop-up menu that appears. For instance, you can set Final Cut Pro to use either Safe RT or Unlimited RT when you're rendering clips in real-time. (Again, see Bonus Chapter 1 on this book's companion Web site for more on these two modes.) You can also set the quality level of real-time–rendered effects that are created in either Safe mode or Unlimited RT mode.

✔ **Snapping control:** By clicking this icon, you can quickly turn the Snapping feature on and off. For more about the Snapping feature, refer to Chapter 7.

✔ **Linking control:** Normally, whenever you select a video clip that has audio clips linked to it (or vice versa) on the Timeline, Final Cut Pro automatically selects all the linked clips at once, as a group. (Refer to Chapter 7 for more about linking.) Clicking this icon turns linking off so that you can select just the clip that you click without selecting all its dependent subclips.

Chapter 9

Editing Wizardry

. . . .

In This Chapter

▶ Using split, roll, ripple, slip, and slide edits

▶ Setting markers in clips and sequences

▶ Using slow- and fast-motion effects

▶ Freezing frames

▶ Nesting a sequence inside another sequence

▶ Recording a voiceover

. . . .

*Y*ou may already know enough about Final Cut Pro to cruise through many projects on autopilot, but if you want to turbocharge your editing work, this chapter has what you need. In fact, this chapter probably has *more* than you need. It all depends on the kind of work you're doing. My advice is to read the topics that are likely to apply to just about everybody — for instance, my coverage of advanced editing tools — and then skim through the rest of the chapter's headings to see what else looks interesting to you.

Going Beyond Insert and Overwrite Edits

In Chapter 7, you read about two different ways to edit a clip to the Timeline: You can either insert the clip (Final Cut Pro scoots over any clips on the Timeline to make room for the new one) or overwrite the clip (brutally erasing any clips or segments of clips that stand in its way). Final Cut Pro offers a few other options — such as replace edits, fit-to-fill edits, and superimpose edits — that can come in handy, depending on the situation.

Replace edits

A *replace edit* works like an overwrite edit, but replaces a single clip on the Timeline with a range of frames from a new clip (called your *source* clip) that you have opened in the Viewer window. That range equals the number of frames that are used by the original clip on the Timeline, so the length of your movie doesn't change when you replace a shot. Preserving the length of your movie is an important feature of the replace edit. Perhaps your client or producer insists that a movie be a certain length, or maybe you have spent lots of time syncing music and sound effects to your video clips and don't want to see those elements go out of sync when you replace a shot.

When you do a replace edit, Final Cut Pro pays particular attention to where you have placed the playhead in the source clip (that is, the clip in the Viewer) and where you have placed the playhead on the Timeline (you see why in a moment). For a quick and easy way to do a replace edit, follow these steps:

1. **Find on the Timeline a clip you want to replace with a new one.**

2. **Position the Timeline playhead on the In point of the clip you want to replace.**

   Make sure that the clip is on a Timeline track that is your destination track. Remember that when you make edits on the Timeline, those edits affect anything on your current destination track. (Refer to Chapter 7 for more about setting destination tracks.)

3. **From the Browser, find the new clip you want to add to the Timeline (this clip replaces the clip that's already there), and double-click to open the new clip in the Viewer window.**

4. **In the Viewer window, position the playhead on the frame that should be the clip's first frame to be moved on the Timeline.**

   This step is similar to setting the clip's In point, but you do this by simply placing the Viewer playhead on that frame rather than set an In point.

5. **Drag the clip from the Viewer to the Canvas window, and select Replace from the Edit Overlay that appears, as shown in Figure 9-1.**

Figure 9-1:
Drag clips from the Viewer to the Canvas window, and select the edit options from the Edit Overlay.

Match Frame button

Final Cut Pro replaces the current clip on the Timeline with the new clip in the Viewer. The first frame of the new clip is the frame on which you positioned the Viewer's playhead in Step 4. Final Cut Pro places the new clip's remaining frames (the frames to the right of the Viewer playhead) on the Timeline until they fill the same number of frames that were occupied by the original clip you're replacing.

If you have excess frames in the Viewer that don't fit within the Timeline's original clip's length, Final Cut Pro leaves these frames off the Timeline. For example, if the Timeline clip is 50 frames, Final Cut Pro adds only 50 frames from the Viewer, even if the clip in the Viewer contains 70 frames.

When you're doing a replace edit, you don't have to position the Timeline's playhead at the first frame of the clip you want to replace — I just suggested doing that so that you can more easily see how replace edits work. In fact, you can position the Timeline playhead on *any* frame within a clip. When you do the replace edit, Final Cut Pro centers the frame at the Viewer's playhead to the frame at the Timeline's playhead and fills in the Timeline clip with frames from both the left and right side of the Viewer playhead. (This process sounds a bit complicated, but it becomes clear after you see this type of edit in action.)

If you see an `Insufficient Content for Edit` error message while replacing a clip (a likely scenario when you're getting used to this feature), Final Cut Pro is telling you that the source clip in the Viewer doesn't have enough frames to replace all the Timeline clip's frames. (The source clip in the Viewer needs the same or a greater number of frames on *each* side of the Viewer's playhead as the Timeline clip has on each side of the Timeline's playhead.)

The Match Frame feature

You can use a replace edit with the Final Cut Pro Match Frame feature to quickly sync an event in a video clip with an event in an audio clip (for example, to sync a dancer's exaggerated step to a beat of music in a music video). Follow these steps:

1. **On the Timeline, place your audio clip in an audio track that's directly below your video clip so that the two clips fall within the same timeframe.**

   Don't try to sync the video and audio events yet — just make sure that your audio clip is directly below the video clip. (However, it doesn't matter which track the audio clip occupies.) It's okay if the video and audio clips aren't the same length and therefore don't line up perfectly. You just want to line them up as best as you can.

2. **Position the Timeline playhead at the point where the audio event takes place.**

For example, you may want to position the playhead on a beat of music. For greater precision, you can display your Timeline clips in a bigger size and set them to show audio waveforms. (To do this, choose Sequence⇨ Settings, click the Timeline Options tab, and make the appropriate selections. Refer to Chapter 7 if these options are unfamiliar to you.)

3. **Make sure that none of your audio tracks is set as a destination track by separating the Source and Destination controls for audio tracks in the Timeline's Patch panel.**

   You can click either the track's Destination or Source control to disconnect them from each other. Refer to Chapter 7 for more about setting destination tracks.

4. **Make the Timeline track that is carrying your video clip into your destination video track.**

   The video track that's carrying your clip must be the destination track. By default, the Final Cut Pro destination video track is V1, but you can switch it to another video track you have created. Refer to Chapter 7 for more details.

5. **Without moving the Timeline playhead, do a match frame by pressing** F. **Alternatively, you can click the Match Frame button in the Canvas window (refer to Figure 9-1).**

   In the Viewer window, Final Cut Pro opens the original master clip that the Timeline's *video* clip came from. (It's as though you found that clip in the Browser and double-clicked it to open it in the Viewer.) Notice that the Viewer playhead is positioned on the same frame of the clip as your Timeline playhead. (In other words, the Viewer and Canvas windows should now display the same frame because each playhead is on the same frame.) This is how the Match Frame feature works: It looks at the frame where you have positioned the Timeline playhead and opens the original clip in the Viewer window, with the playhead positioned on that same frame.

6. **In the Viewer window, move the playhead to the video frame you want to synchronize with the audio event.**

   Remember that you positioned the Timeline playhead on that audio event in Step 2. You're now about to sync the Viewer video frame with the audio that's on the Timeline.

7. **Do a replace edit: Drag the clip from the Viewer to the Canvas window, and select Replace from the Edit Overlay that appears.**

   Final Cut Pro replaces the current video clip on the Timeline with the Match Frame version in the Viewer (and lines up the Viewer playhead frame with the Timeline playhead, which also happens to be positioned where your audio event takes place). The video and audio frames should now be synchronized, as long as the Viewer clip had enough frames available on either side of the Viewer playhead to replace the Timeline clip's frames on either side of the Timeline playhead. (If you run into problems, see the Warning paragraph about `Insufficient Content for Edit` errors at the end of the preceding section, "Replace edits.")

Fit-to-fill edits

A *fit-to-fill edit* is aptly named because that's exactly what this edit does: It forces a source clip to fit any gap or range of frames that you set for it on the Timeline. Final Cut Pro does this by speeding or slowing the clip.

Suppose that you have finished editing your movie, but you're waiting for a fancy animated opening title from a motion graphics artist. You have reserved a 5-second gap in the movie for the title, but when you finally get the animation, it's only 4 seconds long! In this case, you would use a fit-to-fill edit to add an extra second to the title and let it fit the gap you reserved for it. The result? Final Cut Pro figures out how to play the 4-second title animation slower so that it fills its 5-second allocation.

To do a fit-to-fill edit, follow these steps:

1. **On the Timeline, make sure that the track that's receiving your source clip is the destination track.**

   By default, the Final Cut Pro destination video track is V1, and its destination audio tracks are A1 and A2 (unless you have made changes). Refer to Chapter 7 for more about destination tracks.

2. **On the Timeline, set In and Out points to define the range of frames that are to receive the source clip.**

   You do this by setting In and Out points on the Timeline. (The points you set are indicated on the Timeline ruler.) Position the Timeline playhead at the beginning of the range, and press I for In point. Then move the playhead to the last frame of the range, and press O for Out point.

3. **Open your source clip (the one you want to fit to fill) in the Viewer window, and set its In and Out points, if necessary.**

   You don't have to set In and Out points if you want to fit to fill the entire clip.

4. **Drag the clip from the Viewer to the Canvas window.**

   When you drag the fit-to-fill clip over the Canvas, the familiar Edit Overlay appears and displays your edit options.

5. **Select Fit to Fill from the Edit Overlay (refer to Figure 9-1).**

   Final Cut Pro adds the fit-to-fill clip to the Timeline and sets the clip to play at the appropriate speed.

6. **If necessary, render the clip by selecting it and choosing Sequence⇨ Render Selection⇨Both.**

   If the clip needs to play faster than normal (to fit a smaller space than it originally filled), Final Cut Pro plays the clip so that it skips frames while playing. If the clip needs to play slower than normal, the software plays it with some duplicated frames. To see the speed at which the clip now plays, you can select it on the Timeline and choose Modify⇨Speed.

Superimpose edits

When you superimpose a clip, Final Cut Pro moves it to the Timeline and places it on the next available track after the current destination track. If you need to stack multiple clips on top of each other (for instance, if you're about to composite many different images into one shot or add various audio clips that play simultaneously), a superimpose edit is a helpful way to quickly get those clips on separate Timeline tracks.

You perform a superimpose edit in the usual way — by opening a source clip in the Viewer window, dragging the clip to the Canvas window, and selecting Superimpose from the Edit Overlay that appears. A superimpose edit is unique in one important way: Normally, whenever you edit a clip to the Timeline, Final Cut Pro places it where the Timeline's playhead happens to be — but not this time! Instead, Final Cut Pro looks at the position of the Timeline playhead, and if a clip is already at that point on the current destination track, that clip's In and Out points on the Timeline become the In and Out points for your superimposed edit (as you can see in Figure 9-2).

Figure 9-2:
Three clips are super-imposed with the Track V1 clip, matching its In and Out points on the Timeline.

Suppose that you're superimposing a 5-second video clip on the Timeline (it ends up on track V2) and you place the Timeline playhead where you already have a 2-second clip on the V1 target track. When you superimpose the 5-second clip — surprise! — only 2 seconds make it to Track V2 on the Timeline.

This strange functionality may seem like an annoying bug, but when you're in the superimposing mood, you usually want superimposed clips to match each other's durations, so this weird twist works in your favor. If it doesn't, you can set your own In and Out points on the Timeline before superimposing a clip. In this case, Final Cut Pro ignores the length of the clip that's on the current destination target track and edits the new clip into the In and Out edit points you set.

You can superimpose a group of clips, and make each one go to its own Timeline track, by selecting the group in the Browser window and dragging the clips to the Canvas window, where you can select the Superimpose option from the Canvas's Edit Overlay (refer to Figure 9-1).

Splitting Video and Audio Edits

Whenever you edit a clip that has video and audio that are linked (either by setting In and Out points for the clip in the Final Cut Pro Viewer window or by adjusting those points after the clip is on the Timeline), you're usually affecting both the clip's video and audio components the same way. In other words, whenever a video clip begins or ends, so does its audio clip (or vice versa).

By doing a *split edit,* however, you can set different In and Out points for the video and audio segments of a clip. That is, you can end a video clip while letting its audio continue (as shown in Figure 9-3), or you can begin the audio first and then bring in the video a moment later.

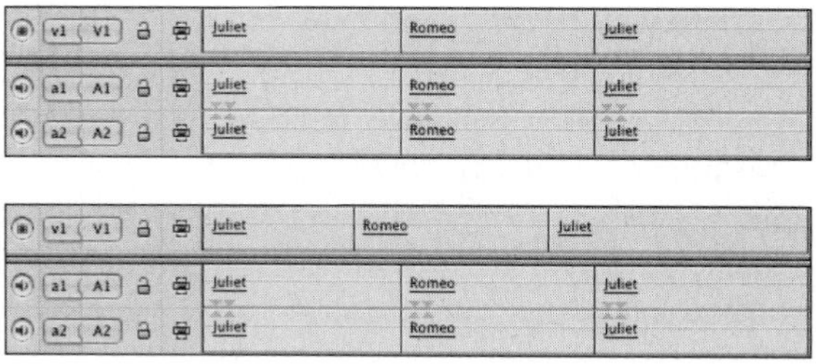

Figure 9-3:
Before and after a split edit on the Timeline.

		Juliet	Romeo	Juliet
v1 (V1)		Juliet	Romeo	Juliet
a1 (A1)		Juliet	Romeo	Juliet
a2 (A2)		Juliet	Romeo	Juliet
v1 (V1)		Juliet	Romeo	Juliet
a1 (A1)		Juliet	Romeo	Juliet
a2 (A2)		Juliet	Romeo	Juliet

Splitting edits from the Viewer

You can set up split edit points in the Viewer. Doing so is almost as easy as marking simple In and Out points, but you can mark as many as four points — In and Out points for video and In and Out points for audio. Follow these steps to set up split edit points:

1. **From the Browser, open in the Viewer window a video clip that also incorporates audio.**

   You have to select a clip from the Browser. Selecting a clip that's already on the Timeline doesn't work. (I don't know why.)

2. **Position the Viewer playhead on the frame where the video will begin, and set an In point by choosing Mark⇨Mark Split⇨Video In from the menu bar.**

   You can also press Control+I to mark the video's In point.

   You have just told Final Cut Pro that the clip's video should start at this frame, but you still have to define the video's Out point as well as the In and Out points for the clip's audio.

3. **Repeat Step 2, and mark the Video Out, Audio In, and Audio Out points by choosing those options from the Mark Split submenu.**

   You can mark these points in any order. You can also skip setting an Out point for either the video or audio — if you skip setting these points, Final Cut Pro just makes the last frame of the clip the Out points. (The software does just the reverse when you set Out points, but not In points, for video and audio.)

   Also, if you want the video and audio to either start or end on the same frame (in many cases, you want to split the beginning of a clip but not the end, or vice versa), place a standard In or Out point on that particular frame.

   Figure 9-4 shows all video and audio In and Out points set.

4. **Move the clip to the Timeline.**

   You can drag the clip from the Viewer directly to the Timeline or drag it to the Canvas window and choose an edit option. After moving the clip to the Timeline, notice that Final Cut Pro sets the video and audio points differently, to reflect how you split them in the Viewer.

   When you have moved the split-edited clip to the Timeline, you can still adjust the clip's video and audio In and Out points by clicking and dragging them on the Timeline.

Figure 9-4:
Split video
and audio
edits in the
Viewer.

Audio In point   Video In point   Video Out point   Audio Out point

To clear split edit points, open the clip from the Browser window and choose Mark⇨Clear Split. The Clear Split submenu lets you clear each In and Out point or all audio or all video points together. Or, as a shortcut, press Control while clicking the Viewer scrubber bar, and clear your split edits from the pop-up menu that appears.

After you add a split-edited clip to the Timeline, you have a limited ability to adjust the clip's split edits by using the Viewer again. If you double-click the clip on the Timeline, it opens in the Viewer, but you can readjust only the clip's two In points (video and audio) together as well as its two Out points (video and audio) together. The easiest way to adjust these linked points is to use your mouse to click them on the scrubber bar and drag them to a new location. Before you do this, read the next section, which shows you how to adjust (and readjust) split video and audio points directly on the Timeline. This method is a bit more intuitive.

Splitting edits on the Timeline

You can also create split edits on clips that are already on the Timeline, as shown in Figure 9-5. I prefer this approach because you can more intuitively see how a clip's video and audio are split, and you can see how those splits integrate with neighboring clips that you eventually place side by side with your split-edited clip.

The easiest way to split-edit a clip on the Timeline is to simply drag the edges of the clip's video and audio components to different points. (The edges of a clip represent its In and Out points.) To set new points, hold down Option and drag the edge of the clip's video or audio to a new point. You can see that the clip's video and audio stay linked (you can move the clip on the Timeline, and its video and audio portions stay together), but the clip's video and audio In and Out points change independently of one another.

Figure 9-5:
Splitting
audio and
video on
overlapping
tracks.

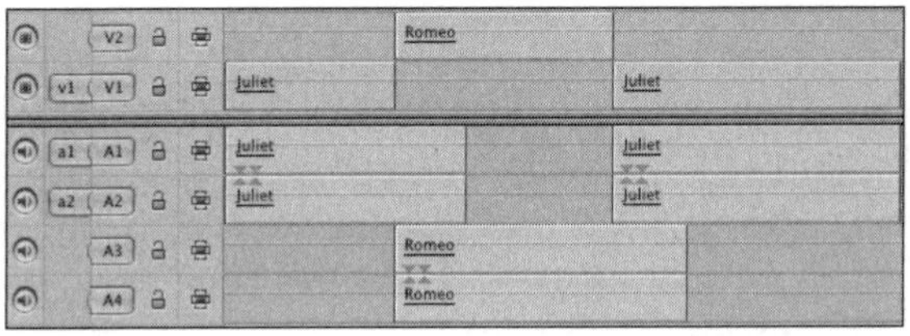

Using Advanced Editing Tools

After you move your media clips to the Timeline, most of your editing energy goes toward tweaking those clips so that they cut smoothly from one to another. In Chapter 7, I introduce you to all the basic tools and techniques to do just that, but you shouldn't stop there! Final Cut Pro sports a range of advanced tools — such as roll and ripple edits or slips and slides — that let you accomplish certain editing tasks in one simple step rather than two, three, or four (as can be the case when you're working with the more basic Final Cut Pro tools).

After you get the hang of using them, you use most of these power tools throughout your editing work. They're especially handy when you want to tweak a few clips (add a few frames here or cut a few frames there) without changing the length of your Timeline sequence (that is, movie). Why is pre-serving length so important? In the late stages of your work, you may have already inserted sound effects or music, for example — all carefully synced with your video. Or, maybe your video just has to fit within an allotted length of time, as does a TV commercial. At any rate, these tools, with the exception of the Ripple Edit tool, all let you tweak clips and minimize the effects of those tweaks on other clips and on your sequence in general.

You can also use these advanced tools in a variety of ways, although the quickest and most intuitive approach is to simply select a new tool from the Tool palette and apply it directly to clips you have already placed on the Timeline. Still, some of these tools and techniques can seem a bit confusing when you're reading about them for the first time, so don't get frustrated if you find yourself saying "Huh?" Just take the time to study the figures I provide, and then try out the tools on your own clips.

Editing clips often means making small, precise changes to them. But, if you have the Final Cut Pro Snapping feature turned on, you may find it hard to be as precise as you want because your mouse pointer keeps snapping to the edges of nearby clips rather than going where you want it to be. If this is the case, press N to toggle off snapping. (You can even toggle snapping while dragging a clip or its edges.)

You may want to apply these new tools to only the video or audio portions of a linked clip. (Normally, any changes you make to a linked clip affect both its video and audio.) That's no problem: Just hold down the Option key while you're using the tools, and your changes affect only the part of the clip you're adjusting. For instance, if you press Option and then apply the Roll Edit tool to the video of a linked clip, you affect only the clip's video, not its audio.

Resizing clips with roll and ripple edits

Roll and *ripple* edits let you resize clips on the Timeline without having to separately move adjacent (side-by-side) clips forward or backward to accommodate your changes. For instance, you don't have to create a gap on the Timeline before extending a clip into that gap, and you don't have to close an unwanted gap after trimming a clip.

Both these edits affect how two adjacent clips are joined on the Timeline. When you perform either a roll or ripple edit, you're either adding or taking away frames from the first clip (known as the *outgoing clip,* which comes earlier) or the second clip (known as the *incoming clip,* which comes later), but you're maintaining the edit point of these clips — that is, the two clips stay connected, never leaving a gap between them.

Rolling edits

A *roll edit* lets you simultaneously move the edit point between two clips, to make one clip longer and the other shorter, all in one fell swoop. (Of course, the clip you're trying to make longer must have extra frames that you haven't already edited onto the Timeline.) For example, you may have Clips A, B, C, and D on the Timeline, side by side, and you want to do a roll edit between Clips A and B. Check out Figure 9-6. The top image shows Clip A and B at the same size, before the roll edit. The next image shows a roll edit that extends Clip B at the expense of Clip A. The bottom image shows you another roll edit in the opposite direction that extends Clip A at the expense of Clip B. No matter which way you move the roll edit pointer, Clips C and D remain unaffected.

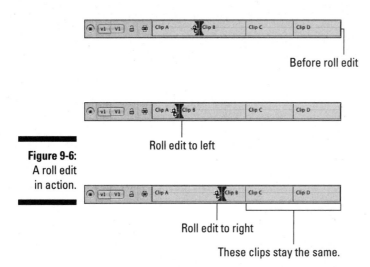

Before roll edit

Roll edit to left

Figure 9-6:
A roll edit
in action.

Roll edit to right

These clips stay the same.

In other words, my roll edit changes the Out point of Clip A and the In point of Clip B, but it doesn't change the combined length of the two clips. Therefore, the Roll doesn't shift any of the following clips (C and D) either forward or backward along the Timeline.

Why would you want to do a roll edit — other than to show off your Final Cut Pro acumen to family and friends? A roll edit is helpful to use when you're trying to match the same action as you cut from one clip to another. Suppose that you have the dubious distinction of editing the next installment of *Rocky* and you want to cut from a medium shot of Rocky throwing his knockout blow to a close-up of his glove landing squarely on the jaw of his hapless challenger. In this case, you place these two clips side by side, to try to match the actions as closely as possible, and then use the roll edit to fine-tune the edit point — and look for the perfect frame to exit the first clip and enter the second clip.

Roll edits are easy to do right on the Timeline. Follow these steps:

1. **Select the Roll Edit tool from the Final Cut Pro Tool palette (as shown in Figure 9-7), or press R.**

   The mouse pointer becomes a Roll Edit symbol.

2. **Click the Roll Edit tool on an edit point between two clips on the Timeline, and drag the edit point either right or left (forward or backward in time).**

Figure 9-7:
The Roll Edit
and Ripple
Edit tools on
the Tool
palette.

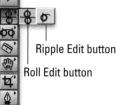

Ripple Edit button

Roll Edit button

As you drag, keep an eye on the Canvas window. As shown in Figure 9-8, the window goes into a two-up clip display. The frame on the left shows the last frame, or Out point, of the outgoing clip (again, the clip to the left of the Timeline's edit point), and the frame on the right displays the first frame, or In point, of the incoming clip. When you release the mouse button, the roll edit takes effect on the Timeline.

Figure 9-8:
The Canvas
window
becomes
a two-up
clip display.

When you use a roll edit to extend an edit point by a certain number of frames, you're also shortening the adjacent clip by the same number of frames, so the two clips continue to share the same edit point. What you give to one clip, you take from the other (and vice versa).

Ripplin' with ripple edits

A *ripple edit* lets you resize a clip by moving its In or Out point on the Timeline — it sounds simple enough, eh? What makes ripple edits so cool — and probably the most handy editing tool that's available to you — is that when you resize a clip, Final Cut Pro automatically ripples that change through the rest of the Timeline sequence, to move clips forward or backward in time (to make room for the clip you have extended or to close the gap that was left by a clip you have trimmed).

For instance, you may have placed Clips A, B, C, and D on the Timeline side by side, but you decide to trim a few frames off the end of Clip B (the Out point) while also moving Clips C and D to the left so that they fill the empty gap left by Clip B's trimmed frames, as shown in Figure 9-9. The top image shows the Timeline before a ripple edit takes place. In the middle image, the ripple edit trims Clip B and moves Clip C over to fill in the gap. In the bottom image, I have used the ripple edit to extend Clip B and move Clip C later in time to make room. See how cool that is? Without the Ripple Edit tool, these kinds of operations would take two or more steps, but now they're boiled down to one. That's progress, folks.

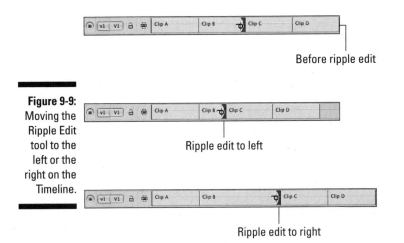

Figure 9-9:
Moving the Ripple Edit tool to the left or the right on the Timeline.

Before ripple edit

Ripple edit to left

Ripple edit to right

Like the Roll Edit tool, the Ripple Edit tool is specifically designed to work with two clips — one on either side of an edit point (an outgoing clip and an incoming clip). You can move either the Out point of the outgoing clip (that is, the first clip) or the In point of the incoming clip. To use a ripple edit on clips on the Timeline, follow these steps:

1. **Select the Ripple Edit tool from the Final Cut Pro Tool palette (refer to Figure 9-7).**

   Alternatively, press R twice. The mouse pointer becomes a Ripple Edit symbol.

2. **Click to the immediate left of an edit point with the Ripple Edit tool to select the outgoing clip, or click to the immediate right to select the incoming clip.**

   Sometimes, you may wonder whether you're selecting the outgoing or incoming clip at the edit point, because the two clips are right next to each other. Watch the Ripple Edit symbol's tail, which looks like a hook. The tail always points toward the clip you're about to select.

   You're letting Final Cut know which of the two clips at the edit point you want to affect. Final Cut Pro responds by highlighting a thin slice of the clip that's next to the edit point. (Figure 9-9 shows Clip B selected in this way.)

3. **Click and drag the selected side of the edit point either forward or backward in time to extend or trim it.**

   As you drag, keep an eye on the Canvas window. It goes into its two-up clip display: The frame on the left shows the last frame, or Out point, of the outgoing clip (again, the clip to the left of the edit point), and the frame on the right shows the first frame, or In point, of the incoming clip.

   When you release the mouse button, Final Cut ripples the effects of your edit through all the following clips in the Timeline sequence. Seeing those clips shift in time can sometimes be disorienting, but go ahead and play the clips you have just affected. You should see that all's well (if not, choose Edit⇨Undo and try again).

Slip-slidin' clips

Slip Edit and Slide Edit are two other specialized tools in your editing arsenal. Although you probably don't use them every day (as you would use the Ripple Edit tool), they can save you a few steps in certain scenarios.

Like roll and ripple edits, slips and slides are easy to do directly on the Timeline, so that's what this subsection focuses on.

Give a clip the slip

A *slip edit* changes the In and Out points of a single clip, but not its duration or its position on the Timeline. Say what?

If this concept sounds a bit abstract, try this example: Suppose that you open a clip in the Viewer, and it's 90 frames long. You decide to edit only its middle 30 frames (31 through 60) to the Timeline. After those frames are on the Timeline, you can use the Slip Edit tool to change the 30 frames that the clip shows — for instance, frames 1–30, 15–45, and so on — as shown in Figure 9-10.

Rectangle frame shows all frames available.

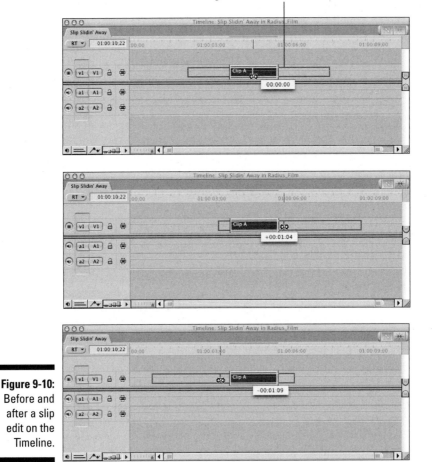

Figure 9-10:
Before and
after a slip
edit on the
Timeline.

So now you're thinking, "Hmmm, that's pretty clever, but what would ever posses me to do that?" You can turn to the Slip Edit tool whenever you have carefully edited a group of clips and you need to change one clip in the sequence but don't want to affect any others. For instance, maybe you have meticulously synced some video to music beats or other sound events, but then you realize that one clip plays a bit awkwardly with the clips around it. If you don't want to extend or trim that clip (because that would change the duration of the sequence and throw off the sync with the audio), you can do a slip edit and try to find a better-looking range of frames within the problem clip — without changing its position or length in the sequence.

That's enough theory. To edit a clip by using the Slip Edit tool, follow these steps:

1. **Select the Slip Edit tool on the Tool palette (as shown in Figure 9-11), or press S.**

   Either way, the mouse pointer becomes a Slip Edit symbol.

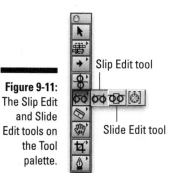

Figure 9-11: The Slip Edit and Slide Edit tools on the Tool palette.

Slip Edit tool

Slide Edit tool

2. **Click a clip on the Timeline, and drag the mouse either left or right to slip its frames.**

   When you click the clip, Final Cut Pro shows a rectangle frame that represents the total frames available to the clip. Drag left to move the latter frames of the clip into position, or drag right to see its earlier frames.

   Also, keep an eye on the Canvas window. As you drag, it shows a two-up display of the new In and Out points for the clip (refer to Figure 9-8).

3. **Release the mouse button when you're happy with those new In and Out points.**

4. **Play the slipped clip from the Timeline to see how it looks.**

Sliding a clip

The Slide Edit tool is an unusual beast in that it moves an entire clip either forward or backward on the Timeline while also moving the edit points on either side of the clip. *Translation:* As you move a clip with the Slide Edit tool, you're at the same time trimming or extending the clips to either side of it to accommodate the clip in its new location while keeping its edit points intact.

Suppose that you have arranged Clips A, B, and C side by side on the Timeline (as shown in Figure 9-12), and each clip is 30 frames long. When you slide Clip B forward in time by 15 frames, you also trim the Clip A Out point by 15 frames and extend the Clip C In point by 15 frames. The result? Clip A is now only 15 frames long, Clip B keeps its original 30-frame length, but is now in a new position on the Timeline, and Clip C is 45 frames long (as long as it had extra frames to extend out to).

Figure 9-12:
Before and after a slide edit on the Timeline.

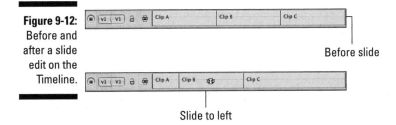

Before slide

Slide to left

Although you're not likely to use the Slide Edit tool regularly (I probably use it once a year), it can be helpful to move an important clip without manually changing the edit points of other clips in the sequence. To use the Slide Edit tool, follow these steps:

1. **Select the Slide Edit tool on the Final Cut Pro Tool palette (refer to Figure 9-11), or press S twice.**

   The mouse pointer becomes a Slide Edit symbol.

Option: The unsung hero

The Option key is the unsung hero of your Timeline editing tools: When you hold it down, it lets you edit the video and audio parts of a clip separately, even though that clip's video and audio are linked. Trust me: The benefit is *huge* because you inevitably want to edit the video of a clip, but not its audio (or vice versa), and would otherwise have to unlink the two elements, do your edit, and then link them again — which is quite time consuming. With Option, it's a no-brainer.

To see Option's prowess, just place on the Timeline a clip that includes video and audio (a clip captured from a DV camera is a good bet). Now, try these simple exercises:

✔ Using the Final Cut Selection tool (press A or choose it on the Tool palette), hold the Option key down, select the video portion of your clip, and press Delete. Presto! The video is gone, but the audio still lives.

✔ With the Razor Blade tool selected, hold the Option key down and click the blade on the audio part of the clip. Cool! You just cut the audio, but not the video.

✔ With the Roll tool selected, hold down the Option key and click and drag an edit point between two video clips. The Roll tool affects your video, but doesn't change the edit point between the clips' audio!

2. **Click a clip on the Timeline, and drag the mouse either left or right to slide it forward or backward in time.**

   The Canvas window switches to a two-up display (refer to Figure 9-8) and displays the new Out-point frame of the clip to the left and the new In-point frame of the clip to the right.

   Also, a pop-up timecode box tells you how many seconds and frames you're sliding your clip away from its original location.

3. **Release the mouse button when you have moved the middle clip to a good spot.**

4. **Play the edited clips from the Timeline to see how they look.**

Using Markers to Highlight Important Moments

Markers are little signposts that you can place anywhere in a media clip or Timeline sequence to identify (or . . . mark!) frames that are important to you. For instance, you may mark a frame where you want to begin changing a clip's volume, by fading it in or out. Or, you may want to place markers at a clip's existing In and Out points so that you always know where they were originally set (in case you plan to change those points and want the option of going back to their original locations later, if you don't like your changes).

In this section, you find out how to use markers to their fullest.

Setting markers

You can set markers inside an individual clip or within a sequence on the Timeline. Set them in clips to flag important moments within that clip, and set them in a sequence to flag important moments in your edited story (for instance, a frame where you may want to insert additional clips or possibly trim or extend a nearby clip). You can set as many markers as you want — Final Cut just numbers them sequentially (Marker 1, Marker 2, and so on) until you rename them. (For more details on renaming markers, see the section "Renaming, deleting, and designating markers," later in this chapter.)

The Timeline can snap clips to markers, as long as you have snapping turned on — press N to toggle it. This feature makes markers helpful aids for lining up clips (or keyframes in clips) with other clips on the Timeline.

Setting markers within a clip

To set a marker within a clip (see Figure 9-13), follow these steps:

1. **Open the clip in the Viewer window.**

2. **Position the Viewer playhead on the frame you want to mark, and press M (for marker).**

   You can also click the Add Marker button in the Viewer window — refer to Figure 9-13.

Viewer Current Timecode box

Figure 9-13: Markers set for a clip in the Viewer window.

Click to add a marker

Individual markers

A marker comment

Keep setting as many markers as you want. When you move your clip to the Timeline, you see those markers within the clip.

You can use markers to break a clip into smaller subclips, which is a useful way to quickly divide a long, unwieldy clip into more-manageable morsels. To take advantage of this cool feature, open a clip by double-clicking it from the Browser window. In the Viewer window, set markers at each frame where you want a new subclip to begin. From now on, the Final Cut Pro Browser identifies that marked-up clip with a small triangle next to its name. If you click the triangle, the Browser lists every marker you set in that clip (as shown in Figure 9-14), although your Browser has to be in List view for this feature to work (choose Edit⇨Browser Items⇨As List).

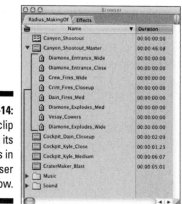

Figure 9-14:
A clip
shows its
markers in
the Browser
window.

Markers in the Browser window

In fact, the Browser now treats each marker as though it's an individual clip.
(Each of these new clips starts at the first frame you marked in the original
clip and ends at the frame before the next marker you set.) All the usual
things you can do to clips apply to these subclips. You can rename them,
open them in the Viewer window, set In and Out points for them, and move
them to the Timeline. Cool, eh?

You can even set markers while Final Cut plays a clip in the Viewer (as
opposed to stopping playback to set the marker). Just start playing the clip,
and press M or click the Add Marker button to place a marker on the fly.
Granted, this method isn't highly precise (unless you have incredible hand-
eye coordination), but it's the best way to insert lots of markers in a hurry —
for instance, to mark beats of music in an audio clip.

Setting markers within a sequence

Setting a marker on the Timeline (that is, a marker that highlights a point in
time, not a frame in a particular clip) isn't much different from setting a marker
in the Viewer window. Follow these steps to set a marker on the Timeline:

1. **Make sure that you haven't selected any clips on the Timeline.**

   To be safe, select the Timeline window and then press ⌘+Shift+A to
   deselect any clips (or choose Edit⇨Deselect All).

2. **Position the Timeline's playhead on the frame to mark, and press M to
   place the marker.**

Even if you're working on the Timeline, you can still set markers within a particular clip (as you would do if you opened the clip in the Viewer). Select the
clip on the Timeline, position the Timeline playhead within that clip, and
press M. The marker appears within the clip itself (see Figure 9-15), not on
the Timeline ruler.

Markers on Timeline

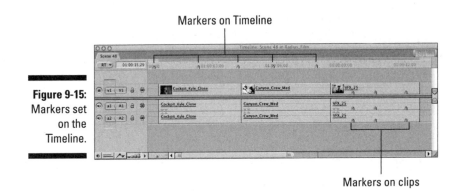

Figure 9-15:
Markers set
on the
Timeline.

Markers on clips

Renaming, deleting, and designating markers

You can edit markers either from the Viewer window (for markers within clips) or from the Timeline (for markers on the Timeline).

Follow these steps to rename markers:

1. **In the Viewer or Timeline window, position the playhead directly on a marker.**

   Watch out: It may look as though you have positioned the playhead directly on a marked frame, but you may still be off by a frame or two. If the playhead is indeed on a marker, you see the marker change color. For guaranteed results, you can also jump the playhead to the preceding and following markers by pressing Shift+↑ or Shift+↓, respectively.

2. **Choose Mark⊃Markers⊃Edit from the menu bar, or press M.**

   Either way, Final Cut Pro opens the Edit Marker dialog box.

3. **In the Edit Marker dialog box (as shown in Figure 9-16), type a new name for the marker and click OK.**

	Edit Marker
Name:	Explosion
Comment:	Dain and Vesay duck as Diamone shield blows from grenade detonation.
Start:	01:00:07;26
Duration:	00:00:00;00

Delete

Add Chapter Marker

Add Compression Marker

Add Scoring Marker

Cancel   OK

Figure 9-16:
The Edit
Marker
dialog box.

You should name markers something meaningful so that you can easily search for a marker by name (which I cover in the following section).

You can also type a comment for a marker. (This habit is helpful when, a few weeks later, you can't remember why you placed the marker in the first place.)

To delete a marker, follow these steps:

1. **In the Viewer or Timeline window, position the playhead directly on a marker.**

2. **Choose Mark⇨Markers⇨Edit from the menu bar, or press M.**

3. **In the Edit Marker dialog box, click the Delete button.**

Besides naming and deleting markers, you can give a marker a special designation that's recognized by other programs you may export your Final Cut movies into. For instance, you may place a marker where you want your musical score to suddenly pick up its pace. By designating that marker as a Scoring marker, it appears in your video when you export it to the Soundtrack application for scoring. (See Chapter 10 for more on Soundtrack.)

You can give three different designations to your markers. Scoring markers are recognized by Soundtrack, whereas Chapter markers are recognized by the Apple DVD Studio Pro (and are handy for noting the beginning of new chapters in your video), and Compression markers can be exported to Compressor and other encoding software to identify frames of a movie that should be encoded with the greatest accuracy. To give a marker one of these three special designations, simply click the appropriate button in the Edit Marker dialog box. Final Cut inserts a special code into the box's Comment field, which is built in when you export your movie from Final Cut.

Searching for markers

You can quickly search for markers you have set in either clips or a Timeline sequence. Here's a word of advice, though: To get the most from these searches, make sure that you rename markers so that they're more descriptive than the default names Final Cut gives them (Marker 1, Marker 2, and so on). See the preceding section for more information about renaming markers.

To search for Timeline markers, follow these steps:

1. **Press Control, and click anywhere on the Timeline ruler (refer to Figure 9-15).**

2. **From the pop-up menu that appears, select the marker you want to search for.**

   Final Cut Pro moves the Timeline playhead to that marker.

To search for markers within a clip, follow these steps:

1. **Open the clip in the Viewer.**

2. **Press Control, click the Viewer's Current Timecode box (refer to Figure 9-13), and choose the marker you want to search for from the pop-up menu that appears.**

You can also search a Timeline sequence for markers by using the Final Cut Pro Find command. Follow these steps to do so:

1. **Make the Timeline or Canvas window active.**

2. **Choose Edit⇨Find from the menu bar.**

   The Find dialog box is displayed, as shown in Figure 9-17.

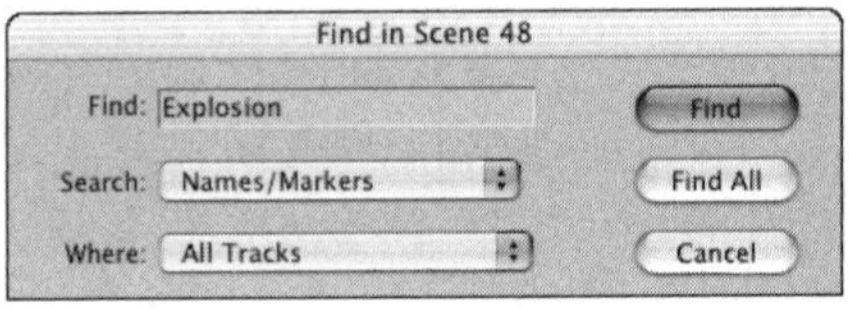

Figure 9-17:
The Find
dialog box.

Find in Scene 48	
Find: Explosion	Find
Search: Names/Markers	Find All
Where: All Tracks	Cancel

3. **Select Names/Markers from the Search pop-up menu that appears, and type part of or the whole marker name in the Find text box.**

4. **Click the Find button.**

   Final Cut Pro moves the Timeline playhead to the first clip or sequence marker that fits the description. (Clips have to be on the Timeline for their markers to be found). You hear a beep if Final Cut Pro can't find any markers.

5. **To move to the next marker that fits the description, choose Edit⇨Find Again.**

From the Viewer, Canvas, or Timeline windows, you can quickly jump the playhead to the next or previous marker: Press Shift+↓ for Next and Shift+↑ for Previous.

Playing a Clip Backward

Occasionally, you may find it handy to play a clip backward rather than forward. For instance, in my movie *Radius,* I needed footage of a timer counting down to zero, but the timer prop could only count up, not down. No problem. The cameraman just filmed the timer counting up, and then I reversed the footage after it was on the Timeline, so it seemed to be counting down. To reverse a clip, follow these steps:

1. **On the Timeline, select the clip you want to reverse.**

   If you also want to keep a version of the clip that plays forward on the Timeline, copy the original clip on the Timeline by using the Final Cut Pro Copy command (on the Edit menu), and then paste its duplicate elsewhere on the Timeline. Remember that you can also create copies of clips in the Browser window and store them there for safekeeping.

2. **Choose Modify⇨Speed.**

3. **In the Speed dialog box (see Figure 9-18), select the Reverse check box and click OK.**

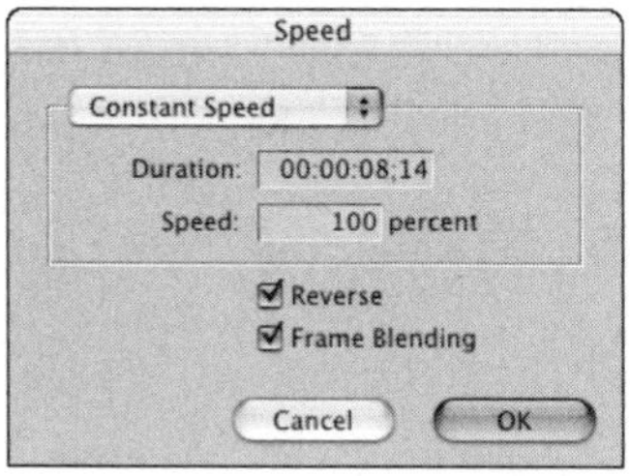

Figure 9-18:
The Speed
dialog box.

Notice on the Timeline that (100%) follows the clip name. This percentage tells you that the clip is playing at full speed (100 percent), but in reverse (as indicated by the parentheses).

4. **If necessary, choose the familiar Sequence⇨Render Selection⇨Both command to render the clip.**

5. **Play the clip on the Timeline to see how it looks.**

Changing a Clip's Speed

Slowing and speeding video clips are useful ways to add drama and suspense or frenetic action to your movie. With Final Cut Pro HD, you have the following ways to change the play speed of a clip:

✔ You can give a clip a constant speed throughout (for instance, 150 percent or 25 percent).

✔ You can vary play speeds within a single clip (for instance, go from slow motion to fast and back to slow again in a single clip). This variable-speed feature is sure to please anyone who does some of those spiffy time-based effects that are popular in commercials as well as in music and sports videos.

Setting a constant speed

When you slow a clip, Final Cut Pro is adding frames to the clip, so it takes more time for the clip to play at the DV 29.97 frames-per-second pace. Likewise, when you increase the speed of a clip, Final Cut Pro tosses out frames, to make the action seem to go quicker. To add either effect, follow these steps:

1. **On the Timeline, select a clip that you want to play slower or faster (but at a constant speed).**

2. **Choose Modify⇨Speed from the menu bar.**

3. **Make sure that Constant Speed is selected on the Speed dialog box's pop-up menu.**

4. **In the Speed dialog box (refer to Figure 9-18), type either a new percentage of speed or a new time duration for your clip.**

   When you change a clip's constant speed, you're also changing its duration. (A clip that plays twice as fast lasts only half as long, and a clip that plays twice as slow lasts twice as long. Right?) Final Cut Pro lets you set speed as a percentage of normal speed or as a new timecode duration for the clip, depending on your needs. For instance, if you're trying to fit the clip into a fixed amount of time, type a new duration value. Or, if you're just going by instinct, try using a percentage. (A rate lower than 100 percent makes the clip play in slow motion, and a higher value increases the speed of the clip.)

   After you change a clip's speed, play it and see how it looks. If it plays a bit stuttery, trying changing its speed to a different but similar number. Final Cut plays certain frames rates a bit smoother than others, and so you might want to experiment with the best play speed for your clip.

5. **Toggle Frame Blending on or off.**

   This option is handy for slow-motion clips. Ordinarily, Final Cut Pro creates a slow-motion effect by duplicating some or all of the original clip's frames, once or many times. But, repeating the same frames many times can create a stuttering effect so that when the Frame Blending option is turned on, Final Cut Pro tries to create new frames that are a blend of the original frames in the movie. For instance, rather than play Frame 1 twice, Final Cut Pro would play Frame 1 once and then draw a new frame that is halfway between Frame 1 and Frame 2 (and so on). The result is a smoother slow-motion effect.

6. **Click OK, and render your clip on the Timeline (if necessary).**

   When you click OK, you see that Final Cut Pro has either lengthened or shortened the clip on the Timeline (as shown in Figure 9-19). If your Mac requires you to render the clip before you can see it play, choose Sequence⇨Render Selection⇨Both.

7. **Play the clip on the Timeline to see how it looks.**

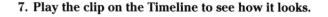

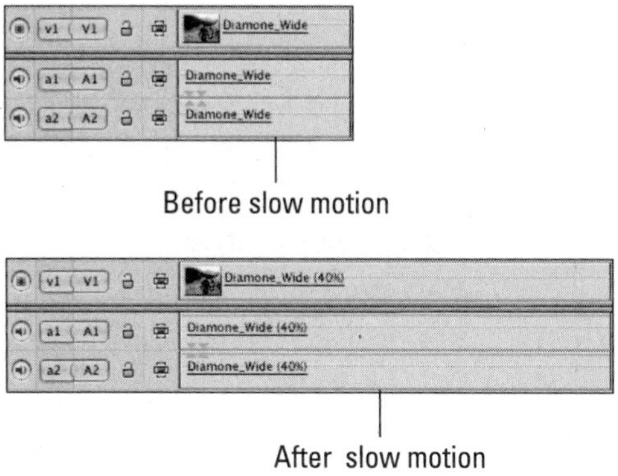

Figure 9-19:
A clip
before and
after a
constant
slow-motion
effect is
applied.

Before slow motion

After slow motion

Setting a variable speed

Rather than play a clip at one, constant speed, you can vary the clip's speed as
it plays (for instance, so that part of it plays in slow motion and then gracefully
increases in speed). But, before diving into the nitty-gritty, it's worth explaining
the underlying concept behind this feature. The key point to remember is that
when you apply variable-speed changes to a clip, the clip's duration doesn't
change. (This concept is different from changing a clip's constant speed, which
always changes its duration.) And the fact that a variable-speed clip's duration
doesn't change means that when you make one part of the clip play slower
than normal, the rest of the clip plays faster than normal (thereby keeping the
clip's overall duration the same).

Put this concept into practice now. Naturally, Final Cut Pro gives you a
number of ways to vary a clip's speed, but the easiest way to do it is by working with a clip directly on the Timeline:

1. **Set the Timeline to display tracks at either medium or large size by
   clicking one of the Timeline's corresponding Track Height buttons
   (see Figure 9-20).**

   This step isn't required, but it's easier to fine-tune a clip's speed settings
   when Timeline tracks are on the bigger side.

2. **Click the Timeline's Clip Keyframes button (refer to Figure 9-20) to
   toggle keyframes on.**

   Clips on the Timeline grow taller so that they can display the speed of
   keyframes that you soon set within a clip. Keyframes let you mark areas
   of a clip where you want speed changes to occur.

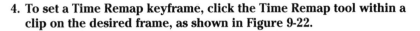

Figure 9-20:
The Timeline as shown with a large track height and with Clip Keyframes toggled on.

Click one of these vertical bars to set your track height.

Clip Keyframes button

3. **Select the Time Remap tool from the Tool palette (see Figure 9-21).**

   This tool is hidden under the Slip Edit tool. To select the Time Remap tool, click and hold your mouse over the Slip Edit tool and then select the Time Remap tool after its icon pops up. Your mouse pointer changes to a Time Remap symbol.

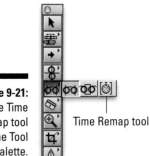

Figure 9-21:
The Time Remap tool on the Tool palette.

Time Remap tool

4. **To set a Time Remap keyframe, click the Time Remap tool within a clip on the desired frame, as shown in Figure 9-22.**

   Final Cut displays your new keyframe within the clip on the Timeline. You see the keyframe on a thin blue horizontal line that appears within the clip, which is called a Motion bar (refer to Figure 9-22).

   If you click the Time Remap tool within a clip and don't see the blue Motion bar and its keyframe appear, your Timeline isn't set to display these elements. Display them by choosing Sequence➪Settings and clicking the Timeline Options tab. On the tab, be sure to select the Motion Bar option in the Clip Keyframes segment of the tab.

Keyframe   Time Remap tool

Figure 9-22:
Figure 9-22:
Click the
Time Remap
tool within a
clip to set a
keyframe.
The
keyframe
appears on
the blue
Motion bar.

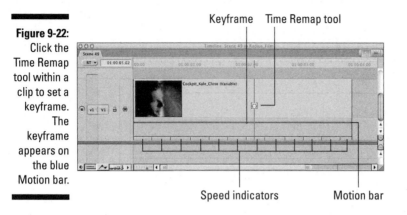

Speed indicators   Motion bar

 To see what a frame looks like before a keyframe is placed on it, click the Time Remap tool on the Timeline's ruler. Rather than set a keyframe, you move the Timeline's playhead to that particular frame, where you can see the frame in the Canvas window.

5. **Click and drag your clip's keyframe to either the right or left to vary the clip's speed (see Figure 9-23).**

Figure 9-23:
The original
keyframe
has been
moved to
the left (that
is, earlier
in time).

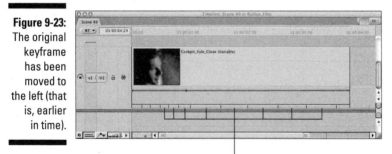

A clip plays faster where speed indicators are more tightly spaced.

This statement is crucial: When you move a keyframe to a new position, it's like you're moving the frame of the clip that the keyframe marks. In other words, a link exists between the Time Remap keyframe and the frame of the clip that the keyframe is placed on. Think of the keyframe as being attached to the particular frame you set it on.

How does this concept affect a clip's speed? When you move a Time Remap keyframe to the left, you're indicating that you want the clip's corresponding frame to move left as well — that is, to move so that it plays earlier in time. To play that frame earlier in time, however, Final

Cut Pro has to play all the frames before it even faster than they normally would play. (It's like those frames are being scrunched into a smaller allotment of time so that they play faster.) And, because a variable-speed clip's total time duration can never change, the frames to the right of your keyframe play in slow motion, to compensate for the frames to the left of your keyframe that are playing faster than normal.

Confused? I don't blame you, because these concepts are a bit abstract. To help you visualize what's going on, Final Cut Pro displays speed indicators along the bottom of your clips. (You can see them in Figures 9-22 and 9-23. If you don't see these indicators, choose Sequence⇨Settings and click the Timeline Options tab. On that tab, make sure that the Speed Indicators option is selected.) When these indicators are evenly spaced, this indicates that your clip is playing at a normal speed. When you drag a keyframe to a new position, however, you see that the speed indicators bunch together (indicating that frames are getting closer together in time — that is, playing faster) or they spread out (indicating that frames are getting farther apart in time — that is, playing slower). You can easily see a clip's speed increasing or decreasing by noting the frequency of the speed indicators.

6. **Play your new speed-varied clip on the Timeline.**

   Position your playhead on the Timeline and click the Play button in the Canvas, or press the spacebar.

   You may have to render the clip first. To do so, select the clip and choose Sequence⇨Render Selection⇨Both.

7. **If necessary, use the Time Remap tool to readjust your keyframe (move it to the left or right again) or to set more keyframes in the clip.**

   Setting more keyframes allows you to vary the clip's speed even more — for instance, to speed it, and then slow it, and then speed it again. You can also set additional keyframes to stretch out (that is, smooth) the acceleration or deceleration of a speed change (see Figure 9-24).

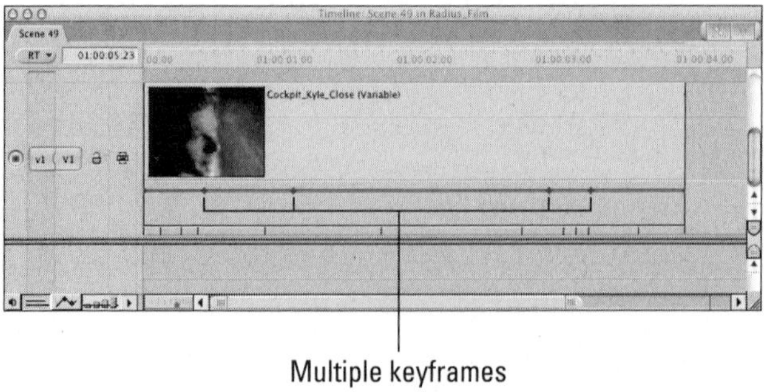

Figure 9-24: Multiple keyframes set within a clip.

Multiple keyframes

So, you have now mastered the basic steps for varying a clip's speed. Still, many more aspects to this feature go beyond the scope of a *For Dummies* book, so if you need more control over these speed effects, I recommend turning to the Final Cut Pro documentation. You can find a large section that covers every nuance of the Variable Speed feature in detail.

Stopping Action with a Freeze Frame

In the course of a movie, you may want to suddenly freeze the action on a single frame of video and hold it for a moment. (This stylistic touch was hot in the 1970s and is coming on strong again these days.) Final Cut Pro lets you easily freeze frames by turning any frame from an existing video clip into a still picture that lasts as long as you like. To freeze a frame, follow these steps:

1. **Open in the Viewer the video clip that you want to freeze.**

2. **Move the Viewer's playhead to the frame you want to freeze.**

3. **Choose Modify⇨Make Freeze Frame from the menu bar.**

   Final Cut Pro opens that single frame in the Viewer and treats it as a new clip of video. By default, the frozen frame has a duration of 10 seconds.

4. **In the Viewer, move the In or Out point of the frozen frame to change the frame's duration (as shown in Figure 9-25).**

   You can see the frame's current duration in the Viewer's Clip Duration box (in the upper-left corner of the Viewer). You can also trim or extend the freeze-frame clip after it's on the Timeline.

5. **Move the freeze-frame clip from the Viewer to either the Timeline or the Browser by clicking anywhere in the Viewer image area and dragging the freeze frame to its destination.**

   When you create the freeze frame in the Viewer, Final Cut Pro doesn't automatically add the freeze frame to the Browser as a clip (as though you had just imported a movie or still picture into the program). You don't have to add the freeze frame to the Browser, but I recommend moving it there so that it becomes a permanent clip in the project and you can quickly reuse it. Otherwise, move the freeze-frame clip to the Timeline and edit it into a sequence, like any other video clip.

   After a freeze frame is on the Timeline, you may have to render it because you're essentially creating a new video clip from what was once just a single frame. (To render the clip, select the freeze-frame clip and choose Sequence⇨Render Selection⇨Both.)

Clip Duration box

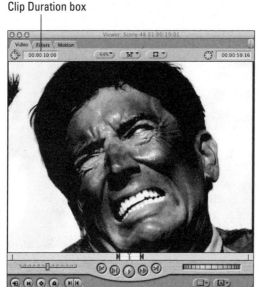

Figure 9-25:
A freeze
frame in
the Viewer.

To save a bit of time, you can freeze a frame directly from the Timeline. Position the Timeline playhead on a frame of video, and choose Modify⇨Make Freeze Frame from the menu bar. You see that frame appear in the Viewer window, ready to be moved to the Browser or back to the Timeline.

By default, Final Cut Pro sets each freeze frame to last for 10 seconds, but you can change that value. Choose Final Cut Pro⇨User Preferences, and type a new timecode value in the Still/Freeze Duration field.

Nesting a Sequence into Another Sequence

Final Cut Pro lets you assemble a group of clips into a sequence, but you can also assemble a group of sequences into *another* sequence (as shown in Figure 9-26). This process is called *nesting* sequences, and it's particularly handy because it lets you break bigger projects into smaller, more manageable parts. For instance, if you're creating a 2-hour feature film, don't try editing the whole thing in a single Timeline sequence. (That would make for one lo-o-ong sequence.) Instead, edit each of the movie's scenes (or acts or any other division) in its own sequence and then edit those finished sequences to assemble your final film.

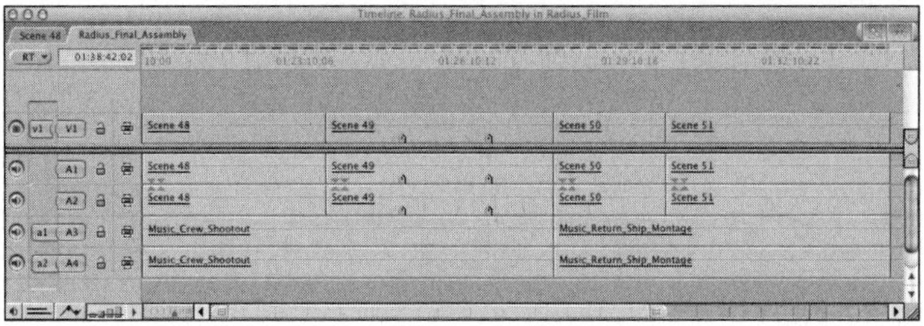

Figure 9-26:
Nested
sequences
on the
Timeline.

To nest one sequence into another, follow these steps:

1. **Double-click a sequence icon in the Browser to open it on the Timeline.**

   This sequence is your master sequence — that is, the one to receive any other sequences you're nesting.

2. **Click and drag another sequence from the Browser window to the Timeline.**

   You have now nested the second sequence into the first as though it were a single media clip (except that it probably already contains lots of preedited clips). *Note:* If your nested sequence contains In and Out points, only the sequence's contents between those points are nested.

That's it! After you have nested another sequence into the Timeline, Final Cut Pro treats that nested sequence like any other media clip. For instance, you can trim or extend the nested sequence on the Timeline, and you can apply the same effects to a nested sequence that you apply to individual clips — add audio and video filters, set volumes and opacity levels, and even animate a nested sequence with motion settings. However, to apply some of these effects, you need to open a nested sequence in the Viewer window — perhaps to tweak filters or motion settings. To open a nested sequence in the Viewer, click the nested sequence on the Timeline while holding Control and choose Open in Viewer from the pop-up menu that appears.

In Final Cut Pro HD, if you drag a sequence to the Timeline while holding Command, Final Cut Pro doesn't nest the dragged sequence but instead adds the individual clips that the sequence contains. It's as though you copied the clips from one sequence and pasted them into a new sequence.

Adding a Voice-Over to a Sequence

The Voice Over tool lets you connect a microphone to your Mac and record your voice (or a narrator's voice) as Final Cut Pro plays a Timeline sequence. The Voice Over tool provides a quick and easy way to add voice narration to any movie. You may be editing a documentary or training program, adding director's commentary to your latest blockbuster, or just going hog wild with those vacation videos.

Having recorded your voice, Final Cut Pro turns it into an .aiff audio clip (saved to your hard drive, naturally) and adds it to the Timeline on its own audio track. You can record a voice-over through the entire Timeline sequence or through just a part of it (by setting In and Out points). Follow these steps to record your voice-over:

1. **Connect a microphone to your Mac.**

   Many Macs have audio-in connectors that you can use to attach a microphone, and many Macs have a built-in microphone too (check your Mac's Help system for more information). Although the internal mic doesn't sound so hot, it works fine for recording placeholder audio.

2. **On the Timeline, position the playhead where you plan to begin recording the voice-over.**

   You can also set In and Out points on the Timeline if you just want to record a segment of the sequence.

3. **Choose Tools⇨Voice Over from the menu bar.**

   Final Cut Pro opens the Voice Over dialog box, as shown in Figure 9-27.

Review button

Record/Stop button

Discard Last Recording button

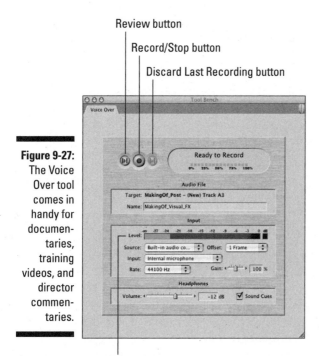

Figure 9-27: The Voice Over tool comes in handy for documentaries, training videos, and director commentaries.

Level meter

4. **In the Voice Over dialog box, in the Name text box, type a name for the voice-over audio clip that you plan to record.**

5. **Click the Source pop-up menu, and choose either Built In Audio Controller (for internal and external mics) or DV Audio (if you have connected a DV camera and are recording live through its microphone).**

6. **Click the Input pop-up menu to select the microphone.**

   Choose Internal Microphone if you're using the mic that's built into your Mac, or select External/Line In if you're using a plug-in mic.

7. **Click the Rate pop-up menu to set the sample rate (that is, the quality) for your voice recording.**

   Choose the rate that matches your current Timeline sequence setting. (You can see the setting by choosing Sequence⇨Settings from the menu bar and noting the audio rate that's listed there.)

8. **By using the Offset pop-up menu, correct for any delays (known as *latency*) that occur between the time when the microphone picks up an audio signal and the time when the device that is capturing that signal records it.**

   Most USB capture devices suffer from a 1-frame latency, so choose an offset of one frame to counteract it. If you're capturing audio from a DV camcorder, try selecting an offset of three frames.

9. **To set the volume level for the recording, move the Gain slider to the left or right.**

   The higher the gain, the louder your voice recording. On the flip side, if your gain is too high, your voice may distort. I discuss this topic further in a moment.

10. **Set the volume level for the headphones by moving the Volume slider to the left or right.**

    Your range is from 0 to 60 decibels; keep the volume low but loud enough to hear the voice through the headphones.

11. **Select the Sound Cues check box.**

    When you select this check box, Final Cut Pro plays a series of beeps a few seconds before recording begins and a few seconds before it ends. These beeps aren't recorded in the voice-over audio; they just help the narrator gauge when to start and stop speaking.

12. **In the Voice Over dialog box, click the Record button to start recording.**

    Don't start speaking immediately. Final Cut Pro first does a 5-second countdown before recording. (You can see the countdown in the Recording Status box.)

    As you record, keep an eye on the Voice Over tool's Level meter (refer to Figure 9-27), and make sure that your recording levels aren't going into the meter's red zone. (If this happens, reduce your gain by moving the Gain slider to the left and try again.)

13. **Click Stop (this button, as shown in Figure 9-27, toggles between Record and Stop) to stop recording at any point or to continue recording until the Timeline playhead reaches an Out point or the end of the sequence.**

    Final Cut Pro places a new audio clip that contains the voice narration on a new audio track on the Timeline.

14. **Review your work, and decide whether to keep it or give it the ol' heave-ho.**

    Click the Voice Over tool's Review button (refer to Figure 9-27) to play the sequence with its new voice narration. Click the Discard Last Recording button to erase that narration clip from the Timeline.

Final Cut Pro records the voice-over to the folder you set as the Scratch Disk. (Choose Final Cut Pro HD⇨System Settings from the menu bar to see where that folder is.) You can find the recordings in that location, within a folder named `Capture Scratch`, and then again in a folder that shares the name of the current project.

When you finish a voice narration, Final Cut Pro adds the new audio clip to the Timeline but not to the Browser window. Therefore, you don't have a permanent version of the narration clip. If you delete the narration clip from the Timeline, you have to dig up its `.aiff` file in some obscure folder on the hard drive and then reimport it. So, I recommend dragging to the Browser window any narration clips that you want to keep, where they become an official audio clip in your Final Cut Pro project.

If you record lots of different "takes," Final Cut records each one to a new audio track on the Timeline. As you record *another* voice-over, Final Cut records it to the Timeline while playing any existing voiceovers in other Timeline tracks. If you don't want to hear those previous voiceovers as you record your new one, refer to Chapter 8 for tips on turning off or muting audio tracks.

Part IV
Adding Pizzazz

The 5th Wave   By Rich Tennant

DAD ADDS MULTIMEDIA SOUND AND GRAPHICS TO THE TRADITIONAL CAMPFIRE GHOST STORY.

In this part . . .

In Part IV, I explain all sorts of audio-related topics: how to set different volume levels for different clips, how to edit out scratches and pops in your audio, and how to use the numerous Final Cut audio filters to create effects. Next, I tackle the new Final Cut Soundtrack application, which lets you compose a musical score for your video — no musical experience required! I then show you how to apply the many Final Cut video transitions, which let you smoothly transition from one video clip to another. I also look at the Final Cut video filters, which can change and enhance the look of video clips in all sorts of ways.

This part concludes by telling you how to use the Final Cut advanced effects engine to scale the size of text, graphics, and video clips; change their positions on-screen; change their opacity; and composite different images into a single shot.

Chapter 10

Audio Excellence

. . . .

. . . .

Audio is one of the most unappreciated and underestimated aspects of filmmaking. Video is a visual medium, so it's easy to get excited about great shots and well-edited sequences, whereas recording and then editing good audio isn't quite as "sexy." Yet, audio can significantly affect the ultimate impact of your movie. Mediocre audio (such as uneven volume levels or distortion and hiss) is the quickest way to make your work seem amateurish.

Fortunately, Final Cut Pro gives you plenty of tools for designing a quality audio experience. The big highlights include the following:

✔ **Mixing volume levels:** Setting the right volume levels for all the audio elements in your movie (called *mixing*) may sound pedestrian, but it's probably the most important audio-related task you do. With Final Cut Pro, you can set volume levels for your entire movie, a single track of audio, a single clip of audio, part of a clip, or even a part of a frame of a clip! By selectively setting volume, you can mix all the audio elements of your movie — that is, multiple dialogue tracks, music, and sound effects — so that they blend smoothly. This process ensures that no element overpowers another unless you want it to. Additionally, by setting an audio clip's volume with superprecision (by increments as small as $\frac{1}{100}$ of a frame), you can edit out subtle glitches, such as the occasional pop of a microphone, or obvious annoyances, like actors breathing excessively or someone's cell phone ringing on-set.

✔ **Audio transitions:** You can also use audio transitions to smooth cuts from one audio clip to another, just as you can use a video transition, such as a Cross Dissolve, to gracefully blend one video clip into another.

✔ **Audio filters:** You can use audio filters to add special effects, such as echoes or distortion, to your audio clips. Other filters help you improve audio quality — for instance, adjusting the audio's dynamic range or cutting unwanted noise, such as the hum of a noisy camera on-set or the dull murmur of street traffic outside.

These three audio highlights are the focus of this chapter. But because audio is such a big topic, I also touch on many audio-related issues throughout this book. To peruse some additional audio topics, check out the following chapters:

✔ **Chapter 2:** Establish audio settings for new sequences with Easy Setup.

✔ **Chapter 4:** Capture audio (along with video) from a DV camera or tape deck.

✔ **Chapter 5:** Import different audio files (and convert audio into formats that work best with Final Cut Pro).

✔ **Chapter 6:** Open and edit audio clips in the Viewer and Timeline windows.

✔ **Chapter 7:** Get audio out of sync and back into sync.

✔ **Chapter 8:** Create, manage, and delete audio tracks on the Timeline.

✔ **Chapter 9:** Use split edits to edit audio separately from its associated video clip.

Some Audio Basics

Before moving on to the meat of this chapter, I cover a few audio basics in case you're completely new to the world of audio.

Capturing and maintaining high-quality audio

Final Cut Pro lets you tweak audio in all sorts of ways, but your audio's quality is largely determined before you do any such futzing. The battle for good audio is, for the most part, won or lost when you record it, so the following list gives you a few tips to help you record audio that sounds great, and to keep it that way:

✔ **Find a good microphone.** If you're shooting video or audio with a DV camera, I suggest buying or renting a separate microphone for the camera. (Built-in camera mics often pick up the hum of your camera's gears and electronics, and these mics have short ranges, so they pick up only what's right in front of them.) Your best bet is to rent clip-on mics that attach to people you're recording (such as someone being interviewed for a documentary) or to get a boom mic, which is positioned over your subject, just outside the camera frame. If these options sound like too much work or money, consider buying a consumer add-on mic for your DV camera (typically, $50–$100). These little mics are attached directly to your camera, and they can significantly improve the audio you would normally get from the camera's internal mic. Also, if you're recording audio outdoors, you can minimize the impact of wind and other background noise by getting a wind sock for the microphone.

✔ **Always work with high-quality audio.** Whether you're capturing audio from DV tapes or CDs or getting digital files from a composer or sound designer, keep the audio in a high-quality format. Audio that's recorded with no compression, and at settings of 48 kHz, 16-bit stereo is the best you can hope for, but a lower rate of 32 kHz, 16-bit does fine as well. Fortunately, DV cameras, as well as other dedicated audio gear, can deliver one or the other of these formats, but make sure that you have set your audio equipment to record at these levels (and that your Final Cut Pro project expects these audio levels as well, by choosing the right Easy Setup — refer to Chapter 2 for more details).

✔ **Get a good pair of headphones.** After you have recorded or captured high-quality audio, it's important to hear all its subtleties. For starters, don't expect your Mac's speakers, or the speakers on an attached TV, to play back your audio faithfully — 'cause they don't. Ideally, you attach a high-grade speaker system to Final Cut Pro and work in a room with excellent audio acoustics. If that's not possible, a relatively inexpensive alternative is to buy a good pair of headphones. You can find them for about $100, and they make a big difference.

Understanding stereo and mono audio

Final Cut Pro can work with mono or stereo audio clips, but what's the difference between the two? Mono audio was used in the early days of media, when radios, record players, and televisions had only a single speaker. In today's stereo world, audio is typically played through two speakers (a left one and a right one), and elements of the overall audio signal play differently on each speaker (for example, louder on one speaker and softer on the other, or slightly shifted in time). The result is that stereo audio sounds fuller and richer because stereo has more of a 3-D spatial quality.

Final Cut Pro treats mono and stereo audio clips differently when you open them in the Viewer window and when you move them to the Timeline. The following points describe these differences:

- ✔ **Mono:** A mono audio clip uses one channel of audio. When you open the clip in the Viewer, you see that single channel represented by a single waveform. And, when you move a mono audio clip (or a video clip with mono audio that's linked), the mono audio occupies only one audio track on the Timeline (see Figure 10-1).

- ✔ **Stereo:** A stereo audio clip uses two channels of audio. What's important to know is that Final Cut Pro can treat stereo audio differently — that is, the two channels that make up stereo audio can be paired or not paired. If stereo audio is paired, Final Cut Pro treats its two channels as a single element. For practical purposes, therefore, whenever you make an adjustment to one channel (such as change its volume or add an audio filter), the same adjustment applies to the clip's other, paired channel. And, if the stereo channels aren't paired, Final Cut Pro treats the two channels as separate elements — that is, you have to adjust each stereo channel separately.

Generally, you want your stereo audio channels to be paired because adjusting both stereo channels at one time is more convenient than adjusting them one at a time. The easiest way to ensure that your stereo audio is paired is to capture video and audio in that form right from the start. (Refer to Chapter 4 for more details on establishing the right capture settings.) If you need to link a stereo audio clip, select it on the Timeline and choose Modify⇨Stereo Pair.

Rendering audio

You may run into a few instances (or many, depending on your project) where Final Cut Pro can't play your audio until you have rendered it. Rendering is necessary when Final Cut Pro doesn't have the processing power to play an audio clip in real-time, so it has to take a moment to calculate how the clip should sound before playing it. You may have to render audio in the following instances:

- ✔ If you import audio that has been compressed (for instance, with an audio codec, such as IMA or MACE), you have to render the audio first. (Refer to Chapter 18 for more about compression codecs.)

- ✔ If you add multiple audio filters to a clip, you may have to render the clip before hearing the filter's effect.

- ✔ If the Timeline sequence tries to play several audio clips at the same time (that is, clips that are stacked together on different tracks), your Mac may not have the processing power to keep up, so you have to render the clips first.

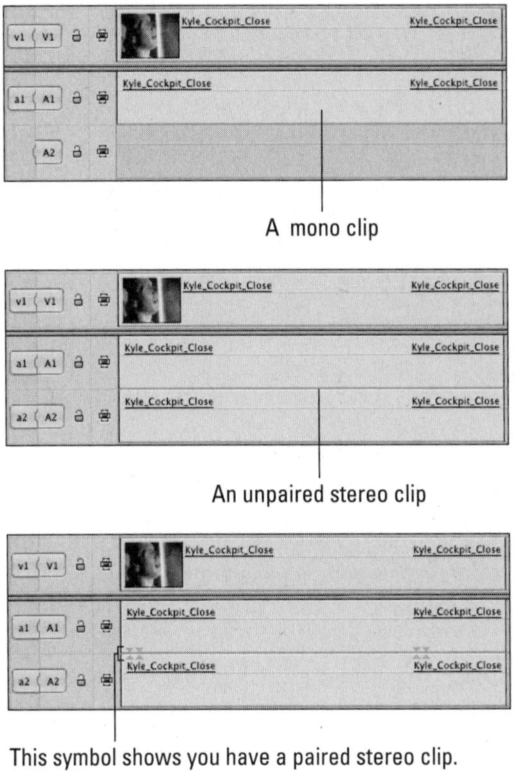

A mono clip

An unpaired stereo clip

Figure 10-1:
Mono and
stereo audio
clips as
shown in
the Viewer
and on the
Timeline.

This symbol shows you have a paired stereo clip.

You know that audio needs rendering when Final Cut Pro plays a series of beeps rather than the audio you're expecting to hear. (You also see a red, horizontal line drawn above the clip on the Timeline Render status bar, as shown in Figure 10-2.) To render that audio, select it on the Timeline and choose Sequence⇨Render Selection⇨Audio.

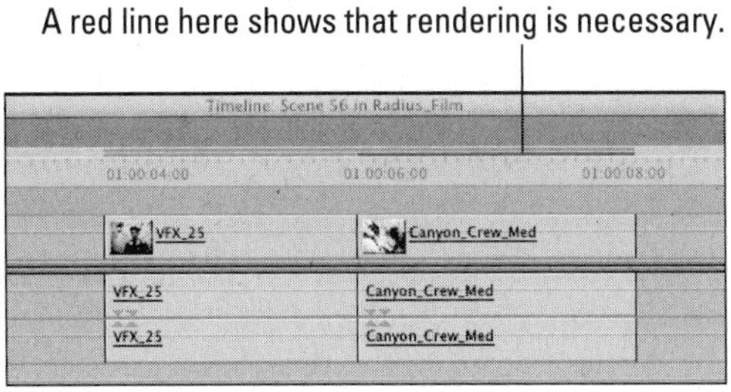

Figure 10-2:
If you see
a red line
on the
Timeline's
Render
Status bar,
you know
that your
audio clip
needs
rendering.

A red line here shows that rendering is necessary.

Three Ways to Set Volume Levels

When you import an audio clip, Final Cut Pro sets its volume at 0 decibels, but you can change that level to as high as 12 decibels (louder) and as low as –60 decibels (silence). Changing the volume levels of individual clips is the essence of audio mixing — that is, deciding which of your audio elements (dialogue, music, or sound effects) to emphasize in a scene and which to leave more in the background. For instance, a quiet, reflective conversation between two friends would most likely emphasize dialogue by making its volume most prominent. On the other hand, if those two friends suddenly found themselves in the middle of an action shootout, the volume of their dialogue may take a backseat to sound effects.

Final Cut Pro lets you change a clip's volume by using three different approaches. I discuss each approach, along with my recommendations for which method makes sense at a given time, in the following list:

- ✔ **The Viewer window:** Use the Viewer to change a clip's volume when you want to make precise, fine-tuned adjustments to a clip's volume (for instance, if you're setting lots of volume keyframes). I discuss more on keyframes in a moment.

- ✔ **The Timeline:** After a clip is on the Timeline, you can easily adjust the clip's volume and even set keyframes. I like using the Timeline to make quick, ballpark volume adjustments.

- ✔ **The Audio Mixer tool:** This handy tool lets you quickly and precisely adjust the volume of any track in your Timeline sequence — in real-time — as it plays against all the other tracks. You have to try the tool to really appreciate it, but it's your go-to guy when you have an elaborate soundtrack and you need to balance all the audio elements in relation to each other.

When you're setting the decibel level of a clip in Final Cut Pro, you should realize that the decibel values are all relative from clip to clip — that is, just because you set two clips at the same decibel level doesn't mean that they play at the same volume. That's because clip volume depends on the following two factors:

- ✔ The decibel level used in the original recording of the clip (for example, by a microphone or by a composer's or sound editor's computer)

- ✔ The decibel level you set for the clip when you bring it into Final Cut Pro

It may seem strange that Final Cut Pro sets a clip at 0 decibels of volume when you first import it (0, it seems, should mean silence), but a level of 0 indicates that Final Cut Pro plays the clip at the volume level that was used in the original recording, without adding or taking away decibels. That's why clips that have the same decibel value (0 or any other value) still may not play at equal volumes.

Changing the volume of audio clips in the Viewer

When you adjust clip volume in the Viewer, you can set a new level for the entire clip or for just a part of it, thanks to keyframes.

Changing the volume for an entire clip

To change the volume for an entire clip, follow these steps:

1. **Open the audio clip in the Viewer window.**

   You can double-click the audio clip from the Browser window or from the Timeline if you have already placed the clip there.

   Either way, the Viewer displays the clip as an audio waveform. (***Note:*** If your audio clip is linked with a video clip, you may have to click the Viewer's Audio tab to see the waveform.)

2. **Change the volume of the clip in one of the following ways (as shown in Figure 10-3):**

   • Drag the Level slider to the left or right to adjust the clip's decibel level.

   • Type a new decibel value in the Viewer's Level text box (a value between –60 and 12 is fine), and then press Return.

   • Click and drag the red line, called the Level Overlay, up or down. (This overlay controls the volume.)

Level slider   Level box   Level overlay

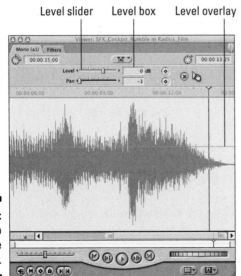

Figure 10-3:
An audio
clip in the
Viewer.

Changing the volume for part of a clip

You can change the volume in only part of a clip rather than change the whole enchilada. You may want to use this technique to briefly lower your music's volume so that a key line of dialogue can be heard more clearly. Or, perhaps an actor is walking toward the camera, and you want to slowly increase the volume of her dialogue as she approaches.

To make these kinds of volume adjustments, you set keyframes within your audio clip. *Keyframes* are like little markers that define a different volume level for your clip at that point. Basically, you set a keyframe in your clip, give that keyframe a volume level, and then set another keyframe elsewhere in the clip and give that keyframe a different volume. The result is that while Final Cut Pro plays your audio clip, it smoothly changes the clip's volume across the range of keyframes you set. Follow these steps to change the volume with keyframes:

1. **Open the audio clip in the Viewer.**

   If the audio clip is linked to video, you may have to select the Viewer's Audio tab before you can see the clip's audio waveform and controls.

2. **Position the Viewer's playhead on the frame where you want the volume change to begin.**

   You're likely to set keyframes on or near noticeable events in the audio (such as a beat of music, a pop of a microphone, or an unusually quiet moment). You can pinpoint these events by studying the clip's audio waveform, which is a visual representation of the clip's loud and soft moments. Spikes in the waveform indicate loudness, and dips indicate more quiet content.

   Sometimes, the waveform seems so compressed (its vertical lines are scrunched together) that you can't see its detail, making it hard to place a keyframe on the perfect frame. To increase the waveform's detail (effectively stretching it out across the Viewer window), drag the Viewer's Zoom control to the left (check out Figure 10-4). On the other hand, you can shrink the view of the waveform (to see more of it at one time) by dragging the Zoom control to the right.

3. **Place a keyframe by clicking the Insert/Delete Keyframe button in the Viewer (refer to Figure 10-4).**

   You can also press Control+K. Either way, Final Cut Pro places a volume keyframe at that frame of audio, setting the volume to the current volume level of the clip. The keyframe looks like a small diamond symbol that sits on the Level Overlay.

4. **Move the Viewer playhead to the last frame where the volume change should end.**

   For instance, to smoothly fade the volume from 0 to –20 decibels across 90 frames, move the Viewer's playhead 90 frames ahead to the frame where the volume should finally reach –20 decibels.

Reset Keyframes button

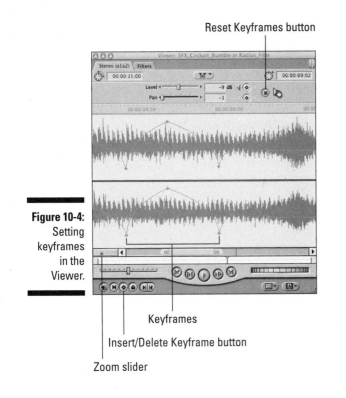

Figure 10-4:
Setting
keyframes
in the
Viewer.

Keyframes

Insert/Delete Keyframe button

Zoom slider

5. **Set a keyframe at that point, and then set its new volume level.**

   Remember that you need at least two keyframes to change a clip's volume over time.

   Again, you can set the keyframe volume level in one of three ways: drag the Viewer's Level slider to the left or right, type a new decibel value in the Level text box, or drag the Level Overlay line up or down (refer to Figure 10-3).

   In the Viewer, you can see the clip's Level Overlay rise or fall from the first to the second keyframe you set.

6. **Play the clip to listen to the volume change.**

   You can listen to the audio clip right in the Viewer. But you may want to play the clip from the Timeline (if it has already been placed there) so that you can listen to it while watching your movie's video and so that you can hear any other audio that may be on the Timeline. This description gives you a good idea of how your volume change works with other elements in the movie.

You can also set keyframes in the Viewer by selecting the Pen tool on the Final Cut Pro Tool palette and clicking any point on the audio clip's Level Overlay. Using the Pen tool is a good way to quickly set many keyframes.

To fine-tune your work, go back to the Viewer and set more keyframes or adjust the ones you already set.

Moving, changing, and deleting keyframes

Final Cut Pro makes it easy to change keyframes you have already placed. With a keyframed audio clip open in the Viewer, you can make the following changes:

- ✔ **Change a keyframe level value (to make it louder or softer):** Click and drag the keyframe either up or down to increase or decrease its level value, respectively. While you drag, watch the keyframe's value change in the Viewer's Level text box (refer to Figure 10-4). Be careful not to accidentally drag the keyframe to the left or right because this action changes the keyframe's location in time.

- ✔ **Set a new volume level for two adjacent keyframes:** Click the Level Overlay between two keyframes, and drag it up or down.

- ✔ **Move a keyframe forward or backward in time so that it affects volume earlier or later:** Click and drag the keyframe to the right or left, respectively.

- ✔ **Delete a keyframe:** Hold down the Option key, and your mouse pointer becomes a pen symbol. When you move the pen symbol over an existing keyframe, you see a minus sign appear next to the pen symbol. While continuing to hold Option, click an existing keyframe to delete it.

Fixing audio glitches with subframe editing

You can set keyframes even more precisely within an audio clip. Rather than set keyframes frame by frame in the Viewer, you can set them every $\frac{1}{100}$ of a frame! This kind of precision is helpful if you want to edit out annoying pops in audio. (These types of sounds may have been recorded by a microphone, but the sounds can also occur at the In or Out points of clips, when you cut from one clip to another.) You can correct these "hiccups" by setting precise keyframes around them and then dropping the volume level between those keyframes: Follow these steps to set superprecise keyframes:

1. **With the clip open in the Viewer, position the Viewer's playhead at roughly the position where the audio glitch occurs.**

   You don't have to position the playhead precisely on the glitch; just get it close.

2. **Zoom in on the audio waveform as much as Final Cut Pro allows.**

   The goal is to see as much detail as possible in the waveform. To see that detail, you have to zoom in your view of the waveform.

You can use the Viewer's Zoom control or press ⌘++ (⌘ and the plus key) to zoom in, or magnify, the view.

When you have zoomed in all the way, you can see that the Viewer's playhead highlights a single frame at a time. A single frame is indicated by the dark bar that follows the playhead, as shown in Figure 10-5.

Playhead   Subframe keyframe

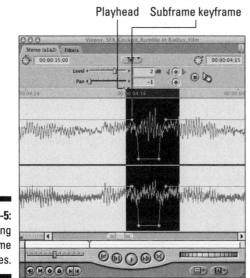

Figure 10-5:
Setting
subframe
keyframes.

Zoom control

3. **Hold down Shift, and slowly drag the playhead to the part of the clip's waveform that indicates a pop.**

   Holding down Shift allows you to move the playhead by fractions of a frame rather than a whole frame at a time.

4. **Set a few keyframes around the pop, and lower their volume levels to silence the pop.**

   Setting four keyframes, and then lowering the volume of the middle two keyframes, usually works best (refer to Figure 10-5).

   Again, you can set a keyframe at the playhead's current position by clicking the Level Insert/Delete Keyframe button.

Alternatively, you can set your keyframes by selecting the Pen tool from the Tool palette and clicking the tool on the Level Overlay. If you take this approach, you don't have to worry about positioning the Viewer's playhead at every keyframe location. Just click the Pen tool at that point, and your keyframe is set.

Adjusting the volume of clips on the Timeline

Sometimes, changing the volume of clips directly on the Timeline is easier than using the Viewer window. Although using the Timeline isn't as precise as using the Viewer, it's quick, and it lets you more easily match volume changes to your video. Follow these steps to adjust the volume of a clip on the Timeline:

1. **Set the Timeline to display clip overlays by clicking its Clip Overlay button (see Figure 10-6).**

   Final Cut Pro shows a thin, horizontal line (called the *Level Overlay*) through each audio clip that's on the Timeline. This overlay represents the volume level of each clip — the higher the line (oops — overlay) within the clip, the louder the clip plays.

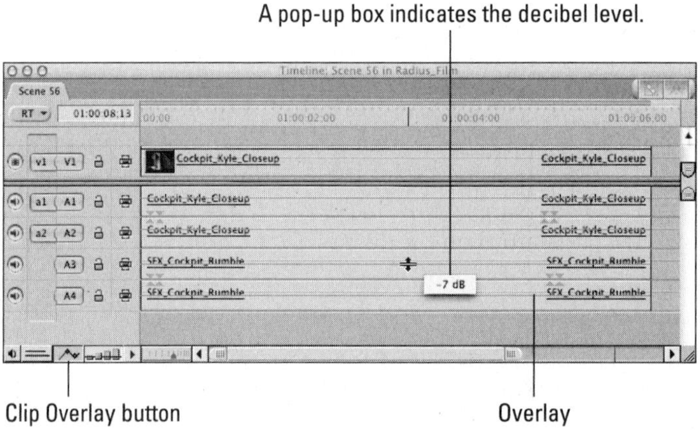

A pop-up box indicates the decibel level.

Figure 10-6: Clicking the Clip Overlay button shows you the volume of each audio clip on the Timeline.

Clip Overlay button   Overlay

2. **Use the Final Cut Pro Selection tool (press A) to raise or lower the volume for the entire clip or just part of it.**

   To change the volume for the entire audio clip: Click and drag the clip's Level Overlay up or down to raise or lower the volume, respectively.

   To adjust the volume for only part of the audio clip: Set different keyframes on the clip's Level Overlay. (See the section "Changing the volume for part of a clip," earlier in this chapter, where I explain the concept of keyframes.) Here's how to set and adjust keyframes on the Timeline:

- **Set a keyframe:** To set a keyframe, first make sure that the Selection tool is active (press A if it isn't). Then, Option+click the audio clip's Level Overlay (the mouse pointer becomes a pen symbol when you're holding Option), and Final Cut Pro adds a keyframe at that point on the overlay (the keyframe symbol looks like a diamond).

- **Adjust a keyframe:** To adjust a keyframe, click and drag the Keyframe icon on the audio clip's Level Overlay to the left or right to change the keyframe location in time or up and down to adjust the keyframe volume.

- **Adjust the volume for two keyframes at one time:** You can click the Level Overlay between two keyframes and move it up or down to adjust the volume for both keyframes at one time.

- **Delete a keyframe:** To delete an unwanted keyframe, press Option and click the unlucky keyframe. (A small minus sign appears next to the pen pointer when it hovers over the keyframe, to let you know that you're in Delete mode.)

Final Cut Pro can show a clip's audio waveform directly on the Timeline; this helps you set keyframes more precisely (as shown in Figure 10-7). The quickest way to toggle waveforms on and off is to click the Track Layout control (it's the arrow between the Track Height control and the Zoom slider toward the bottom of the Timeline) and choose Show Audio Waveforms from the pop-up menu that appears. To see those waveforms as large and clearly as possible, choose the largest track size by clicking one of the taller bars within the Track Height control on the Timeline (refer to Figure 10-7).

Figure 10-7: The Timeline with waveforms and keyframes displayed.

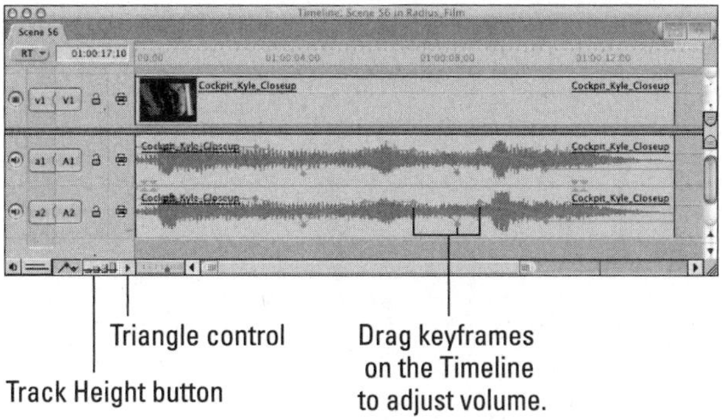

Triangle control

Track Height button

Drag keyframes on the Timeline to adjust volume.

Adjusting the volume for stereo clips that are set as stereo pairs is much easier than adjusting them separately. This way, you don't have to adjust the volume for each channel of a stereo audio clip — if you adjust one channel, the other channel automatically reflects that adjustment too. If a clip's stereo channels aren't set as a stereo pair, select the clip and choose Modify⇨Stereo Pair. See the section "Understanding stereo and mono audio," earlier in this chapter, for more information.

Many volume changes may simply be fading out volume at the end of a clip, or fading in at the beginning. A quick and easy way to do this is to use an audio transition, which I talk about later in this chapter.

Mixing with the Audio Mixer

The new Final Cut Pro Audio Mixer is a useful tool for quickly and precisely balancing the volume of many audio clips, and it doesn't hurt that using the Audio Mixer is straightforward. In Figure 10-8, you see that the Mixer's window is divided into track strips, with each track strip representing an audio track on the Timeline. (If you have six audio tracks on your Timeline, for instance, you see six track strips in the Audio Mixer.) Each track strip in the Mixer features a fader control. As your movie plays, you can drag a track strip's fader to a new decibel level. As you drag, you instantly hear the volume level change in the clip that is playing in the Timeline's corresponding track, and Final Cut Pro applies that new decibel level to the clip as well. Suppose that you select the Audio Mixer's fader for Track A4 and drag the fader up to 5 decibels. Yep, you guessed it: The clip that's playing on Track A4 in your Timeline gets a new volume of 5 decibels.

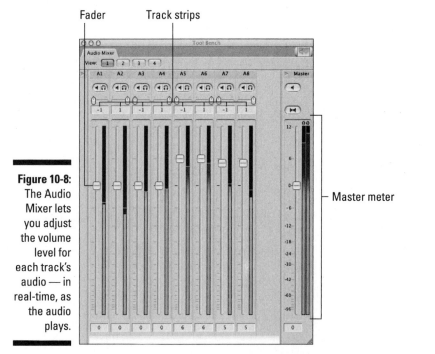

Figure 10-8:
The Audio Mixer lets you adjust the volume level for each track's audio — in real-time, as the audio plays.

Before getting started, I recommend that you do the following things to make working with the Audio Mixer easier:

- ✔ **Clip Overlays:** Set your Timeline to display Clip Overlays by clicking the Timeline's Clip Overlay button (refer to Figure 10-6). This way, when you make volume changes with the Audio Mixer, you see the Level Overlays within each clip on the Timeline change as well. This feature provides nice feedback.

- ✔ **Stereo pairs:** Make sure that any stereo audio clips on your Timeline are set as stereo pairs. (See the section "Understanding stereo and mono audio," earlier in this chapter.) Your stereo audio clips must be paired so that a volume change you make to one channel of stereo audio is automatically made to the clip's other channel. (You probably want each channel of a stereo audio clip to play at the same volume.)

- ✔ **Lose the keyframes:** If you have already set keyframes within audio clips you plan to mix, you should clear the keyframes because you make new adjustments to the volume of the clips. To do so, Control+click the clip on the Timeline and choose Remove Attributes from the pop-up menu that appears. In the Remove Attributes dialog box, select Levels under the Audio Attributes heading and click OK.

Follow these steps to do some mixing:

1. **Position your Timeline's playhead at the point where you want to begin mixing audio.**

   To give you some lead time, you may want to position the Timeline a few seconds before the point where you want to begin adjusting audio.

2. **Choose Tools⇨Audio Mixer from the menu bar.**

   The Audio Mixer window appears (refer to Figure 10-8), usually directly over the Viewer window. In the Mixer, you see track strips that represent all your Timeline's audio tracks, running from left to right (A1, A2, A3, and so on).

3. **Begin playing your Timeline sequence (press the spacebar or press L).**

   You don't have to reselect the Timeline to do this. Just press the spacebar or L, and your Timeline begins playing, even though the Audio Mixer window is still selected.

   Listen carefully to your audio as it plays. You may notice that the Audio Mixer's volume faders move up and down their track strips, as though possessed. In fact, they move to indicate the volume level (in decibels) of the particular clip that's playing in each track.

4. **In the Audio Mixer window, adjust a track's volume level by clicking and dragging its volume fader up (to increase volume) or down (to reduce volume).**

As you drag a track's volume fader, you can hear the results. The clip that happens to be playing on that Timeline track at that moment in time immediately plays either louder or softer, at the decibel level to which you have dragged the fader.

You can also see your changes immediately reflected in the meters for the track you're changing. In this case, you don't have to worry if the track's meters go into the red areas. (The meters for individual tracks measure sound a bit different from what you're used to.) The only meters you have to worry about are the Audio Mixer's Master meters (refer to Figure 10-8). If those meters go into the red areas as a result of a track adjustment you make, you must lower that track's volume until the Master meters don't reach into the red.

5. **Watch the Timeline's playhead position, and make sure that you have finished your volume adjustment when the Timeline's playhead reaches the end of each clip.**

This step is important: When you drag the Mixer's fader, you're adjusting the volume level of the clip that the Timeline is playing (that is, the clip on the track that corresponds to the track fader you're adjusting). For example, if you're dragging the A1 fader in the Audio Mixer, you're affecting the volume of the clip that is on Track A1 in the Timeline.

By default, Final Cut Pro records your volume change for the full duration of each clip. In other words, while a clip plays on the Timeline, suppose that you drag the Audio Mixer's fader up and down drastically. Those extreme changes in volume aren't ultimately recorded to the clip. Instead, the clip's volume is set at the point of the Mixer's fader when the Timeline reaches the clip's last frame (or when you stop Timeline playback).

For instance, if you used the Mixer to adjust Track 1's fader to −10 decibels as the Timeline was playing a clip at its middle point, and then you moved the fader to −15 decibels by the time the Timeline reached the end of the clip, that entire clip is set at a volume of −15 decibels because that's the position of the Mixer's fader when the Timeline reaches the clip's last frame.

This is why it's important to not get distracted by all the pretty lights and controls in the Audio Mixer. Instead, pay attention to the Timeline's playhead position so that you know that the volume you're setting is in fact the one that's recorded to the particular clip that's playing.

6. **Stop the Timeline's playback by pressing the spacebar again.**

7. **Notice how clip volumes have changed on the Timeline.**

Your Timeline should be set to display Clip Overlays. If so, you can see that the volume adjustments you made in the Audio Mixer are reflected in the Level Overlays for each clip on the Timeline — that is, the clip's Level Overlays are raised or lowered on the Timeline, according to your adjustments in the Audio Mixer.

8. Reposition your Timeline's playhead, and repeat Steps 3 and 4 to adjust the volume levels for other Timeline tracks.

To quickly reset a fader's values to 0 decibels (so that you can try a mix again from scratch), Option+click that fader. To reset all faders to 0 decibels, Control+click at the top of any track strip and choose Reset All Faders from the pop-up menu that appears.

Recording volume changes as keyframes, in real-time

By default, the Audio Mixer records only a single volume setting for the duration of each Timeline clip. For instance, as a clip is playing on the Timeline, you can move the Audio Mixer's fader up and down all you like, and only the last setting is recorded to the clip. But, what if you want a clip to slowly fade up or down? Can this kind of change in volume be recorded as well? Fortunately, the answer is yes.

The Audio Mixer can, in fact, record each audio adjustment you make to a clip. Even if you drag a track's audio fader up or down a tiny bit, that change is recorded in real-time as a volume keyframe that's placed in the clip that's now playing (see Figure 10-9).

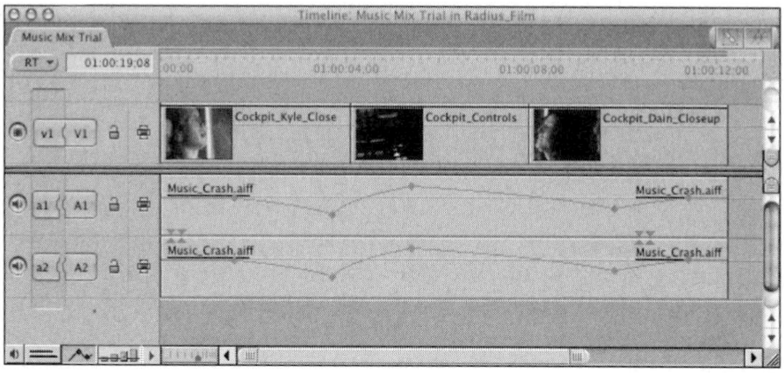

Figure 10-9:
These volume keyframes were set in real-time when using the Audio Mixer.

To get this real-time functionality, click the Record Audio Keyframes button in the upper-right corner of the Audio Mixer (see Figure 10-10). Clicking this button toggles the feature on and off. Be advised: You should generally use this mode only when you want to record volume fades within clips or across adjacent clips. If you're simply trying to establish the right volume for a clip, you don't want the Mixer to record keyframes each time you adjust a fader, because those adjustments are merely necessary to find the right volume for the clip.

Visibility controls

Track Selection pane

Disclosure triangle Mute control

Views Solo control

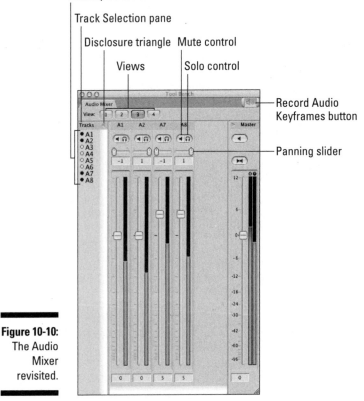

Record Audio
Keyframes button

Panning slider

Figure 10-10:
The Audio
Mixer
revisited.

More audio mixing stuff

Here a few more handy features you can put to use in the Audio Mixer.

✔ **Track selection:** If your Timeline sequence features lots of audio tracks, seeing them all in the Audio Mixer can be bewildering — especially if you intend to mix only a few tracks at a time. Fortunately, you can use the Audio Mixer's Track Selection pane (refer to Figure 10-10) to hide any tracks you don't need to work with. To do so, make sure that the Track Selection pane is visible (you can click the pane's disclosure triangle) and then toggle any track on or off by clicking its Visibility control.

✔ **Customized views:** A *view* is a group of audio tracks that you can display together in the Audio Mixer; any tracks that aren't part of that view are hidden. For instance, you can create a custom view that shows only dialogue tracks in the Audio Mixer and another view that shows only sound effects tracks. The Audio Mixer can display one of four views. To select the desired view, click one of the four View buttons at the top of the Audio Mixer (refer to Figure 10-10). At first, each of these views displays all the Timeline's audio tracks, but you can hide some of those tracks to create the customized views you want. (See the first bullet point in this list to find out how to toggle tracks on and off.)

✔ **Muting and soloing a track:** As you mix volume levels, it can be helpful to either mute a track (or tracks) that you don't immediately want to work with or to solo a single track so that it's the only one you hear. (*Note:* Doing so doesn't affect the volume levels of your audio clips.) To toggle a track's muting on and off, click its Mute control (the Speaker icon located at the top of each track strip — refer to Figure 10-10). To solo a single track, click its Solo control, which looks like a pair of headphones.

✔ **Panning control:** You can also use the Audio Mixer to adjust the panning of an audio clip. Drag the Panning slider (refer to Figure 10-10) for any track whose clips you want to affect. (The next section discusses panning in general.)

Panning an Audio Clip

If you have never worked with audio, you have probably never heard of the term *pan*. Tweaking the pan lets you move your movie's audio from one speaker to another, to create a more sophisticated stereo audio experience.

For example, imagine editing a scene in which a character speaks off-screen. To make the character's dialogue seem to come from the right or left (rather than from front and center), you can pan the dialogue voice clip so that it plays on only one speaker or the other. Or, suppose that your character is caught in a violent storm. You can pan your sound effects to move howling wind from one speaker to another, heightening the sense of the storm's movement.

Pan works a bit differently when it's applied to stereo-linked audio, or mono audio. If the audio is linked stereo, adjusting pan lets you swap the stereo channels — and therefore the speakers — that the audio clip plays through. For instance, adjusting pan would cause the left stereo channel to suddenly play through the right speaker, and the right stereo channel to play through the left speaker (if there's no difference in the audio of each channel, you don't notice any difference when panning occurs. However, if the audio in one channel is louder than the other channel, you definitely notice the audio's movement as the two stereo channels switch speakers).

Panning mono audio clips (such as dialogue) is very noticeable — by panning the mono clip, you allow it to play more loudly on one speaker than the other (for instance, to make an actor's voice seem like it's coming from the left or right of the camera).

Changing audio clip pan is easy. Open the clip in the Viewer, and drag the Pan slider. Or, use the Pan text box to enter a value in the following three ranges, as shown in Figure 10-11:

✔ The value –1 plays the left channel through the left speaker and the right channel through the right speaker. (This setting is the Final Cut Pro default.)

✔ The value 0 plays the left and right channels equally in each speaker.

✔ The value 1 swaps the channels so that the left channel plays on the right speaker and vice versa.

You can enter pan values in very small increments (such as 0.80 or –0.65). Doing so plays an audio channel mostly on one speaker and partially on the other.

You can also use keyframes to change the audio pan over time, for interesting effects.

You may import a stereo audio clip, only to notice that it's playing through only one of the two stereo speakers. This usually means that although the clip is in stereo, no audio data appears in one of its stereo channels. (Maybe the clip was originally recorded in mono and then converted to stereo, or a technical glitch occurred during recording and only one channel was captured.) To fix this problem, set the clip pan to 0. Final Cut Pro plays the clip's single working channel on both speakers, making it essentially mono (because each stereo channel is playing the same thing).

Pan slider   Pan box

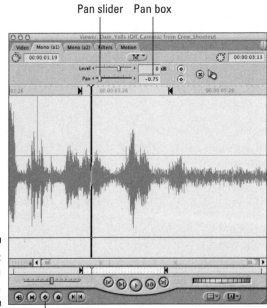

Figure 10-11:
Pan levels in
the Viewer.

Insert/Delete Keyframe button

Creating Audio Transitions

You can use the Final Cut Pro cross-fade transitions to smooth awkward or obvious cuts in the audio (that is, when one audio clip ends and the next one begins). You have two cross fades to choose from. Each one essentially fades out the volume for the outgoing clip while fading in the incoming clip (as shown in Figure 10-12), but each type of cross fade works slightly differently.

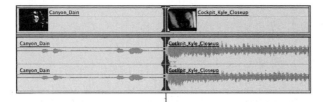

Edit point

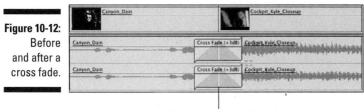

Figure 10-12:
Before
and after a
cross fade.

Cross Fade transition

Applying an audio transition is easy. Follow these steps:

1. **Select an edit point between two adjacent audio clips.**

2. **Choose Effects⇨Audio Transitions.**

3. **Choose either Cross Fade (0 dB) or Cross Fade (+3 dB) from the Audio Transitions submenu.**

   What's the difference between the Cross Fade (0 dB) and Cross Fade (+3 dB)? It's subtle, but Cross Fade (0 dB) briefly dips the volume while the first clips fades out and the second fades in. Cross Fade (+3 dB) keeps the volume steady throughout the transition. Don't fret over which cross fade to use. Give each one a try, and use the one that sounds best. You can easily replace one transition with another by selecting the transition on the Timeline and then choosing a new transition from the Audio Transitions submenu. Or, you can press Delete to toss out the selected transition.

If you get an `Insufficient content for edit` error message while you try to apply a cross fade, consider this: To apply a fade between two audio clips, each clip needs to have additional frames available to it beyond its Timeline edit points. The default cross fade lasts 1 second. Therefore, the first clip (the outgoing clip) needs an additional 15 frames beyond its Out point, and the second clip (the incoming clip) needs to have an additional 15 frames available before its In point. The cross fade uses these extra frames to make a smooth transition between the two clips.

You can use a cross fade to fade up the volume at the beginning of a clip, or fade it out at the end of a clip — just apply the cross fade to the beginning or end of any clip that's not adjoining another clip.

After you have applied a cross fade, you can customize it to play over more or fewer frames on the Timeline — just drag the transition edges to stretch or shrink the cross fade. When you resize a cross fade, you can save it as a Favorite in case you want to apply a transition of that size elsewhere. To save a cross fade as a Favorite, follow these steps:

1. **Open the Final Cut Pro Effects tab in the Browser window (see Figure 10-13).**

   Choose Windows⇨Effects from the menu bar, or click the Effects tab in the Browser window.

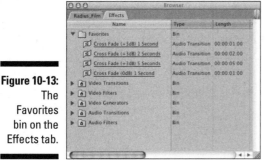

Figure 10-13: The Favorites bin on the Effects tab.

2. **Click and drag the customized transition from the Timeline to the Favorites bin on the Effects tab to add the transition there.**

   You should rename the transition now, as you would with any clip in the Browser window (refer to Chapter 6), so that you can recognize the transition later. After you name the transition, you're free to use it whenever you like. Just open the Effects tab and drag the transition from the Favorites bin to any new edit point (between two clips) on the Timeline.

Working with Audio Filters

When you bring audio into Final Cut Pro, you may want to change its sound in some way — for instance, to add some reverb to a sound effect, to add an echo to a character's voice, or to tone down the hum of some electrical equipment that your microphone picked up on-set. You can do it all, thanks to the Final Cut Pro library of 16 audio filters.

If you have never tweaked audio, figuring out the Final Cut Pro audio filters can be daunting. For starters, most of them use not-so-user-friendly names like DC Notch, High Shelf Filter, and Parametric Equalizer, leaving most of us with no idea about what each filter does. Second, most of these filters give you a number of technical parameters to adjust — settings such as frequency, threshold, ratio, and attack time — which make the filters even more daunting.

Don't fret! After you get past this initial bewilderment, getting a grip on the Final Cut Pro audio filters isn't difficult. You just need to take some time to understand the purpose for each one and to see what settings you use to finesse it.

Describing each filter in detail is beyond the scope of a *For Dummies* book, but later in this chapter I cover the major categories of available audio filters, and I tell you how they generally work. This understanding should give you a good foundation to build on. In the meantime, this section tackles the mechanics of applying audio filters to your clips.

Earlier versions of Final Cut Pro required you to render all filtered audio clips before hearing them, but Final Cut Pro HD makes rendering much more rare. Still, rendering audio filters is in the cards if your Mac's CPU isn't very fast or if you apply more than a few filters to an audio clip at one time. If you have to render an audio clip, Final Cut Pro displays a thin red line above the clip on the Timeline's Render status bar. The software doesn't play the clip until you select it on your Timeline and render it (choose Sequence⇨Render Selection⇨ Audio).

Applying an audio filter and changing its parameters

You can apply a filter to an audio clip in a variety of ways, but the following steps outline the easiest, most straightforward approach:

1. **Select an audio clip on the Timeline, choose Effects⇨Audio Filters from the menu bar, and then choose a filter from the Audio Filters submenu.**

   You have just applied the filter to your clip. If you played the clip on the Timeline, you may or may not hear the filter's effects, depending on the filter's settings. Generally, you have to change a filter's default settings before the filter is noticeable.

2. **Double-click a filtered audio clip on the Timeline to open it in the Viewer.**

3. **Click the Viewer's Filters tab (as shown in Figure 10-14).**

   On the Filters tab, you can now see every filter that's applied to the clip as well as controls for each filter's parameters.

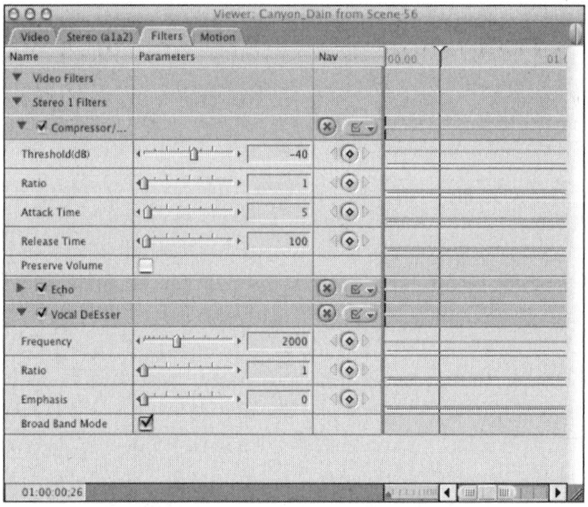

Figure 10-14: Three filters are applied to a clip, as shown on the Filters tab in the Viewer.

4. **Change a parameter for the filter.**

   You usually drag a slider to change a parameter. Also, you can often type values into each parameter's numeric field.

5. **If necessary, render the filtered audio clip.**

   Make sure that the clip is still selected on the Timeline, and choose Sequence⇨Render Selection⇨Audio to render it.

6. **Play the clip on the Timeline, and listen to the filter's effects.**

   If you don't like the results, you can undo your changes (choose Edit⇨Undo), return to the Viewer's Filters tab, and further tweak your settings.

You can also apply a filter to an audio clip on the Timeline by dragging filters from the Effects window. Follow these steps:

1. **Open the Final Cut Pro Effects window (as shown in Figure 10-15).**

   Click the Effects tab in the Browser window, or choose Windows⇨Effects.

Figure 10-15:
Audio filters
on the
Effects tab.

2. **In the Effects window, drag any filter in the Audio Filters bin to an audio clip on the Timeline.**

3. **Tweak your filter's parameters by using the Viewer's Filters tab.**

TIP

When you apply more than one filter to a clip, you see the filters stacked on the Filters tab (refer to Figure 10-14). The top filter is the first one you applied, followed by the second, and so on. This order is important because when Final Cut Pro plays your multifiltered clip, it works out the first filter's effect and then adds the effect of the second filter to that one, and so on. In other words, the order in which you apply the filters can seriously affect how a clip sounds when Final Cut Pro plays it. With that in mind, you can rearrange the order of any filters within the Filters tab by clicking and dragging them into a new order.

Changing filter parameters over time with keyframes

You can change an audio filter's parameters over time by creating keyframes within the filter and giving each keyframe a different value. To review the concept of keyframes, see the section "Changing the volume for part of a clip," earlier in this chapter. However, because setting keyframes in audio filters is handled a bit differently, I cover what's appropriate here as well. Follow these steps to set keyframes within your audio filters:

1. **Open a filtered audio clip in the Viewer, and click the Filters tab so that you can see the filter you have applied.**

2. **Play your audio clip from the Canvas or Timeline windows (not the Viewer).**

   You can click the Play button in the Canvas window or press the spacebar for play/stop. As your movie plays, notice that the Filters tab has a Timeline ruler and playhead of its own and that the playhead moves in sync with the playheads for the Timeline and Canvas windows (see Figure 10-16). Think of these playheads as one big happy family — but keep your eye on the Filters tab playhead from now on.

3. **Stop the Filters tab playhead where you want to place a keyframe.**

   You can most easily control the playhead by pressing the spacebar to play or stop, or you can press the familiar J, K, and L keys to control playback. If you didn't stop the filter's playhead at the perfect frame, you can position the playhead more precisely by pressing ← and →.

4. **Set your first keyframe by clicking the Insert/Delete Keyframe button that corresponds to the filter parameter you want to affect.**

   You see a keyframe symbol appear at the filter's playhead position. (The symbol looks like a diamond, as shown in Figure 10-16.) Make sure that you're pressing the keyframe button associated with the parameter you want to change! If a filter has six different parameters, for instance, you see six keyframe buttons. Be sure to click the right one.

   When you set this first keyframe, it uses the current value set for the parameter associated with that keyframe. You change that value by using the next keyframe.

   Make sure that you're setting keyframes within the In and Out points of the audio clip. If you're not careful, you can move the filter's playhead outside the In and Out points of the clip you're working with. You can then set a keyframe outside the clip (resulting in a keyframe that has no effect). Fortunately, the Filters tab uses black vertical lines to indicate the selected clip's boundaries (refer to Figure 10-16).

5. **Move the Filters playhead to the next frame where you want to set a keyframe.**

   You need to set at least two keyframes to change a parameter from one value to another over time.

6. **Change the parameter's value, and Final Cut Pro automatically creates a new keyframe that is set at that new value.**

   To change a parameter's value, type a new number or use any slider controls that are available. When you change the parameter's value, Final

Cut Pro automatically sets a new keyframe at that point in time. (You don't have to click the Insert/Delete Keyframe button.)

Notice how the parameter's Overlay line moves either up or down from your first keyframe to this new one; the line shows you how the parameter's value changes from one keyframe to the next. The change is sudden or gradual, depending on how many frames lie between your keyframes as well as how much the parameter's values are changing between the keyframes.

7. Repeat Steps 5 and 6 to set more keyframes.

You're free to set more keyframes so that you can change a parameter's value as often as you want. Experiment to find the settings that achieve the effect you're looking for.

8. If necessary, render your keyframed audio clip before listening to it.

Make sure that the clip is selected on the Timeline, and choose Sequence⇨Render Selection⇨Audio.

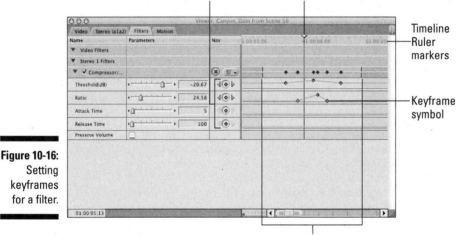

Insert/Delete Keyframe buttons   Playhead

Timeline
Ruler
markers

Keyframe
symbol

Figure 10-16:
Setting
keyframes
for a filter.

Boundaries of the clip's In and Out points

As you would expect, you can easily edit keyframes you have already set in a filter. Simply click an existing keyframe on the Viewer's Filters tab. Then, drag the keyframe up or down to change its value, or drag it left or right to change its position in time. You can also delete keyframes by pressing Option and clicking the unwanted keyframe. (Your mouse pointer becomes a pen symbol while you're holding down Option.)

Disabling and deleting filters

If you want to turn off a filter temporarily — without losing any of its settings — you can toggle it off and on by selecting the check box that's next to the filter's name (refer to Figure 10-14).

To delete a filter (and lose any settings you have adjusted), click the filter's name to select it and press Delete.

Getting quick access to your favorite filters

If you take the time to tweak filter settings and you know that you want to apply those same custom settings to another audio clip, you can save that filter as a Favorite by following these steps:

1. **Open the Final Cut Pro Effects window.**

   To open the Effects window, choose Window⇨Effects or click the Effects tab in the Browser window.

2. **Click and drag the customized filter from the Viewer's Filter tab to the Favorites bin in the Effects window.**

   Technically, you can drag the filter anywhere in the Browser, but custom filters are easier to find if you know that you always keep them in your Favorites bin. Also, filters in the Favorites bin are available to all your Final Cut Pro projects, not just the current one.

3. **Rename the filter now (as you would rename any clip in the Browser window) so that you can recognize it later.**

That's it! Now you can apply the filter to any clip on the Timeline by choosing Effects⇨Favorites from the menu bar and then choosing the custom filter from your Favorites submenu. *Note:* The Effects menu has two Favorites menu items. Make sure that you choose the one on the Audio Filters menu.

Exploring Audio Filters

The preceding section explains how to apply and edit audio filters. In this section, I look at the different kinds of filters that Final Cut Pro offers, and I show how you can use these filters to improve and stylize your movie's audio. The Final Cut Pro audio filters are grouped into the following major categories:

✔ Equalization filters

✔ Echo and reverberation filters

✔ Compression and expansion filters

✔ Noise-reduction filters

Equalization filters

Equalization filters (that's *EQ filters,* for short) let you raise or lower the volume, not of an entire clip but of individual sound frequencies within that clip. Having that capability is very useful because sound is made up of a wide range of frequencies and each frequency determines the *pitch* (the highness or lowness) of the sound. For instance, a man's deep voice has a lower frequency than the higher pitch of a woman's voice, and the rumble of a car engine has a lower frequency than the hiss of recording tape.

You may want to use audio that has been marred by some unwanted element — for instance, the buzz of fluorescent lights on-set or the hum of traffic. Fortunately, you can use an EQ filter to isolate a certain troublesome frequency within the audio and lower the volume of this frequency so that it's less noticeable.

That's the good news about EQ filters. Now, for some bad news: First, don't expect these filters to solve major audio problems because the filters make only subtle audio shifts (that is, the filters aren't helpful if you recorded dialogue while a neighbor ran his leaf blower). Second, getting good results from these filters takes lots of trial and error, and if you're not careful, you can end up distorting your audio. In other words, experience is a big plus.

Final Cut Pro sports three equalization filters that specialize in working with different ranges of frequencies, and each filter offers different parameters you can tweak. If you want to explore each of these, I suggest that you read a more comprehensive book, such as *Final Cut Pro 4 Bible,* by Zed Saeed, J.J. Marshall and Jeffrey Chong (Wiley).

Echoes and reverberations

You can use the Final Cut Pro Echo and Reverberation filters to better match sound to the physical setting of a movie scene. Reverb in particular is useful in matching the acoustics that are found in a wide variety of enclosed settings — for instance, a sprawling auditorium. Because Echo is a bit more extreme, use it to match the sound of a big outdoor setting, such as a huge canyon.

Both filters let you set the following parameters so that you can hone your effect to perfection:

- **Effect Mix slider:** Sets how much of the original, unfiltered sound that Final Cut Pro mixes with the effect the filter creates. The higher the number, the more affected the sound.

- **Effect Level slider:** Sets the volume of the affected sound in decibels (as opposed to the volume of the original, unaffected sound).

- **Brightness slider:** Gives the effect more punch (without changing its volume). Experiment with this parameter to get a feel for its effects.

If you're using Reverb specifically, click the Type pop-up menu to set the style of reverb you want, depending on the kind of environment you're trying to acoustically match (a tunnel, a medium-size room, or a long hallway, for instance).

For the Echo filter, you can also use its Feedback slider to set how long each echo lasts; use its Delay Time slider to set the time between each echo.

Compression and expansion filters

You may want to expand or limit an audio clip's *dynamic range,* which is the range between the clip's softest and loudest volume levels.

By choosing the Compressor/Limiter filter, you can *compress* (reduce) a clip's dynamic range by lowering the volume of its loudest points. Of course, you can always try adjusting the clip's volume by setting keyframes — see the section "Changing the volume for part of a clip," earlier in this chapter — but the Compressor/Limiter filter can do the same thing with a more subtle touch, and you can apply the filter to many clips quickly.

On the other hand, you could use the Final Cut Pro Expander/Noise Gate filter to decrease a clip's dynamic range by raising the volume of only its softest parts — for instance, if an actor goes from whispering to shouting and the shouts are at a perfect volume but the whispers are barely audible.

When you use either of these filters, you can fiddle with the following controls:

- **Threshold slider:** In the case of the Expander filter, this control sets how low, in decibels, a clip's volume can go before the filter does its job. For the Compressor filter, this control sets how high the clip's volume can go before the filter goes to work.

- **Ratio slider:** Sets the amount of compression or expansion that's applied to the clip after its high or low volume passes the threshold point.

✔ **Attack Time slider:** Sets how quickly the filters react to changes in the volume of the clip.

✔ **Release Time slider:** Sets how slowly the filter eases out of its volume change.

Noise-reduction filters

The three Final Cut Pro noise-reduction filters help reduce unique kinds of noise you record accidentally — perhaps a microphone wasn't tuned right or some electrical conflicts occurred in your recording setup. You can also use an equalization filter to reduce other kinds of noise (such as the dull hint of distant traffic). Final Cut Pro offers the following noise-reduction filters:

✔ **The Vocal De-Esser:** This filter eases any heavy *S* sounds your microphone picks up while an actor speaks.

✔ **The Vocal De-Popper:** This filter reduces the harsh pop of spoken *P* sounds that were picked up by an overly sensitive mic.

✔ **The Hum Remover:** This filter is a bit more obscure. Use it to reduce the hum from electrical equipment in your audio's background. (You can't hear these hums on-set, but your recording equipment picks them up nonetheless.) Make sure that you have good headphones — you need them in order to pick up and adjust the subtleties of hum.

Copying and Removing Audio Attributes

After you set an audio clip's volume level, determine its pan, or apply audio filters to the clip, you can quickly copy those attributes to any number of other audio clips (saving you from manually applying the same settings repeatedly). For instance, you may have dozens of audio clips that make up a voice narration on the Timeline. After you change the volume level for one of those clips, you can apply the same volume setting to all the other narration clips.

Follow these steps to copy and paste audio attributes:

1. **Select a clip on the Timeline that already has attributes you want to copy to other clips.**

   Those attributes can be volume levels, pan settings, or specific audio filters you have applied to the clip.

2. **Copy the clip by choosing Edit⇨Copy or pressing ⌘+C.**

   Don't worry if your audio clip is linked to video.

3. **Select on the Timeline all the other audio clips to which you want to apply the original clip's settings.**

   Refer to Chapter 7 for all the ways you can select multiple clips on the Timeline. A quick option is to use the Selection tool and hold down ⌘ while selecting each clip.

4. **Choose Edit➪Paste Attributes.**

   The Paste Attributes dialog box appears, as shown in Figure 10-17.

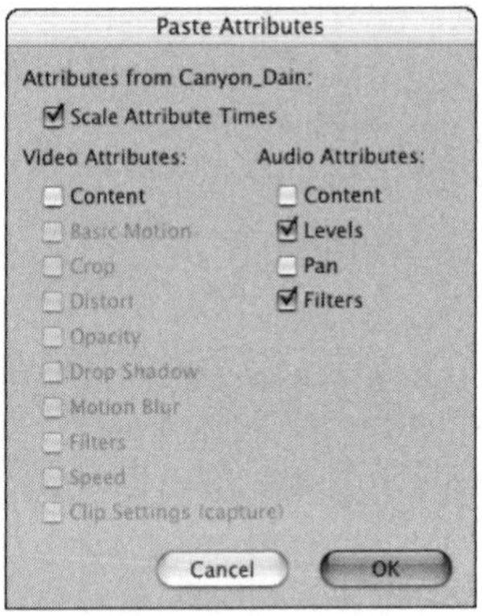

Figure 10-17: The Paste Attributes dialog box.

5. **In the Audio Attributes section of the Paste Attributes dialog box, select the check box next to the attribute you want to paste from the original clip to the selected clips.**

   For instance, to paste volume levels from the original clip, make sure that you select the Levels check box. If you don't want to paste the original clip's audio filters, don't select the Filters check box.

   By selecting these attributes, you decide which attributes from the original, copied clip are pasted to the selected clips on the Timeline. If you don't want to copy certain attributes from the original clip to your new clip (such as video attributes, in case you copied a clip that had video as well), simply leave the check boxes next to those attributes unchecked.

   If the original, copied clip used keyframes in its settings, Final Cut Pro applies those keyframes to the new clips as well. You may or may not want this, but if you do, you can select the Scale Attribute Times check box to scale the distances between those keyframes so that they fit any longer or shorter clips that the keyframes are pasted to.

6. **Click OK.**

   The clips you selected on the Timeline now have the desired attributes from the original, copied clip. If you don't like the results, you can undo your actions by choosing Edit➪Undo.

Chapter 11

Composing a Soundtrack

· ·

In This Chapter

▶ Importing video into Soundtrack

▶ Taking a tour of the Soundtrack interface

▶ Finding and editing loops to the Timeline

▶ Setting volume, pan, and key

▶ Exporting your finished score

· ·

As though being a great video editor weren't enough, Final Cut Pro HD includes a separate, stand-alone application named Soundtrack, which lets you compose original musical scores for your Final Cut Pro movies — no musical experience required!

The way Soundtrack works is simple: The application contains a database of hundreds of musical *loops* — recordings of a particular instrument, like a drum or guitar, that play a short rhythm or melody. Each loop typically lasts just a few seconds, but Soundtrack lets you repeat them (*loop* them) as many times as you want so that a single loop, like a bass drumbeat, can fill as much time as you want. And, you can, of course, easily layer multiple loops so that they play together — for instance, a bass drum loop, with a funky snare drum, with a catchy guitar riff, with some other loops added for musical background.

Soundtrack doesn't stop there. It offers lots of flexibility to make composing music as easy as possible. For instance, you can set your music to play at any pace you want (measured in beats per minute), and the loops automatically adjust to play at that pace, without changing pitch. (Usually, when you play audio faster or slower, its pitch changes.) What's more, if you want to change the musical key in which a loop plays (so that it plays a few notes higher or lower), Soundtrack make this adjustment without breaking a sweat.

Of course, not all movie soundtracks can be pieced together with loops. For instance, if you're looking for music with a well-defined, original, melodic theme or music that's tightly integrated to your video, your best option may be to use original music that has been scored by a real, live composer. Loops are suitable for lots of other scenarios too — for instance, to create background music that you can use in a corporate video or infomercial or in a fast, driving track for an action sequence.

Even if a composer scores your final music, Soundtrack is great for creating a placeholder score. You can then get a better feel for how your story plays with music (you can even edit your video to the placeholder music), and your composer can get an idea of what you want your final, custom score to do.

 Soundtrack can work with loops that are made for Sonic Foundry's ACID product line (popular in the PC world). Tons of unique loop libraries are available that cover different genres, such as jazz, trance, and country. To browse and buy loop libraries, start by visiting the following Web site:

```
www.sonicfoundry.com/loop_libraries/default.asp
```

 You may wonder what the difference is between Soundtrack and Apple's GarageBand, which ships with its iLife suite of software. Although both programs offer thousands of loops for building music, the big difference between the two is that Soundtrack can import video (so that you can compose music to your final edit), and GarageBand can't. On the other hand, GarageBand, in addition to using loops, lets you compose original music with a large variety of software instruments (you can piece together any sequence of individual notes you want), which is quite a nice feature. Ideally, Apple really needs a program that combines the Soundtrack video playback feature with the GarageBand software instruments. In fact, that program is Apple's LogicAudio Pro, but, unfortunately, it costs hundreds of dollars and has a steep learning curve.

Getting Started

Let's get some basics out of the way before you score music with Soundtrack.

Installing and launching

Soundtrack is a stand-alone application. If you chose to do a full install of Final Cut Pro HD (or Version 4), you should see the Soundtrack icon in the Applications folder on your hard drive (see Figure 11-1). Double-click the icon, and Soundtrack launches.

If Soundtrack wasn't installed, you have to dig up your Final Cut Pro Install DVD, launch the Final Cut Pro Installer, and then choose the Custom Install option. Doing a custom install lets you add only certain components of Final Cut Pro to your hard drive, one by one.

Figure 11-1:
Look for the
Soundtrack
icon in your
Applica-
tions
folder.

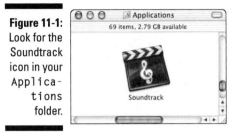

A quick overview of the interface

When you launch Soundtrack, you're greeted by its impressive interface, an untitled project. I advise you to save your project right away by choosing the familiar File➪Save As command.

The Soundtrack interface is composed of two major elements: the Media Manager and the Project Workspace (see Figure 11-2). The following sections give you a quick summary of what each element does, along with unique features that are within the elements.

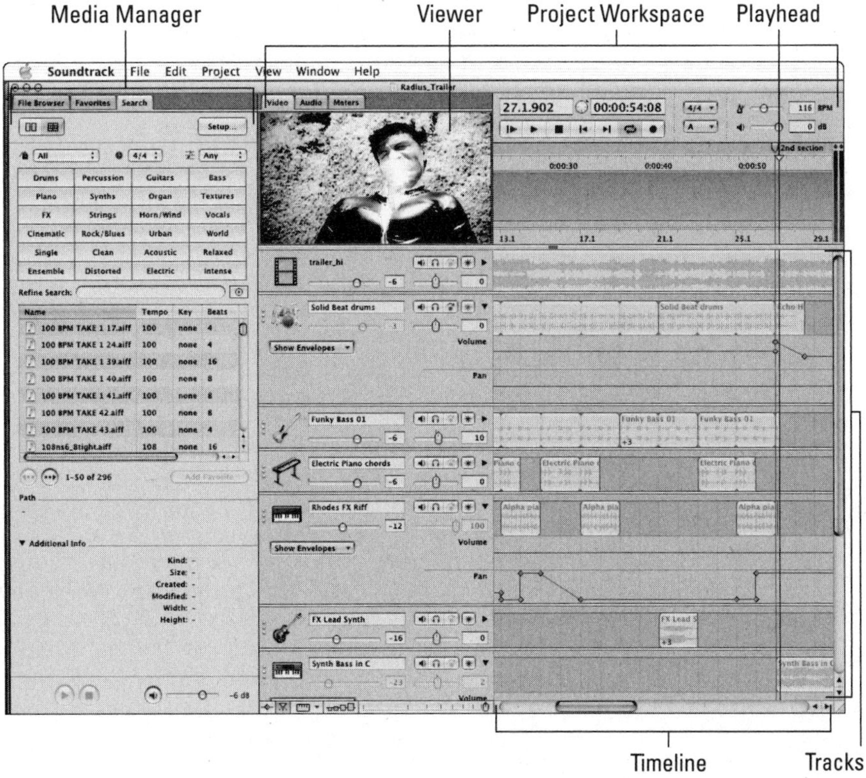

Media Manager   Viewer   Project Workspace   Playhead

Figure 11-2:
The
Soundtrack
interface.

Timeline   Tracks

The Media Manager

The Media Manager is a bit like the Final Cut Pro Browser in that you go to the Media Manager to select media before adding it to your score. For the most part, you use the Media Manager to search for loops (usually, according to keywords, such as *drums* or *strings*) and to load video files on your hard drive (typically, video exported from Final Cut Pro that you want to score).

The Project Workspace

The *Project Workspace* is where you assemble your score. The Workspace is divided into the following key components:

- ✔ **The Viewer:** The *Viewer* displays the video you're scoring music to.

- ✔ **The Timeline:** The *Timeline* is where you assemble all your music loops into a real, live score (just as you would assemble clips of media on the Final Cut Pro Timeline). The Timeline has the following familiar elements:

  - **The playhead:** When you play the Timeline, it plays from the point where the playhead is. You can move the playhead to any point by clicking that point on the Timeline.

  - **Timeline tracks:** The Timeline is divided into *tracks,* which are used to stack different loops together so that multiple loops can play during the same period. (A track is also dedicated to the movie you're scoring, and this track always resides at the top of the Timeline.) Each track is identified by its track header, which you can see on the far left side of each Timeline track. The track header features a number of controls that affect each track; I explore them shortly.

  - **Measurements of time:** The Timeline also lists measurements of time, running from left to right. This Timeline shows not one, but two, measurements of time. The first, displayed above the Timeline video track, measures minutes and seconds. The other measurement, above the first loop track, lists musical measures and beats. (For instance, the measurement 9.1 on the Soundtrack Timeline means that you're in the ninth measure, at the first beat of your score.)

    If you know how to sight-read music, you should be comfortable with beats and measures. If you don't, consider this: When music is composed, the notes are arranged according to beats, which are like intervals of musical time. Even if you know nothing about music, you have the magical ability to detect these beats as music plays, by simply tapping your foot (each tap falls on a beat). And, beats of music are grouped into *measures.* Depending on the music, you may have 3, 4, or 8 beats in every measure. (As you tap the beats with your foot, you can almost feel the beginning of each measure.) But, these details are a bit unnecessary. The truth is that you never have to think about beats and measures to make great music with Soundtrack. These measurements merely make musically experienced composers feel more comfortable in Soundtrack.

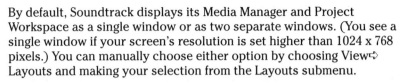

By default, Soundtrack displays its Media Manager and Project Workspace as a single window or as two separate windows. (You see a single window if your screen's resolution is set higher than 1024 x 768 pixels.) You can manually choose either option by choosing View⇨ Layouts and making your selection from the Layouts submenu.

✔ **Play controls:** You can control the playback of your musical score in progress (and its accompanying video) by using the Play and Stop buttons (see Figure 11-3). Buttons are also available to jump your playhead — and with it, the view of the Timeline — to the beginning or end of your score and to set your score to loop.

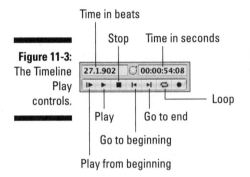

Figure 11-3: The Timeline Play controls.

Time in beats
Stop   Time in seconds
27.1.902   00:00:54:08
Loop
Play   Go to end
Go to beginning
Play from beginning

Creating Your Soundtrack

Now, I come to the good stuff. You're just moments away from scoring some video!

Getting video into soundtrack

You can import any QuickTime video into Soundtrack, regardless of its compression, frame rate, or pixel resolution. Generally, though, the video you bring into Soundtrack comes directly from a Final Cut Pro Timeline sequence that you've finished editing and are ready to score.

Exporting video from Final Cut Pro

When you export a movie meant for Soundtrack, Final Cut exports it as a .ref (*reference*) file. The file itself doesn't contain the video and audio data that is used by your movie, but the file contains pointers to the real media files that are elsewhere on your hard drive. This way, the size of the exported movie stays very small (because it doesn't contain any media). However, be sure that the media the file references stays put on your hard drive — if you move the media, rename it, or delete it, the reference file no longer works.

To export video from Final Cut, follow these steps:

1. **In the Final Cut Pro Browser, select the Timeline sequence you want to export.**

   If you've already set In and Out points in the Timeline sequence, Final Cut Pro exports only the video and audio between those points. Any Timeline tracks you've turned off or muted aren't recorded in your export.

2. **Choose File⇨Export⇨For Soundtrack.**

3. **From the Save Exported File As text box, name your exported movie, navigate to the folder you want to save it in, and click Save.**

   Final Cut Pro then exports your Timeline sequence as a reference movie. Unlike standard QuickTime movies, this file has an icon indicating that it's a Final Cut Pro reference file.

   You're now ready to import your Timeline video into Soundtrack!

Importing video into Soundtrack

Follow these easy steps to import any QuickTime video into Soundtrack, ready for scoring:

1. **Click the File Browser in the Soundtrack Media Manager (see Figure 11-4).**

   The Media Manger is on the leftmost side of the Soundtrack interface (refer to Figure 11-2).

2. **Use the File Browser to find your video file, as follows:**

   • Click the File Browser's Computer button to see the contents of your entire hard drive.

   • Click the Home button to see the contents of your user account's Home folder.

   • Double-click the folders to see their contents, and use the Back button or Path pop-up menu to backtrack through open folders.

3. **If you want to see a preview of the video, just double-click its file to play a preview.**

4. **Drag the video file from the File Browser to the Soundtrack Viewer.**

   Or, you can drag the file to the Timeline video track. Either way, Soundtrack displays the movie file in its Viewer and in the Timeline video track. Soundtrack also places the audio of your imported movie (if any exists) in a new audio track. You can identify this track by the filmstrip icon that's displayed in the track's header, as shown in Figure 11-5.

Back button

Forward button   Computer button

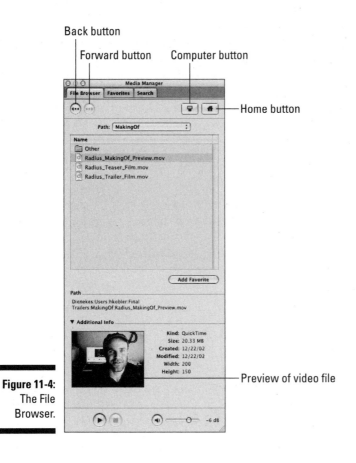

Home button

Preview of video file

Figure 11-4:
The File
Browser.

Filmstrip icon   Viewer   Video track

Figure 11-5:
The Viewer
and the
Timeline
video track.

Audio tracks   Video track audio

You can also drag any video file from your Mac's Finder directly to the Soundtrack Viewer. With Soundtrack on-screen, click the Finder icon in the OS X Dock and locate your video file in a Finder window.

Establishing your score's master settings

A few key settings define the musical character of your score. The important thing to remember about these major settings is that you can change them at any time, and Soundtrack instantly adjusts the loops to reflect your change. Don't worry about locking in the right settings for your score right from the start. You can start working and make adjustments as you go along.

You can apply several major settings to a score by using controls in the upper-right section of the Timeline, as shown in Figure 11-6.

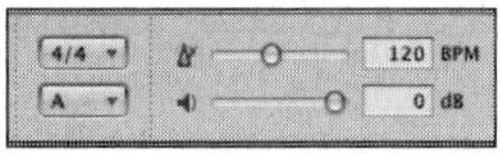

Figure 11-6:
Master
settings for
your score.

If you have musical experience (even from piano lessons that were forced on you as a kid), these elements should be familiar. Even if they're not, no sweat, they're straightforward. The master settings are as follows:

- **BPM:** This term refers to *b*eats *p*er *m*inute. The higher your score's BPM, the faster the music's tempo and the faster it generally feels.

- **Key:** The *key* of a score determines the pitch in which your loops play. The individual Soundtrack loops are all recorded in various keys, but when you move them to the Timeline, they're automatically converted to the Timeline master key. (That's a good thing because if loops were to play together in different keys, they would probably sound horrible together — something like what happens when most of us sing along with our favorite songs.) If you have a specific key in mind for your score, you can set it here. Otherwise, you should keep the default key of A. After you lay down some loops, you can always change your score's master key and see whether a new key is more pleasing to you.

- **Time signature:** The first number in a time signature tells you how many beats are in each measure. The second number tells you what kind of musical note gets a full beat (4 = a quarter note, and 8 = an eighth note, for instance). A 4/4 time signature, for instance, means that you have 4 beats in a measure, and a quarter note gets a full beat (4 quarter notes would make a full measure). If this description is getting too technical for you, don't worry: You can compose a great score without thinking one bit about time signatures.

✔ **dB:** This term stands for *decibels*. This value sets the volume level of your entire score. See the section "Changing volume, pan, and key," later in this chapter, for more details.

Finding the right loops

The first step in composing a score is to choose the loops you want to use. Because Soundtrack includes more than 4,000 loops, you could spend a day "auditioning" them all. Fortunately, you can use the Soundtrack Media Manager (see Figure 11-7) to refine your search and find the right sound more quickly.

View as Buttons button

Favorites tab

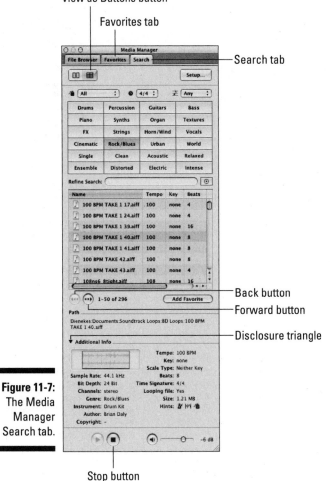

Search tab

Back button

Forward button

Disclosure triangle

Figure 11-7:
The Media
Manager
Search tab.

Stop button

Follow these steps:

1. **Click the Media Manager Search tab.**

2. **Click the Search tab's View as Buttons button.**

   The Search tab works in two different views, but I think that its View as Buttons mode is the easiest for beginners.

3. **Click a keyword button to display any loops that are described with that keyword.**

   Any loops that match the keyword you select are displayed on the Search tab. For instance, clicking the Drums keyword button shows all available drum loops.

   You can easily miss available loops. By default, the Search tab displays only 50 loops at a time, although many more may match your keyword search. To see those extra loops, click the Search tab's Forward button. Likewise, use the Back button to see the preceding set of 50 loops. Alternatively, you can set Soundtrack to display as many as 250 loops at one time: Just choose Soundtrack➪Preferences, and use a new value from the Search Results pop-up menu.

4. **Click any loop on the Search tab to play it.**

   While you're listening to your loop, you can also note some somewhat irrelevant information about it, such as the tempo (in beats per minute) and the key in which the loop was originally recorded. I say that this information is "somewhat irrelevant" because Soundtrack ultimately makes the loop fit in with the key and the tempo you've set on the Timeline. (In fact, when you play a loop from the Search tab, Soundtrack automatically plays it in the Timeline's key and tempo, to give you the clearest sense of how the loop works with your overall score.)

   What may be more useful to you is to note the loop's beats (8 or 16, for instance). This number tells you how many beats the loop lasts; the more beats, the longer the loop — and the more musical variety the loop is likely to offer.

   You can see even more information about a selected loop by clicking the disclosure triangle next to the Additional Information heading (refer to Figure 11-6).

   You can get the best idea of how a loop works in your score by listening to it while simultaneously playing your movie and any other loops you've placed on the Timeline. To do this, play the loop from the Search tab, and click the Play button in the Timeline Play controls to start your movie's playback.

5. **Click the Search tab's Stop button to stop playing a loop.**

6. **To add a loop to the Timeline, drag a loop to an empty track, or empty space, on the Timeline.**

Expand or limit your search

You can refine your search by using the following tools on the Search tab:

- ✔ **Multiple keywords buttons:** You can select multiple keywords buttons by holding ⌘ while clicking each button. For instance, if you select both the Drums and Intense buttons, you see only the loops that use both keywords in their descriptions.

- ✔ **Refine Search field:** You can type portions of a loop's name in this field (and press Return) to search for those elements.

- ✔ **Further search refinements:** You can make selections from the Keywords, Time Signature, and Key drop-down menus to limit your search results. For instance, you can use the Keywords drop-down menu to search all loops solely by genre (jazz or orchestral, for instance), or you can use the Key drop-down menu to show loops that were originally designed in a minor key. (Minor keys are typically good for music with a more subdued and darker emotional feel.)

Designating loops as favorites

As you get familiar with the many Soundtrack loops, you develop a preference for some over others. Rather than fish for them in the humongous Soundtrack database, you can designate your cream-of-the-crop loops as Favorites so that you can easily access them from any Soundtrack project. Consider the following points when organizing your Favorites:

- ✔ To designate a loop as a Favorite, select it on the Soundtrack Search tab and click the Search tab's Add Favorite button.

- ✔ To access your favorite loops from any project, click the Media Manager Favorites tab. You can play a favorite loop and add it to the Timeline, just as you would from the Search tab.

- ✔ To kick a loop out of your Favorites list, select it on the Favorites tab and click the tab's Remove Favorite button.

Editing loops on the Timeline

After you've found a good loop, you should add it to the Timeline (and therefore to your soundtrack). In this section, I describe how to add loops to the Timeline and how to edit loops after they are there.

Moving a loop to the Timeline

Select the loop from the Soundtrack Media Manager, and drag the loop to an existing Timeline track. Or, you can drag the loop to the empty area on the Timeline below the last track, and Soundtrack automatically creates a new track to accommodate your loop. Remember that you can place different loops on the same track. In other words, each distinctive loop doesn't require its own track.

Repeating a loop

After you've added a loop to the Timeline, you probably want it to play multiple times — that is, you want it to loop! You can create a looping effect by dragging the same loop from the Media Manager to the Timeline repeatedly — but you have an easier way. Drag the right edge of a loop to extend it. As you drag, you see that the loop extends across the Timeline. You can drag the loop to repeat only its first beat or so, or you can keep dragging until you see the extended loop's rounded edge, which indicates that the loop has fully repeated (see Figure 11-8).

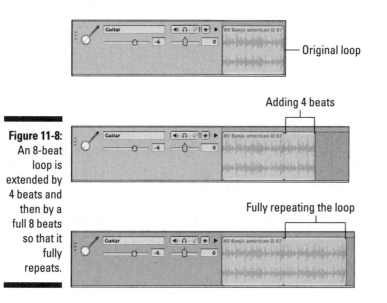

Original loop

Adding 4 beats

Figure 11-8: An 8-beat loop is extended by 4 beats and then by a full 8 beats so that it fully repeats.

Fully repeating the loop

Resizing a loop

You can resize a loop on the Timeline by dragging its edges either inward (toward the center of the loop) or outward. If you resize a loop so that it overlaps another loop, the overlapped loop is overwritten because two loops that share the same track can't play at the same time.

Selecting single and multiple loops

You can select any loop by clicking it, at which point the loop is highlighted on the Timeline. You can select multiple loops by holding down ⌘ as you select each one.

Moving a loop

You can select a loop (or multiple loops) and drag it to a new position on any track on the Timeline. Again, if you move a selected loop so that it overlaps an existing loop, that overlapped loop is overwritten.

Copying a loop

The easiest way to copy a loop is to select it on the Timeline and, while holding down Option, drag the selected loop to a new position. By holding down Option, you make a copy of the selected loop. You can also use the Mac's standard Copy and Paste commands: Select any loop, choose Edit⇨Copy, position the Timeline playhead in a new spot, and choose Edit⇨Paste.

Deleting a loop

To delete a loop, select the loop (or multiple loops) on the Timeline and press Delete.

Splitting and joining loops

You may want to split a loop on the Timeline so that it's treated as two independent parts (see Figure 11-9). You may do this to separate the two parts of the loop (to put other loops between them) or perhaps to transpose a small segment of the original loop. (See the section "Changing volume, pan, and key," later in this chapter, for more details.)

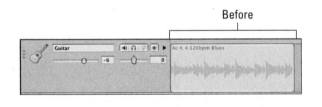

Figure 11-9: A loop that has been split into two parts.

To split a loop, select it on the Timeline and position the Timeline playhead at the part of the loop you want to split. Then, choose Edit⇨Split (or press S).

Likewise, you can join two adjacent loops by selecting them both (click each one while holding down ⌘) and then choosing Edit⇨Join (or press J).

Adding a track

You can Control+click an existing track on the Timeline (you can more easily Control+click the track itself rather than its heading) and choose either Add Track Above or Add Track Below from the pop-up menu that appears.

Deleting a track

To delete a track, Control+click anywhere within the unwanted track and select Remove Track from the pop-up menu that appears.

Looking at your Timeline options

In this section, I provide some helpful tips and tools for working more effectively with the Soundtrack Timeline.

Track options

You can edit or affect your Timeline tracks in the following ways:

✔ **Naming tracks:** Although new tracks normally take on the name of the first sound loop you place on the track (see Figure 11-10), you can change a track's name, if you want. Why do that? Sometimes, working with lots of tracks is easier when they have clear, well-defined names. For instance, finding your snare drum track is much easier when it's named Snare Drum rather than named with the long, formal name of your snare drum loop. To change a track's name, highlight its current name (triple-click the name to highlight the whole thing quickly) and type a new name.

Track Selection area

Solo control

Mute control Track None field

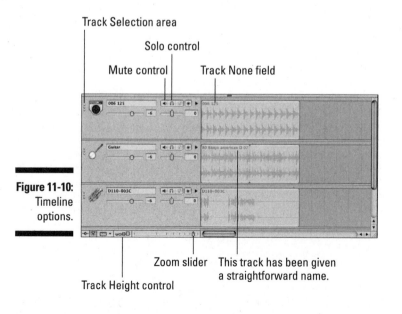

Figure 11-10:
Timeline
options.

Zoom slider   This track has been given
a straightforward name.

Track Height control

✔ **Setting track height:** As in Final Cut Pro, you can change a track's height so that it appears taller or shorter on the Timeline. (You may want a larger track height to better see a loop's audio waveform.) To customize the height of your Timeline tracks, click one of the vertical bars in the Track height control in the lower-left corner of the Timeline (refer to Figure 11-10).

✔ **Mute and Solo controls:** You can quickly choose to mute a track by clicking the Mute control in that track's header. (Look for the small Speaker icon; refer to Figure 11-10.) To solo the track so that it's the only one that plays, click its Solo control (it's the small Headphones icon).

✔ **Rearranging track order:** You may want to rearrange the order in which the tracks appear on the Timeline. (You usually do this to group all related tracks for easy management — for instance, you may place all percussion tracks in the same vicinity.) To rearrange a track's position on the Timeline, click the track header's Track Selection area (the three vertical dots — refer to Figure 11-10) and drag the track to a new spot.

Snapping, revisited

Like Final Cut Pro, Soundtrack has a Snapping feature that makes it easy to position loops (and other things) at precise points on the Timeline. You can toggle snapping on and off by choosing View➪Snapping (or by pressing G).

You can also decide what Timeline elements Soundtrack snaps to. (For instance, you can snap to increments on the Timeline ruler or to musical increments, like quarter notes or eighth notes.) Choose View➪Snap To, and take your pick from the submenu that appears.

Zooming the Timeline view

You can also zoom your view of the Timeline in or out by dragging the Timeline Zoom slider (refer to Figure 11-10). Dragging the slider to the left zooms in on your Timeline so that you see a smaller, but more detailed, slice of time. Dragging to the right zooms out to show you a bigger slice of time.

You can also zoom in and out directly from the keyboard by using the familiar Final Cut Pro shortcuts. Press ⌘+− (that's ⌘ plus the minus key) to zoom out, and press ⌘++ (that's ⌘ followed by the plus key) to zoom in.

Changing volume, pan, and key

You have many ways to control the volume of your tracks and overall score. You can also change the musical key your loops play in.

Changing constant volume

You can adjust the volume of your entire score or that of a single track. You can also change these volume levels over time by fading the levels up or down at any moment you choose. The volume controls are described as follows:

✔ **Score volume:** You can set the volume level of your entire score by dragging the Master Volume slider left or right or by typing a new decibel value in the corresponding text box (refer to Figure 11-6).

✔ **Track volume:** You can set a track's volume by adjusting that track's volume slider or by entering a new value in the Volume text box (see Figure 11-11). By default, Soundtrack assigns each track a volume of –6 decibels. This setting gives you some leeway in increasing a track's volume to about 0 decibels without risking distortion.

Volume slider   Solo control

Figure 11-11:
Various
track
controls.

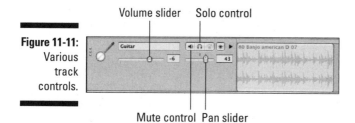

Mute control Pan slider

Changing volume over time

You can fade volume in and out over time by setting *envelope points* that affect individual tracks or your entire score. (Envelope points are just like the volume keyframes you set in Chapter 10, so refer to that chapter if you need a refresher on keyframes.) Follow these steps to set envelope points:

1. **Display the volume envelope for a particular track or for your entire score.**

   The volume envelope is the equivalent of the Volume Overlay in Final Cut Pro — again, refer to Chapter 10.

   • For a track, click that track's Show/Hide Envelopes disclosure triangle, as shown in Figure 11-12.

   • For your entire score, choose View⇨Show Master Envelopes (again, see Figure 11-12).

2. **Double-click the volume envelope where you want to place an envelope point (a keyframe).**

   Soundtrack places a point on the track's or score's volume envelope.

3. **Move the envelope point up or down, to adjust its decibel setting.**

Disclosure triangle   Volume envelope

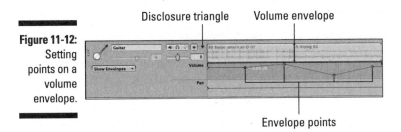

Envelope points

4. **Repeat Steps 2 and 3 to set more envelope points at other places in time.**

   By creating two or more envelope points with different volume settings, you create a fade-in or fade-out.

Control+clicking an existing envelope point displays some handy shortcuts on a pop-up menu.

You can delete unwanted envelope points by clicking them and pressing Delete.

If the Soundtrack Snapping feature is turned on, any envelope points you set position themselves at the nearest snap point. If you want Soundtrack to set your envelope points exactly where you click them, turn off snapping by choosing View⇨Snapping.

Changing pan

Pan refers to how stereo audio is balanced between the left and right speakers as it plays. Each track on the Soundtrack can have a custom pan setting. By default, a track's pan is set to 0, which means that the two stereo audio channels of any loop on the track play equally as loudly on the left and right speakers. You can create interesting (and, often, more realistic) effects by adjusting the pan so that some tracks play louder on one speaker and other tracks play louder on the other speaker. (This advice assumes that your audience hears your score played on stereo speakers positioned far enough apart. For instance, only the most extreme pan effects register through tiny laptop speakers that sit next to each other.)

You can adjust the pan of any track on the Timeline by dragging that track's Pan slider (refer to Figure 11-11). For instance, to make a track's pan favor the right speaker, drag its Pan slider farther to the right. (Dragging all the way in either direction makes that track play as loudly as possible on one speaker and makes it silent on the other.)

You can also change a track's pan settings over time to make loops sound as though they're moving from one speaker to another. To do so, use the same steps I present in the preceding section to change a track's volume over time, and apply those steps to the track's pan envelope.

Changing a loop's key

When you add a loop to the Timeline, Soundtrack converts (or *transposes*) the loop from the original key in which it was recorded to the master key your overall project uses. (Again, think of a loop's key as the pitch it starts playing from.) After a loop is on the Timeline, you can transpose it to its original key or to any other key. For instance, you may place two copies of the same loop on different Timeline tracks so that they play simultaneously. By transposing one of the loops up a full octave (so that it plays at a higher but complementary pitch), the two loops in effect play a chord, creating a richer sound in your music. On the flip side, transposing a loop into a key that's completely incompatible with the key of your other loops can create some weird and disturbing musical effects. (But maybe that's what you want!)

To transpose a loop, click it on the Timeline while pressing Control and choose Transpose from the pop-up menu that appears. You can transpose the loop by *semitones*, which is a musical term for the increments of different musical keys. If you aren't familiar with semitones, don't worry. Choosing a positive value raises the pitch of the loop, and choosing a negative semitone value lowers the pitch. (Soundtrack displays this new semitone value on any Timeline loop you've transposed — see Figure 11-13.) With some trial and error, you should find a new transposed key that works for you.

Figure 11-13:
The same loop is transposed up by one semitone and then transposed by two semitones.

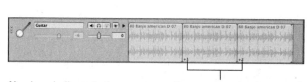

Numbers indicate by how many semitones a loop is transposed.

Sometimes, you can make a repeating loop more interesting by changing its key at some point in the loop and either returning to the original key later on or changing the key again (refer to Figure 11-13). But, because each loop can have only one key at a time, you have to split the loop into different parts so that you can assign each one a unique key.

You can transpose your entire score's key over time. To do so, use the same steps I present in the preceding section to change your score's volume over time, and apply those steps to the score's Transpose envelope.

Other Stuff

This section points out some other Soundtrack tools that can help refine your score or make scoring to key moments easy.

Markers mark important moments

Soundtrack lets you set markers throughout its Timeline to mark important moments in your score and its accompanying video. For instance, you may mark a place on the Timeline where you want to change your score's tempo or begin to fade volume, or where a dramatic musical hit (such as a heavy drum or cymbal crash) should occur. Setting markers reminds you of, and helps you keep track of, all the special moments you should be aware of as you compose your score.

As in Final Cut Pro, markers appear at the top of the Timeline; they look a bit like downward-pointing arrows (see Figure 11-14).

Markers and marker names

Figure 11-14: Markers on the Timeline.

You can work with three kinds of markers in Soundtrack, and each type is displayed in a unique color, as follows:

- **Beat marker (purple):** Use a Beat marker to mark an important beat in your score (for instance, beat 9.1.000). If you ever change the tempo of your score, the beat marker moves to stay with the specific beat you've marked.

✔ **Time marker (green):** Use a Time marker to mark an important event or moment in your video track. Time markers mark a specific timecode (01:00:24.30, for instance) and stick to that timecode, no matter what changes you make to your score's tempo. For that reason, if you want to mark an important moment in your video, use a Time marker.

✔ **Scoring marker (orange):** *Scoring markers* are markers you set while you're working in Final Cut Pro, as you edit your video. (Refer to Chapter 9 for more details about setting Scoring markers.) When you export a movie from Final Cut Pro to Soundtrack (see the section "Exporting video from Final Cut Pro," earlier in this chapter), any Scoring markers you've set are automatically "recorded" in the export and show up on your Soundtrack Timeline when you import that video. (Keep in mind that you can't move or delete Scoring markers in Soundtrack because they're considered part of the exported video.)

Setting markers

Setting markers is easy. Follow these steps:

1. **Position the Timeline playhead at the point where you want to place a marker.**

2. **Set the appropriate marker, as follows:**

   • To set a Time marker, choose Project⇨Insert Time Marker or press M.

   • To set a Beat marker, choose Project⇨Insert Beat Marker or press B.

Managing markers

The following are some handy tips for editing and managing all the markers you may set on the Timeline. Just remember that you can edit only Beat and Time markers; you can't edit Scoring markers that were imported with your video from Final Cut Pro.

✔ **Naming markers:** If you're setting lots of markers, you can more easily remember what they all mark by naming them. Control+click any marker that's already on the Timeline and choose Edit from the pop-up menu that appears. In the dialog box that appears, type a descriptive name for your marker and click OK. You can set Soundtrack to display a marker's name directly on the Timeline by choosing View⇨Show Marker Titles.

✔ **Moving markers:** To move a marker, click and drag it to a new spot on the Timeline ruler.

✔ **Delete markers:** To delete a marker, just click it and press Delete!

Using Time markers to synchronize video and music

You can use a Time marker to automatically change the tempo of your score so that a particular moment of the score occurs at a particular moment in your video. Follow these steps:

1. **Place a Time marker to mark in your video a moment you want to synchronize with a moment in your score.**

   Position the Soundtrack playhead at that particular spot in your video, and press M to place a Time marker.

2. **Select the marker you just placed by clicking it.**

3. **Position the Timeline playhead at the location of the music you want to match to your marked video.**

4. **Choose Project⇨Score Marker to Playhead.**

   Soundtrack either speeds or slows the tempo of your score so that the music at the Timeline playhead now occurs at the position of the marker you placed in Step 1.

   You can see the tempo change by looking at your score's tempo envelope. Choose View⇨Show Master Envelopes, and note how the tempo envelope changes suddenly at the position of the marker you matched to the playhead. Clicking one of the envelope points on the Tempo envelope displays the new tempo value that's used at that moment. If the tempo changes that now occur feel too abrupt for you, click and drag the tempo envelope points to smooth the transition over more time.

Soundtrack can't make extreme changes to tempo, so if the playhead and your Time marker are too far apart, Soundtrack can't match the playhead and marker.

Applying effects

Soundtrack includes a wide variety of audio effects you can use to stylize and adjust the sound of individual tracks or your entire score (see Figure 11-15). For instance, you can use a delay effect to create echoes or even make a single violin sound more like an orchestral section of strings. Likewise, you can use a distortion effect to add a bit of "grit" to a sound and change its emotional impact.

As is the case with the Final Cut Pro audio filters (which I discuss in Chapter 10), the trick to using Soundtrack effects is understanding how a myriad of effects parameters affect your sound, and that broad topic is outside the scope of a *For Dummies* book. If you're interested in exploring the wide world of Soundtrack effects, I suggest that you consult the extensive Soundtrack online help system or a comprehensive reference book, such as *Final Cut Pro 4 Bible*, by Zed Saeed, J.J. Marshall, and Jeffrey Chong (Wiley).

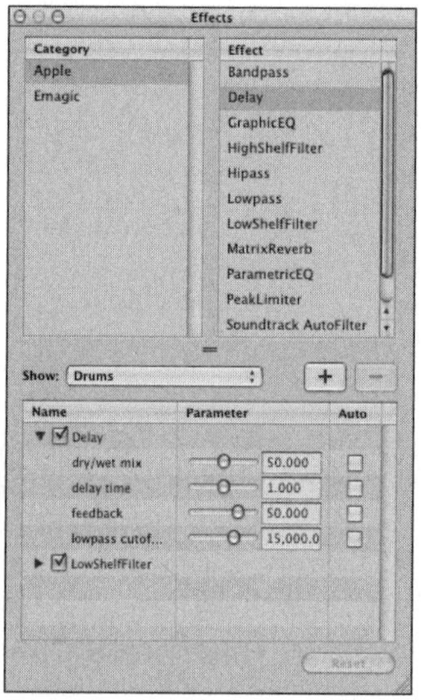

Figure 11-15:
The Effects
window lists
all available
effects.

Making your own loops and one-shots

If you really want to get fancy with Soundtrack, you can add your own music and sounds to the software's "factory installed" loops. You can import this audio as an AIFF file and use it in one of two ways: You can use the Soundtrack Loop Utility tool to turn the AIFF file into a repeatable loop that works like all the other loops available to you, or you can treat the audio as a "one-shot" — an element of music or sound that's not designed to repeat, but that complements the other loops already in your score (such as a single drum hit or cymbal crash, or spoken dialogue).

A description of this level of customization is outside the scope of a *For Dummies* book, but I want to let you know that it's possible, in case you want to customize your scores as much as possible. For more information, check out your Soundtrack documentation.

Exporting Your Score

After you have finished composing your score, you're ready to export it in a format that your Final Cut Pro (as well as any other video or audio editing program) project can work with. When you export, you're presented with a Save As dialog box so that you can name the exported file and save it to your hard drive.

You can export your score back to Final Cut by using the following two options, which are on the Soundtrack File menu:

- **Stereo Mix:** This option saves your *score* as a stereo audio file. (When you import your score into Final Cut, it occupies two of your sequence's audio tracks.) You should choose this option only if you don't plan to adjust the volume of elements in your score, after the score has been imported into Final Cut Pro. For instance, you can't change only the volume of the score's drums because those drums are no longer recognized as an individual element.

- **Export Tracks:** This option saves *each track* in your Soundtrack score as a stereo audio file. (For instance, if your score uses 10 tracks, you end up with 10 stereo audio files.) You can therefore import all these individual stereo files to the Final Cut Pro Timeline and tweak each track's volume separately. In other words, you have the most flexibility in mixing your musical score with other audio elements, such as dialogue or sound effects, that are on the Final Cut Pro Timeline. The drawback is that the Final Cut Pro Timeline can quickly become crowded with lots of audio tracks — and be a bit disorienting.

After you've exported your score as an audio file (or files), open the Final Cut Pro project that it's meant to work with, import the new audio file as you would do with any other media, and place the audio file on your movie's Timeline.

After you've imported your score into Final Cut Pro, you may decide to edit your movie's video. You also have to adjust the Soundtrack score you created, therefore, so that the score stays in sync with the freshly edited movie.

This task isn't a problem. You can export your edited Timeline sequence as I describe in the section "Exporting video from Final Cut Pro," earlier in this chapter. As you do this, Final Cut Pro recognizes that your Timeline sequence already features audio tracks that were created earlier in Soundtrack, and the software assumes that you want to leave these tracks out of the Final Cut Pro sequence you're about to export. (Because you need to re-edit your score, you don't want an earlier version recorded with the exported Final Cut Pro video.) If you want your export to include the Soundtrack score, Final Cut Pro begins its export by presenting a dialog box that lets you select the earlier Soundtrack score for inclusion.

Chapter 12

Creating Transitions

· ·

In This Chapter

▶ Understanding the types of transitions

▶ Applying transitions

▶ Rendering and previewing transitions

▶ Modifying transitions

▶ Creating and saving custom transitions

▶ Using transitions effectively

· ·

*T*ransitions are special effects for shifting smoothly from one video clip to the next rather than simply cutting away from one clip and starting another on the next frame. You're probably familiar with some of the more common transitions, such as Cross Dissolve and Wipe. The Cross Dissolve fades one clip out as it fades a new clip in, and makes the two appear to merge for a moment, whereas a Wipe slides one shot in over the other. (George Lucas uses these transitions a lot in his *Star Wars* movies.)

Final Cut Pro places a dizzying and exotic array of transitions at your disposal, which you can easily apply and customize.

Exploring the Types of Transitions in Final Cut Pro

The following list details some of the most important transition types that Final Cut Pro provides:

✔ **3D Simulation:** As this name implies, these six transitions create a motion in three dimensions. You can use them to zoom in and out of video clips or to create different types of spins and swings. These transitions have an animated, high-tech feel, which you often see in commercials or short news clips.

The 3D simulation transitions are Cross Zoom, Cube Spin, Spin 3D, Spinback 3D, Swing, and Zoom.

✔ **Dissolve:** A *dissolve,* the most common type of transition, is an equal fading out of one clip as another is fading in. These transitions change the image from one clip into the next by modifying the transparency of clips as they overlap.

The dissolves that are available to you are Additive, Cross, Dip to Color, Dither, Fade In, Fade Out, Non-Additive, and Ripple.

✔ **Iris:** An *iris* transition concentrates the focus of a clip in the center by moving the edges of its frames inward. This effect is similar to closing and opening the shutter of a mechanical camera. You can create an iris transition by using several shapes, including Cross, Diamond, Oval, Point, Rectangle, and Star.

✔ **Map:** By selecting or inverting specific channels with Channel or Luminescence (Color) maps, you can create a transition with dramatic, effects similar to solarizing. (*Solarizing* appears to "burn out" the edges of images, reminiscent of a psychedelic effect from the 1960s.) You can also fill portions of an image with black, depending on how two clips interact with each other.

✔ **Page peel:** In a *page peel* transition, the first clip strips away to reveal the second. Make sure to consider the relationship between the two images as each one is peeled away, and make any necessary adjustments to the transition. If you peel too slowly between talking-head shots, the effect may look similar to Mr. Potato Head.

✔ **QuickTime:** The Apple QuickTime video format has its own set of transitions, which any program that uses QuickTime (including Final Cut Pro) can access. Some of these transitions, such as Zoom, are similar to the native Final Cut Pro transitions; QuickTime, however, has some unique ones as well, such as Explode, in which the first clip is shattered to reveal the second.

The main QuickTime transitions are Channel Compositor, Chroma Key, Explode, Gradient Wipe, Implode, Iris, Matrix Wipe, Push, Slide, Wipe, and Zoom.

✔ **Slide:** Your uncle's old slide projector could never move slides like this collection of transitions does. Final Cut Pro can push video frames around in a variety of ways — from the top or bottom or even from a split in the middle.

The slide transitions in Final Cut Pro are Band, Box, Center Split, Multi Spin, Push, Spin, Split, and Swap.

✔ **Stretch and Squeeze:** The names say it all. These transitions are great for creating extreme effects that are psychedelic and fun.

This set of transitions includes Cross Stretch, Squeeze, Squeeze and Stretch, and just Stretch (for those mellow days!).

✔ **Wipe:** *Wipes* move one clip out of the way by using another. Wipes differ from dissolves in that wipes don't blend. Also, wipes give you more options than slides, which move a frame in simple directions. Wipes are fun — for instance, the Jaws wipe is a great way to amuse your friends when you're showing video from that fishing trip.

The 14 wipes available to you are Band, Center, Checker, Checkerboard, Clock, Edge, Gradient, Inset, Jaws, Random Edge, V, Venetian Blind, Wrap, and Zig-Zag.

Here's one bit of stylistic advice: Don't get carried away with all the crazy transitions offered in Final Cut Pro. Let the mood and emotions of your story dictate the kind of transitions you use. Just because you have access to a transition that makes people say "Wow!" doesn't mean that it's the best transition for your project. Also, if your project requires transitions, try to keep the transitions you pick within the same family: Choose a type of transition (such as a Cross Dissolve) and stay with it so that you don't distract the viewer with a variety of different transition styles.

Applying Your First Transition

Although Final Cut Pro gives you tons of different transitions to use in your movies, you probably use a simple Cross Dissolve the most, fading one movie clip gracefully into another clip. However, before you can apply a Cross Dissolve, you need to trim the clips, as follows:

1. **In the Browser window, first double-click one clip and then the other to load them both into the Viewer window.**

2. **For the first clip, mark an Out point about 1 second before the end of the clip.**

   Position the Viewer playhead on the frame you want, and press O. (Refer to Chapter 7 for more details about In and Out points.)

3. **For the second clip (the later clip in the transition), mark an In point 1 second after the beginning of the clip.**

   Position the Viewer playhead on the frame you want, and press I.

   This trimming is crucial because Final Cut Pro uses the trimmed, unseen frames of a clip to create a transition from one clip to another. Untrimmed clips placed on the Timeline (clips that show all their frames on the Timeline) don't have any unused frames for Final Cut Pro to use in creating the transition. See the nearby sidebar "Understanding unused frames," for more information.

Now that you have trimmed the clips, you can try out a Cross Dissolve by following these steps:

1. **Place two trimmed clips side by side on the Timeline, as shown in Figure 12-1.**

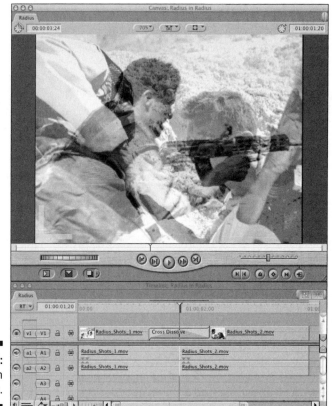

Figure 12-1:
A transition
in progress.

2. **Click the edit point (where the two clips meet on the Timeline) to select it.**

3. **Choose Effects⇨Video Transitions⇨Dissolve⇨Cross Dissolve.**

   The Video Transitions submenu has transitions galore. Subcategories include dissolves, irises, wipes, and lots more, but for now, stick with the basic Cross Dissolve. Final Cut Pro responds by placing a transition over the edit point between the two clips (refer to Figure 12-1).

4. **Play the transition on the Timeline.**

Understanding unused frames

All transitions have one thing in common: handles. *Handles* are the extra frames (outside the In and Out points of the selected clip) that you need at the end of one clip and the beginning of the next clip for a transition to work.

A transition takes a specific amount of time to unfold. (The Final Cut Pro default for all transitions is 1 second — about 30 frames.) If one clip disappears over the course of 1 second while another appears during that same 1 second, the transition involves a total of 60 frames — 30 frames from the outgoing clip (the earlier clip on the Timeline) and 30 frames from the incoming clip (the following clip). When the transition is half a second, you need the same amount of time present at the ends of both clips as extra frames for the transition. (*Note:* Final Cut Pro always tries to create a transition with all the extra frames that are available to it. When the transition doesn't have enough extra frames available, Final Cut Pro shortens the transition.)

The way to deal with handles is to always leave enough extra footage (frames outside the clip's In and Out points) so that you have a handle. The simplest way to leave handles on clips is to use the Viewer window to mark the In point a bit into the clip (as opposed to the first frame of the clip) or mark the Out point a few seconds earlier than the end of the clip. You don't have to create handles at both the beginning and end of a clip — just the part of the clip you want to incorporate into a transition. You can also create handles by trimming clips after they're on the Timeline. (Refer to Chapters 7 and 9 for more information about trimming from the Timeline.)

If you have a Mac with a newer G4 processor, and if you're not watching video through a television that's hooked to a DV camera, you should be able to play the transition in real-time. Place the Timeline playhead before the transition and press the spacebar so that you can see the transition play in the Canvas window.

If you're using a Mac with a G3 or an older G4 processor, you may have to render (or process) the transition before playing it. (Final Cut Pro warns you by drawing a thin red line over the transition on the Timeline.) To render a Cross Dissolve, click the transition on the Timeline to select it and then choose Sequence⇨Render Selection (or just press ⌘+R).

Looking at the Many Ways to Apply Transitions

Final Cut Pro usually offers more than one way to accomplish a task, and transitions are no exception. This section describes some alternative methods you can use to apply transitions.

Dragging transitions from the Browser to the edit point on the Timeline

One of the quickest ways to create a transition is to drag the transition from the Browser to the edit point — the place where your two clips meet on the Timeline. Just follow these steps:

1. **In the Browser, click the Effects tab to display the Final Cut Pro effects, grouped by category into bins.**

2. **Click the small triangle next to Video Transitions, for instance, to see all available transition families (also in bins); see Figure 12-2.**

3. **Open a transition bin, and drag a transition to an edit point on the Timeline (in other words, the place where two clips meet).**

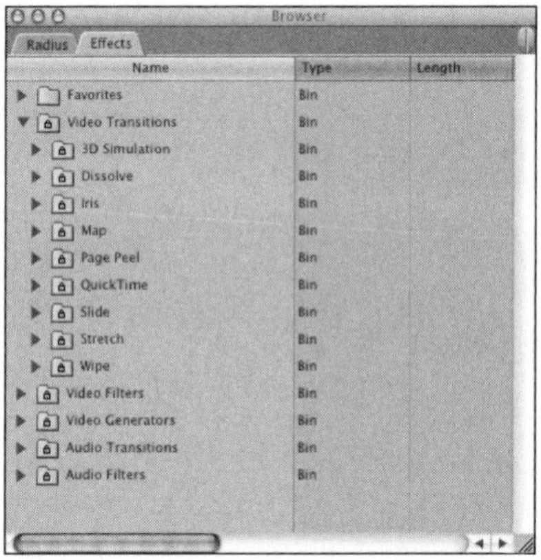

Figure 12-2:
The Effects tab on the Browser window tab stores all transitions.

If you hate to dig through all those bins each time you want to find your favorite transitions, drag the transitions to the Favorites bin in the Browser (or anywhere else in the Browser, for that matter). Final Cut Pro makes a copy of the transition in this new location and leaves the original where it belongs. Now, you can use this copy and not jump through as many hoops each time you need a transition.

Using the keyboard shortcut

You can apply the Final Cut Pro Cross Dissolve transition (which is considered its default transition) with a keyboard shortcut. What could be simpler? Just follow these steps:

1. **Select the edit point on the Timeline where you want to add a transition.**

2. **Press ⌘+T (*T* for *t*ransition, of course).**

Copying and pasting a transition

You can copy and paste a transition from one edit point to a new edit point you have prepared. This method is handy if you have a custom transition at the second edit point and want to apply it at the 20th edit point in the sequence (I tell you more about custom transitions later in this chapter). To copy and paste a transition, follow these steps:

1. **Make sure that you have handles at the new edit point!**

   If you're not sure what handles are, see the sidebar "Understanding unused frames," earlier in this chapter.

2. **Click an existing transition on the Timeline to select it, and then press ⌘+C to copy it.**

3. **Move the Timeline playhead to the exact position between the two clips where you want to copy the transition.**

   The Final Cut Pro Snapping feature can be very helpful at this point because it automatically (when you click the Timeline) selects the nearest edit point for you. To toggle snapping on and off, press N. Or, press ↑ and ↓ to jump the Timeline playhead between clips.

4. **Press ⌘+V to paste the transition.**

   Alternatively, you can Option+drag-and-drop the transition from one edit point to another to make a copy of the transition in the new location.

Editing Clips and Adding Transitions

In Chapter 7, I explain how to insert or overwrite a clip from the Viewer window to the Timeline. You can also perform these edits while automatically adding the default Final Cut Pro transition (the trusty Cross Dissolve) to the clip you're editing, without having to manually apply the transition. Follow these steps to edit two clips together and, in the process, perform an insert edit with a transition:

1. **Locate a clip in the Browser and double-click the clip to load it into the Viewer.**

2. **Set both an In and an Out point in the clip.**

   Remember that you can press the letters I and O to set the edit points. Make sure that Final Cut Pro has enough extra frames past the Out point to accommodate the transition time.

3. **To add this clip to the Timeline, drag the clip into the Canvas window (while still holding down the mouse button) and choose either an Overwrite or Insert edit from the context menu that appears.**

Final Cut Pro either inserts or overwrites your clip to the Timeline.

Note that you can also drag the clip directly into the Timeline, but make sure that you have positioned the Timeline playhead at the end of the edited clip. The playhead *must* be positioned right after the clip you just edited.

4. **Locate a second clip in the Browser and double-click the clip to open it in the Viewer.**

5. **Set In and Out points for your second clip in the Viewer.**

Make sure that Final Cut Pro has enough extra frames before the In point to accommodate the transition time.

6. **Drag the clip from the Viewer to the right side of the media area in the Canvas window.**

Final Cut Pro reveals a set of options, as shown in Figure 12-3.

7. **Drag the clip into the Canvas window (while still holding down the mouse button) and choose Insert with Transition from the context menu that appears.**

You can also choose to overwrite the clip. Either way, Final Cut Pro adds the clip to the Timeline, but with a Cross Dissolve already attached at the beginning of the clip, so the clips transition seamlessly with each other.

Figure 12-3:
Dragging a clip to the right side of the Canvas window reveals overwrite and insert options.

Rendering Transitions

After you've placed a transition on the Timeline, you may have to render it before you can see the results. *Rendering* is the process by which Final Cut Pro calculates how to create an effect, such as a transition, and then writes a new video clip (which incorporates the new frames that the transition uses) to the hard drive. A thin red line over any clip on the Timeline's Render Status bar (refer to Chapter 8) indicates that the clip needs rendering.

However, you may never see that little red line over a clip because Final Cut Pro 4 has introduced a new technology named RT Unlimited, which offers a whole new way of showing real-time previews of transitions and other effects. (With this technology, no rendering is required — at least until you're ready to export your final movie or record it to tape.)

RT Unlimited is discussed more fully in Bonus Chapter 1 on this book's companion Web site; however, understanding the render settings for working with transitions is particularly useful. Begin by checking to see whether the render bar over your transitions is a thin red, green, or gray line. If the line is red, you need to render the transition first or switch from Safe RT to Unlimited RT by selecting the latter from the RT drop-down menu in the upper-left corner of the Timeline window (refer to Chapter 8). When Unlimited RT is activated, the render bar above the transitions changes to orange, indicating that you can watch a preview, although the software may drop frames on slower machines. A green or gray line means that you can preview a transition without rendering or switching settings.

At any rate, using Unlimited RT can spare you from ever rendering another transition for preview purposes (to see how it looks as you experiment with its duration or other factors). If the real-time preview of a transition isn't playing smoothly or it appears too blurry, you may want to render the transition to see it at its best quality level. The remainder of this section discusses how to render a transition the old-fashioned way.

Rendering a single transition

To render a single transition on the Timeline, follow these steps:

1. **Select the transition on the Timeline.**

   Use the Selection tool (it's on the Tool palette) to select the transition.

2. **Choose Sequence⇨Render Selection⇨Both from the main menu.**

   You may also choose Sequence⇨Render Selection⇨Video if you're not concerned about any audio effects or transitions. It's often easier, though, to get in the habit of rendering both audio and video, in case any changes in either one could affect smooth playback.

Alternatively, you can press ⌘+R.

The rendering process begins, and a Render Status bar shows you the progress. Click Cancel on the status bar or press Esc to cancel the rendering.

Rendering all transitions in a range

If you have lots of transitions in a sequence, you may want to render them all at one time rather than process them individually. By following these steps, you can render everything in the sequence at one time after you finish applying transitions:

1. **Select or open a sequence in the Timeline window.**

2. **Choose Sequence⇨Render All⇨Both from the main menu.**

   You can also press Option+R to begin rendering everything on the Timeline.

If Final Cut doesn't render your transitions, you may need to give it a bit more guidance. Check the color of the line that appears above your clip on the Timeline's Render Status bar (it's probably green or orange). Then, choose Sequence⇨Render Selection or Sequence⇨Render All and make sure that the same color is checked on the Render menu. By doing this, you're telling Final Cut not to ignore clips that fall into certain render classifications. Now, try to render your transitions again, and they should render right away.

Modifying Transitions

After rendering and previewing a transition, you may decide to change it to suit your needs. Final Cut Pro enables you to modify transitions in numerous ways. You can change the duration of transitions, alter their alignments with respect to the edit point, or simply move them around.

Changing the duration of a transition

You can use several methods to modify the duration of a transition. One of the most common methods is described in these steps:

1. **Control+click the transition on the Timeline.**

   Make sure that you're clicking the transition itself, not the edit point between the two transitioned clips.

2. **Choose Duration from the pop-up menu that appears, as shown in Figure 12-4.**

   The Duration dialog box appears.

3. **In the Duration dialog box, type a new duration and click OK.**

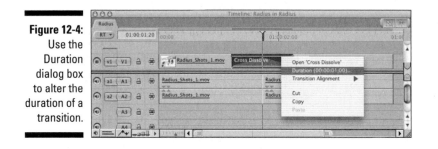

Figure 12-4: Use the Duration dialog box to alter the duration of a transition.

Another way to change the duration of a transition is to simply drag the ends of the transition (as shown on the Timeline) to change its overall duration, as follows:

1. **On the Timeline, click and drag either end of the transition.**

   A timecode pop-up tip appears, as shown in Figure 12-5.

2. **Drag the edge of the transition, and watch the timecode change.**

   With a little practice, you can change the duration of fades on the fly. What's really cool is that Final Cut Pro displays the results of this customization in the Canvas window as you drag.

Figure 12-5: Modifying the duration of a transition.

If you find that Final Cut Pro doesn't allow you to make longer transitions, it may be because you don't have enough unused frames on either side of your edit points. Before adding clips with transitions to the Timeline, make sure that you set In and Out points for your clips in the Viewer with enough frames on both sides to accommodate longer transitions.

Changing the alignment of a transition

By default, Final Cut Pro centers transitions on an edit point between two clips. That is, the transition straddles the edit point equally on both sides — half the transition on the outgoing clip and the other half on the incoming side.

However, after you've placed a transition and previewed it, you may want it to occur earlier or later. For example, you may want the transition to start immediately after an edit point rather than occur squarely in the middle of the edit. On the other hand, you may want a transition to begin and end before it even reaches the edit point between two clips. Fortunately, Final Cut Pro allows you to quickly change the alignment of a transition so that it occurs immediately before or after an edit point.

You can change the alignment of the transition by following these steps:

1. **Control+click a transition, and choose Transition Alignment from the pop-up menu that appears.**

   Make sure that you're not clicking the edit point between the two transitioned clips.

2. **Using the submenu that appears, choose to either start, center, or end the transition on the edit point between the two Timeline clips.**

   Figure 12-6 shows the method of transition-alignment selection and its results.

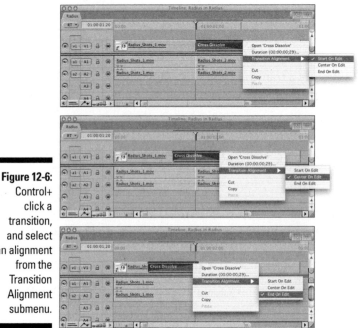

Figure 12-6: Control+ click a transition, and select an alignment from the Transition Alignment submenu.

Moving transitions

In Final Cut Pro, you can move a transition from one edit point to another. This process removes the transition from the first edit point and moves it to the new one. If you have a transition at the next edit point, Final Cut Pro replaces the transition. To move a transition, click and drag it from its current location to the new edit point.

Note that you can even align the transition to center, end, or start on the edit point. As you drag the transition to the new edit point, you can feel the transition snap to the edit point (center, beginning, or end).

Replacing and removing transitions

Many times, you may be unhappy with your choice of a transition. In that case, you can easily replace the current transition on the Timeline with another one. Final Cut Pro keeps the duration of the preceding transition as well as the alignment to the edit point and simply applies a different type of transition. To replace a transition, follow these steps:

1. **On the Timeline, select the transition you want to replace.**

   Use the Selection tool to select the transition. The Selection tool is at the top of the Tool palette, to the right of the Timeline window.

2. **Choose Effects⇨Video Transitions, and select another transition from the submenu options.**

   The new choice replaces the older transition. Unhappy with this one too? Keep replacing it until you get the effect you're searching for.

If you decide not to use a transition you've already applied, just select it with the Selection tool and press Delete. It's simple!

Fading In and Out

Fading into or out of a clip in Final Cut Pro couldn't be easier. You can use a transition at one end of the clip, which automatically creates a fade-in or fade-out. Although you have other options to fade in and out of a clip, the transition that's most commonly used for this purpose is Cross Dissolve.

To fade into or out of a clip, follow these steps:

1. **Locate a clip in the Browser and double-click the clip to load it into the Viewer.**

2. **Set an In and an Out point in the clip.**

3. **Drag the clip from the Viewer onto a video track on the Timeline.**

   Make sure that no clip is adjacent to this clip on either its left or right side. The clip must not touch any other nearby clip on the Timeline.

4. **Drag a Cross Dissolve transition from the Effects tab in the Browser window, and drop the transition at the beginning of the clip (see Figure 12-7).**

   This step gives you a fade-in from black into the clip.

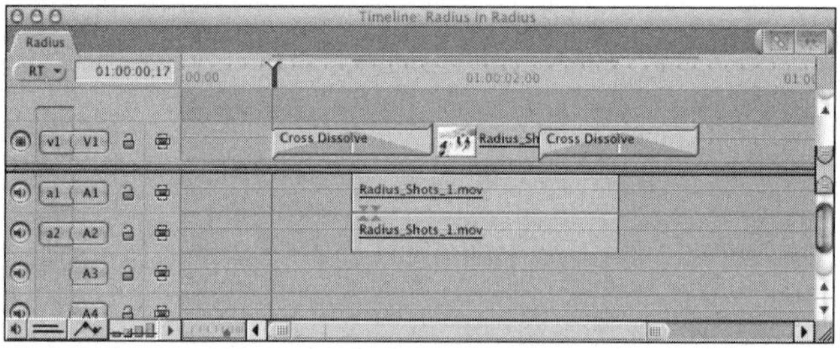

Figure 12-7:
Fading in and out on a clip on the Timeline.

5. **Drag another Cross Dissolve transition from the Effects tab in the Browser to the end of the clip.**

   This step gives you a fade-out to black from the clip.

6. **Preview the transition. (You may need to render it if your Mac isn't generating a real-time preview.)**

   You have just created, as shown in Figure 12-7, a fade-in and fade-out for the clip. Remember that you can increase or decrease the amount of time that these fades last by clicking the ends of the Cross Dissolve and dragging to make them longer or shorter.

When you're creating a fade-in or fade-out, click and drag the transition from the Browser to a clip's edit point on the Timeline and then press ⌘ to force the transition to be placed at the start or the end (whichever you've chosen) of a clip's edit point. This way, you don't have to precisely position the transition yourself — Final Cut Pro does it for you.

Saving and Organizing Custom Transitions

You soon find that you use certain transitions more often than others. In addition, these transitions often have different durations than the 1-second timespan that Final Cut Pro offers by default.

Using the following steps — assuming that you have a few transitions on the Timeline that have been modified to your preferred duration — you can save transitions and rename them as you see fit:

1. **Drag the Effects tab out of the Browser window so that it's a separate window.**

2. **Press ⌘+B to create a new bin in the Browser window.**

3. **Name this bin something intuitive (Custom Fades, for instance) by clicking it once to highlight it and then clicking a second time to edit its name.**

4. **Drag and drop the new bin into the Favorites bin in the now-separate Effects window.**

5. **Drag a transition from the Timeline where you applied it into the new bin you just created.**

   This step saves the name of the transition as well as its duration.

6. **Rename the transition according to its purpose so that you can remember what it does.**

   To rename the effect, double-click its name and type a new name for it. Editors commonly rename transitions to indicate their duration as well. For example, `Cross Diss10fr` means a Cross Dissolve with a 10-frame duration.

Using the Transition Editor to Customize a Transition

The Transition Editor window provides a number of tools and options for more precise control over transitions. These customizing features increase in number, depending on the complexity of the transition you're using. The advantage is obvious: You can set up a special transition for repeated use (maybe a 3D-cube spin for a short commercial or a precise type of Cross Dissolve for a movie project) and then save it for repeated use.

You can load a transition into the Transition Editor window (see Figure 12-8) in one of two ways: by double-clicking a transition on the Timeline or double-clicking a transition on the Effects tab of the Browser window. Each method allows you to change and modify transitions. However, when you double-click a transition from the Timeline, you modify only that existing transition on that particular sequence; you don't modify all transitions of that type.

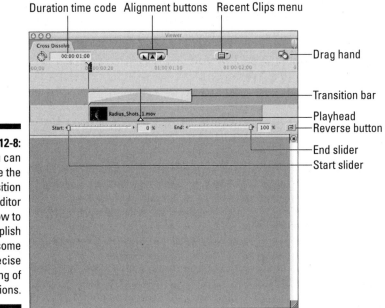

Duration time code   Alignment buttons   Recent Clips menu

Drag hand

Transition bar

Playhead
Reverse button

End slider
Start slider

Figure 12-8:
You can
use the
Transition
Editor
window to
accomplish
some
precise
tweaking of
transitions.

The following list presents some tasks you can accomplish in the Transition Editor window:

- **Change the duration of a transition:** Enter a new duration in the time-code field in the upper-left corner of the Transition Editor window (refer to Figure 12-8).

- **Drag a transition:** Using the Drag Hand icon, you can either drag the transition into the Timeline to apply it to a edit point or drag it back to the Browser into the Favorites bin, which is on the Effects tab.

- **Reverse a transition:** Click Reverse to switch the direction of a transition from forward to backward.

- **Change the start and end percentage:** Use the Start and End sliders to change the starting and ending percentages of a transition. This method is especially useful during some wipes in which you may want the transition to start out at 50 percent (halfway through the transition) rather than at 0 or end at a value other than 100 percent.

- **Change the edit point around a transition:** For instance, you can drag at the ends of the two clips that are shown in the window and change the location of the edit point between the clips. The transition automatically moves to the new location of the edit point.

- **Change the alignment of a transition:** Click the Start on Edit, Center on Edit (the default selection), or End on Edit button at the top of the Transition Editor window to modify the alignment of a transition.

Chapter 13

Adding Text to Your Videos

*F*inal Cut Pro has always allowed you to create text for all kinds of occasions. You could create title cards to open and close your movie, and you could create captions, subtitles, and logos to superimpose over video. You could animate *crawls,* which are like the running news ticker tape at the bottom of a news broadcast, or scrolling credits. You could go conservative with any of these features, by playing it cool with respectable typefaces, or you could create treatments so wild that they would make your eyes hurt.

Now, thanks to the new LiveType application included with Final Cut Pro, you can create titles that dance and move unlike anything you have ever seen. The LiveType text pulses with energy and can add excitement to any production. You can also quite easily create high-quality animated titles, which were previously the domain of graphics experts, using complex software.

What you do with your text and the tools that are included with Final Cut Pro depends entirely on your vision. This chapter is designed to show you how to accomplish that vision.

Formatting Text for Display on a TV

One of the first things you should know about text and titles for your videos is that, because computer monitors and TV sets work differently, text that looks good on a Mac monitor (or liquid crystal display (LCD) screen) may not look so hot when displayed on a television set. This situation isn't important if you never expect your video to be seen on a TV. This may be the case if, for example, you're making videos just for your Web site or for a CD. However, if you expect someone to watch your movie on a TV, you should keep a few things in mind. I cover these items in the following sections.

If you expect your movie to end up on a TV, make sure that you test and preview on a TV all the text you're creating, to ensure that everything looks good. (Refer to Chapter 2 for details about how to connect a TV to your Mac via FireWire.)

Selecting the right font size

Tiny print doesn't cut it in video. Small print, whether it's used for closing credits or the fine print of a copyright notice, may look good on your Mac's screen but ultimately appears fuzzy and illegible on a television because a TV screen's resolution isn't good enough to clearly display the thin lines that make up small text. (See the following sidebar, "Text can look bad on a TV but good on a computer," for more information.) How do you know what font size works well? Selecting font size is as much art as science, so, unfortunately, I can't give you any hard-and-fast rules. Fonts vary in size among typefaces. Saying that 12 points is the smallest size font you should use isn't necessarily true for all font typefaces; you may be able to get by with 10 points in some fonts. However, I don't recommend going much below 10 points, regardless of the typeface. The bottom line is to test small font sizes on a decent TV before you commit to using them.

Avoiding thick and thin

For best results on a TV, try to avoid fonts that have thick and thin parts in each letter. For example, take a closer look at the Cheltenham font — the font face you're reading right now. Look at the letter *O,* and notice how its vertical lines are thick but the horizontal lines that form the top and bottom of the letter are much thinner.

In addition to having thicker and thinner parts of letters, the Cheltenham font has little turns, or *serifs,* such as those at the ends of the top of a capital *T.* Fonts with these little curlies at their ends are called by their family name: *serif fonts.* The narrow lines of the serifs on these fonts can *buzz* (flicker) or disappear on a television (at least at smaller font sizes). For example, the *e* may look like a *c* or an *o. Sans serif* fonts, such as Arial, Helvetica, and Futura, don't have these serifs (*sans* means without); therefore, these fonts are easier to read on a TV. For easy readability, stay with the sans serif family of fonts. In fact, a proverbial Cult of Helvetica exists in the television business. This cult is made up of people who use nothing but endless variations on the Helvetica font. Hey, it works!

Text can look bad on a TV but good on a computer

TVs and computer screens (both monitors and LCDs) work differently. Standard NTSC video images, the video signal that's used for North America (it's PAL in Europe), are made up of horizontal lines *(scan lines)* that are drawn across a screen at a very high rate of speed. Scan lines create a video frame on the screen about every ⅟₃₀th of a second. (Technically, the frame rate for NTSC video is 29.97 frames per second.)

When a computer displays an NTSC image, it shows all the scan lines that make up a frame of video together — in one fell swoop. When a television set shows an NTSC video frame, however, it creates the frame by quickly displaying two semiframes, called *fields;* the TV flashes one field for ⅟₆₀th of a second and then flashes the next field for ⅟₆₀th of a second. Each of these two fields that make up a frame are slightly different. One shows only the odd-numbered scan

lines that make up an image (lines 1, 3, 5, and so on), and the other shows the even-numbered lines (2, 4, 6, and so on). These two fields are said to be *interlaced;* it's like their even- and odd-numbered scan lines are laced or meshed together to create an image. Your TV flashes these two fields so quickly that your eye and brain can't tell the difference and accepts them as one frame.

In fact, these two interlaced frames don't match up perfectly. The brightness and position of the lines vary slightly, which isn't a problem when the screen displays a large object. A thin line, however, which is what small text is made up of, doesn't fare so well. Because of those fields, small text can appear to vibrate or buzz, especially in the case of a light vertical line on a dark background.

Using textures and colors sparingly

As you can see, Final Cut Pro and LiveType give you the capability to do some amazing things with a font typeface, such as create bizarre shapes or apply colored, patterned textures to the lines that make up a font. (You can also use LiveType to make fancy, animated type for your videos.) However, when these effects are viewed on a TV, you can run into the same buzzing and legibility problems that occur with a serif font: Thin, precise lines may fuzz out, bright vibrant colors may buzz, and darker colors may seem to disappear when they're superimposed over video that's also on the darker side. The key, again, is to view the final output on a TV monitor so that you know that you're safe!

To avoid flickering artwork on final video output, avoid using artwork with lines thinner than 1 pixel. If you're using Adobe Photoshop or Illustrator files, be sure to make the lines in the artwork about 2 to 3 pixels thick.

Getting Started with a Text Generator

The first step to building a simple text title is to select a text generator for the text clip. In Final Cut Pro, a *text generator* is the main tool for creating text. A generator is just like any effect, except that unlike an effect, which can be applied only to a clip, Final Cut Pro treats the generator like a clip. Final Cut Pro can add the generator to the Timeline like any other media you have.

Final Cut Pro offers a number of text generators that do different things, such as create static text and create scrolling or crawling text. I cover those topics shortly, but the important thing to know now is that you can select a text generator in one of the following ways:

✔ **Generator pop-up menu:** You can choose a text generator from the generator pop-up menu that's in the lower-right corner of the Viewer window (see Figure 13-1). When you make your choice, the text generator you choose opens into the Viewer (like any other clip opens into the Viewer), and you can then edit the text.

You can also find text generators in the Effects tab.

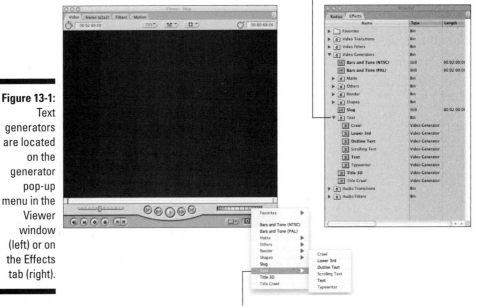

Figure 13-1: Text generators are located on the generator pop-up menu in the Viewer window (left) or on the Effects tab (right).

Select a generator from the Text submenu.

✔ **Effects tab:** Alternatively, you can locate the text generators on the Effects tab of the Browser. Click the Video Generators bin to open it, and in the Text bin, double-click the text generator of your choice to open it in the Viewer. (You can also drag the text generator from the Browser's Effects tab directly into the Viewer, and then edit the generator's text.)

Creating Text with Final Cut Pro

The best way to get a feel for how to create text is to look at the process from start to finish. This section explains how to choose the most common Final Cut Pro generator, open it in the Viewer, and use the Viewer Controls tab to tweak the text to your liking. I then describe how to apply the text to the Timeline in two different ways so that the text appears over a solid-colored background (good for opening title cards) or is superimposed over a clip of video (good for captions and subtitles, for instance).

If you mess up any of these steps, don't worry about it! You can always undo an action by pressing ⌘+Z.

Creating text and adding it to a video

The following steps use the Final Cut Pro generator called Text, which is the quickest, easiest way to get basic, static text up on the screen. However, these steps work the same way if you want to apply other generators, which I look at in the section "Touring the Text Generators" later in this chapter.

1. **Open the Viewer window by choosing Window⇨Viewer from the main menu.**

   You can also press ⌘+1 to open the Viewer.

2. **Click the Effects tab in the Browser window.**

3. **Twirl down the small triangle next to the Video Generators bin, and open the Text sub-bin, which contains the text generators.**

4. **Double-click the generator named Text (which looks like a small clip with some color bars on it) to open it in the Viewer.**

   After you open the Text text generator in the Viewer, you can see white text that reads SAMPLE TEXT on the Viewer's Video tab; the Viewer window also sports a new tab titled Controls.

5. **Drag the Viewer Controls tab outside the Viewer so that it opens in its own window (the Control tab, which is originally a part of the Viewer window, is shown in Figure 13-2).**

This new Controls tab window lets you type text and edit it, but the Video tab in the Viewer is where you see what the text actually looks like while you finesse it. By dragging the Controls tab outside the Viewer (so that it's in its own window), you can tweak the text and see it displayed in the Viewer's Video tab at the same time.

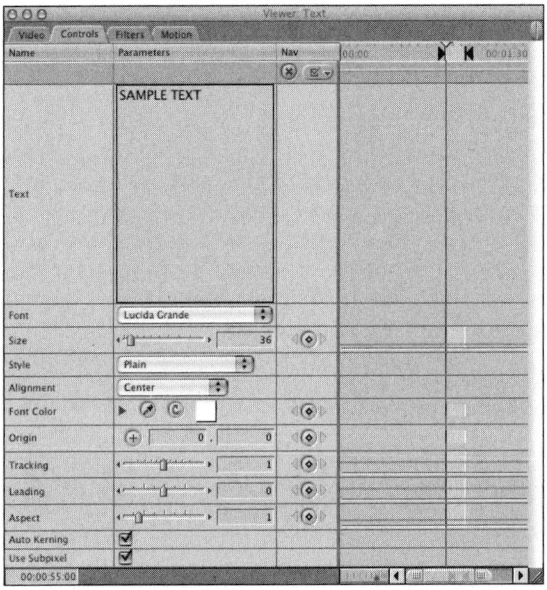

Figure 13-2: You can change attributes for the Text text generator on the Controls tab in the Viewer window.

6. **On the Controls tab (now in its own window), replace** SAMPLE TEXT **and make changes to your text.**

   To do so, highlight SAMPLE TEXT in the Text field on the Controls tab window and replace it with your own text. For example, you may want to type **The End**.

7. **Tweak the other settings on the Controls tab, if you want.**

   The other settings in the Text text generator Controls tab work like a basic word processor. For example, you can change the font by using the Font pop-up menu. You can also change the location where your text appears on-screen by clicking the Origins cross hair in the Controls tab. Your mouse pointer becomes a cross-hair symbol, and you can then click anywhere in the Viewer window to reposition your text at that spot. See the section "Understanding the options on the Controls tab," later in this chapter, for details on modifying these settings and many more.

Unfortunately, the Achilles heel of the standard Final Cut Pro Text text generator is that it doesn't let you apply different settings to different parts of the text. All the text has to be the same font, size, and style. For more advanced text effects, check out the LiveType application, in the section "Creating Titles with LiveType," later in this chapter.

When you make changes, you should see them reflected in the Viewer Video tab. If not, click the Viewer window once, and this should wake it up so that it shows changes while you make them. Then go back to the Controls tab window and tweak away!

8. Change the duration of the generator's text.

By default, all generators create a clip of text that lasts for 10 seconds (after you add the generator's text to your Timeline). To change this setting, highlight the timecode in the Duration field (located in the upper-left corner of the Viewer Video tab) and type a new duration, such as **5:00** for a duration of 5 seconds. Of course, after you place your text on the Timeline, you can also adjust the text clip's length by dragging the clip's edges, just like any other media clip.

9. Move the generator's text to the Timeline to superimpose it over an existing video clip or to make the text appear over a black background, as follows:

- **Superimposed over video:** To superimpose the text clip over a video clip (for example, to display the name of a person who is currently on camera), first move your video clip to the Timeline, making sure that the Timeline playhead is over this clip. Next, drag the generator's text from the Viewer to the Canvas window, and then select the Superimpose option from the Edit Overlay that appears over the Canvas. The Superimpose edit places the text in a new video track, above your video clip. What's more, Final Cut Pro automatically adjusts the duration of your text to match that of the underlying video clip. Figure 13-3 shows a text clip superimposed in the Timeline over a video clip.

- **Appearing over a black background:** If you want the text to appear over a black background (for instance, if you're designing an opening title card), you can drag the text from the Viewer Video tab down to a video track in the Timeline.

10. If necessary, render the text and play it on the Timeline.

If Final Cut Pro is set up for real-time previews of effects (see Bonus Chapter 1 on this book's CD for more details), you don't have to render the text to play it. If you see a thin, red bar drawn over the text generator clip in the Timeline, the text clip needs rendering. Select the text generator clip on the Timeline, and then choose Sequence⇨Render⇨Both from the main menu. After Final Cut Pro completes the rendering, place the playhead just before the text generator clip in the Timeline and press the spacebar to play through the text.

Figure 13-3:
When placed on top of another clip on the Timeline, the text generator clip is superimposed on the clip beneath it on the Timeline (in this example, a plain-colored background).

If Final Cut Pro is set up to show real-time previews of text without rendering, the Timeline shows a thin, green bar over the text clip. The text quality you see playing from the Timeline may seem a bit soft or otherwise rough because Final Cut Pro is showing you a lower-resolution preview of the text. When you finally print the movie to tape or export it to a QuickTime digital file (see Chapters 17 and 18), Final Cut Pro renders the text. To see how clearly the text clip appears when it's rendered, select it on the Timeline and choose Sequence⇨Render⇨Both.

11. **Make further adjustments to the text generator by double-clicking it on the Timeline.**

    Like any clip, the generator opens in the Viewer window, and you can use its now-familiar Controls tab to make tweaks.

After altering any of the text generators, you can drag the text from the Viewer Video tab back to the Browser and rename it in the same way you would rename any old clip. (This way, you have a copy of the clip to apply elsewhere in the project.) Later, you can drag this text as many times as you like into the Timeline. This approach is handy when you need to reuse the same title more than once.

Understanding the options on the Controls tab

After you open any text generator in the Viewer window (see a rundown of the different generators in the section "Touring the text generators," later in this chapter), the Controls tab appears in the Viewer. On the Controls tab, you can find the various options you can tweak for that text generator.

Discussing each setting for every text generator is beyond the scope of a *For Dummies* book, but that's okay because many of the controls are common among all the generators, and they're pretty intuitive as well. The following list outlines some of the most common settings you see when you're using the Final Cut Pro text generators:

- **Text:** The Text pane in all text generators contains the text SAMPLE TEXT by default. To add your own text, highlight the default text and then type the new text you require. Some text generators, such as Lower 3rd, have two separate areas for text entry: one for the top line and one for the bottom.

- **Font:** Select the font from the drop-down list. Final Cut Pro uses all the TrueType fonts that are loaded in your system. (Again, if you have Adobe PostScript fonts installed on your Mac, you can't use 'em in Final Cut Pro. Sorry.) After you select a font from this list, the Text pane updates the font to show you what the font looks like.

- **Size:** To select the font size, click in the Size text box and then type the size (in points). You can also use the slider to change the font size.

- **Style:** Use the drop-down list to select the style that works for your project. Options include Plain, Bold, Italic, and Bold/Italic. Italicizing a font is generally not a good idea for video because it can create flickering on the screen.

- **Color:** The Color pane offers really cool features, as you can tell by the detail of the color options shown in Figure 13-4. (Refer to Figure 13-2 to see where the Color pane is on the Controls tab.) For most video work, you should avoid highly saturated colors, particularly bright yellow or red. These colors tend to bleed and do not look very good when played back on a television or video monitor.

    - **Eyedropper:** The Eyedropper button is right next to the small drop-down triangle. Clicking the Eyedropper button changes the cursor to an eyedropper. Click anywhere in the Canvas window with this Eyedropper tool to select any color you like from the video that's displayed in the Canvas. Presto! The color selection is now in the color swatch to the right of the Eyedropper button back on the Controls tab. And Final Cut Pro applies this selection to the text.

Click triangle to reveal HSB sliders.

Eyedropper for color selection

Hue direction

Figure 13-4:
The Font
Color pane
on the
Controls tab.

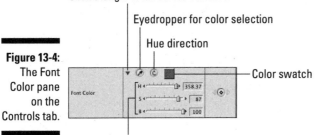

Color swatch

HSB sliders for text color

You have the following ways to select the color of your text:

- **Color Picker:** Click the small, square color swatch that is located to the right of the Eyedropper tool, and the Color Picker wheel opens. The Color Picker displays many small squares of various colors. You can click any color to select it. The Color Picker also displays the RGB values for the selected color. (*RGB values* are numeric descriptions of color that relate to the amounts of red, green, and blue in that color.) You can modify any of the preset colors by fiddling with their values. If you happen to know the values for the color you want, you can type them in the Color Picker. When you're finished working in the Color Picker, click OK to close it.

- **Hue, Saturation, Brightness:** Not enough options for you yet? Click the small triangle text to the Eyedropper tool, and down drops a menu with the HSB sliders. The *H* stands for hue (or tint), which changes the actual color, *S* is for saturation (the intensity of a color), and *B* is for brightness. Changing these sliders changes the color of the small color swatch and gives you direct feedback about your color choices. Close the menu by clicking the triangle.

✔ **Spacing or Tracking:** *Spacing* refers to the space between the letters. When you drag the slider to the right, the spacing between the letters in a word increases. Be careful, however, because you don't want to move the slider so far that your audience can no longer make sense of the words that are crawling across the screen. Note that for tight spacing, you can type negative numbers in the text box to the right of the slider. However, some headline fonts bunch up when you use negative values.

✔ **Leading:** Leading controls the space between lines of text. You can type a percentage or use the slider to affect this setting. The higher the percentage, the bigger the space between lines of text.

✔ **Origin or Center:** You can precisely set where text appears on-screen (lower-right corner, upper-left, and so on). Click the cross hair in the Controls tab, and the mouse pointer becomes a cross-hair symbol. Click the mouse anywhere in the Viewer Video tab (where you can see your text) to position the text at that point. (Final Cut Pro centers your text at the point.) You can also offset text horizontally and vertically, respectively, by typing values (positive and negative) in the two text boxes to the right of the Origin cross hair.

✔ **Location:** You can choose where you want the text to appear on-screen. The higher the number, the lower the text is placed on the screen.

✔ **Direction:** In the case of a Crawl generator, select either Left or Right from the drop-down list. Left means that the crawl heads for the left side of the screen, which is almost always the best option. A crawl that heads right makes your audience go nuts. In the case of a Scroll, the choices in the Direction menu are Up and Down, which indicate whether the text scrolls up or down.

✔ **Auto Kerning:** Kinda sounds like the name of a World War I field general, doesn't it? When you turn on the Auto Kerning feature by selecting this check box, the general lines up the characters in an automatic and precise way so that they're all nice and tidy. Some fonts don't respond well to the general's commands, so sometimes you may just want to send him packing.

Note that the Auto Kerning setting affects the Spacing setting as well. If you have the Auto Kerning setting selected, you can use the Spacing slider. Turning off the Auto Kerning setting causes the font to use its default spacing, and the Spacing slider has no effect.

More handy tips about text generators

Use video filters. You can apply any of the Final Cut Pro video filters to a text generator. (For instance, you may add a Wind Blur filter to text to make it seem out of focus.) See Chapter 14 for more about filters and how to apply them to clips, including generators, because hey! they're clips, too.

Animate text. You can animate text (make it grow bigger and smaller or move all over the place) by using some settings that are found in the Final Cut Pro Motion tab and its motion keyframes. See Chapter 15 for how to animate clips, including the text generators.

Use only TrueType fonts. Final Cut Pro works only with fonts in the TrueType format (unless you're using the LiveType application, which has its own format). Mac OS X already ships with a lot of TrueType fonts built in, but the thousands of fonts that are in the PostScript format (also known as Type 1) don't work. The good news is that if you have a PostScript font that you just have to use, you can get a shareware program, such as TransType (www.fontlab.com), that can convert fonts from one format to another (even between Macs and PCs).

Touring the text generators

Again, Final Cut Pro offers a number of text generators with different characteristics, purposes, and features to appreciate (and some hazards to watch out for as well). Some of these may be handy; you may never touch others. The following sections give you a rundown of all the text generators that are available in Final Cut Pro and describe their features and benefits.

Crawl

The Crawl text generator in Final Cut Pro produces a line of text that moves horizontally across the screen. It emerges like a ticker tape from the side of the screen. In this generator, you can also select the font, size, style, spacing, color, and vertical location of the text. More details are as follows:

- ✓ **Typical use:** Having text crawl is a common practice on TV news programs to warn viewers of breaking news. This consists of just a single line of text crawling across the bottom of the screen from right to left.

- ✓ **Feature notes:** You can do virtually anything with the Crawl text generator, including all the usual text variations. You can also use it with the myriad of filters, such as Drop Shadow and Blur.

If you installed the Boris Calligraphy generators from your Final Cut Pro CD, you also have a supercharged text crawl generator available called Title Crawl. It's better than the standard Final Cut Pro Crawl text generator in that you can apply a deflicker treatment to text, and you can easily set a mask that lets the text crawl across only part of the screen rather than the whole thing. The Boris generator also enables you to set a Blend value, which makes text appear to gently fade in and fade out while it crawls on and off the screen.

Lower 3rd

As the name of this text generator suggests, it enables you to draw two lines of text in the lower-third portion of the screen. As in most other text generators, you can select all aspects of the type, including the font, style, size, tracking, and color. More details are as follows:

- ✓ **Typical use:** This text generator displays text that identifies the name and organization of a news-feature personality or interviewees in a documentary. This is a common device that is used during news shows in which an interviewee is being identified. Of course, as an alternative, you could also use another text generator and simply change its Origin value to position it anywhere on-screen.

- ✓ **Feature notes:** Using a bit of a drop shadow when using this text effect can make the text stand out from the background image. In fact, you should add a drop shadow to any text you create, unless you're using white text over a black background.

Outline Text

The Outline Text text generator in Final Cut Pro creates an outline around the letters; for example, you can create black text with a white outline or vice versa. This generator dresses the text for greater on-screen visibility. More details are as follows:

- **Typical use:** Outlining makes text easier to read over a busy background.

- **Feature notes:** The Outline Text text generator has the basic features of text-editing software, such as changing the font, the size, and so on. These features make Final Cut Pro a tool of choice for creating outlined text. The Final Cut Pro sliders and other tools enable you to create an outline text clip quickly. Best of all, clip controls for text and line graphics enable you to fill either the text or the outline with an image of a clip you apply, not just a solid color.

Scrolling Text

The Scrolling Text text generator creates titles that run from bottom to top, as though on a scroll. You can also flip-flop them to run from the top down. More details are as follows:

- **Typical use:** Scrolling is commonly used for displaying credits at the end of a video.

- **Feature notes:** The length of the clip to which you apply this text effect determines how fast the text goes by. When you have long text credits but the generator you place on the Timeline is only a few seconds long, the credits flash by. When you have only a few text credits but the credit's generator lasts a minute on the Timeline, the credits go by slowly. You have to experiment with the amount of text and the length of the text's clip before you find what works in your project. Layout, spacing, type style, font, and even the color influence the effectiveness and legibility of the scroll. You have control over all these and more in this Final Cut Pro text generator. You can also try slowing or speeding the scroll up a little bit to compensate for the flicker.

Text

We cover this generator earlier in this chapter, so you're probably familiar with it. For starters, the Text text generator creates static text in the center of the screen. (You can adjust the generator's Origin value to later move the text to anywhere else in the screen.) Like a full-featured word processor or a good drawing program, this text generator enables you to control virtually everything about the text, such as the font, size, and color. The only real limitation is that you can't mix and match fonts, sizes, or styles together — any settings you make affect all the text in the generator. If this text generator is too limiting, you can try using an application like BorisFX or the LiveType application, which is discussed in the section "Creating Titles with LiveType," later in this chapter. Boris' title tools are superior to many titles created with the Final Cut Pro built-in titling tools. In fact, you can install the BorisFX tools (which are included on the Final Cut Pro install disks) and use them exclusively in place of the text generated by Final Cut Pro.

More details on text generators are as follows:

- ✔ **Typical use:** The Text text generator creates text on-screen between scenes, like in those reruns of *Law & Order* or *The X-Files*.

- ✔ **Feature notes:** You can create beautiful, detailed text by using the Subpixel feature. (Refer to Figure 13-2 to see this setting on the Controls tab.) The Subpixel feature in this text generator calculates the text drawing down to a minute and refined (hence, *subpixel*) level. This type of calculation is important if the text needs a polished, refined look. The text takes longer to render when the Subpixel feature is enabled, but it's worth it. Don't miss the Use Subpixel check box, which is at the bottom of the Controls tab (and easy to overlook). The default view leaves the check box hidden at the bottom of the Controls tab.

Typewriter

Although typewriters have become boat anchors and doorstops for most people, they're still the perfect metaphor for words that are presented one letter at a time. That's what this little generator does; it creates one letter at a time any way you want. More details are as follows:

- ✔ **Typical use:** This text generator mimics an old Teletype machine by displaying one letter at a time on the screen or by splattering letters and words in a wave. Maybe you're making a *film noir* detective film set in 1939 Los Angeles, and you want to indicate the time and place in a style that's evocative of the period. You can do this with the Typewriter text generator. Just keep in mind that getting carried away with this generator can kill readability.

- ✔ **Feature notes:** The Typewriter text generator defaults to a timing of 10 seconds, which means that the text you type into the generator takes 10 seconds to type onto the screen. Be aware that when you first apply this generator, you don't see any text. To see the text move across the screen, you have to play the effect. Press the spacebar to play the Typewriter text generator in the Viewer window.

In some instances, you may want to start collecting your favorite titles so that you can easily apply the same kind of title to different projects. Start by creating a new Final Cut Pro project, and name it something like *Favorite Titles*. Now, whenever you generate a title that you may want to save for later use, copy and paste the title from the Timeline into your new Favorite Titles project. (You can paste it into the Browser window of this new project and organize the collection of titles into bins.) This way, when you decide to use a favorite title, you can just open this Favorite Titles project and then copy and paste the desired title clip into the new project you're working on. (Again, you can paste into the new project's Browser window or straight to its Timeline.)

Creating titles on colored backgrounds

If you add a text generator to the Timeline without superimposing it on another clip, the text appears against a black background (as shown earlier, on the left side of Figure 13-3). To change the color of the text's background, you can use another generator, named Color, to create a *matte,* as follows:

1. **Open the Effects window.**

   You can choose Windows⇨Effects from the main menu or click the Effects tab in the Browser window.

2. **Open the Video Generators bin, and then open the Matte sub-bin.**

3. **Double-click the generator called Color to open it in the Viewer.**

4. **Set the generator color to the color you want to use as the background for your text.**

   Click the Viewer Controls tab, and use the color controls to set the color you want.

5. **Move the generator from the Viewer to the Timeline.**

   Clicking the Viewer Video tab and then dragging the generator directly to the Timeline is a quick approach. By doing this, you're creating a colored matte on the Timeline. (The matte displays just a single color on the screen.)

6. **Move a text clip (containing the title you want) to a track that's directly above the matte you just placed on the Timeline.**

   You're basically superimposing the title on top of the colored matte. Refer to the right side of Figure 13-3 to see how two clips look on the Timeline. Make sure that the text uses a color that works well with the color of the matte. You can change the text color by following the steps I outline in the section "Understanding the options on the Controls tab," earlier in this chapter.

7. **If necessary, render the two clips on the Timeline to see how they look.**

   Select one of the clips, and then choose Sequence⇨Render⇨Both from the main menu.

Rather than superimpose the text over a solid-color matte generator, you could use a different generator, such as Gradient or Custom Gradient, to create colored backgrounds that involve a range of custom colors rather than just one solid color. You can find these generators in the Final Cut Pro Effects window by going to the Video Generators bin and then looking in the nested Render bin.

Practicing safe text

Home televisions use a cathode ray tube to display the images of a video. These tubes have a slight overscan (approximately 10 to 15 percent), where certain items that are closer to the edges are cropped off and are not seen by the viewer. The overscan on televisions varies from one TV to another. Over the years, engineers have come up with a safety-area grid, which assures editors that their text isn't cropped off on some TVs.

The safety-area grids, called Title Safe and Action Safe, are available to you via the Final Cut Pro overlays. To select an overlay, click the Video tab in the Viewer. Next, choose View⇨Show Overlays (so that the feature is turned on), and then choose View⇨Show Title Safe so that that menu option is on, too. You see two aqua-colored rectangles in the Viewer window. The inner rectangle is the Title Safe grid; don't lay any text outside the edge of this inner rectangle. The outer rectangle is the Action Safe grid; don't place any action of importance outside the outer rectangle. In short, when shooting a video, don't place a critical element outside the Action Safe grid; otherwise, many home viewers may never see the critical element.

When laying out titles in Final Cut Pro, be sure to have these overlays turned on and make sure that no text is placed outside the Title Safe grid.

One more thing: If you like working with Title Safe overlays, you can also apply them to the Canvas window. Just select the Canvas, and follow the steps I outline earlier in this chapter to turn on the overlays.

Creating Titles with LiveType

Since the introduction of Final Cut Pro 4 (the precursor to HD), you have not only the capabilities of quite a competent video editor and text generator, but also some new applications to make your projects even better. LiveType is one of these new applications that ships with Final Cut Pro 4 (and HD), and it's definitely worth checking out. In fact, you may find it so addictive that you wouldn't consider using any other application (including plain-old Final Cut Pro) to create your video's titles!

What exactly is LiveType? Well, LiveType is a complete text-generation and -animation program that uses a new kind of cool "motion" text called LiveFonts. Now, rather than select a typically static font, you can choose from a wide range of font sets that produce interesting movements and fun animations, or you can even create your own font using its FontMaker utility. Starting with one of the default sets, you can customize a default font to suit the needs of your project, or you can assemble your own animation for manipulating one of your old system fonts or graphic images. For example, you could import a custom background, choose the Times font, apply a shimmering gold surface to it, and then warp it to make it move along a path you define. The number of things you can do with your text is seemingly limitless! Hopefully, this type of text-creation package will catch on and other companies will continue to add to its already large variety of styles and presets.

In this section, I demonstrate how to use LiveType (see Figure 13-5) to create a simple text animation using a few of the presets included with the application. Although this book cannot possibly cover the entire range of capabilities in this full-featured program (I already have my hands full with Final Cut Pro!), in the next section, I demonstrate the range of features that are available in this powerful and incredibly fun application. By using the following steps as a guideline for future exploration (and by consulting the Help menu as necessary), you can create text and titles for your videos that are sure to impress your friends and maybe even a few clients.

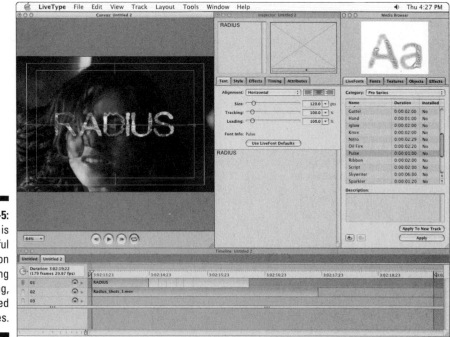

Figure 13-5: LiveType is a useful application for creating exciting, animated titles.

Exporting a movie from Final Cut Pro to use with LiveType

If you want to use a video clip you created in Final Cut Pro as the background for a title sequence created in the LiveType application, you first need to export a movie from Final Cut Pro. This is easy to do by following the steps below:

1. **Select the clip or sequence you want to export by clicking on it in the Timeline window.**

Your clip or sequence must already be added to the Timeline for this export function to work. If you don't already have a clip or sequence added to the Timeline, you can do so by double-clicking a sequence in the Browser or dragging a clip directly to the Timeline or Canvas window. (You can add a clip to the Timeline in Final Cut Pro in a number of ways, as discussed in earlier chapters of this book — just choose the one that's most convenient for you!)

2. **Choose File⇨Export⇨For LiveType.**

3. **In the Save dialog box, choose a location for the video you're exporting.**

4. **Click Save to begin the export process.**

If your video hasn't been rendered, you may experience a longer wait while Final Cut Pro renders and writes the video and audio to your hard drive.

Using LiveType to create a new title

Ready to give LiveType a try? Just do the following:

1. **Locate the LiveType application on your hard drive, and click its icon to launch the application.**

2. **Choose File⇨New from the application's main menu to create a new project, or simply use the blank project that opens by default.**

You can use a template for your project by choosing File⇨Open Template. The Template Browser should open and present you with a few categories and a variety of existing templates. Select an option from the Category window and the Template window. You can also create a new template of your own by starting with a new project, making modifications, saving it, and making sure that the .ipr project file is in the appropriate location on your hard drive (`Library\Application Support\LiveType\Templates`).

3. **Choose Edit⇨Project Properties.**

The Project Properties window duly appears.

4. **Choose NTSC DV 3:2 (or another video standard, like PAL, depending on your country of origin) from the drop-down menu, at the top of the Project Properties window.**

The Project Properties window includes a variety of general settings for size, frame rate, quality, background color, and opacity as well as ruler and grid settings for layout. If you're using a preset, you can keep the preset or tailor the settings to meet your needs.

5. **Click OK to accept the new settings.**

6. **Choose File⇨Place Background Movie.**

The Open dialog box appears.

You use the movie clip you exported from Final Cut Pro as the background for your Live Type project (although you can use any video you want), and the Open dialog box is there to help you navigate to the clip you want.

7. **Use the Open dialog box to navigate to an appropriate movie file on your hard drive.**

   Select a video clip that you have previously created to add texture to your background. The clip can be a video specially designed for use in a title sequence, or it can be any video clip that is relevant to your project, such as a movie you exported from Final Cut Pro.

8. **In the Open dialog box, click Open to accept the choice of a background movie.**

9. **Create a new track in the LiveType Canvas window by choosing Track⇨New Text Track.**

   Although many users may use just one track of text in LiveType, you can create even more complex title sequences by using several tracks of text. Just perform this step again to create the text tracks you need for your project. After multiple text tracks have been added, you can follow the steps for creating individual tracks, and repeat them for each new text track you have.

10. **Click the LiveFonts tab in the LiveType Media Browser window to select an animated font for your project.**

    You can also click the Fonts tab to select a more standard font. One cool feature of LiveType is that you can also work with any PostScript or TrueType fonts you have on your system. In addition, the Fonts tab is useful when you decide that an animated font is too lively for your project or when you want to customize your own effect.

11. **Choose an appropriate font.**

12. **Click Apply to accept the selection.**

13. **Enter your text into the text-entry boxes at the bottom of the LiveType Inspector window.**

14. **Click the text track in the LiveType Canvas window or its Timeline to select the text track (it appears in both).**

    It's usually easiest to select the text track in the Timeline window at the bottom. Selecting text in the Canvas window can be tricky, because you often end up choosing individual letters rather than the entire track. To select an entire track in the Canvas window, click and drag the mouse to make a box around the track you want. Of course, selecting individual letters can be helpful for more advanced use of the application, which allows you to animate each letter separately rather than just as complete blocks of text.

15. **Adjust the formatting of your text in the LiveType Inspector window.**

    Several tabs are available in the Inspector window with settings for your text that you can modify. The main categories are Text, Style, Effects, Timing, and Attributes. Text includes basic font settings, such as alignment, size, tracking, and leading. Style lets you make adjustments to the shadows and outlines that surround your text as well as the color and amount of warp, which stretches the text. The Effects tab lists any effects you apply from the other Effects tab in the LiveType Media Browser window. (You can test these effects by clicking them in the Media Browser and adding them by dragging into the Canvas window.) Finally, Timing allows precise adjustments to speed and duration of the text track, and Attributes offers settings for the color, opacity, scale, and color of your text (to name a few).

16. **Stretch the text track in the LiveType Timeline window to modify the duration of the animation.**

    Grab the ends of the clip in the text track (it's similar to modifying the length of clips on the Final Cut Pro Timeline), and expand or contract the track to suit the length of your title sequence. Note the duration in the upper-left corner of the Timeline window. You can also move the text track around by clicking it and dragging it forward or backward on the Timeline.

17. **Press the Play button in the LiveType Canvas window to preview your project.**

    LiveType automatically generates a RAM preview, which can be pretty slow depending on the speed of your Mac and the amount of memory you have installed. To get just a general idea of the animation, you can refer to the small wireframe (the simple, wire-like outlines that represents an object or the placement of text) bounding boxes in the upper-right corner of the LiveType Inspector window, or you can generate a wireframe preview by choosing File⇨Render Preview⇨Wireframe. You can also render a preview movie by choosing File⇨Render Movie, which is a good way to check out a more complex animation that quickly eats up RAM.

18. **Choose File⇨Render Movie to output a finished version of your project.**

19. **Type a filename for your project in the Save As field of the Save dialog box.**

20. **Choose a location for your project on your hard drive.**

21. **Uncheck the Render Background radio button to create a video of your text sequence with an alpha channel in place of the background.**

    One outstanding feature of LiveType is its ability to render title sequences with alpha channels. By using alpha channels, which define a transparent layer, you can seamlessly composite your text over a track of video in Final Cut Pro. By unchecking the option to render a background along with your titles, you have more flexibility when working with the clip in Final Cut Pro. For instance, you could choose to replace the background with another video, or easily add other elements to the composite. Of course, if you're set with the video and text the way it is, you can select the Render Background option and still use the clip as part of a Final Cut Pro sequence.

22. **Click the Create New Movie File button.**

    If you have any missing program files, LiveType prompts you to insert the appropriate disc. After the project is rendered, it should open in a separate window so that you can view it. After you have rendered and output your project, you can import it to Final Cut Pro for inclusion in a Timeline sequence.

Although I have covered in this section a basic method for working with LiveType, many more capabilities are waiting to be explored. For example, you can add keyframes to animate your text, making it perform exactly as you want. Of course, you can also start by checking out all the fun LiveFont types and effects in the Media Browser window and then creating your own projects to use your favorites.

Using Titles and Text Created Outside Final Cut Pro

You can create titles and text in other programs, aside from LiveType, and import that text into Final Cut Pro. However, overlaying such text over video (where the video is shown behind the text) requires special considerations.

Many software packages are available that can help you design cool typeface treatments, and an entire library of books has been written on creating and manipulating images in these various programs. One product, Adobe Photoshop, is recognized as the leader in this field. This program lets you do some incredible things with typefaces (and logos, not to mention images and graphics of any sort) that you could never do with Final Cut Pro alone. The details of working in Photoshop are outside the scope of this book. Refer to *Photoshop 7 For Dummies,* by Deke McClelland and Barbara Obermeier (Wiley), for an excellent guide on the many features of Photoshop.

Working with Photoshop and Final Cut Pro

Adobe Photoshop and Final Cut Pro work well together, but they're still different applications. When you move between the two, you may experience some bumps along the way. Remember the following important points about creating files in Photoshop and then bringing them into Final Cut Pro:

- ✔ **Pixel type:** DV video(the Final Cut Pro native format) uses rectangular *pixels* — that is, tiny dots of light — to describe an image (remember that DV video uses 720 horizontal pixels and 480 vertical pixels to describe a frame of NTSC video), whereas photo and graphics programs, such as Photoshop, use square pixels. Even though you create an image in Photoshop that measures 720 × 480 pixels (perhaps to fill a full video frame), when you import the image into Final Cut Pro, therefore, it looks distorted because Final Cut Pro converts those 720 × 480 pixels into DV video's rectangular pixels (the image was initially designed with square pixels). Don't worry, though: A fix is available for this, and I discuss it in a moment.

- ✔ **Colors:** DV video doesn't work well with certain colors you may create in Photoshop, rendering those colors in a way that makes them appear too bright or washed out. Fortunately, Photoshop displays a yellow exclamation icon (!) in its Color Picker when the color you select exceeds the video spectrum that's safe for DV video. When selecting colors in Photoshop, avoid this warning by toning down the colors.

- ✔ **Editability:** Final Cut Pro can't change text and images that are imported into it from Photoshop (although it does a pretty good job of animating and reassembling layers). To edit the text and images, you must open the original files in Photoshop, edit, and then reimport them into Final Cut Pro.

Preparing Photoshop Text for Final Cut Pro

This section outlines how to prepare text files created in Adobe Photoshop that are headed for a DV video project in Final Cut Pro. As you go through these steps, bear in mind that the frame size for DV video is 720 × 480 pixels. But, in Adobe Photoshop, you need to start out working with an image size of 720 × 534 pixels. You need this odd size to prevent Photoshop images (which use those square pixels) from becoming distorted when you import them into Final Cut Pro (which, thanks to the DV video format, uses rectangular pixels).

The following list provides you with steps and tips for bringing text that was created in Photoshop into Final Cut Pro:

1. **Create the text as an image in Photoshop. (Refer to *Photoshop 7 For Dummies* if you need help.)**

   The image should have the following dimensions: a width of 720 pixels and a height of 534 pixels.

2. **When you're finished with your creation, save the file.**

Make sure that you save the file as a Photoshop file, with the .psd extension. In the Save As dialog box, you can choose Photoshop from the Format pop-up menu that appears.

3. **Make a copy with the same name as the original, and add *version 2* or *import* to the filename.**

You can make a copy by choosing File⇨Save As in Photoshop. By entering a name that's different from the original file, you're creating a copy. Again, make sure that you're saving the file as a Photoshop file with the .psd extension.

4. **Working with the image copy, choose Image⇨Image Size from the main menu.**

The Image Size dialog box opens.

5. **Deselect the Constrain Proportions check box.**

6. **In the Pixel Dimensions area, change the height from 534 pixels to 480 pixels.**

Remember these numbers; you need them every time you want to prepare a text in Adobe Photoshop for use in Final Cut Pro.

Figure 13-6 shows the Photoshop file before and after the height change. In the After state, the *O*s appear distorted, although importing them into Final Cut Pro corrects the distortion automatically.

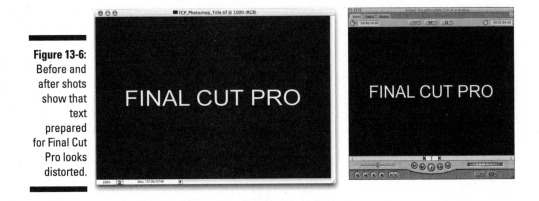

Figure 13-6: Before and after shots show that text prepared for Final Cut Pro looks distorted.

7. **Select Resample Image in the Image Size dialog box.**

Whoa! Someone flattened the image! Rest assured, though: That's just the way it should look now to look good in Final Cut Pro.

8. **To make sure that the colors in the Photoshop image look good in video, choose Filter⇨Video⇨NTSC.**

You can choose a PAL option if that's the standard in your country of origin, or stick with NTSC — which does a good job of limiting many dangerous colors.

9. **Save the file.**

   Again, make sure that the file is saved with a Photoshop extension (.psd). If not, do the Save As operation again to add this extension to the filename.

10. **Open the Final Cut Pro project that is to receive the Photoshop file.**

11. **In Final Cut Pro, choose File⇨Import⇨Files and then locate the Photoshop file.**

12. **In the Choose a File dialog box, select the Photoshop file and then click Choose.**

   The Photoshop file is imported into the Final Cut Pro Browser. Use this Photoshop still as a clip anywhere on the Timeline. Final Cut Pro automatically compensates for the distortion you created in the text, and the text appears correctly proportioned. However, one of the coolest features is that layered Photoshop graphics that are added to the Timeline in Final Cut Pro have each of their layers automatically placed on separate tracks. This makes it possible to animate and position your original graphic layers any way you want in Final Cut Pro, similar to working in After Effects or a similar compositing application. Final Cut Pro makes working with graphic layers almost as simple and fun as working with multiple video tracks.

Chapter 14

Special Effects with Filters and Color Correction

*I*t seems like someone has taken the "special" out of special effects these days: What was once strange and wonderful on the screen has become commonplace. For instance, applying a vast array of color filters and treatments to a video was once considered cutting-edge and required the services of an expensive postproduction shop. Now, you can do it all in spades — right from your desktop! Indeed, Final Cut Pro hands you a bag of tricks that would make Houdini green with envy.

In this chapter, I cover the video filters and other tools that are available to help you create special effects. You can think of a *filter* as an effect that modifies a clip in some way, such as adding a color or blur to it. You discover how to use filters to control the look, color, and consistency of a movie. You also acquire some tricks for enhancing or fixing the color in clips (to create a mood or to match the look of lighting from one shot to another).

In fact, the word *color* comes up a lot in this chapter. There's no doubt about it: Color is a deep subject, and some people spend their entire lives learning about it. One cool feature of Final Cut Pro is that it offers tools for controlling color at many levels without requiring a Ph.D. on the subject. Yet, as easy as the tools are to use, these same controls and tools can satisfy the expert as well as the novice. Try out the steps in this chapter on a clip or two, and play with your new magic wands. Color has never been so easy or just plain fun to control.

To see your special effects, Final Cut may require you to render them in advance, depending on your Mac hardware. I give you the steps necessary for rendering out these effects when necessary, but, if Final Cut doesn't successfully render what you tell it to, see Bonus Chapter 1 on this book's companion Web site for rendering-related troubleshooting tips (The address for this site is in this book's Introduction.)

Shooting Video with Effects in Mind

Before shooting video for a project, try to plan ahead. Think about the look you want the movie to have before you ever take out your trusty camera. If you're doing an artsy short in *film noir* (that dark, shadowy look that Alfred Hitchcock and others made so popular in the 1940s), high-contrast lighting and appropriate camera settings can do much more for the project than any filter in Final Cut Pro. If you want a high-contrast clip that emphasizes primary colors for an instructional video for children, for instance, make sure that you shoot with lots of light. Giving you a rundown of all the considerations for shooting footage is outside the scope of this book, but you can check out more information in *Digital Video For Dummies,* 3rd Edition, by Keith Underdahl (Wiley).

Special-effect video filters and controls in Final Cut Pro can do some amazing things, but they definitely have limits. Postproduction isn't the place for turning lead into gold. If the video is ugly to start with, it may be ugly after you edit it.

Making a Colored Clip Black and White

A great place to start with this whole color thing is getting rid of it. That's right — go black and white. Although many, if not most, cameras now offer the option to shoot in black and white, this option is rarely used. Why? The color shot contains so much information that you would be silly not to take advantage of it, even if you plan to drop the color in the postproduction process.

Why go black and white? Removing color is a way to give punch to a video, resurrect *film noir,* create a background for a color object or text, or simply "go retro." Going black and white is easy to do. Just follow these steps:

1. **In the Viewer window, open the clip you want to convert to black and white.**

   You can also double-click the clip in the Browser to load it into the Viewer.

2. **In the Browser window, click the Effects tab and then click the small triangle next to the Video Filters bin.**

3. **In the Video Filters bin, click the small triangle next to the Image Control bin to open it.**

   In the Image Control bin, you can find the Desaturate filter, as shown in Figure 14-1.

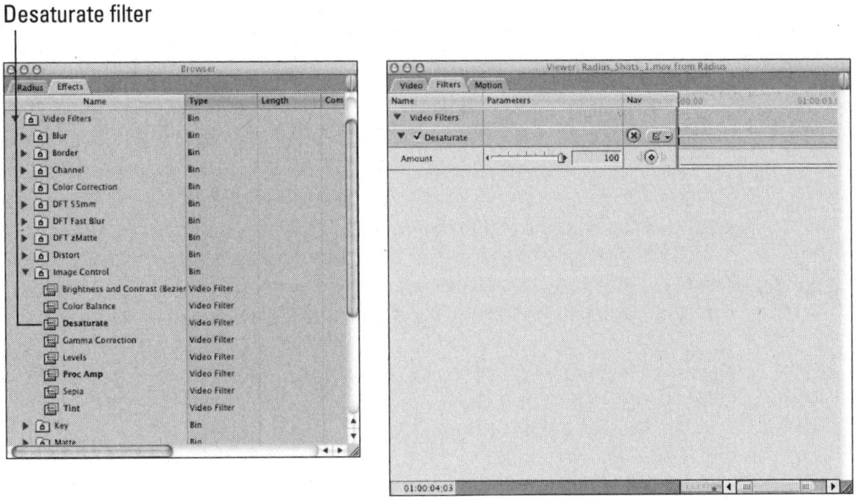

Desaturate filter

Figure 14-1: The Desaturate filter creates a black-and-white clip or sequence.

4. **Click and drag the Desaturate filter from the Browser to anywhere in the Viewer window.**

   The clip immediately becomes black and white because the Desaturate filter is applied at a 100 percent strength by default. To *desaturate* means to take away the color.

5. **Click the Filters tab in the Viewer window.**

   On the other hand, you can drag the Filters tab outside the Viewer window so that you can make adjustments to the filter while seeing the effects on the video clip in the Viewer window.

6. **Use the Amount slider (refer to Figure 14-1) to set the level of desaturation to your liking.**

   Placing the slider in the middle creates a value of 0, or no change. Dragging the slider to the left creates negative values and supersaturates the color in the clip. If you move the slider all the way to the right (and it has a numerical value of 100), all the color is removed and only a black-and-white image remains. Experiment with several values: Sometimes, just removing a little, but not all, of the color from an image can create a unique effect.

7. **Drag the clip from the Viewer to the Canvas window, and drop the clip on the Overwrite overlay, which appears over the Canvas window.**

   Final Cut Pro sends the clip to the Timeline. Alternatively, you can drag the clip from the Viewer to the Timeline if you feel comfortable with that approach.

8. **Select the clip on the Timeline, and choose Sequence⇨Render⇨Both.**

9. **After Final Cut Pro renders the clip, position the playhead just before the clip on the Timeline and press the spacebar to play the clip.**

Getting That Old, Grainy Video Look

Getting people's attention is hard in a media-crowded world. Not everyone or every project needs to go high-tech with videos that look like something from the 22nd century. Some projects make more sense looking old or oddly out of fashion. A video with a different look — if it fits the video and its message — can get the right kind of attention from its viewers.

Suppose that an old video you caught on cable TV really inspires you. How did the video get that gritty, grainy look? Who knows, really, but you can use the Noise generator in Final Cut Pro to get the same or similar effect. Just follow these steps:

1. **Drag a clip from the Browser to the Timeline into a video track.**

   (Refer to Chapter 7 if you need a refresher on how to put clips on the Timeline.)

2. **Click the Effects tab in the Browser window.**

3. **Click the triangle next to Video Generators to open this bin, and then click the triangle next to Render to open this bin.**

   In the Render bin, locate the Noise generator.

4. **Drag the Noise generator to the track that's above the clip on the Timeline.**

   Generators work just like clips in that you can place them directly on the Timeline.

5. **Drag the ends of the Noise generator so that the clip stretches out to cover the entire clip or sequence on the tracks beneath it, as shown in Figure 14-2.**

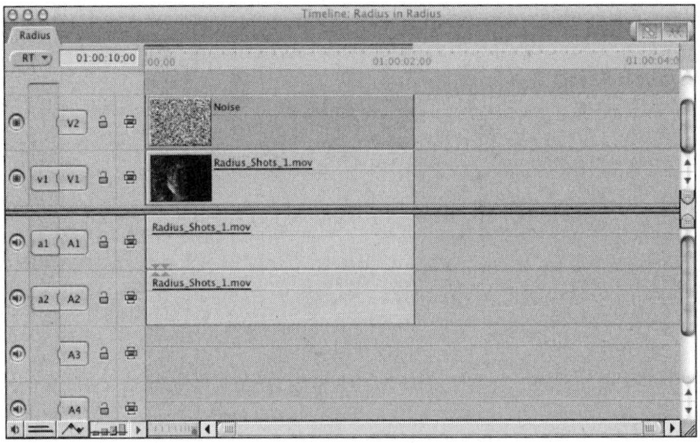

Figure 14-2:
Drag the
Noise
generator
from the
Effects tab
to the track
that's above
the clip on
the Timeline.

If the Noise generator on the Timeline track is so long that you have to scroll to find its start zand end points (which can be disorienting and a bit time consuming), go back to Step 3 and double-click the Noise generator from the Browser. Final Cut Pro opens the Noise generator in the Viewer window (like any other clip), and from there, you can set narrow In and Out points before dragging the generator to the Timeline.

6. **On the Timeline, drag the playhead over the Noise clip.**

   You see the Noise generator noise in the Canvas window.

7. **Double-click the Noise generator clip on the Timeline so that it loads into the Viewer window.**

8. **In the Viewer window, click the Motion tab and click the small triangle next to the Opacity setting.**

9. **Move the Opacity slider, as shown in Figure 14-3, to get the grainy look you want.**

   The Canvas window shows this effect as you move the Opacity slider. Keep moving the slider until Final Cut Pro generates the amount of grain you want.

10. **Select the Noise generator clip on the Timeline, and choose Sequence⇨Render⇨Both.**

11. **After Final Cut Pro completes the rendering process, move the playhead just before the clip on the Timeline and press the spacebar to play the clip.**

After the Noise generator is on the Timeline, a quicker way to adjust noise levels is to click the Overlays button (the button that looks like a bar graph), which is in the upper-left corner of the Timeline window (refer to Figure 14-2) and then simply drag the opacity line of the Noise clip up and down.

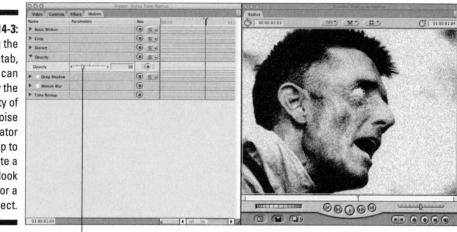

Figure 14-3:
By using the
Motion tab,
you can
modify the
opacity of
the Noise
generator
clip to
create a
grainy look
for a
project.

Opacity sliders

Changing Colors

Changing the colors in a clip can be very handy and easy. First, a note of caution: This section is *not* about color correction. You can find info on that topic later in this chapter. This section is about giving a colored look to a clip or a project and about shifting colors to match a particular look and feel. These tools give you the power to change the color of the sun (really). That washed-out, golden-autumn look in *O Brother, Where Art Thou?* isn't far out of reach. You can also make an ever-so-subtle change in a clip to warm it or cool it.

I discuss video generator matters and the RGB balance filters in this section. Later, in the section "Checking Out More Handy Filters," I tackle a third tool, the Tint filter, which can help you achieve the look you want.

Using mattes

An easy way to create a color change effect is to simply add a *filter,* which is something like a digital version of those tinted plastic color filters that you may have clamped over the lens of a 35mm camera. But, the Final Cut Pro filter is much easier to use, and you have all the colors of the rainbow at your disposal! In Final Cut Pro, a filter can be an effect that alters the clip in some way, such as adding a sepia tint or a glow to the clip. This type of filter is called a *matte.* Specifically, to place a glow over a particular clip, as though the subjects were in a kind of golden fog, follow these steps:

1. **Drag a clip from the Browser to a video track on the Timeline.**

2. **Click the Effects tab in the Browser window.**

3. **Click the small triangle for the Video Generators bin to open it, and then click the Matte triangle to open the Matte bin.**

4. **In the Matte bin, find the Color matte.**

5. **Drag the Color matte to the track that's above the clip on the Timeline.**

   Again, generators work just like normal clips on the Timeline.

6. **Drag the ends of the Color matte so that the matte clip stretches out to cover the entire clip on the track beneath it. (This is similar to Figure 14-2.)**

7. **On the Timeline, place the playhead anywhere on the Color matte so that you can preview the effect.**

   If you do this, you can later see in the Canvas window any changes you make to the Color matte.

8. **Double-click the Color matte on the Timeline, and then click the Controls tab in the Viewer window.**

9. **In the Color Parameters area of the Controls tab, click the triangle to reveal the color controls, as shown in Figure 14-4.**

Click the color swatch to access the Color Picker

Eyedropper tool

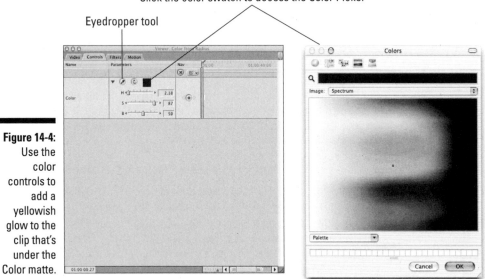

Figure 14-4:
Use the color controls to add a yellowish glow to the clip that's under the Color matte.

Final Cut Pro offers the following ways to select a color:

- **Color swatch:** You can click the small, square color swatch and select a yellowish color from the Color Picker selection box that pops up (refer to Figure 14-4).

- **Eyedropper tool:** You can click the Eyedropper tool. After the cursor turns into an eyedropper, you can click any color you like in the clip, as displayed in the Canvas window. The Color matte then picks up the color you selected with the Eyedropper tool.

- **Sliders:** You can use the sliders labeled *H, S,* and *B* to alter the hue, saturation, and brightness settings of a color. You can preview any changes you make by looking in the square color swatch above the sliders (refer to Figure 14-4). After you have settled on a color you like, it's applied to the Color matte.

10. **Click the Motion tab in the Viewer window, and click the small triangle next to Opacity.**

11. **Move the slider in the Opacity pane until the transparency of the Color matte is just right.**

    Note that when the playhead is located over the clips on the Timeline, the Canvas window shows you an update of the final color effect.

12. **Select the Color matte clip on the Timeline, and choose Sequence⇨ Render⇨Both.**

13. **After Final Cut Pro renders the clip, position the playhead just before the clips on the Timeline and press the spacebar to play the clip.**

Using the RGB Balance tool

Rather than use a low-opacity matte, you can change the color of any given part of the spectrum in the video by using the RGB Balance tool. The controls are precise, and the numbers next to the sliders let you track and record edits. To change color with the RGB Balance filter, follow these steps:

1. **Drag a clip from the Browser to a video track on the Timeline.**

2. **On the Timeline, drag the playhead anywhere on the clip so that you can later see a good preview of the effect in the Canvas.**

3. **Double-click the clip.**

   This step opens the clip in the Viewer window.

4. **Click the Filters tab in the Viewer window.**

5. **Click the Effects tab in the Browser window.**

6. **On the Effects tab, click the Video Filters bin to open it, and then click the Color Correction bin.**

7. **Find the RGB Balance filter in the Color Correction bin, and drag it onto the clip on the Timeline.**

You can avoid Steps 5 through 7 by choosing Effects⇨Video Filters⇨Color Correction from the menu bar and then selecting the RGB Balance filter. It's just another way to do things.

8. **On the Filters tab in the Viewer, use the RGB balance parameters to adjust the colors and thus achieve the look you want (see Figure 14-5).**

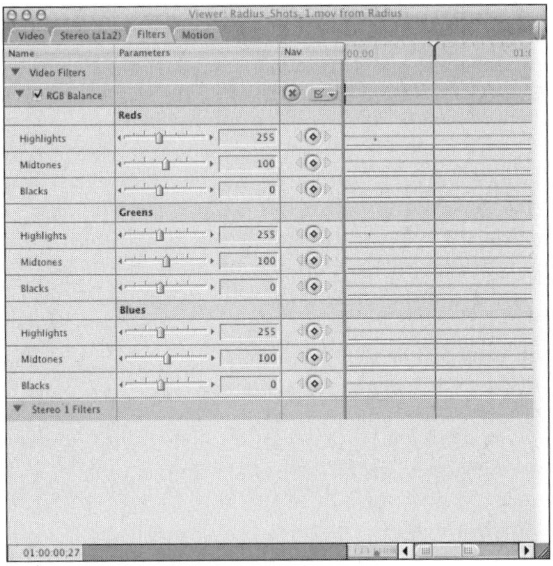

Figure 14-5: RGB color balance provides controls to change the red, green, and blue color balance in black, white, and midtone (gray) values.

Any video image is made up of three color channels: red (R), green (G), and blue (B). The red set of sliders, for instance, changes the amount of red in the highlights (whites), midtones (grays), and blacks of the image. So, you have individual control of the amount of R, G, or B in the highlights, midtones, and blacks. To create a golden glow, increase the highlights and midtones for both red and green. Red plus green equals yellow, and tweaking just the highlights makes the overall look lighter, giving the clip a sunny yellow feel.

The tiny color sliders can be a pain to use, but they have one redeeming feature: Those tiny arrows at the ends of each slider enable you to change the numeric color values one unit at a time. Use the numbers to keep track of where you were and where you are. If you make a mistake, use the tiny Reset button at the top (marked with a red X, as shown in Figure 14-5) to reset everything to the default settings.

9. **Select the clip on the Timeline, and choose Sequence⇨Render⇨Both.**

10. **After Final Cut Pro completes the rendering process, position the play-head just before the clip on the Timeline and press the spacebar to play and view the clip.**

If you have used Adobe Photoshop, you should feel right at home with the RGB balance controls. The RGB Balance tool in Final Cut Pro is, in many ways, identical to the Color Balance tool that's in Photoshop.

Working with Color-Correction Tools

Final Cut Pro gives you surprisingly powerful color-correction tools that were available only on very high-end editing systems (or from dedicated postpro-duction shops) only a few years ago. The Final Cut Pro Color Corrector filter, in particular, is helpful for improving the look of DV video. For instance, you can use the filter to lighten shots that are too dark and to change orange, blue, or green tints that were caused by shooting in lighting conditions that the DV camera wasn't expecting. (The white balance of a camera usually needs to be set for shooting in different lighting situations, such as sunny daylight, cloudy daylight, indoor light, and light cast by fluorescent lights that are in many offices.)

Keep in mind that the Final Cut Pro Color Corrector can't make poorly shot video look perfect. There's no substitute for knowing what you're doing with a videocamera. In other words, make sure that scenes have adequate light and are exposed properly, and anticipate the kind of light you're shooting in by adjusting the white balance of a camera. However, the Final Cut Pro Color Corrector can push "bad video" into "okay video" territory and can turn "okay video" into "polished video."

Before you start, you should view the output on a television or professional video monitor. (For the details on setting it up, refer to Chapter 2.) An RGB monitor or LCD display isn't the best device to base color corrections on (unless you expect the finished movie to be shown only on a computer — for instance, a video you may post only on your Web site).

Now you're ready to get started with some basic color correction. Just follow these steps:

1. **Drag a clip from the Browser to a video track on the Timeline.**

2. **Position the Timeline playhead anywhere on the clip so that you can see the clip in the Canvas window.**

3. **Select the clip on the Timeline, and apply the Color Corrector filter to it.**

   You can choose Effects⇨Video Filters⇨Color Correction⇨Color Corrector from the menu bar. Alternatively, you can find the filter on the Effects tab of the Browser window and drag it to your clip on the Timeline.

4. **Double-click the clip on the Timeline to open the clip in the Viewer.**

   A new Color Corrector tab appears in the Viewer window.

5. **In the Viewer window, click the Color Corrector tab.**

   The Color Corrector filter defaults to Visual view (as shown in Figure 14-6). If you find yourself in Numeric view (with just numbers and sliders), click the Visual button in the upper-left corner.

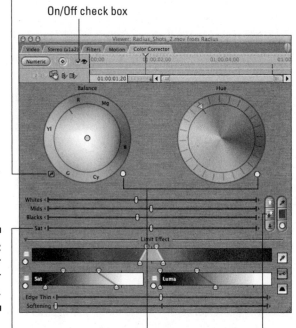

Select Auto Balance Color button

On/Off check box

Saturation slider   Reset buttons   Auto-Contrast button

Figure 14-6: The Color Corrector filter.

6. **Click the Auto Contrast button for the filter (refer to Figure 14-6).**

   This step maximizes the range from black to white in the clip, which is the starting point for any color correction for the clip. Notice that the Blacks, Mids, and Whites sliders automatically move to achieve the best overall luminance distribution in the image. An image is essentially made up of dark tones (blacks), light tones (whites), and tones in between (grays, or *midtones*).

   If a video clip seems dark, clicking Auto Contrast can make a big improvement, and you can then fine-tune the clip by further adjusting the Whites, Blacks, and Mids sliders. For instance, you may increase the Whites and Mids of a dark image. If the clip gets too washed out, increase the Blacks slider a bit to compensate.

You can quickly compare the corrections against the original, uncorrected image by selecting the On/Off check box for the filter (refer to Figure 14-6).

7. **Click the Select AutoBalance Color button.**

   This button looks like a tiny eyedropper next to the Balance color wheel.

   When you select this button, the pointer turns into an eyedropper when you place it over the Canvas or the Viewer window.

8. **In the Canvas or Viewer window, use the Eyedropper cursor to click an area of the picture that's supposed to be pure white.**

   You're looking for an object that *should* be pure white (or close) but may have a color tint because of poor lighting or white balance problems in the camera. Be careful not to select an overexposed area, such as a highlight or a white, blown-out light source. Instead, select a well-exposed surface.

   When you click the white in an image (or what you want to be white), the Color Corrector filter analyzes the RGB mix of colors in areas that share that color throughout the image and adjusts the center knob of the Color Balance wheel to offset the mix of colors that are tinting the whites.

   In most cases, you immediately see a change for the better in the whites. If they were green or bluish, they're closer to white after this step, even if they're not pure white.

9. **Tweak the Color Balance and Hue controls to make additional, small adjustments to color.**

   Both of these controls effectively let you change certain colors in an image into new ones. You can adjust the color balance by dragging the small circle in the middle of the Color Balance dial from the middle area toward a surrounding color, such as red, magenta, cyan, or green. To speed the dragging, hold down ⌘ while you drag across the colors. Whites become the color you drag toward.

   Similarly, you can change the *hue* (the color of an image) by dragging the Hue dial to a new color value.

   You probably don't make big adjustments with these tools (unless you're going for a completely unrealistic look in the color). They're more for nudging color a bit here and a bit there to give it a bit of punch or to soften it slightly.

   In any event, if you make some adjustments you don't like, you can reset any changes by clicking the Reset buttons, which are in the lower-right corners of the Color Balance and Hue controls (refer to Figure 14-6).

10. **Adjust the saturation by using the Saturation slider in the Color Corrector.**

You may want to adjust the saturation (which makes colors appear a bit more vibrant). I find it helpful in some cases — for instance, to bring out the red in someone's cheeks or to slightly brighten the color of a shirt or the blue of the sky. But, be subtle with these saturation adjustments. Otherwise, the scenes and subjects may appear to glow!

11. **To see how the newly color-corrected clip plays, select it on the Timeline, and choose Sequence⇨Render⇨Both. Then, after Final Cut Pro completes the rendering process, position the playhead just before the clip on the Timeline, and press the spacebar to play and view the clip.**

If you apply a color corrector to a clip and then decide not to use the filter, you can remove the filter from the clip. Switch the Color Corrector filter to Numeric mode (click Numeric in the upper-left corner of the Color Corrector tab), select the filter as it's listed in Video Filters, and press Delete.

You're probably wondering why, in the preceding steps, I didn't address the Mids controls (the slider in the center). To adjust the Midtones, you usually need a cinematographer's gray *chip chart,* which is a piece of cardboard with a neutral gray on it. If you didn't use a chip chart during the shooting process, leave the Mids controls alone in the Color Corrector.

Selecting and changing the color of an object

Although most people use color-correction tools to adjust the overall look of a video, these tools can be equally effective in altering the color of specific objects in a scene. This capability can be useful in a number of situations. Perhaps you just shot a commercial for a client that features a red car. Unfortunately, the client comes back to you a week later and says that she wants the car to be purple rather than red. Without adequate color-correction tools, you would have to reshoot the car, losing lots of time and money in the process. What should you do in this situation? Let Final Cut Pro come to the rescue! Using the Color Corrector filter, the Eyedropper tool, and a few careful adjustments, you can select a colored object and change it to any color your heart desires.

Follow these steps to select and change the color of an object with the Final Cut Pro Color Corrector filter:

1. **Drag a clip from the Browser to a video track on the Timeline.**

2. **Position the Timeline playhead anywhere on the clip so that you can see the clip in the Canvas window.**

3. **Select the clip on the Timeline, and apply the Color Corrector filter to it.**

   You can choose Effects⇨Video Filters⇨Color Correction⇨Color Corrector from the menu bar. Alternatively, you can find the filter on the Effects tab of the Browser window and drag the filter to your clip on the Timeline.

4. **Double-click the clip on the Timeline to open the clip in the Viewer.**

   A new Color Corrector tab appears in the Viewer window.

5. **In the Viewer window, click the Color Corrector tab.**

   The Color Corrector filter defaults to Visual view (refer to Figure 14-6). If you find yourself in Numeric view (with just numbers and sliders), click the Visual button in the upper-left corner.

6. **Click the eyedropper tool, under the Limit Effect area of the Color Corrector window (refer to Figure 14-6).**

   If the Limit Effect area isn't visible, click the arrow on the left side of the screen to twirl down this option.

7. **Click in the Canvas window the solid-color object you want to change.**

   Of course, it's easiest to choose an object with a unique color that's not used in other parts of the same clip. For instance, if you choose a green shirt in a scene that was shot in the woods, Final Cut Pro selects all similar colors in the clip, which means that some of the trees become part of your selection. To preview your selection, you can click the key-shaped button on the right side of the Color Corrector window to better inspect the areas of color you have selected. A black-and-white matted image makes it clear which areas are selected. White sections represent the color that was selected with the eyedropper tool, and the black sections represent those areas that are unselected and not affected by changes in color.

8. **Adjust the Color Selection, Saturation, Luminance, Edge Thin, and Softening controls to improve the precision of your selection.**

   Tweak the selection area of the object and color you have selected. The top set of handles under Limit Effect adjusts the overall color tolerance, the Saturation controls affect the amount of color in an image, and the Luminance controls affect the amount of brightness. Edge Thin and Softening affect the outline of the selected color area to make it more or less defined. A little experimentation can produce good results.

9. **Use the Hue wheel to select a new color, and watch the effect it has in the Canvas window.**

   The original color you selected changes to a different color.

Copying color-correction settings to other clips

After you have adjusted a master clip with the color-correction filters to look the way you want, you should adjust the look of other clips in your sequence to match the master clip. For instance, if you have dialogue in your movie between two actors, you probably shot multiple angles to cover the scene. Switching between these different shots reveals inconsistencies in color and lighting. That's why you would copy color-correction adjustment from a master shot to the other clips you edit. This is where the Copy Filter controls come into play.

Use the Copy Filter controls in the upper-left corner of the Color Corrector window (they look like arrows with the numbers 1 or 2 inside) to apply the same filter to other clips in your Timeline sequence, based on their relative positions from the clip you have selected. For instance, to apply the effect from the selected clip to a clip that comes next in your sequence, click the Copy Filter To 1 Forward button. To copy the filter that was applied two clips before your selected clip, press the Copy Filter From 2 Back button, for instance. Other options include Copy Filter To 2 Forward and Copy Filter From 1 Back.

Of course, you can just click and drag the Drag Filter button (the button in the upper-left corner that looks like a hand grabbing a clip) onto a clip on the Timeline to apply the current settings to it. If you have a long or complex sequence, copying filters can seriously reduce the headaches of making manual adjustments to every occurrence of a clip. To compare frames side by side, you can also use the Frame Viewer, which I discuss in the section "Comparing Results with the Frame Viewer," later in this chapter.

You can easily compare the color-correction effects that are applied to your clips by using keyboard shortcuts to jump among them. For instance, pressing Control+↑ temporarily moves the playhead one edit back to the preceding clip (until you release ↑), and Control+↓ moves the playhead ahead one edit to the next clip in your sequence. Other keyboard shortcuts are available for moving the playhead two edits back (Control+Shift+↑) and forward (Control+Shift+↓).

Fixing or Adjusting Exposures

Occasionally, you come across a situation in which you aren't happy about the exposure of some video you're working with. (*Exposure* refers to the range of bright to dark values in the image.) Perhaps the image is a bit too dark (see Figure 14-7) or too bright because the camera operator who shot it didn't do a good job of setting the exposure level for the given scene. On the other hand, the video exposure may look decent when viewed by itself, but when you try to mix it with footage taken from another camera, the two don't match. One camera may have recorded things a bit brighter than the other, which can be a bit jarring for viewers.

Figure 14-7:
An under-
exposed
shot: before
and after
treatment
in Final
Cut Pro.

Of course, Final Cut Pro can help you adjust the video exposure to help compensate for these headaches. With one obvious filter and another that's somewhat obscure, you can make serious strides in fixing problem video clips.

Be aware that extreme exposure problems can't be fixed. Glaring errors in exposure have to be prevented when you're shooting the video. For more information on how to regulate exposure while shooting, see *Digital Photography For Dummies,* 4th Edition, by Julie Adair King (Wiley).

Two effects filters can help you in this correction process: Proc Amp and Brightness and Contrast. Proc Amp, which sounds like the opening band at a rock concert, stands for *process amp*lifier. The Proc Amp filter enables you to adjust aspects of exposure during the editing process. (If you're a Photoshop user, you may notice that Proc Amp is similar to the Photoshop Adjust Hue/Saturation control.)

Follow this step-by-step guide to editing exposure levels in a project:

1. **Drag a clip from the Browser to a video track on the Timeline.**

2. **Position the Timeline playhead anywhere on the clip so that you can see the clip in the Canvas window.**

3. **Select the clip on the Timeline, and apply the Brightness and Contrast filter and the Proc Amp filter to it.**

You can apply the filters by choosing Effects⇨Video Filters⇨Image Control. Alternatively, you can find the filters on the Effects tab of the Browser window (in the Image Control bin) and drag them to the clip on the Timeline.

4. Double-click the clip on the Timeline to open it in the Viewer.

5. In the Viewer window, click the Filters tab.

You should now see the two filters — with accompanying controls — that you just applied to the clip on the Timeline (as shown in Figure 14-8).

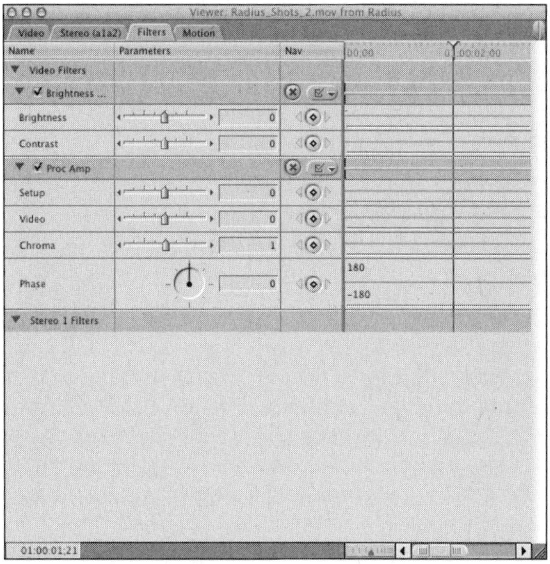

Figure 14-8: The Brightness and Contrast filter and the Proc Amp filter help you fix clips with exposure problems.

6. On the Filters tab, adjust each of the filters you just applied.

Move the filters' sliders or repeatedly click the small arrowheads that are at the end of each slider until you get the results you want. Alternatively, you can type numeric values into the filters' fields.

The Brightness and Contrast filter controls are pretty self explanatory. The Proc Amp filter controls aren't as easy to figure out, so the following list describes what these controls do:

- **Setup:** Changes the black level in a clip. Blacks should be deep and dark with no grays in them. Look for blacks in hair or dark areas of the shot.

- **Video:** Affects the whites in an image. Adjust this slider until the whites start to glow in the image, and then back off a bit until they're just below that glowing level.

- **Chroma:** Affects the color level or saturation. Be sure to check on an NTSC or PAL video monitor to determine the final amount of color you want to add to the clip.

- **Phase:** Gives you control over the hue (color) in a clip. Whether you want to make the colors greener or redder, the Phase control can help.

7. **To see how the newly color corrected clip plays, select it on the Timeline, choose Sequence⇨Render⇨Both. Then, after Final Cut Pro completes the rendering process, position the playhead just before the clip on the Timeline and press the spacebar to play and view the clip.**

 A handy reference to use is another shot in a movie whose exposure and colors you like. Compare the two shots, and make adjustments until you like what you see.

Comparing Results with the Frame Viewer

Comparing frames from different clips is the best way to make sure that your video maintains a consistent look, especially if you use color-correction tools or need to line up shots for a special effect. Of course, adjusting all your video clips to look the same, regardless of how they were shot or where they occur in a sequence, can be difficult without viewing them together. Using the Frame Viewer in Final Cut Pro, you can see a side-by-side comparison of two frames from different clips in your sequence. Using the Frame Viewer together with the color-correction tools mentioned in this chapter is a helpful way to get harmonious results.

Follow these steps to open and compare two clips with the Frame Viewer:

1. **Place two clips from the Browser on a video track on the Timeline.**

   If you want, you can also use two clips that are already placed on the Timeline. For instance, if you have already used the color-correction tools to adjust a single clip, you may decide to compare it with any other clip that's on the Timeline.

2. **Position the Timeline playhead anywhere on the first clip so that you can see the clip in the Canvas window.**

3. **Choose Tools⇨Frame Viewer from the menu bar.**

   The Frame Viewer opens to reveal a window with your current frame or (depending on your default settings) a split screen of your current frame (on the right) and a frame from another edit (on the left), as shown in

Figure 14-9. You can choose from several options, depending on which frames you want to see side by side. Although a vertical alignment (V-Split) is usually the default, you can choose to view clips horizontally (H-Split).

Figure 14-9: The Frame Viewer is a handy tool for comparing frames from different clips.

4. **Open the pop-up menu in the lower-right corner, and select Current Frame.**

   Choosing an option from this menu automatically displays your current frame (or another edit point) in the right half of the Frame Viewer window.

5. **Select Previous Edit from the pop-up menu in the lower-left corner.**

   The Out point of the preceding clip in your sequence is shown on the left side of the screen. To toggle between right- and left-side views of your clips, click the Swap button to move between them. Other frame-viewing options are 2nd Edit Back, Current w/o Filters, Next Edit, 2nd Edit Forward, In Point, and Out Point. Depending on what you need to see, you can choose any of these options for either side of the frame. You may also switch between horizontal (H-Split) or vertical (V-Split) positions by pressing the corresponding buttons.

Checking Out More Handy Filters

In this section, I discuss more cool filters and other special effects that can help give your video a unique look. Here's an abbreviated guide to applying these effects — for more detail, check out earlier steps in this chapter:

1. **Place a video clip on the Timeline.**

2. **Position the Timeline playhead over the clip so that you can see it in the Canvas window.**

   This way, you can preview the changes in the Canvas.

3. **Double-click the video clip to open it in the Viewer.**

4. **Click the Filters tab in the Viewer window.**

5. **Click the Effects tab in the Browser window, and drag any desired effects to either the Viewer window or the selected clip on the Timeline.**

   Each filter and its controls appear on the Filters tab in the Viewer window.

6. **Adjust the controls for each filter on the Filters tab of the Viewer window while watching their effects in the Canvas window.**

Just a dash of any of the following filter combinations can set your project apart. ***Remember:*** These are just the tip of the iceberg.

Final Cut Pro offers many other filters that, with some tweaking and combining, may give you exactly the look you want. Try adding multiple filters to a clip and making adjustments to each one on the Filters tab in the Viewer window to obtain complex and precise results. Just make sure that you don't apply filters more than once by mistake. You can easily lose track of several filters on the same clip. When you're not working on adjusting a particular filter, twirl up its arrow (to the left) to make room for the filters that are above and below it in the Viewer window.

- ✔ **Tint, Sepia, and Desaturate:** Combining these three filters (in the Image Control filters bin) at one time can create some interesting effects.

  The Sepia filter tints a clip with a sepia tone, the yellowish-brown color that's often visible in old photos. You can change the color of the tint by clicking a color picker or by using two sliders (labeled Amount and Highlight) to control the amount and the brightness of the tint you apply. The Tint filter is less useful than the Sepia filter because you can select only the color and the amount. You may want to switch between the Tint and the Sepia filters to see which effect you find more pleasing. As mentioned, the Desaturate filter allows you to remove some color from the image. At the highest saturation setting (100), the image becomes completely black and white.

- ✔ **Channel Blur, Channel Offset, Color Offset, and Invert:** You can find these filters in the Channel bin. Blurring on a color channel (by adjusting just one of the RGB blur sliders in the Channel Blur effect) and leaving the rest alone can give a poorly focused shot a deliberate soft focus in one or more parts of the color spectrum. The Channel Offset filter shifts one color layer to one side and creates a double-exposure look that can work as a dream effect. The Color Offset filter alters the color values in the red, green, and blue channels with sliders, and Invert looks like something from an old science fiction movie; it inverts all colors to their complementary colors (colors that are opposite each other on the color wheel).

✔ **Sharpen and Edge Detection:** These tools, in the Video Filter QuickTime bin, have a sharpening effect. They can also make a scene look more three-dimensional and give fuzzy or slightly out-of-focus elements more clarity. Rather than use sliders, you adjust these filters by selecting values from a drop-down menu. You need to experiment with the extremes in the numbers here to see the possibilities for these filters. Used together, these filters can also produce dramatic, deliberately grainy results.

✔ **Emboss and Lens Flare:** Also in the QuickTime bin are several unusual tools for dramatically changing the look of a scene. Emboss mimics the Photoshop filter of the same name and turns the scene gray with hard edges. Lens Flare does just what it says: It gives you hundreds of possible lens flares, like the rays and circles of light from the sun that sometimes appear on video or in photographs. You can select the size, shape, and color of the flare.

Blurring the Action

If you want shots to convey movement and speed, you may want to add a little blur to the action. By using the Final Cut Pro blur filters, you can help create or enhance the sense of motion. Follow these steps to achieve a blurry scene:

1. **Drag a clip from the Browser to a video track on the Timeline.**

2. **Position the Timeline playhead anywhere on the clip so that you can see it previewed in the Canvas window.**

3. **Double-click the clip to open it in the Viewer.**

4. **Click the Filters tab in the Viewer window.**

5. **Click the Effects tab in the Browser window.**

6. **On the Effects tab, click the triangle next to the Video Filters bin to open it, and then do the same to open the Blur sub-bin.**

7. **Drag each of the blur filters (Gaussian, Radial, Wind, and Zoom) from the Effects tab to the Filters tab in the Viewer window.**

   Alternatively, you can drag the filters onto the clip on the Timeline. Hey, you make the choice, but the results on the Filters tab should look like those shown in Figure 14-10.

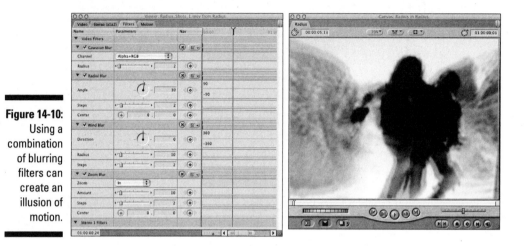

Figure 14-10:
Using a
combination
of blurring
filters can
create an
illusion of
motion.

8. **Start by selecting only the check box next to the Wind Blur filter.**

   You can see that the Wind Blur filter is checked in Figure 14-10.

9. **Move the wind direction indicator and the sliders until you get the desired effect.**

   The Canvas window shows the results. You can move the playhead around in the Canvas window to see what the results look like in other parts of the clip — but you can't judge this kind of effect well until you see it in motion.

10. **Try turning on the other blurring filters (by selecting the check boxes next to them) to exaggerate the blurring effect.**

11. **Select the clip on the Timeline, and choose Sequence⇨Render⇨Both.**

12. **After Final Cut Pro completes the rendering process, view the newly rendered effect on the Timeline.**

    You probably want to make some tweaks to the blurs, so return to the Effects tab in the Viewer window, change some settings, and render again.

Saving and Applying Customized Filters

If you have taken the time to tweak the parameters of a video filter, you can save that tweaked filter as a Favorite so that you can easily apply it to other clips that need the same filter treatment. This process saves you from having to repeatedly apply the same filter and adjust its settings each time it's applied. To save a filter as a Favorite, follow these steps:

1. **Open the Final Cut Pro Effects tab.**

   You can click the Effects tab in the Browser window or choose Window⇨Effects to activate that tab in the Browser.

2. **Open an already filtered video clip in the Viewer window, and click the Viewer Filters tab.**

3. **Click the name of the filter you want to save, and drag it to the Favorites bin in the Effects window (see Figure 14-11).**

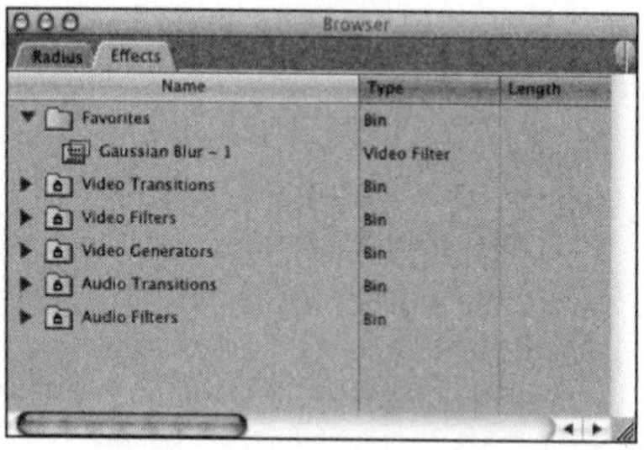

Figure 14-11: A customized filter is saved to the Favorites bin in the Effects window.

Final Cut Pro saves the filter to the Favorites bin, with all the unique parameters you set for it. You can now apply the filter to new clips just as you would do with any other filter. (You may want to rename the customized filter while you're in the Browser window.)

Technically, you can drag your filter anywhere in the Browser, but I recommend putting it in the Favorites bin, where it's easy to find and is available to all your projects. If you want to make this customized filter available only to your current project, consider placing it in another bin within your project.

Chapter 15

Motion Effects

• •

In This Chapter

▶ Understanding advanced effects tools

▶ Creating effects in Wireframe mode

▶ Creating effects with the Motion tab

▶ Using keyframes to change effects over time

▶ Zooming and panning for the Ken Burns effect

• •

Some projects call for you to do crazy things to your video clips, such as resize them, rotate them, reposition them, overlap them, change their opacity (to make them seem partially transparent), and more. You typically see these kind of effects in stylized montages that are featured in commercials, music videos, and the opening credits of TV news shows, sports programs, or even documentaries.

Creating these types of effects is the topic of this chapter. I cover how to manipulate video clips in all sorts of advanced ways. I also explain how to use handy tools, called *keyframes*, to add motion to these effects so that the effects change over time.

Manipulating Images in Wireframe Mode

Wireframes are thin outlines (like wires that define the shape of an object) in the Canvas window that simply represent the motion or relative position of a video clip or graphic. Using wireframes greatly speeds the creation and preview of composites or other motion effects. To tap in to advanced Final Cut Pro effects work, you need to shift into Wireframe mode, which then lets you quickly change the size, rotation, position, and shape of any video clip in your project. To switch Final Cut Pro to Wireframe mode, make sure that either the Canvas or Timeline window is active and then choose View➪Image+Wireframe from the menu bar.

If you didn't notice a change after switching to Wireframe mode, try selecting a video clip on the Timeline (move a clip there, if necessary) and make sure that you've positioned the Timeline playhead over the clip you've selected.

When you select the clip, you see the Canvas window display boundaries around your video clip, along with a big X that runs through the image (see Figure 15-1). In this mode, the boundaries of video and still images appear as thin blue lines that also serve as handles for the media. You tweak these handles to change the look and position of the imagery on-screen, as I explain in the next subsection.

Drag any side to rotate

Clip's current track number

Drag interior to move

Drag any corner to scale

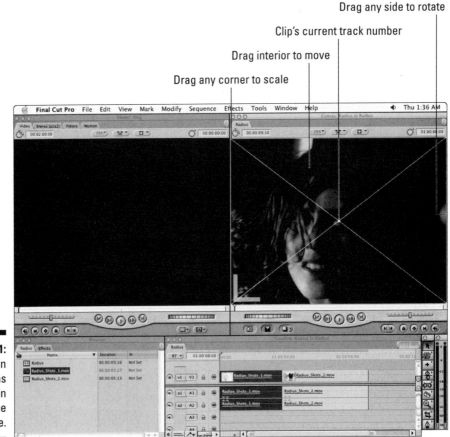

Figure 15-1:
An image in
the Canvas
window in
Wireframe
mode.

Scaling, rotating, and moving images

You can create some impressive video effects simply by scaling, rotating, and repositioning images on-screen. In fact, these straightforward tasks are the building blocks for most of the advanced effects you're likely to create in Final Cut Pro.

To start manipulating an image clip that's already on the Timeline, follow these steps:

1. **Make sure that you're in Wireframe mode.**

   Remember, choose View⇨Image+Wireframe.

2. **Choose the Final Cut Pro Selection tool.**

   The Selection tool is the topmost tool on the Tool palette (it looks like an arrow).

3. **Select the clip on the Timeline, and make sure that you can see it in the Canvas window.**

   You see the clip in the Canvas window when you position the Timeline playhead over it. But you must select the clip you want to work with on the Timeline. You need to select it to see its wireframe in the Canvas window.

4. **Click and drag the clip in the following ways in the Canvas window (see Figure 15-2):**

   • **Scale:** To change the size (or scale) of an image, click one of its four corners in the Canvas window and drag the mouse pointer away from the center of the image to make it larger, or toward the center to make it smaller.

   • **Rotate:** To rotate an image, click the image in the Canvas anywhere on its wireframe border (but not the corners) and drag your mouse.

   • **Move:** To move an image (so that it's off-center), move your mouse into the center of the image (anywhere away from its edges) and drag the image to a new spot in the Canvas window.

5. **Select the clip on the Timeline, and choose Sequence⇨Render Selection⇨Video to render the clip, if necessary.**

   Depending on the changes you've made and the render mode (Safe RT or Unlimited RT) Final Cut Pro is in, you may have to render before playing the clip from the Timeline (see Bonus Chapter 1 on this book's CD for more information on rendering).

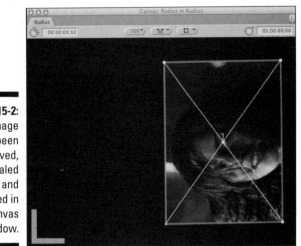

Figure 15-2:
An image
has been
moved,
scaled
down, and
rotated in
the Canvas
window.

Cropping or distorting an image

You can crop an image so that it ends at any point you choose. You can also distort images to make them appear warped, stretched out, or compressed (see Figure 15-3).

Figure 15-3:
An image
that has
been
cropped
and
distorted.

To crop or distort an image, follow the same steps you use for scaling, rotating, and moving images (as described in the preceding section), except that rather than use the Final Cut Pro standard Selection tool when manipulating an image in the Canvas window, you use its custom Crop or Distort tools, which are described as follows:

- **Crop:** Select the Crop tool from the Final Cut Pro Tool palette (see Figure 15-4). Crop any side of an image in the Canvas window by clicking and dragging that side of the image inward, toward the center of the Canvas window. When you crop at the corner of an image rather than its side, you crop two adjacent sides at one time.

- **Distort:** Select the Distort tool from the Final Cut Pro Tool palette (see Figure 15-4). Click the tool on any corner of the wireframe that surrounds the image in the Canvas window, and drag your mouse to distort the image.

Figure 15-4:
The Crop and Distort tools.

Crop tool   Distort tool

If you hold down Option while you're using either the Crop or Distort tool, you can scale, move, or rotate an image by its wireframe, as though you were using the Final Cut Pro standard Selection tool. This shortcut saves you from having to switch back and forth between the standard Selection tool and the Crop or Distort tool.

Working in Wireframe mode in the Viewer

You can do all of these manipulations to a clip (scaling, moving, cropping, rotating, and distorting) in the Viewer window as well, not just in the Canvas window. I recommend doing them in the Canvas window after a clip is on the Timeline because the Canvas window simultaneously shows you the clip you're trying to manipulate as well as any other clips that happen to share the same sliver of time. (Final Cut Pro places these clips on different tracks of the Timeline.) This way, as you manipulate a clip, you see how the changes affect the whole scene of your movie.

However, you may want to quickly manipulate a clip that's directly in the Final Cut Pro Viewer without dragging the clip to the Timeline and viewing it from the Canvas window. In this case, open the clip in the Viewer (double-click it from the Browser window) and choose View⇨Image+Wireframe from the menu bar. As a result, Final Cut Pro displays the same familiar wireframe outline on top of your clip. At this point, you can make any manipulations you want by following the steps I just covered.

Changing Images with the Motion Tab

Using Wireframe mode to manipulate images in the Canvas window is the most visual and intuitive way to move, scale, rotate, crop, and distort clips. However, you can accomplish the same thing by entering numerical values for a clip on the Viewer Motion tab. The Motion tab also offers a couple of new effects, such as Drop Shadow and Blur, which you can apply to a clip.

I usually prefer the visual appeal of Wireframe mode, but sometimes, using the Motion tab is helpful (especially when you have to be precise). For instance, I recently used Final Cut Pro to mock up a Scenes menu for a DVD. I wanted four thumbnails of the DVD movie scenes to appear on the menu simultaneously. Of course, I wanted the thumbnails (which were just clips on the Final Cut Pro Timeline) to be the same size and to be perfectly aligned. Creating this menu was easier to do by entering the scale and position information for the clips on the Motion tab than by attempting to use Wireframe mode to arrange all the thumbnail clips visually in the Canvas window.

To alter a clip by using the Viewer Motion tab, follow these steps:

1. **Place a clip on the Timeline.**

2. **Position the Timeline playhead over the clip to see it in the Canvas window.**

   This way, as you make changes to the clip on the Viewer Motion tab, you see the changes in the Canvas window.

3. **Double-click the clip on the Timeline to open it in the Viewer.**

4. **Click the Viewer Motion tab.**

   The Motion tab has all sorts of clip settings you can adjust, including scale, rotation, and crop values (see Figure 15-5). The numeric values on the Motion tab reflect any adjustments you already made to this particular clip when it was in Wireframe mode.

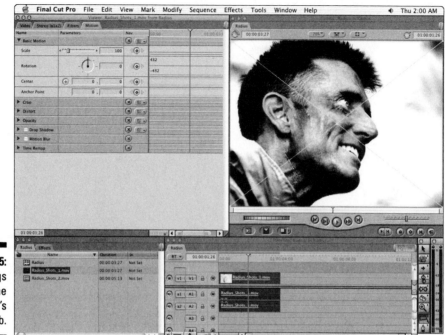

Figure 15-5:
Clip settings
on the
Viewer's
Motion tab.

5. **Change the Scale, Rotation, and Center settings of the clip, and see the changes in the Canvas window, as follows:**

   • **Scale and Rotate:** To set the scale and rotation of a clip, drag the respective slider or dial or type a numeric value into the respective field.

   • **Center:** To center the clip in a new position on-screen, click the cross-hair button in the Center area of the Motion tab, and the mouse pointer becomes a cross-hair symbol. Then, click your mouse anywhere in the Canvas window to center the clip at that new point.

6. **For the other controls, either click the small triangle next to each control name or select a check box to reveal any other controls available on the Motion tab, as follows:**

   • **Crop:** You can set the number of pixels to crop off the side of an image. Even better, you can set a value to feather each side of an image so that its edges appear to gracefully fade away (a nice, sophisticated look).

   • **Distort:** You can define the position of each of the four corners of an image by adjusting their X and Y coordinates. If you're thinking, "Wow! That's too many numbers to worry about," I agree wholeheartedly and recommend distorting an image visually in Wireframe mode (as discussed in the section "Manipulating Images in Wireframe Mode" earlier in this chapter).

- **Opacity:** Remember that the less opacity you give to a clip, the more you can see through it to other clips that are behind it (if you've stacked clips together on different Timeline tracks). Drag the Opacity slider, or enter a value between 0 and 100. The higher the number, the less transparent the clip.

- **Drop Shadow:** Adding drop shadows to images creates neat 3D effects, which often make the images seem more realistic. For instance, you can add drop shadows to text generators you place on the Timeline to make the text stand out more. As another example (in making the DVD mock-up menu that I referred to earlier in this section), I placed a drop shadow under each Scene thumbnail to make the thumbnails appear to float above the menu background. Final Cut Pro gives you lots of drop shadow control. The Offset value defines the number of pixels that a drop shadow appears away from its subject. You can set the angle of a shadow from its subject, color, opacity, and softness (how gracefully the edges of the shadow blend with what the shadow falls on).

- **Motion Blur:** You can create a stylized sense of motion by applying a motion blur to clips. You can control the power of the blur and the number of steps that the blur uses. Leave some time to render a few experiments before finding the right settings for this one, because it can take a while for the computer to process.

If you tweak settings on the Motion tab and then decide that you don't like those tweaks and want to quickly reset the changes so that you can start over, click the Reset button next to each value on the Motion tab (refer to Figure 15-5). This action brings each setting back to the Final Cut Pro default value.

7. **Select the clip on the Timeline, and choose Sequence⇨Render Selection⇨Video to render the clip.**

   You don't have to close the Motion tab. After playing the rendered clip on the Timeline, you can go right back to the open Motion tab and tweak the settings some more, although you need to render again to see your changes in action (depending on your processor speed, memory use, and render settings).

Using Keyframes to Change Motion Settings over Time

The first half of this chapter outlines how to do all sorts of fancy things to your images, by using either intuitive wireframes in the Canvas or the numerically precise approach of the Motion tab in the Viewer. These two methods may be enough for the projects you tackle, but you can do more. In fact, considering the power of the Final Cut Pro effects and compositing features, the rubber doesn't really meet the road until you combine the techniques I described in the previous sections with the concept of keyframes, which let you change a clip's motion settings (with all the things you can control on the Motion tab) over time.

Assume that, using the skills you have just acquired in this chapter, you scale a video clip to 50 percent of its original size. When that clip appears in your movie, its size (or any other settings you define for it, such as opacity, position, cropping, or distortion) doesn't change, unless you use keyframes to adjust it over time. What if you want that clip to appear in your movie at 50 percent of its original size and then, over a few seconds, begin slowly growing to dominate the scene? The only way to change the Motion tab values, such as Scale, over time is by setting keyframes for each of them.

Keyframes are essentially marks you place in your movie that describe any motion settings you want to give a clip at a particular time. Final Cut Pro notices the keyframes you place in your movie and, if the motion values in those keyframes change over time, Final Cut Pro smoothly changes the value between the two keyframes over time. For instance, if the Scale value in Keyframe A is 50 percent and the Scale value in Keyframe B is 100 percent, Final Cut Pro continuously scales the clip from 50 percent to 100 percent between those keyframes.

The speed of the changes between keyframes depends on how much time (in seconds and frames) exists between each keyframe you set. For instance, if you set a keyframe in your movie at 5 seconds and another at 10 seconds, any values that change between those keyframes change over 5 seconds (the time between the two keyframes). To go back to the preceding scaling example, the video clip gracefully scales from 50 percent to 100 percent over 5 seconds. However, if you set a keyframe at 5 seconds in your movie and set the next keyframe at 6 seconds, the scaling effect takes place in only a split second, and the clip scales up very quickly. In other words, the more time between keyframes, the slower the transition (that is, the more slowly a clip changes its scale, opacity, position, or any other value you may have changed between the keyframes).

Using keyframes to set clip opacity

If you have read Chapter 10, you're probably already comfortable with keyframes. (Chapter 10 covers how to use keyframes to change the volume level of clips over time to make some parts of a single clip soft and others louder.)

To use keyframes to dynamically change the opacity level of a clip (so that it appears to get more or less transparent over time), place keyframes on an overlay, which is a fancy word for a line. After this overlay is activated, it appears on the clips on the Timeline. Follow these steps to make your changes:

1. **Place a clip on the Timeline.**

2. **Click the Clip Overlay button on the Timeline to toggle on the overlay that controls opacity for a clip.**

   The Clip Overlay button is in the lower-left corner of the Timeline (see Figure 15-6), and it toggles the overlays (for audio and video) on and off. When it's on, you should see a thin black line representing the opacity level for video appear at the top of all video clips on the Timeline — it appears white for video clips that are already selected.

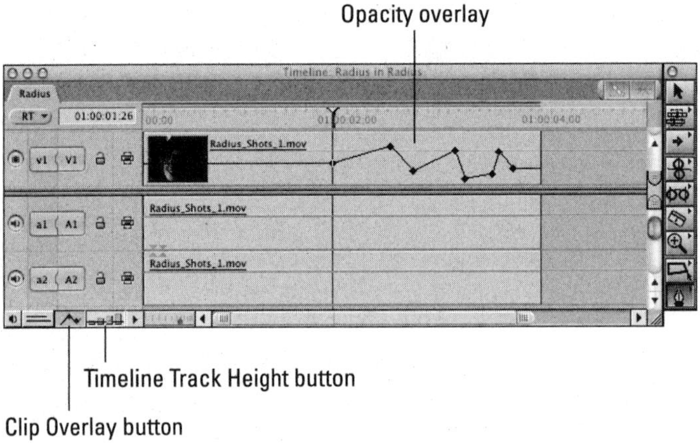

Opacity overlay

Figure 15-6:
Turn on the
Clip Overlay
to view and
set
keyframes.

Timeline Track Height button

Clip Overlay button

   To better see the Opacity Overlay and the keyframes you're about to put on it, you may want to enlarge your view of the Timeline tracks. To do so quickly, click one of the taller vertical bars on the Timeline Track Height button, to the right of the Clip Overlay button.

3. **Select the Pen tool from the Tool palette.**

   The mouse cursor turns into a pen symbol. The Pen tool lets you create keyframes in the Timeline window.

4. **To place a keyframe, click the Pen tool on an Opacity Overlay.**

   You should place a keyframe at a place in time where you want to set a new opacity level. When you place a keyframe, you see a small black diamond icon placed at that point on the Opacity Overlay.

5. **Adjust the opacity level of the keyframe you just placed.**

   Move your mouse over the keyframe, and the pointer becomes a crosshair symbol. Click and drag the Keyframe icon (the small diamond icon) up to increase the opacity level of the clip for that keyframe or down to decrease the opacity (in other words, to make the clip more transparent). As you drag your mouse, a tiny pop-up box tells you the opacity level.

The change you make to the opacity level carries through for the rest of the clip unless you set another keyframe at a different opacity level.

6. **Place another keyframe within that clip, and adjust its opacity level.**

   You're just repeating Steps 4 and 5 — with this exception: When you adjust the opacity level of the second clip, you should notice that the Opacity Overlay line moves from one keyframe to another over time. (It begins to form what looks like a mountain range — refer to Figure 15-6.) That's keyframing in action!

7. **Place any other keyframes you want within the clip.**

   The more keyframes you set now, the more practice you get for free.

8. **Play the clip on the Timeline to see the opacity changes in action.**

Editing existing keyframes

You can change the opacity setting for an existing keyframe, and you can change where the keyframe is located in the clip (in other words, when in time the keyframe occurs). To make either change, click the keyframe (make sure that you have the Pen tool selected) and drag the keyframe to either the left or right to move its location within the clip (so that it plays earlier or later in time). Or, you can move the keyframe up or down to adjust its opacity level. To adjust the levels of adjacent keyframes simultaneously, hold down ⌘ and drag the keyframe line between two keyframes up or down.

To delete an existing keyframe, make sure that you have the Pen tool selected, hold down Option, and click a keyframe. Final Cut Pro then gives the keyframe the boot and adjusts its Opacity Overlay as if the keyframe were never there.

If you're doing quick-and-dirty keyframe adjustments (moving them in time or changing the level of their opacity), you can do so without selecting the Pen tool. With the standard Selection tool, just click the keyframes and adjust them.

Using keyframes to set other motion values

The easiest way to change the opacity levels of a clip over time is by adding keyframes to the clip's Opacity Overlay, as described in the section "Using keyframes to set clip opacity," earlier in this chapter. If you need to create keyframes for other motion settings — such as Scale, Origin, Rotation, Crop, or Distort — Final Cut Pro requires you to use a different approach.

Setting keyframes on an overlay (such as the Opacity Overlay on the Timeline), where you can see the values of each keyframe relative to each other over time, is fairly natural and intuitive. You can also use keyframes with options on the Motion tab to create a cool effect that you see in lots of Ken Burns–style documentaries, which move and scale a large photograph around the screen (rather like zooming and panning). In fact, the Apple iMovie 4 does something like this effect and even calls it the Ken Burns effect; however, Final Cut Pro can do it with more control. Remember that if you're not interested in doing Ken Burns–style effects, you can still use these same principles and steps to make other motion keyframes do anything you want. Just follow these steps:

1. **Click and drag a still image from the Browser window to the Timeline.**

2. **Select the clip on the Timeline, and position the Timeline playhead over the clip so that you can see its image in the Canvas window.**

   Watch the Canvas window to see how the Motion settings you make affect the image. The results should look something like Figure 15-7.

   Some black areas appear around the edge of the image if the proportions of the image aren't exactly the same as the video frame. This appearance is normal, so don't worry.

Figure 15-7: Importing a still image and dropping it into the Timeline makes the image look like a video clip in the Canvas window.

3. **Double-click the still clip on the Timeline to open it in the Viewer.**

   This step opens the clip on the Motion tab and activates the motion tools for the clip.

4. **Click the Viewer Motion tab.**

   Ah, yes, the Motion tab. You should feel right at home here. If not, flip back a few pages to the section "Changing Images with the Motion Tab."

5. **Position the playhead on the Timeline at the beginning of the clip.**

   You place the first keyframe at this position. Technically, you can place this keyframe anywhere in a clip, but this time you're starting at the beginning of a clip. By the way, turn snapping on (pressing N toggles it on and off) to help snap the playhead to the edges of clips.

6. **Back on the Viewer Motion tab, set the clip starting values for settings such as Scale, Rotation, and Center.**

   For instance, you can set the scale at 100 percent (which, if the picture comes from a large-scan or megapixel camera, makes the picture too large to fill the 720 x 480–pixel video frame for DV). Starting with a large image is often the best approach because you may want to begin by showing just a small part of the picture, which fills the entire video frame.

   At any rate, you see the current state of the image in the Canvas window.

   Rather than make these adjustments on the Viewer Motion tab, you can make the same kind of changes by clicking and dragging the image in the Canvas window, just as you do earlier in this chapter. (See the section "Manipulating Images in Wireframe Mode.") Just make sure that you've set the Canvas window to Wireframe mode (choose View⇨Image+Wireframe) and that you've selected the clip you're working with on the Timeline. We often use both approaches to change images. We use the mouse in the Canvas window to make a general change and then use the Motion tab (with its numerical precision) for precise tuning.

7. **Click the Add Keyframe button in the Canvas window to insert the first keyframe (refer to Figure 15-7).**

   By doing this, you're placing the first keyframe where the Timeline play-head happens to be and assigning the keyframe values on the Motion tab at that time.

8. **Drag the Timeline playhead to the next place in the clip where you want to set a keyframe.**

   The more time between keyframes, the slower the changes when the clip plays.

9. **On the Viewer Motion tab, enter the values you want for this new keyframe so that Final Cut Pro can automatically place the keyframe.**

   If you've moved the Timeline playhead after setting the first keyframe (as you did in Step 8) and then you change one of the motion settings, Final Cut Pro guesses that it should throw caution to the wind and place a keyframe for you. Handy, eh?

   You can change as many of the motion values as you want. Two natural values to tweak are Scale, to make the picture appear to zoom in or out, and Center, which centers the picture in a different spot, to make it appear to move or pan across the screen as your clip plays. These changes all become part of the keyframe you've just placed.

10. **To set more keyframes in the clip, repeat Steps 8 and 9.**

    You can create simpler animations and effects with just two keyframes, but fancier ones involve several keyframes.

11. **Select the freshly keyframed clip on the Timeline, and choose Sequence⇨Render Selection⇨Video to render it.**

    You're now ready to play the clip. Depending on your real-time settings and the number and types of motion values the various keyframes require, you may not have to render before previewing the finished effect. In many cases, you can play a real-time preview directly from the Timeline. Lucky dog!

When you play your rendered clip, you can see the motion you created. For instance, an image can be made to scale from one size to another and move across the screen.

That's how to set motion keyframes in a clip. I oriented this example toward zooming and panning a still picture à la Ken Burns, but you can apply these steps to any other kind of motion effects you have in mind.

Just about any parameter in Final Cut Pro can be keyframed, including filter settings and even text properties such as kerning and text size. For your next project, you may want to try experimenting with your titles by keyframing various text properties to create interesting effects.

Editing motion keyframes

As you animate motion effects, you probably should tweak keyframes a bit to fine-tune your effects. To edit keyframes you've already placed on the Timeline, use keyboard commands to jump the playhead to existing keyframes in a clip and then use the Viewer's Motion tab to review and change the motion values of any keyframe. Follow these steps to edit motion keyframes:

1. **Double-click a keyframed clip on the Timeline to open it in the Viewer.**

2. **Click the Viewer Motion tab, which allows you to see the clip's current motion settings.**

3. **Position the Timeline playhead near the clip you just opened in the Viewer.**

4. **Press Shift+K to move the Timeline playhead forward to the next keyframe in a clip, or press Option+K to move it back to the preceding keyframe.**

   As the Timeline playhead jumps to the nearest invisible keyframe, the values on the Viewer Motion tab change to reflect the settings of each keyframe.

5. **To edit a keyframe, change its values on the Viewer Motion tab.**

   You don't have to reapply the keyframe; just change its values.

6. **To edit more keyframes, repeat Steps 4 and 5.**

7. **Select the clip on the Timeline, and choose Sequence⇨Render Selection⇨Video to render the clip, if necessary.**

Do you want to delete a keyframe? If you set it recently, you can always undo the placement of a keyframe by choosing Edit⇨Undo. If, for instance, you set the unwanted keyframe during another work session, which is often the case, you can't use the Undo command. In the Viewer window, make sure that the Motion tab is selected and choose the Delete Point tool (the pen with a minus sign next to it) from the Pen tool pop-up menu to the left of the Timeline. Click any keyframe to delete it.

Creating a Multiple-Screen Effect

In the steps in this section, I tell you how to produce a fun effect by creating multiple-screen segments in your sequence. This effect was advanced stuff for movies in the 1960s. In recent years, this technique has been used for cutting-edge advertising and to simulate a retro look that's associated with older films. Follow these steps to create a multiple-screen effect:

1. **Place two clips on the Timeline, one over the other (one in Track V1 and the other in Track V2).**

   It doesn't matter which clip is in which track, but keep in mind that the clip you see in the Canvas window is the clip in Track V2 (the top track) because it's the top clip. The clip in Track V1 is hidden behind the clip in Track V2.

   If the Canvas window isn't visible, press ⌘+2 to open it.

2. **Place the playhead anywhere over your clips on the Timeline.**

   This step ensures that the Canvas window displays your clips and updates the effect you're about to create.

3. **Select the clip in Track V2 (the top track) by clicking it.**

   This step is important because wireframe handles show up only on clips that are selected and only if the playhead is in the selected clip on the Timeline. Many times, users get frustrated trying to figure out why they're not seeing wireframes. Almost always, the problem is that they don't have the clip selected on the Timeline.

4. **In the Canvas window, choose View⇨Image+Wireframe.**

   The wireframe appears around your image. The number 2 in the center of the frame lets you know that the clip in Track V2 is displayed.

5. **Click and drag any corner handle on the wireframe toward the center of the frame so that the image is approximately 40 percent of its original size.**

   Don't be concerned about the precise size. Simply drag until the clip is smaller than approximately half its original size. Note that as the image of the top clip shrinks, the clip behind it (on the lower track) appears.

6. **Click the Track V2 (top) clip, and drag it to the upper-right corner of the Canvas Window, as shown in Figure 15-8.**

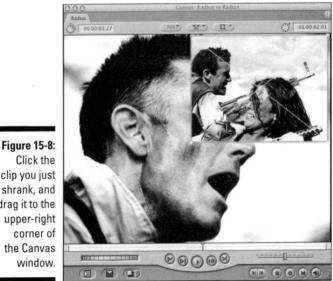

Figure 15-8:
Click the clip you just shrank, and drag it to the upper-right corner of the Canvas window.

7. **In the Canvas window, select the video clip from Track V1 (the lower clip) and resize the clip by dragging one of its corners.**

Without worrying about precision, make this clip about the same size as the first one you shrank.

When you click the background clip in the Canvas window, this clip automatically becomes selected on the Timeline as well. Wireframe view is turned off from the first clip and is presented on the clip you just selected.

8. **Move the lower clip you just shrank to the lower-left corner of the Canvas window by clicking the image and dragging it (see Figure 15-9).**

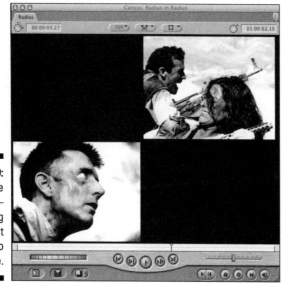

Figure 15-9:
Multiple
screens —
a swinging
1960s effect
brought to
life.

9. **To render, select the top clip and choose Sequence⇨Render Selection⇨ Video.**

10. **After the rendering is complete, place your playhead just before the clips on the Timeline and press the spacebar to play your clip.**

The 1960s are back!

You can continue to layer clips in the video tracks and to size them as shown in the preceding example. Final Cut Pro allows you to have as many as 99 video tracks, which lets you create complex layering effects. Multiple tracks can create the look of a surveillance video, with several screens showing at one time, as well as a similar effect that was produced in the movie *Timecode* and the TV series *24*. This effect presented real-time action that was created by four synchronized videos playing at the same time on-screen.

Chapter 16

Compositing

· ·

· ·

*T*his chapter discusses *compositing*, which is the merging of two or more different images into one. A classic example of compositing is the trick of making an actor appear in front of a background that he was never in. First, you film the actor in front of a solid-color background, such as a blue screen. Later, you remove the blue screen and place the actor over a new background, such as a beach, an exploding building, or other object. Compositing can also be used to create a collage of images and text, such as the titles you typically see at the beginning of a news or sports program or a documentary — all moving and fading in and out gracefully. (This kind of work uses the skills I describe in Chapter 15 for scaling and moving images and changing their opacity.)

In this chapter, I cover how to do compositing as well as discuss some related compositing topics, such as *mattes,* which let you selectively crop parts of an image. When you combine the information in this chapter with the details in Chapters 14 and 15, you can create some impressive visual work!

If you expect people to watch your finished movie on a TV, make sure that you also preview and check all your compositing work on a TV! Composited images can appear subtly different on a TV, particularly in the way that colors interact and in the sharpness of an image's edges, compared with the way they're displayed on your Mac's computer screen.

Get ready to render! If you don't like to sit around waiting for clips to render, this chapter isn't for you! The advanced effects work that I show you how to do in this chapter requires you to render your clips with every tweak you make. The good news is that when you're willing to put in a little extra time, you can achieve some very cool results!

Choosing a Composite Mode

Composite modes allow you to set how the colors of one clip mix with the colors of a second clip. For this discussion, Final Cut Pro has many composite modes that I loosely group in two categories: practical and artistic.

Multiply composite mode, which eliminates white pixels from an image, is an example of Practical mode. You may want to use it if, for example, you want to separate a still image from a white background. Screen composite mode is similar, but it drops out black pixels.

Artistic composite modes, on the other hand, are good for creating a pretty, colorful picture that's based on the interaction of the colors in the two clips. For example, Difference mode subtracts the color values of a clip from a clip in the Timeline track above it. Figure 16-1 shows the results of two clips when combined with Difference mode. As you can see, Difference mode is best reserved for moments when you want to be "artistic" and achieve fantasy effects.

Figure 16-1:
The clip on the left was placed on top of the middle clip, and the Difference mode was applied to create the clip on the right.

Final Cut Pro offers 13 composite modes. In this section, I explain the effect of each mode on your images. If you can't grasp what these modes do just by reading, don't worry about it. Even the most experienced composite-mode users don't go by mathematical descriptions of pixel behavior when it comes to choosing composite modes. Most just try out a few until they find one they like. You can do the same.

When discussing compositing, I often use the term *layer*. A layer is simply a video clip that's on its own Timeline track. Compositing involves merging clips, and each clip is considered a layer in the overall composited effect. (Other programs, such as Photoshop, use the concept of layers, and the concept here is the same: A layer is an element that can be merged with another.)

Also, when I use the term *bottom clip* or *top clip,* I'm referring to how Final Cut Pro stacks clips together on different tracks of the Timeline. A bottom clip may be on Track V1 on the Timeline, and a top clip may be on Track V2.

The following list provides a brief explanation of each composite-mode effect:

- **Normal:** This mode is the default for all clips that are edited into the Timeline. Normal mode shows the clip on the topmost Timeline track, without any modifications.

- **Add:** This mode combines the values of the color pixels of the top clip with those of the bottom clip and creates a final image that is brighter than the two combined.

- **Subtract:** This mode subtracts the values of the color pixels of the top clip from those of the bottom clip. The final image is darker than the original two.

- **Difference:** Difference mode subtracts the color values of the bottom clip from those of the top clip. This mode can give you some artistically interesting combinations, depending on the colors of the two clips.

- **Multiply:** This mode compares the color values of the pixels of the top clip with those of the clip below it and then multiplies the two values together. If the image is dark, this mode has little effect. This mode darkens a light image. Multiply, commonly used to drop out white backgrounds from stills and other images, is one of the more useful modes. For example, if someone gives you a Photoshop still with a logo against a white background, you can use Multiply mode to drop out the white and place the logo over the video layer of your choice. (Hopefully, the logo doesn't have any white in it, because that gets lost too!)

- **Screen:** This mode is another one of those useful modes that can save the day in a pinch. Screen mode drops out the black pixels of a clip. If you have a video clip or a still that has an element you want to save over a black background, you can apply this mode to the clip to eliminate the black pixels. If you find a mathematical explanation of this mode easier to understand, here it is: Screen mode compares the color values of the pixels in the top clip to those of the bottom clip and multiplies the inverse of each. Now you know!

- **Overlay:** Overlay mode combines the color values between the two layers and maintains the highlights and the shadows. You can use this mode to combine images so that they appear to merge into one another.

- **Hard Light:** Hard Light mode multiplies the colors, depending on the color values of the clip. This mode often creates a slightly dramatic, colorful look to the final composite. Again, the result depends on the colors you have in the layers, and experimenting can produce quite a pleasing effect.

- **Soft Light:** This mode darkens or lightens the layers. The colors that result from this compositing mode depend on the original layer color.

✔ **Darken:** Darken compares the color values of two composited clips and displays the darker of the two.

✔ **Lighten:** The opposite of Darken, this mode compares the color values of the two composited clips and displays the lighter of the two.

✔ **Travel Matte-Alpha:** This mode applies a matte to the top clip, using information from the bottom clip. You can use travel mattes to create halos or cutout borders that combine the two layered clips. The Alpha option of this mode ignores the RGB channels and looks for only the alpha channel — if one is present. I discuss alpha channels in a moment, but they define colors that are intended to be transparent, and you can create them using Adobe Photoshop or another photo-editing application.

✔ **Travel Matte-Luma:** This mode works just like the preceding one except that it uses luminance values (black and white values) rather than the alpha channel to create the final matte . The advantage here is that you don't need an alpha channel in an image beforehand. Anything that is black in the image is invisible (transparent), whereas anything that is white is visible (or opaque).

For readers who have worked with Adobe Photoshop or After Effects, keep in mind that the 13 Final Cut Pro composite modes behave exactly as they do in the Adobe applications.

Applying a Composite Mode

Composite modes are used on layered clips (clips that are stacked together on different tracks) on the Timeline. To apply a composite mode, you must first add two clips to the Timeline, right on top of one another. (Refer to Chapter 7 if you need a refresher on how to do so.) Figure 16-2 shows how these layered clips appear on the Timeline.

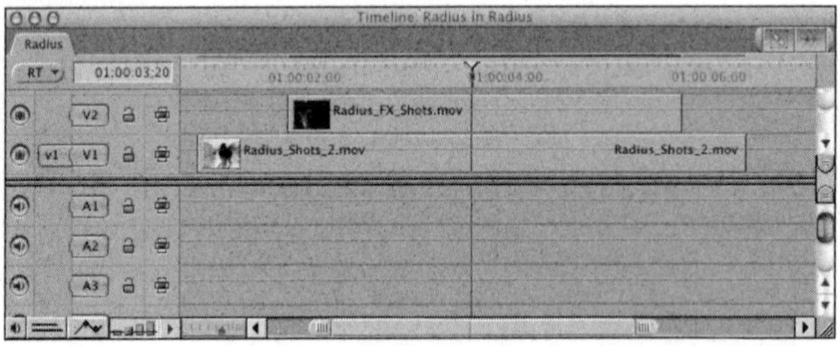

Figure 16-2:
Composite modes are applied to the topmost clip in a layered setting.

After you have placed two clips in different tracks on top of each other, follow these steps to apply a composite mode:

1. **Select the top clip.**

2. **Choose Modify⇨Composite Mode from the menu bar and then select one of the composite modes, as shown in Figure 16-3.**

   Final Cut Pro applies the composite mode to the topmost clip.

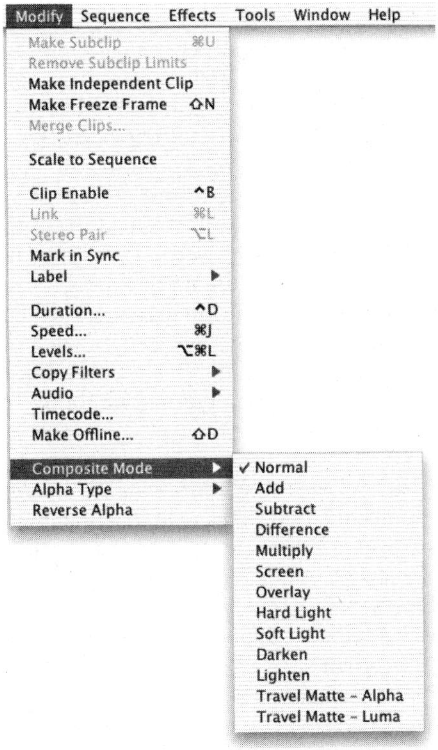

Figure 16-3:
Choosing a composite mode.

Note that composite modes create an effect between two layers, working *downward*. In essence, the layer (that is, the clip) that has the composite mode applied to it needs another layer (clip) beneath it to create an effect. You can technically apply the composite mode to the bottom layer, but it doesn't show any changes because it has no layer beneath it.

Understanding Alpha Channels

Channels are layers that create a final image when they're combined. Most video clips have three channels of color: red, green, and blue. These color channels combine to create all the other colors you see in the clip. However, you can create some video and still images with a fourth channel, the *alpha channel*. This alpha channel contains information that pertains to the transparency of the clip. Alpha channels tell Final Cut Pro which parts of the image to make visible and which parts to make invisible.

For example, you may be working with an artist who is using Adobe After Effects to create a movie of an animated logo against an alpha-channel background. You can import this movie (assuming that it's saved in the QuickTime format) into Final Cut Pro and layer it above an existing video track. Final Cut Pro recognizes the animation's alpha-channel background and makes it transparent, and the logo remains visible and composites it cleanly over your video track. If the artist had created this animation without an alpha-channel background (for example, with a solid-black background), it would be more difficult to composite the logo with your video in Final Cut Pro. (In truth, you can use a different compositing mode to knock out the logo's background, as discussed earlier in this chapter, but that topic is more complicated and can lead to some problems.) The point is that by building artwork with built-in alpha-channel backgrounds, you make it very easy to composite that art with your Final Cut Pro video.

In some situations, Final Cut Pro may misinterpret the alpha channel that's built into some artwork you're trying to use. This problem may be obvious in some artifacts, such as edge-fringing or halos around your final composited image. These artifacts make your final composite look grungy and rough at the edges. If you have these problems, select the clip on the Timeline, choose Modify➪Alpha Type, and select a different type of alpha from the submenu (Straight, Black, or White). Experiment with different alpha types. The problem disappears and the edges appear smooth when you choose the correct type.

Compositing with Mattes and Keys

Mattes and keys are common in software programs that are devoted to compositing and creating special effects. Even though Final Cut Pro is mainly a nifty editing program, it also has many built-in features and functions that allow you to create these interesting compositing effects. Mattes and keys are described as follows:

✔ **Mattes:** *Mattes* are still images that are used to create various cutout effects. In fact, you can think of mattes as cardboard cutouts. (Imagine a cardboard sheet with a circle cut out in the middle that reveals any image behind it.) In fact, digital mattes get their name from the old-fashioned mattes that surround a professionally framed art print or photograph. Of course, mattes in the digital world are much more versatile than cardboard mattes. In Final Cut Pro, you can fill the inside or outside of the matte with different video or stills. You see this feature in effect in the next section.

✔ **Keys:** *Keys,* which are essentially another type of matte, eliminate certain color or luminance values from an image to create transparency. You use keys to create, among other things, the "weatherperson effect" on your local news: A meteorologist is photographed in front of a blue or green background, and later, that particular color is keyed out (made transparent) so that the image of a satellite weather map can appear behind the meteorologist.

Creating a simple matte

You can easily apply simple mattes to your clips in Final Cut Pro. This section discusses how to apply a quick-and-dirty matte, such as the one shown in Figure 16-4, just to get your feet wet. As an extension of these steps, I explain how to composite your matted clip over another image so that you can see how the two different clips interact.

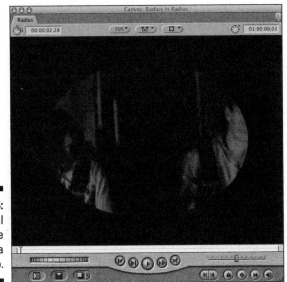

Figure 16-4:
An oval matte applied to a video clip.

Follow these steps to create a simple matte:

1. **Drag a video clip from the Browser to the Timeline.**

2. **Position the Timeline playhead over the clip so that you can see the clip in Canvas window.**

3. **Select the clip on the Timeline, and choose Effects⇨Video Filters⇨ Matte⇨Mask Shape.**

   Notice that an invisible rectangular matte automatically crops your clip, as shown in the Canvas window. You can adjust the shape of the matte in just a moment.

   By the way, you can find all the Final Cut Pro matte-related filters by choosing Effects⇨Video Filters⇨Matte, but for now, I stick with the Mask Shape filter because it illustrates the basics of a matte so well.

   You can also apply a filter to your clip by opening the Final Cut Pro Effects window (choose Window⇨Effects), opening the Matte bin, and dragging the Mask Shape filter onto the Timeline clip.

4. **To fine-tune your matte, double-click the video clip on the Timeline to open the clip in the Viewer.**

5. **Click the Viewer Filters tab.**

   Remember that you can use the Filters tab in the Viewer to tweak any filter you apply to a clip.

6. **From the Viewer Filters tab, adjust the matte settings (see Figure 16-5):**

   • **Shape:** Adjust the matte shape by clicking the Shape drop-down menu. (You can change it to an oval, round, rectangle, or diamond shape.)

   • **Size:** Change the matte size by tweaking its Horizontal Scale and Vertical Scale values. (You can drag the respective sliders or type a value up to 200.)

   • **Center:** To center the matte in a new position on-screen, click the cross-hair button in the Center area of the Mask Shape filter. (The mouse pointer becomes a cross-hair symbol.) Then, click your mouse anywhere in the Canvas window to center the matte at that new point.

   • **Invert:** You can invert a matte (swap the areas of the clip that the matte hides and reveals) by selecting the Invert check box.

   When you position the Timeline playhead over the clip, you see in the Canvas window the changes that were made.

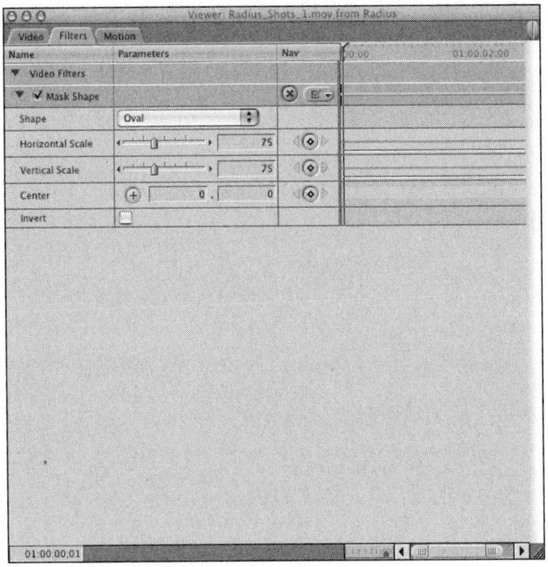

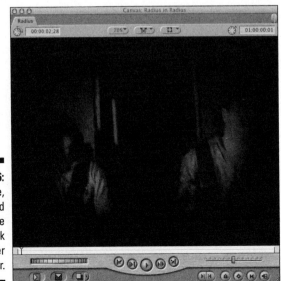

Figure 16-5:
Tweak
these filter
settings to
customize
the matte.

Softening the edges of your matte

By default, the edges of a matte are *hard,* meaning that the edges appear to
have been cut with a very sharp knife to create well-defined lines. You can
soften those edges so that your video clip seems to gracefully fade into the
edges of the matte, as shown in Figure 16-6. This option is especially handy
when you want to composite the matted clip with another image (which I
explain how to do in a moment).

Figure 16-6:
The matte,
softened
with the
Mask
Feather
filter.

You can easily soften the edges of a matte you have already applied to a clip by following these steps:

1. **Position the Timeline playhead over the matted clip whose edges you want to soften.**

   This way, you can see the clip displayed in the Canvas window.

2. **Select the clip on the Timeline, and choose Effects⇨Video Filters⇨ Matte⇨Mask Feather.**

   When you apply the Mask Feather filter to a matted clip, you notice a subtle softening of the matte edges. You can increase this effect.

3. **Double-click the video clip on the Timeline to open it in the Viewer.**

4. **Click the Viewer Filters tab.**

5. **From the Viewers Filters tab, adjust the Soft settings of the matte.**

   Drag the filter slider, or type a number as high as 100. The larger the Soft number, the softer the edges of the matte become.

Compositing your matted video clip with another clip

Now that you have applied a matte to a video clip (effectively hiding some areas of the clip behind the matte), you can composite this matted clip with another video clip so that the areas hidden by the matte reveal the second clip behind it, as shown in Figure 16-7. Just follow these steps:

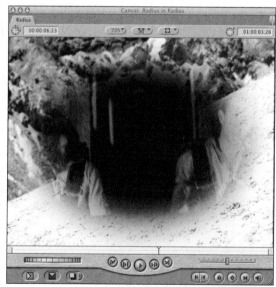

Figure 16-7:
The matted clip composited with a new clip.

1. **Place the second, new clip on the Timeline.**

2. **On the Timeline, drag the matted clip onto the track that's directly above the new clip.**

   In other words, if the new clip is on Track V1, drag the matted clip onto Track V2 so that Final Cut Pro stacks the two clips together.

Final Cut Pro composites (combines) your matted clip with the new clip. Remember that the clip that's on a higher track number appears first, but the clip matte is transparent, so you can see through to the new clip below!

Using intricate mattes

As you can see, the Final Cut Pro filter tools let you create mattes with simple shapes. To create a more sophisticated matte design — such as a design featuring rows of vertical columns, something that resembles Venetian blinds, or a matte featuring lots of random cutouts — you can use a graphics program like Adobe Photoshop to create the matte (in black and white, typically), save it as a Photoshop file (or even a .tiff or .jpeg file), and then import the graphic into Final Cut Pro. Then, on the Final Cut Pro Timeline, you can stack the matte on top of another video clip, select the matte, and then choose Modify⇨Composite Mode⇨Travel Matte-Luma. If you created the matte using an alpha channel in Photoshop, try choosing Modify⇨Composite Mode⇨Travel Matte-Alpha.

Compositing with keys

Another way of creating composites is by using keys. You create a *key* by using a clip in which the subject is filmed against a blue or green background. (Green backgrounds tend to be the color of choice these days, but blue can have advantages too.) You later replace the colored background with another background element, such as a computer-generated scene. (Virtually no recent special-effects movies, such as *Star Wars* or *The Matrix,* could have been made without the use of keys.)

This process may sound simple, but creating a clean key is quite a bit of work. Many companies, such as Ultimatte and others, specialize in creating high-end software that has the sole purpose of creating clean color keys. The Final Cut Pro tools aren't nearly as sophisticated as some on the market, but they're not a bad place to start.

To create a key, follow these steps:

1. **Drag the foreground and background shots from the Browser, and stack them on different tracks on the Timeline.**

   Place the key (the subject that's shot against a green or blue background) on the top track, and place the background you want to insert on the bottom video track (see Figure 16-8).

Shooting for green or blue screens

If you're struggling to create a good green- or blue-screen effect, remember this adage from the keying pros: Most of the work for green-screening is already done by the time the video ends up in your hands. The real trick, therefore, to getting a clean key is to shoot your video right in the first place.

Filming actors or other elements in front of a green screen is an art as well as a science. Some of the best directors in Hollywood call on companies and professionals who specialize in shooting green-screen. Use the following guidelines to achieve the best results:

- **Green or blue:** The general rule is that if you have lots of flesh tone in the shots, use a green color. (This is one reason that green screens have become fairly popular these days.) Also consider the colors your subject will feature. If an actor is wearing a loud, neon-green shirt, you don't want to film her in front of a green screen, because removing the green-screen color without taking out part of your actor's shirt may be difficult.

- **Use the right color grade:** The blue or green you may see in a green-screen shot is not just any green or blue. These paints are a standard color that don't occur naturally in the majority of subjects, and they're used to calibrate most keying software. You should

obtain paints for keying from a photo-supply or specialty-paint store. (In other words, don't use that old house paint that's on the shelf in your garage.) Many photo-supply shops also sell background cloth with the right shade of blue or green. This hanging cloth saves you the trouble of painting and gives you the ability to set up virtually anywhere.

- **Light and paint the background evenly:** A crucial task is lighting and painting the screen evenly so that no part is lighter or darker than the rest. Uneven areas make it very hard for Final Cut Pro to key out what you want keyed out, because the software is, ideally, looking for a single color to separate, and it doesn't interpret uneven areas (such as light green and dark green) as a single color. To get a good key, you should also avoid shadows caused by wrinkles and creases in the fabric.

- **Keep your distance:** Maintain a distance of at least 10 feet between your subjects and the green- or blue-screen background. The distance prevents the color of the screen from reflecting subtly onto your subjects. Without such a distance, you'll complicate your efforts to get a proper key later and can make your subjects look as though they have strange skin conditions!

2. **Position the Timeline playhead over the stacked clips so that you can see them in the Canvas window.**

   This way, you can use the Canvas window to preview the clips as you tweak them.

3. **Select the green-screen layer (for example, the hand shown in Figure 16-8) by clicking it and then choosing Effects⇨Video Filters⇨Key⇨ Blue and Green Screen.**

   Final Cut Pro applies the Blue and Green Screen filter to the top clip.

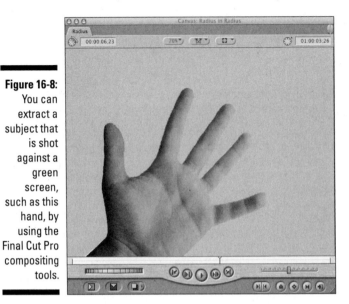

Figure 16-8:
You can extract a subject that is shot against a green screen, such as this hand, by using the Final Cut Pro compositing tools.

4. **To adjust filter settings, double-click the green-screen key layer to open it in the Viewer window.**

5. **Click the Filters tab, as shown in Figure 16-9.**

   The settings for the Blue and Green Screen filter appear.

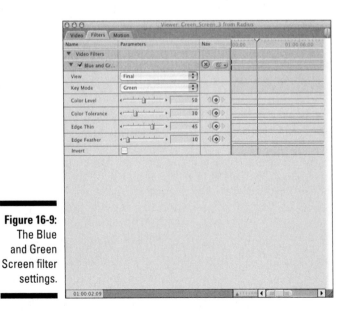

Figure 16-9:
The Blue and Green Screen filter settings.

6. **From the Key Mode drop-down list, select Blue or Green, depending on the color of the background of the video.**

    See the sidebar "Shooting for green or blue screens," earlier in this chapter, for more details about the blue-versus-green debate.

7. **While keeping an eye on the image in the Canvas window, click and drag the Color Level slider to a lower setting until the color of the blue or green screen disappears.**

    Drag the slider slowly so that you can see the green color in the video drop out bit by bit. You may have to tweak this setting to your satisfaction. The slider defaults to 100. You may also move the Color Tolerance slider to remove shades that are adjacent to the key color you have chosen.

8. **Click and drag the sliders to adjust Edge Thin and Edge Feather parameters and tweak your work, as follows:**

    • **Edge Thin:** The Edge Thin parameter creates a choking-in or -out of the outer boundaries of your subject.

    • **Edge Feather:** The Edge Feather parameter creates a slight feather to an edge.

Tips for getting clean keys

The basic key filters in Final Cut Pro are just the first step in getting a clean key. You can use many other tools on the Effects⇨Video Filters⇨Key menu to help clean up the key. The following list gives you a brief rundown of a few of these tools:

✔ **Luma Key:** The Luma Key filter allows a key based on luminance values (such as black and white) as opposed to color values (green or blue). For example, if you shot an all-white element against a solid-black background, you may want to use this key to drop out the blacks and retain the white element.

✔ **Difference Matte:** This type of key compares two layers and eliminates what they have in common. You need to prepare for using this matte when you're in the shooting phase. The Difference Matte requires you to film a shot twice: once with the subject in front of the background and the second time with just the background and without the subject. Ideally, these shots are identical (except for the presence of the subject, of course). In other words, you don't want even a slight difference in the camera position or angle, for example. (That's why it's important to use a good tripod.) The final results compare the two layers and eliminate the background while retaining the subject.

    The main advantage to the Difference Matte method is that the background doesn't have to be blue or green. It can be any color, as long as it doesn't change.

✔ **Spill Suppressors:** In many cases, when you finish filming the green or blue-screen shots, you may notice that your subjects have a little of the screen color reflected on them (this is called *spill*). Final Cut Pro has two filters that can help correct this spill — one for green and one for blue. These suppressors eliminate color spills, which are otherwise difficult to get rid of by using a simple key. To apply a suppressor, click your clip on the Timeline to select it and then choose Effects⇨Video Filters⇨Key⇨Spill Suppressor⇨Green or Blue.

The following matte tools are also useful for creating clean keys:

✔ **8-Point and 4-Point Garbage mattes:** Garbage mattes are rough mattes that eliminate parts of the image that aren't used in the final key. For example, in some keying work, you may notice a black line at the edge of your video frame. By using a Garbage matte, you can quickly mask out the areas around your subject and get rid of the distracting edges on the frame.

To apply the Garbage matte, select a clip on the Timeline and then choose Effect⇨Video Filters⇨Matte menu. After you apply the 4-Point or 8-Point Garbage matte, double-click the Timeline clip to open it in the Viewer. On the Viewer Video tab, you should see each point that the filter controls labeled clearly with a number, as shown in Figure 16-10. (You can adjust these points to crop offending parts from a frame; my example is exaggerated to illustrate the point.) Drag the Viewer Video tab outside the Viewer, and then click the Viewer Filters tab. (This way, you can adjust the filter while seeing its results at the same time on the Video tab.) The Filters tab displays coordinates for four or eight points (clearly labeled). You can move these points by clicking the cross hair in the Filter setting and clicking different portions of the image on the Viewer Video tab to create a new matte shape.

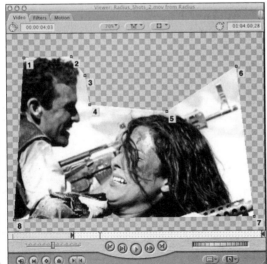

Figure 16-10: An 8-point Garbage matte, as shown on the Viewer Video tab.

✔ **Matte Choker:** The Matte Choker is the ideal substitute for the Edge Thin slider that is found in some of the Final Cut Pro key filters. *Edge thinning* is the process of removing the outer edges of your subject. The Edge Thin sliders in the Final Cut Pro key filters often produce a harsh edge. Use the Matte Choker instead to slightly *choke* (move the matte inward around the subject) the matte in to cut out some of the green or blue fringes that may appear around the edges. You apply the Matte Choker by selecting a clip on the Timeline and then choosing Effect⇨Video Filters⇨Matte⇨Matte Choker. The slider settings allow you to decide how much edge thinning you want to do and how much you want to feather or soften the edge.

Part V
Outputting Your Masterpiece

The 5th Wave   By Rich Tennant

"What do you mean you're updating our Web page?"

In this part . . .

*W*hen you're finished editing and adding any music, transitions, titles, effects, or other elements, you're ready for Part V, which focuses on outputting your movie to its final destination. I show you how to record your finished masterpiece back to videotape (for tape duplication or broadcast) and how to save your finished movie to a QuickTime digital file, which you can later burn to a DVD or CD-ROM or broadcast over the Internet.

Chapter 17

Recording to Tape

· ·

In This Chapter

▶ Setting up for recording

▶ Recording directly from the Timeline

▶ Printing to video

▶ Editing to tape

▶ Editing online versus offline

· ·

*O*ne of the last stages of working on a project in Final Cut Pro is to record your edited project from a sequence to tape. Recording your final edited project to tape is the most common method for delivering your project to a broadcast house or to a client.

As with anything else in Final Cut Pro, you have numerous options and choices available to you at this stage. Make your final choice based on your equipment and the needs of your clients or whoever is awaiting the delivery of the final master tape.

Setting Up for Recording

Before you record your edited project to tape, you must first set up your equipment for recording to tape. You must also check some equipment issues and verify settings in Final Cut Pro before you proceed. Check the following items before preparing to record your project to tape:

1. Connect your equipment.

   If you have a basic DV setup — which simply entails connecting a DV device, such as a camera, directly to your computer with a FireWire cable — your life becomes rather simple. Because a FireWire cable handles both the in and the out of video and audio, you should just confirm that your Mac and DV device are hooked together by a FireWire cable, which plugs into each device's FireWire port.

If you're recording to a VHS tape, skip ahead to the sections "Recording to VHS" for more information.

Remember that part of the beauty of the Panasonic DVCPRO HD format, which Final Cut Pro HD supports so well, is that it permits you to easily hook a compatible HD deck to your Mac via a simple FireWire cable. In other words, with the DVCPRO HD format, you can get HD video into your Mac just as easily as you can get DV video into it. But, because most *For Dummies* readers use DV equipment, that's what I focus on here.

2. Set the proper mode.

Check to make sure that your DV deck or camera is in VCR mode. Sometimes, VCR mode is also labeled VTR (Video Tape Recorder). Final Cut Pro cannot record to your DV device if it is set to Camera mode. If your DV device has multiple inputs (often labeled Video 1 or Video 2, or Line 1 or Line 2), be sure to check that you're on the right input. Video decks often have an Input button that switches the inputs to the deck or the camera. The indications for the selected input appear either on the front panel of the deck or inside the viewfinder of the camera.

3. Check the Final Cut Pro settings.

Choose Final Cut Pro HD➪Easy Setup. In the Easy Setup window, check out the summary of the Easy Setup you have set for Final Cut. (Refer to Chapter 2 for more information about Easy Setups.) Make sure that under Playback Output Video, you have chosen Apple FireWire, as shown in Figure 17-1. The External Video For Recording option should show the Same as Playback setting. This setting indicates that you're ready to output via FireWire. If your Easy Setup doesn't indicate these settings, you can choose Final Cut Pro HD➪Audio/Video Settings and make the necessary adjustments. (Again, refer to Chapter 2 for more.)

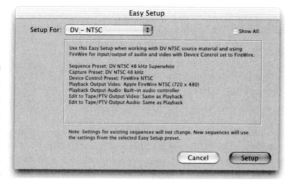

Figure 17-1:
Check the Easy Setup box before recording to tape.

4. Render your sequence by double-clicking it to open it and choosing Sequence➪Render All➪Both.

You may not need to render, depending on your project, but to be safe, take this step to prepare your sequence for recording. Rendering both audio and video ensures that any items that need rendering are ready for output. Without rendering, some of the items, such as effects, may not play in your sequence. Also, audio that isn't rendered may cause your sequence to drop frames or stutter during playback. See Bonus Chapter 1 on this book's companion Web site for more about rendering.

Looking out for dropped frames!

Many other editing systems come with video cards that perform most of the processing tasks that are otherwise done by the computer, but this isn't the case with Final Cut Pro. It relies almost entirely on the processing power of your computer. In some cases, if the requirements of the video overwhelm the processing power of your computer, Final Cut Pro can drop some video frames, which results in jittery playback and stutters in your video. *Dropped frames* are simply frames that Final Cut Pro has missed in playback or capture because your computer's processor had too many things to manage at one time.

To be sure that you're notified if frames are dropped as you record to tape, choose Final Cut Pro HD➪User Preferences and, on the General tab, make sure that the Report Dropped Frames During Playback option is checked, as shown in Figure 17-2.

Figure 17-2:
Checking
this box
ensures that
you receive
a warning if
frames are
dropped.

☑ Report dropped frames during playback

Checking this option ensures that Final Cut Pro warns you about any frames that may be dropped during recording to tape. If you get this warning, you need to take steps to prevent frames from being dropped, such as increasing the memory allocation for Final Cut Pro, closing all other applications, and suspending any network tasks that may be taking place. Also, check to make sure that your scratch-disk settings aren't set to render to your internal drive, which is a common cause of dropped frames (because you're reading and writing to the same drive, it's liable to have more errors). Then restart your computer and attempt to record to tape again.

Recording to DV tape with a camera or deck

If you're recording to a DV device, such as a camera or deck, you have much less to worry about compared to someone who is recording to a format such as Betacam SP or others. With a DV camera or deck, you only need a single FireWire cable to connect the device and the computer. Traveling over this FireWire cable is your video, audio, timecode, and even device control information. The *device control information* is what allows Final Cut Pro to control the transport mechanism (play, rewind, and fast forward, for example) of your deck or camera.

You must be sure that your DV device is switched to VCR (or VTR, depending on your deck or camera), as opposed to camera. A basic DV camera often has a setting that allows you to choose between a camera and a VCR function. Final Cut Pro doesn't record to a camera that is in Camera mode.

You may also want to check the recording-prevention tab on your DV tape to be sure that it isn't on the Save setting. DV tapes have a small tab on one side that switches between Record, which means that you can record over existing material, and Save, which means that you cannot record on the tape.

Recording to VHS

VHS remains one of the most common video formats, and you may want to record your Final Cut Pro movies to VHS rather than to DV tape. Fortunately, Final Cut Pro offers a quick and easy way to do this, as long as you have a DV camera or deck as well (I use the term *DV camera* from now on). Most DV cameras have analog video and audio output connectors, which allow you to play your camera signal *out* to a TV set. But, rather than connect a TV to your DV camera, you can hook up a VHS VCR and use it to record the video or audio signal that's coming from your camera to a VHS tape. The DV camera effectively works as a middleman between your Mac and the VHS deck: The camera receives a DV video signal from your Mac through its FireWire cable, converts that signal to analog, and then sends the signal to the VHS deck for final recording.

The connectors that are used to connect a DV camera to a VCR are the same RCA connections that are found on the back of your home stereo, as shown in Figure 17-3. Most VHS decks have RCA video and audio inputs. (These inputs should be on the back of your VCR. Usually, the video input is yellow, and the audio inputs are red and white — one carries the left channel of stereo audio, and the other carries the right channel.) All you need is a pair of RCA connectors to connect the video and audio outputs of your DV device to the video and audio inputs of your VHS deck. Your DV camera may have already shipped with the cables that you need — a common cable these days has three (yellow, red, and white) RCA connectors on one end and a single small connector at the other, which connects to your DV camera. If you don't have these connectors, you can get them from Radio Shack or any other store that sells stereos.

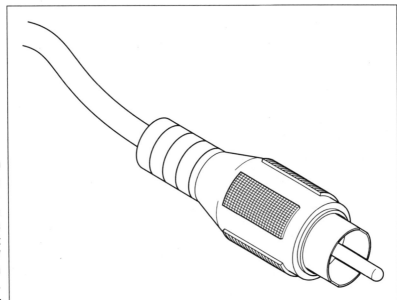

Figure 17-3:
Use RCA-
type
connectors
to connect
your DV
camera to a
VHS deck.

If your DV camera and your VHS VCR both have S-Video connectors, you may want to consider using an S-Video cable to connect the two devices. S-Video is desirable because its signal quality is better than that provided by RCA connectors, and this increased quality results in a better-looking video image being transferred from your camera to the VHS tape (not significantly better, but a little sharper to the discerning eye). S-Video carries only a video signal, though, so you still need to attach two RCA connectors between your camera and VCR to transfer stereo audio (one connector for the audio's left channel and one connector for the right channel).

To connect your equipment using RCA connectors, follow these steps:

1. **Connect your RCA cables to the video or audio inputs on your VCR deck.**

   You need to connect three cables to your deck: one for video and two for audio.

   If you opt to use an S-Video cable to transfer video, connect that cable to the S-Video input on your VHS deck.

2. **Attach the other ends of your RCA cables to your DV camera's audio or video input connector.**

   Many DV cameras — particularly small ones — have only one connector port for both RCA video and audio. These cameras often provide you with a special cable that has three RCA connectors at one end (these go to your VCR in Step 1) and a single connector at the other end (this goes into your camera).

   Again, if you opt to use S-Video, connect this cable to your DV camera's S-Video connector.

3. **Be sure to hook up the output of your VHS deck to a television so that you can see whether the recording is proceeding successfully.**

   That's it! You should be ready to record your DV camera signal to a VHS tape.

Just because you attach a VCR to your DV camera doesn't mean that the recording works. Some VHS decks have multiple inputs (sometimes labeled Line 1 and Line 2), which means that they can have more than one device attached to their inputs at a time. These VCRs have to know which input to record a signal from, so you may need to tell your VCR to record the signal from a different input. (You can usually find a button on the VCR or remote control that lets you switch from one input source to another.) To make sure that your VCR is getting a signal from your DV camera, you should be able to see and hear your Final Cut Pro project via the TV that's connected to your VCR; this confirms that the DV signal is making it into the VCR. To be sure, do a test recording and then play your VHS tape to see that the DV camera signal made it to the tape.

If you don't have a DV camera or deck but need to record your Final Cut Pro video to a VHS VCR (or any other analog device), you have one last resort: You can get a media converter box (a small device made by Sony and a few other companies) that connects to your Mac via a FireWire cable and converts the DV signal that's coming through the FireWire cable to an analog signal that VHS decks can understand. By attaching a VHS deck to the RCA connectors on this type of media converter box, the box can fill the same middleman role as a DV camera. Of course, the quality of the box you use varies as much as the price (devices can range from around $100 to more than $1,000), so be sure to investigate your purchase carefully.

Although having the option of recording DV video to VHS tape is nice, keep in mind that the quality of the VHS video format is pretty low. (That's why so many people prefer to watch movies on DVDs.) Also, converting a signal from one format to another (DV to analog) tends to slightly deteriorate the signal, resulting in even lower quality. On the other hand, some viewers may not notice this loss of quality, or it may be acceptable, given your purposes.

A few words on resolution and compression

If you captured DV video into your Final Cut Pro workstation, you should output it as DV as well. You can certainly use your DV camera or a media converter box to convert the DV signal to analog and then record to a VHS deck. However, sending that analog signal to a Betacam SP or higher tape format doesn't increase the resolution of the DV signal.

DV video has a compression ratio of 5:1. DV, therefore, compresses the video to one-fifth the size of its uncompressed state. This compression is efficient, and the video resolution looks quite good. But sometimes the DV format can show its limitations, such as during recompression with text and other effects. When used with some effects, especially after it's rendered a few times, DV can show blockiness and slight deterioration around the edges of text and objects. Certain broadcasters may not accept DV formats, although more are accepting this format every day.

To avoid the limitations of DV and work with high-end formats like Digital Betacam or Betacam SP, you should purchase an Apple-approved, third-party card that is meant for capturing high-end video and then outputting your video to the deck of your choice. This path can be fairly expensive because you need to purchase the video card and a high-end tape deck as well as faster drives, perhaps, to handle the high data rate. But, depending on your needs, this may just be the ticket for you.

Recording to Tape

When you're ready to record your show to tape, you can use three main approaches. In the next few sections, I explain the pros and cons of each of these approaches. The three possible recording methods from Final Cut Pro are as follows:

- ✔ Play back from the Timeline.
- ✔ Print to video.
- ✔ Edit to tape.

Each of these methods has its advantages and disadvantages. But, more than anything else, the path you take is dictated by the type of equipment you have and the ultimate destination of your tape.

Recording directly from the Timeline

This method may sound too good to be true, but it's real, and it works like a charm. In this method of recording to tape, you just press the Record button on your deck or camera and play your Timeline in Final Cut Pro. If the settings in Final Cut Pro are correct and all your hardware is set up correctly (see the section "Setting Up for Recording," earlier in this chapter, to verify your setup), your Timeline records to tape. The pros and cons of this method are as follows:

- ✔ **Pros:** The most obvious pro is that this method is fast and easy. In our opinion, this is the Official *For Dummies* recording method. You don't have to bother with any dialog boxes or struggle with incomprehensible settings. Your entire Timeline is simply sent to tape. This method also frees you from worrying about timecodes or control tracks on your tape. In some other methods of recording to tape, your tape needs to be *striped;* that is, it needs to have a timecode or control track laid down on it. This isn't the case when you record from the Timeline. (Read more about control tracks in the sidebar "Insert versus assemble edits," later in this chapter.)

- ✔ **Cons:** The main disadvantage of this method is a lack of control. You can't specify whether you want to simply edit one shot into a tape that already has a project on it, also known as *insert editing.* You also cannot specify leader elements, such as color bars or slates, to go before your show. If you want bars and other elements in the beginning of your tape, see the next section, "Printing to video," for details about how to do it.

To record directly from the Timeline, follow these steps:

1. **Open your sequence and render all items by choosing Sequence⇨ Render All⇨Both or by pressing ⌘+R.**

   Before you record to tape, you must make sure that all items have been properly rendered. This step ensures that all effects and other items have been rendered and are now ready to go to tape. Without rendering, some effects may not play. Rendering audio is also critical to avoid dropping frames during your recording process. Computer processing demands that are created by audio tracks in your sequence can cause frames to be dropped. Rendering your audio mixes the audio tracks and creates a single file that Final Cut Pro plays during the playback. This avoids on-the-fly recalculations for audio sampling rates.

2. **Place the playhead at the start point.**

   You should place the playhead on a blank area of the Timeline just before your project starts. Anything that is under the playhead is recorded to your tape, so placing the playhead just before your movie starts helps to avoid an abrupt beginning.

3. **Press Record on your deck or camera.**

   Wait a few seconds after you press Record. Some decks take a few seconds to get up to speed, and you don't want your project to start the moment your tape plays. After a few seconds, you're ready to play your Timeline.

4. **Press the spacebar to play your Timeline.**

5. **Press the spacebar to stop playback.**

When you're done, press the spacebar again to stop playback. You can also press the Stop button on your deck to stop recording.

 Rather than press the spacebar for playback, you can also choose other playback options from the Mark⇨Play submenu. You have choices such as In to Out, which plays only from In to Out points you may have marked in your sequence, and Play Reverse, which plays backward from the current position.

Printing to video

You can also record your Timeline to tape by choosing File⇨Print to Video. This option lets you add industry-standard color bars, countdowns, and slates to the beginning of the tape. In essence, this method differs from playing your Timeline in the sense that it allows you to add some elements before and after your sequence. The pros and cons of this method are as follows:

- ✔ **Pros:** A simple dialog box allows you to add bars, a slate, and other options to your edited movie without adding them to the Timeline. You can also loop your sequence, which may be important in some situations. (Venues such as video kiosks and convention booths often require videos to be looped for playback throughout the shows.) Finally, the timeline is automatically rendered because it's required in order to accurately playback effects and transitions.

- ✔ **Cons:** The cons of this method are a lack of precise controls, such as insert editing, a type of editing that allows you to insert shots with frame accuracy into a tape that already has material on it.

To print to video, follow these steps:

1. **Render all the items on your Timeline by double-clicking the sequence to open it and choosing Sequence⇨Render All⇨Both.**

2. **Choose File⇨Print to Video.**

   The Print to Video dialog box appears, as shown in Figure 17-4.

3. **Select your options in the Print to Video dialog box.**

   The Print to Video dialog box is divided into Leader, Media, Trailer, and Duration Calculator sections, which are described as follows:

   - Leader choices are elements that appear before your movie, whereas the trailer choices follow your movie. For example, in the Leader area, you can check the Color Bars option and then specify how many seconds of color bars you want. (For more on working with color bars, refer to Chapter 14.) You can also use these sections to add a few seconds of black at the end or beginning of your tape to avoid an abrupt start or stop of your movie. (I recommend that you use this feature.)

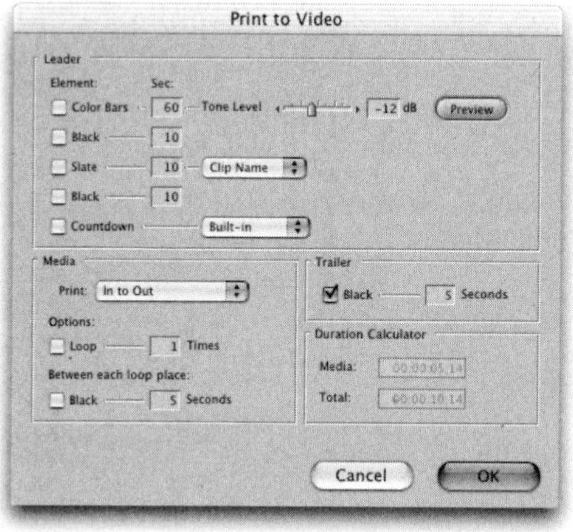

Print to Video

Leader

Element: Sec:
☐ Color Bars   60   Tone Level ◄───◻───► -12 dB   (Preview)
☐ Black   10
☐ Slate   10   (Clip Name ⬍)
☐ Black   10
☐ Countdown   (Built-in ⬍)

Media   Trailer
Print: (In to Out   ⬍)   ☑ Black ─── 5 Seconds
Options: Duration Calculator
☐ Loop ─── 1 Times   Media: 00:03:05:14
Between each loop place: Total: 00:00:10:14
☐ Black ─── 5 Seconds

(Cancel)   (OK)

Figure 17-4:
The Print to
Video dialog
box.

- A slate is a single page or graphic placed at the beginning of a sequence that contains information about the program. You can include information about a clip or sequence that includes various titles, credits, running times, starting timecode, and dates.

- The Duration Calculator shows you the final length of the media you have selected when printing to tape. The Media box shows the total length of all your media clips; the Total box displays the Media length plus the length of all extra elements you may have added, such as color bars or black.

- The choices in the Media section allow you to loop a sequence and specify the media you want to have printed to tape. For example, you can print the sequence from the In point to the Out point or loop it 10 times.

4. **Click OK when you have made your selections.**

5. **When Final Cut Pro displays a message that you can start recording, press Record on your deck.**

   Depending on your choices in the Print to Video dialog box, Final Cut Pro may take some time to render some of these elements. After you get a message to start recording, press Record on your deck. Wait a few seconds, and then click OK in the dialog box that gives you the message to start recording. Final Cut Pro begins playing back the leader, and then your show, and, finally, the trailer choices you made.

In some cases, you may want Final Cut Pro to start recording on your deck and stop recording automatically. To use this feature, choose Final Cut Pro⇨ Audio/Video Settings. On the Device Control tab, edit your Device Control preset by clicking the Edit button. In the Device Control Preset Editor, turn on the Auto Record and PTV After option and enter a time in the time field. After Final Cut Pro has edited the video to tape, it stops after the time you specified.

Editing to tape

The third option, Edit to Tape (on the File drop-down menu), lets you do sophisticated, frame-accurate insert and assemble edits, if you have the right kind of deck. (See the sidebar "Insert versus assemble edits," later in this chapter.) This option is best reserved for high-end decks, such as the ones that use Betacam SP or Digital Betacam tapes, or new HD decks, like the Panasonic AJ-HD1200A. These decks tend to be quite sophisticated (with a price to match) and are common in production companies and broadcast environments. The pros and cons of this method are as follows:

✔ **Pros:** The Edit to Tape method allows the most sophisticated control of any of the recording options. You can choose to just insert a shot into the middle of a project that exists on tape. You can even edit just the video or the audio portion of that shot as well. Another advantage to this type of editing is that you can specify in which frame of the tape you want the edit to occur and what timecode to use. For a production environment and broadcast situation, this type of control is critical.

✔ **Cons:** If the Edit to Tape operation has a disadvantage, it is that on DV tapes, you cannot easily (or cheaply) perform an insert edit (some more-expensive professional decks, such as the Sony DSR-1800, can do this). Sophisticated setups are required in order to ensure accuracy, such as devices with serial control and black-burst generators. Also, the frame accuracy of the insert edit depends on the frame accuracy of the deck you're using. In some cases, the decks may have a slight offset and may be a frame or two off from being frame-accurate. For the general user, however, the most significant drawback is the high cost of the required equipment.

Performing an Edit to Tape operation

To perform an Edit to Tape operation, follow these steps:

1. **Choose File⊳Edit to Tape from the menu bar.**

   The Edit to Tape window appears. This window looks similar to the Final Cut Pro Canvas window, except for some critical differences. Figure 17-5 shows the Edit to Tape window.

2. **Choose Editing from the drop-down list at the top of the Edit to Tape window to do an insert edit. For an assemble edit, choose Mastering.**

   If you're unsure of the difference between editing and mastering, see the sidebar "Insert versus assemble edits," later in this chapter.

3. **Double-click the sequence in the Browser that you want Edit to Tape to open.**

   You can set an In and an Out point in your sequence by pressing I and O. When you perform the Edit to Tape operation, only the video that is between the In and Out points is edited to tape. In the absence of an In or an Out point, the entire sequence is edited to tape.

Figure 17-5:
The Edit to
Tape
window.

4. **Set your In and Out points on the tape.**

By using the Shuttle or the Jog sliders, you can move around on your tape and set In and Out points. (*Note:* If you're in Mastering mode, you can set only an In point. If you're in Editing mode, you can set both In and Out points.) To set In or Out points, cue the tape to the desired spot and click the Mark In or Mark Out buttons, as appropriate. You can also manually set In and Out points by entering timecodes in the In and Out Timecode fields. If you're going to perform an insert edit, correctly selecting these In and Out points is critical. For a more detailed explanation of setting In and Out points, refer to Chapter 7.

5. **If you're in Mastering mode (for an assemble edit), click the Mastering Settings tab at the top of the Edit to Tape window.**

On the Mastering Settings tab, you can choose your leader and other options for recording. Add leader and trailer elements, such as color bars and black, as you desire.

6. **Click and drag your sequence from the Browser window to the Edit to Tape window.**

As you drag your sequence over the window, the Edit Overlay appears. The choices in the Edit Overlay are Insert, Assemble, and Preview. Drop your sequence on the appropriate choice.

The Edit to Tape operation begins automatically. You can press Esc to cancel an Edit to Tape operation at any time. If any rendering is required before the Edit to Tape operation, a dialog box appears to step you through the process of rendering.

Insert versus assemble edits

If you're a DV user and you work exclusively with DV cameras and decks, you can skip this sidebar and not miss a thing. If, on the other hand, you're working in a broadcast environment and are staring at a Betacam SP, Digital Betacam, or HD deck, you should read this sidebar before you attempt to record your video from Final Cut Pro to tape.

You can perform two types of edits when recording your video to tape by using the Edit to Tape option in Final Cut Pro: insert and assemble.

During an insert edit, you can select between audio and video tracks (or make edits to both audio and video). An insert edit doesn't record control or timecode tracks. During an assemble edit to tape, on the other hand, all tracks are recorded (audio, video, control, and timecode).

Why should you care which tracks are recorded? All videotapes have video and audio tracks on them. Videotapes also have a control track and a timecode track. A *control track* is a simple track of tick markers that the deck uses to maintain the proper speed. If you use the Print to Video command to record to a videotape, this control track is also recorded on the tape on its own track. Breaks usually occur in the control track when you stop recording. You

want to avoid these breaks on your master tapes. Broadcast engineers don't like tapes with broken control tracks because they can cause glitches and rolls when they're played through equipment. A *timecode track* is simply the frame-accurate time information added to a tape as you record. This timecode track must be present on a tape so that the edit knows where to place a clip or piece of video in time (for example, if your timecode doesn't go to 4 minutes, you can't record a new clip at 5 minutes).

To avoid breaks during an assemble edit, you first need to make sure that you have at least 6 seconds of tape before the In point of your video. At the end of an assemble edit, you should let the edit run a few seconds longer, to avoid any breaks in the tracks.

Here's where it gets tricky: Although an insert edit doesn't record control or timecode tracks on a tape, these tracks must be present on the tape for the insert edit to be successful. For this reason, editors often use *black and coded tapes*. These tapes have had black and timecode previously recorded on them. Note that insert edits cannot be performed on DV tapes. For DV tapes, only assemble edits are possible, unless you have a relatively expensive professional deck.

Performing insert edits with frame accuracy

Another feature of insert edits in the Edit to Tape window is that they are *frame-accurate*. Under proper conditions, therefore, you can replace just one shot on your tape that lies in the middle of a recorded project. This feature allows a greater degree of control — many editors use it to fix issues with their projects. For example, you may have edited an entire hour-long show to your tape and later decided to replace the video of just one shot in the show, which you have already put on tape. Using the Insert Edit overlay in the Edit to Tape window, you can replace just the video of a single shot on your tape.

However, before you take the severe step of insert editing onto your master tape, you need to be sure that your Final Cut Pro setup is frame-accurate. Video decks can occasionally end up with a slight offset on frame accuracy, and this offset can cause a glitch when you perform an insert edit.

To confirm the frame accuracy of your system, you need to create a sequence that consists of a series of single frames. These single frames can be colored slugs or color bars and other clearly identifiable frames. The important thing is that each of these shots needs to have a duration of just one frame. Of course, you can also use the countdown that Final Cut Pro provides as a reference, but doing this exercise should accurately demonstrate the frame-accurate nature of Final Cut Pro using a sequence you create.

Follow these steps to create a frame-accurate test of the Final Cut Pro insert editing capabilities:

1. **Line up five of these frames in a sequence, such as a white frame, a frame of color bars, a black frame, a red frame, and a yellow frame.**

2. **Use the Edit to Tape function to perform an insert edit to a specific timecode (such as 1:00:10;00) on a test videotape.**

3. **Slowly jog back on your tape, and see which frame has edited to the starting point on tape.**

   If a frame is earlier than what you wanted to have edited to tape, your system has a *drift* of –1 frame. If a frame is later than what you wanted to have edited to 1:00:10;00, your system has an *offset* of +1.

4. **Choose Final Cut Pro⇨Audio/Video settings, and then select the Device Control Preset window.**

5. **Select your preset, and click the Edit button.**

6. **In the Device Control Preset window, edit the Playback Offset setting to account for the frame offset.**

   Figure 17-6 shows this setting in the lower-left corner of the dialog box. For example, if the offset were –1, enter **1** as the Playback Offset setting. On the other hand, if the offset were +1, enter **–1** in the Playback Offset field.

Figure 17-6:
The Device
Control
Preset
Editor.

Now that you have made these adjustments, you too can be a slick and sophisticated editor, doing insert edits with frame accuracy. That is, of course, if you have a frame-accurate deck. Unfortunately, many decks are not frame-accurate.

Editing Online versus Offline

When working with Final Cut Pro and editing in general, you may come across the terms *offline* and *online*. These terms are important to understand because producers often ask you to work offline in Final Cut Pro. In this section, I explain these terms.

The terms *offline* and *online* originated a few years ago when nonlinear editing (NLE) systems, such as Final Cut Pro, had not achieved data rates that were high enough for broadcast resolution. In other words, you could capture and edit at a low resolution, using the earlier manifestations of NLEs, but these systems weren't capable of working at high enough resolutions to go directly to broadcast. These may sound like the dark days of video technology, but that was life for many of us.

In those days, the rough, low-resolution edit was considered an *offline* edit. After an offline rough draft was done, the entire show was re-created in an *online* setup. The Online Room could be a very expensive tape-to-tape edit room or just a more expensive NLE that could handle the high data rates that were required for broadcast.

In many ways, these terms perhaps no longer apply because you can do both your offline and online editing in Final Cut Pro. However, in some cases, the term *online* may still indicate an expensive and very sophisticated edit room, where high-tech features, such as real-time color correction or audio sweetening facilities, may be available.

In some cases, an offline edit may simply consist of creating a rough cut, which you later want to refine and finalize in an online edit room. This online room may consist of a much higher-end Final Cut Pro system, which uses third-party video cards and provides higher-quality video. Or, the online room may be a tape-to-tape edit room.

With Final Cut Pro 3, Apple introduced a new feature called OfflineRT, which stands for Offline Real Time. Using this feature, you can capture video into Final Cut Pro at extremely low resolution, which allows large quantities of media to fit on small drives, and then edit your project. The effects work in real-time when you use this feature; hence, the term *RT*. Later, you can recapture just your edited show at a higher resolution.

Another common method for moving from an offline to an online process is the export of Edit Decision Lists. *Edit Decision Lists* (EDLs) are a data record of your edits. EDLs enable you to do your rough cut at home on a basic Final Cut Pro system and then export the EDL and enter an expensive and high-end editing environment to refine your project. With an EDL and your original media, you can re-create your rough edit on a high-end system and add all the bells, whistles, and polish that a high-end system offers.

Chapter 18

Exporting Your Movie to a Digital File

*I*n the multimedia world we live in, many Final Cut Pro projects never end up on videotape. Instead, they're exported to a digital file so that they can be broadcast on the Internet or played back on DVDs and CDs. DVDs have become a popular format for watching movies at home, and a DVD is a good way to show someone a high-quality version of your edited video.

The process of preparing material for the Web, DVDs, and CDs is full of confusion and myths. In this chapter, I tackle some concepts and techniques for outputting digital video and dispel a few myths about this difficult topic.

For instance, many people think that if you export a project into a QuickTime file, it's ready for the Internet. Right? Wrong. Why not? Because raw digital video files are *way* too big to send over the Internet, unless you expect your audience to spend several days downloading them! Raw video still needs to be compressed into a smaller file size before it can be transferred digitally. This compression can be done with QuickTime, which uses complex schemes to toss out much of the video data. The result of this compression is a video file that is usually not full-screen, and not 100 percent sharp, but the compressed video is small enough to be conveniently transmitted via a modem or DSL service.

Anyway, Final Cut Pro HD takes a number of approaches to exporting your finished movies as digital media files. It can export them into media files that are appropriate for Internet distribution or DVD distribution, for instance. It can also give you manual control over how your exported video is compressed, or it can make those decisions for you.

If you're really interested in learning about the nitty-gritty of video compression, I suggest that you read this entire chapter. If all you want to do is export video in a painless way, without learning what's going on behind the scenes, or how to control every nuance of the exporting process, I suggest that you skip to the section "Easy Exporting with the Compressor Application," later in this chapter. The standalone Compressor program works with Final Cut (and is included on your installation CDs), which lets you compress video into all sorts of different shapes and sizes.

Working with QuickTime Video

QuickTime has often been described as the Swiss Army knife of multimedia applications. That description is certainly a fitting one, although QuickTime is even more than that. Most people think of QuickTime as the player that allows you to watch movies and clips of video on your computer (see Figure 18-1). In fact, QuickTime is an entire multimedia architecture. This versatile and vast architecture allows media creation, delivery, and translation of all kinds. QuickTime consists of more than 200 separate components. QuickTime is simultaneously a file format and a set of applications, plug-ins, and much more that enables users to seamlessly work with many types of multimedia.

Figure 18-1:
The QuickTime Player represents only the tip of the QuickTime iceberg.

What does all this have to do with Final Cut Pro, and why should you know about QuickTime? Final Cut Pro is based entirely on the QuickTime architecture. If you're working with Final Cut Pro, you have access to all the components of QuickTime. Don't worry: You don't have to launch any special applications or learn to use a new interface (unless you choose to work with Compressor, a new application for Final Cut Pro that I discuss at the end of this chapter). QuickTime works seamlessly and transparently, which means that it works behind the scenes without your knowing it. Also, no additional purchase is necessary, because the QuickTime components are installed with Final Cut Pro. Of course, QuickTime offers upgrades and add-ons, such as an MPEG-2 component, which allows you to work with the file format that's used by DVDs and some new cameras, without needing the special Apple DVD Player.

In the next few sections, I show you how to use this multimedia tool to take the movies you edited in Final Cut Pro and prepare them for all kinds of other formats. Web streaming and CD or DVD playback, as well as any other multimedia uses you can think up for your video, are easily within reach.

Getting to Know Codecs

If you're going to prepare your video for the Web or CD, the word *codec* fast becomes part of your vocabulary. Video files, as they exist when you edit them in Final Cut Pro, are simply too large to stream over the Web or even to download in a reasonable amount of time. (*Streaming* means to send video as a continuous stream that is played back on the fly as it's being transmitted, as opposed to *downloading,* where the viewer's computer waits to begin playback until the entire movie has been transmitted to the viewer's hard drive.) Hence, compression is used to reduce the size of the video files and, at the same time, to preserve as much of the quality as possible. You use QuickTime for compressing and selecting your codec as well.

The components that compress the video are called codecs. The word *codec* is short for *coder-deco*der. Several codecs exist for audio and video. Also, many kinds of codecs are specifically intended for streaming, and others are strictly for capturing and playing back video. Some codecs are hardware-based, but a description of those types is outside of the scope of this book. I focus on software-based codecs in this chapter. The particular codec you choose and how you use it have an impact on the final outcome of your compression, and throughout this chapter I tell you some things you need to consider before you decide which codec you want to use.

Using compression also requires paying special attention to the quality of your source footage. In fact, starting with high-quality footage is one of the best ways to get great results, especially when you're planning to compress video to extremely small file sizes. The adage "garbage in, garbage out" is important to keep in mind. For instance, to achieve better video compression, you should keep the backgrounds of your shots simple and use a tripod. If you're interested in why this strategy helps (and for other suggestions), see the sidebar "Shooting with compression in mind," later in this chapter.

Because so many codecs are available, I briefly cover a few basic ones that you can choose from when preparing your material. Bear in mind that this tour of the codecs is done in the context of preparing your video for Web streaming or CD playback. I say that because many video codecs are designed for video capture and playback but are not suitable for streaming or low-data-rate playback, such as the type needed for CDs. Data rates are important because you can use very high data rates for video that plays in your computer. But CDs or DVDs, as well as the Internet, require low data rates. I discuss data rates later in this chapter.

If you're working on a Mac and you're using Final Cut Pro and QuickTime, many video and audio codecs (including the most widely used formats) are automatically loaded onto your computer. Later in this chapter, I show you where in the export process you select the proper codec for your project. Also, many companies make and sell other codecs you can purchase and install on your Mac. After installation (which, in OS X, involves dragging the codecs to your `Library/Quicktime` folder), these codecs are instantly available through the usual QuickTime export methods, which I outline later in this chapter.

Looking at the Video Codecs

The goal of a video codec is to compress your video to a smaller file size so that it can be played on the Web, a CD, or a DVD. The trick for a codec is to maintain as much of the quality as possible while eliminating the least important (or visually noticeable) information.

Apart from quality and size issues, the most important consideration is whether a user has the necessary codec installed on their computer. Without a corresponding codec, a user could not view the content you created. Fortunately, the majority of the most popular codecs (discussed in the following list) are commonplace on most systems. If you have any question about compatibility, you should include a link on the Web page that hosts your file for downloading the necessary driver or player software.

The most common codecs that are used to compress video are as follows:

- **Sorenson Video:** Sorenson Video is by far one of the best codecs, particularly for the Web and CDs, because it delivers extremely good quality and very low data rates. *Data rate* is the amount of data that the compressed video passes through a computer or modem every second that it's being played (generally, you want the highest-quality video produced by the lowest data rate possible). When I first tried Sorenson Video, I was surprised by how low a data rate I could use while still managing to get a very good image from my compressed movies.

- **H.263:** Because this codec was created for videoconferencing, it's an extremely efficient and smart codec that can deliver good quality with a lower data rate. I have tested Sorenson and H.263 under certain conditions, such as high-motion video, and I have noticed that H.263 provides a better finished product. It's definitely a codec to consider.

- **MPEG-1:** *MPEG* stands for Motion Pictures Experts Group, and it represents a new type of codec. The MPEG-1 codec has good quality, but it's generally not the preferred choice for Web streaming. (The reasons have to do with how MPEG creates intermediate frames that don't work well over the low bandwidth that's available through modems.) However, MPEG-1 is a good choice if you want your audience to download the video and then play it from their computer drives. It's also the standard format for VCDs, or Video CDs, which are like lower-resolution DVDs recorded on CD media.

- **MPEG-2:** MPEG-2 is becoming popular because it's used for compressing movies for DVD playback. Although this codec isn't well suited for Web streaming, it provides high quality at DVD playback rates. MPEG-type compressions are ill suited for Web streaming because the type of compression it uses creates intermediate frames that require other full frames to be present. The result is much more data than is necessary for Web applications, but this codec is perfectly suited for use in a home theater. In fact, MPEG-2 is quickly becoming the format of choice for producing videos for commercial release or home playback. Because almost anyone can produce a DVD now, look for more MPEG-2 software and hardware to emerge in the coming months and years. Even video camcorders are beginning to incorporate a flavor of MPEG-2 into their recording devices. Also, if you're using iDVD or DVD Studio Pro to create discs, this codec is the one for you. With the new Compressor application, you have much more control over the MPEG-2 encoding process than you previously had.

- **MPEG-4:** The MPEG-4 format is designed for video over the internet and other low-bandwidth applications (the latest generation of mobile phones incorporates MPEG-4 video, and it's appearing in a number of other places as well). If you're looking for an alternative to the Sorenson codec, MPEG-4 is a great choice. It can produce extremely small file sizes and can be scaled to meet the needs of a variety of user connection speeds.

Looking at the Audio Codecs

Numerous audio codecs are already installed on your Mac. These codecs, like others, are accessible via the QuickTime dialog box, which I guide you through later in this chapter. Many companies also sell advanced versions of their audio codecs that are useful for professional work. You can purchase and install these codecs, which you can then access via the QuickTime dialog box.

Some of the more common codecs for compressing audio are as follows:

- **QDesign music codec:** This is the codec of choice if you have instrumental music to compress. It can produce extremely high-quality files and still maintain a data rate so low that you can stream it over a very slow (14.4 Kbps) modem. Using music with vocals in it is also fine with this codec, but avoid it if you have only voice to compress.

- **Qualcomm PureVoice:** If you have voices in your file that you want to compress, use this codec. It works to create very small and streamable files at very low data rates. This codec is best reserved for the human voice; it doesn't work well with music.

- **MP3:** MP3 is short for MPEG Layer 3 audio. MP3 music files have become the big thing on the Web in the past few years. This codec is helpful for compressing music files to a small size, although it's not always an ideal codec for streaming audio over slow Web connections. However, MP3s are useful for streaming over broadband connections, which are rapidly increasing in number. Even the popular Flash application includes the ability to include MP3s in your Web page designs for faster connections. Also, for downloading over the Web, MP3s are an ideal format.

- **IMA:** A decent audio codec that works easily on both Mac and Windows machines, IMA is good for older machines, but it creates slightly larger files because of its low compression. On the other hand, its lower compression delivers good-sounding audio.

- **AAC:** *AAC,* or Advanced Audio Coding, is a new audio format engineered by Apple that improves on the MP3 codec. Although AAC isn't widely available yet (especially for PC users), it may eventually become the successor to the MP3 because it produces better audio at lower data rates. If you have downloaded music to your iPod from the Apple music store, you have already encountered AAC files (they usually have an .m4p file extension).

Shooting with compression in mind

Compression is a sophisticated and complex science, and codecs perform very tricky computations at blinding speeds. Knowing how video codecs work can help you shoot material for better compression. Video codecs perform spatial and temporal compression. *Spatial compression* means that a codec takes large areas of similar color and compresses them to tiny numbers. Codecs love large areas of solid colors. If you're preparing to shoot a video to be compressed later for the Web, make sure that the subject of your video isn't sitting in front of a complex or patterned background. Keeping the background simple helps the codec to work more efficiently and to create smaller video files of higher quality.

Video codecs also do *temporal encoding* — that is, they save a complete frame only every so often. Instead, they save only areas of an image that change between successive frames. Incomplete frames are compared to a reference frame, which fills in the missing details without adding unnecessary data. If a shot stays the same with just a person's head moving in the frame, that shot will compress well. However, if you use a handheld camera and the framing of the shot keeps changing, that shot will make the codec work much harder, resulting in low-quality files that may also be quite large. In short, for best results, keep your background simple and use a tripod to minimize change from frame to frame.

Knowing Your Data Rates

Before I plunge into exporting movies from Final Cut Pro, you need to know about one more critical item: data rates. Imagine that each modem that's connected to the Internet is a pipeline. Think of slow modems (for instance, 14.4 Kbps) as thin pipelines and fast modems (such as cable and DSL) as fat pipelines. Each of these pipelines can handle a certain data rate. If your compressed movie goes above the data rate for a particular connection, proper playback of the movie is in jeopardy. The movie may choke and stutter during playback or can even stop playing.

Knowing the limits of your data rates is the key to creating movies that play efficiently and without problems. In addition to a maximum data rate, each pipeline (or modem on the Internet) also has a preferred frame size for compressed movies. When you export your movie from Final Cut Pro into QuickTime, you can select a data rate for it. You need to stay with the proper data rate and frame size for the modem type you expect your audience to use if you want your streaming movie to play correctly. To be on the safe side, cater to the slowest modem rate you expect your viewers to have. That way, you cover any faster connections as well. You may also use an application such as Compressor to batch-process a video for distribution to several different Internet connections. You should give your viewers a choice between a low-bandwidth version of your video and a high-bandwidth alternative because many people now have the benefit of a faster connection.

Table 18-1 shows the rates and frame sizes for various types of Internet connections. When exporting a QuickTime movie from Final Cut Pro, you can control the frame size of your final output.

Table 18-1	Data Rates for Common Internet Connections		
Connection Type	*Data Rate, Kilobits per Second*	*Data Rate, Kilobytes per Second*	*Frame Size, Pixels*
28.8 Kbps*	20	2.5	160 × 120
56.6 Kbps	40	5	160 × 120
ISDN	96	12	192 × 144
DSL	140	17	240 × 180
T1	160	20	240 × 180
Cable modem	1000	125	320 × 240

* Kilobits per second

If you're referring to other literature or learning about streaming video on the Web, be aware that data rates are often listed in both Kbps (kilo*bits* per second) and KBps (kilo*bytes* per second). The difference between bits and bytes is critical: A byte is 8 times larger than a bit. If you see rates listed in KBps, multiply the number by 8 to get Kbps. Similarly, if you see data rates reported as Kbps, divide the number by 8 to get KBps.

The data rates for modems are usually lower than advertised. For instance, your 56K modem rarely approaches the 56 Kbps rating. The reason has to do with the analog phone lines that modems use and the overhead from both your computer's software and the server's software.

Export Away!

Final Cut Pro enables you to export video files from a sequence that are compressed for various kinds of deliveries. You can also select and export files directly from the Browser window. For instance, after editing and finishing your DV-based video, you can then compress it for playback on a CD or over the Web.

Follow these steps to export a video for CD or the Web from Final Cut Pro:

1. **In Final Cut Pro, click to select a clip or a sequence in the Browser.**

2. **Choose File➪Export➪Using QuickTime Conversion from the menu bar.**

   The Save dialog box appears, as shown in Figure 18-2.

3. **In the Where drop-down list, indicate where you want to save the exported file and then type a name for your movie in the Save As text box.**

   If you plan to embed this movie into an HTML document for the Web, be sure to give your movie a .mov extension. You should generally add the .mov extension at all times when exporting for the Web or to CD.

4. **From the Format drop-down list, choose QuickTime Movie.**

5. **Select a setting from the Use drop-down list.**

   The settings on the Use menu are divided into a few simple categories, which can be modified on the Options menu, as discussed in the next step. The categories are Modem, DSL/Cable (Low, Medium, and High), and LAN (local-area network). See Figure 18-3. Specify LAN for use over an intranet or other networked environment.

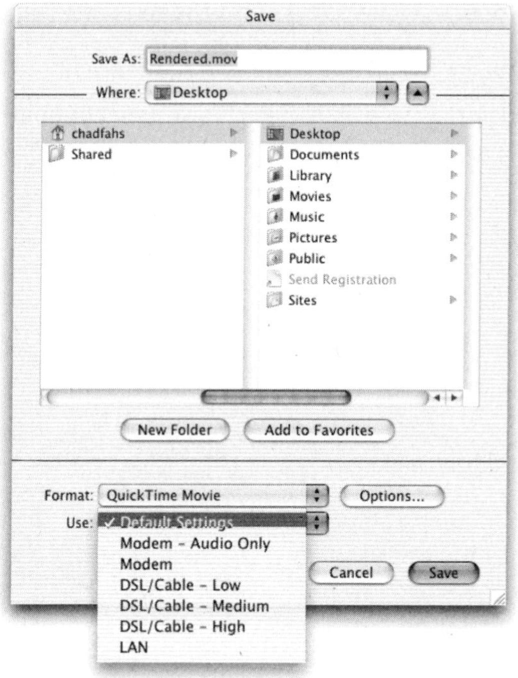

Figure 18-3:
The Use
choices
that are
available in
the Save
dialog box.

6. Click the Options button to access the codec and size options.

The Movie Settings dialog box appears, as shown in Figure 18-4.

Note that if you have selected a setting on the Use menu in the preceding step, you can skip Step 6. Resort to Step 6 only if you have a better understanding of your requirements and want to skip the presets that are offered on the Use menu.

The Movie Settings dialog box enables you to select custom video and audio settings. For instance, click the Settings button inside the Video section, and you see the Compression Settings choices. Here, on the Compressor menu, you can select the appropriate codec, such as Sorenson, MPEG-4, Cinepak, and others. You can also choose a different frame rate for your video or adjust the data rate (if you know your requirements).

In the Movie Settings dialog box, you can click the Size button and then select the Use Custom Size option. This option enables you to set the width and height of your movie. At this point, you can also use any special QuickTime filters you have installed to make last-minute adjustments to the look of your video.

After selecting the desired settings, click OK in the Movie Settings dialog box.

7. When you're ready to export the movie, click Save.

The progress of your export appears on a status bar. You can cancel this export at any time by pressing Esc. To play your movie, double-click the movie file after it has been exported and view it in the QuickTime Player.

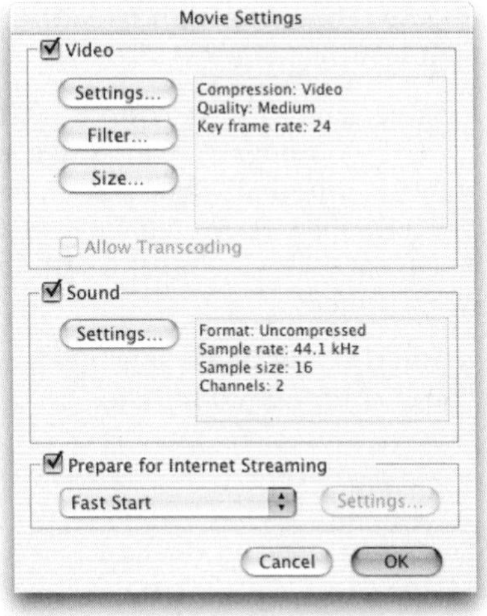

Figure 18-4:
The Movie
Settings
dialog box.

Movie Settings
- ☑ Video
  - Settings... Compression: Video / Quality: Medium / Key frame rate: 24
  - Filter...
  - Size...
  - ☐ Allow Transcoding
- ☑ Sound
  - Settings... Format: Uncompressed / Sample rate: 44.1 kHz / Sample size: 16 / Channels: 2
- ☑ Prepare for Internet Streaming
  - Fast Start Settings...
  - Cancel OK

Exporting a Batch of Movies

Rather than export one movie at a time, you can export a batch of movies. This capability can help you set up a queue, which can export your movies while you do something else, like shop for a director's chair. Exporting by the batch is a good idea if you have lots of movies to export, because exporting several movies one at a time can be time consuming.

To batch-export your movies, follow these steps:

1. Select in the Browser window the items you want to export.

You can select multiple clips by holding down ⌘ and clicking each clip (⌘+clicking). You can also select clips or sequences within one or more open projects.

2. Choose File⇨Batch Export from the menu bar.

The Export Queue window appears and displays your selected items, as shown in Figure 18-5. A new bin is automatically created for each batch of your selections. Settings in the Export Queue window are applied on a bin-by-bin basis, so the same settings apply to all clips in a particular bin. If you don't like the default bin structure, you can create new bins by choosing File⇨New⇨Bin and move items between the bins.

3. **Select a bin in the queue, and click the Settings button at the bottom of the Export Queue window.**

   The Batch settings window appears, as shown in Figure 18-6.

4. **Click the Set Destination button in the Settings window, and select a location to save the exported files.**

5. **Select QuickTime Movie or QuickTime (Custom) from the Format drop-down menu in the Batch settings window.**

   To select a particular video codec, QuickTime (Custom) is the setting to use. Final Cut Pro allows you to do things in many ways, and you can choose your QuickTime settings in different ways as well. Some investigation into the Format and Settings drop-down menus reveals several custom formats and presets you can use. Choose the settings that are best suited to the needs of your project.

6. **Use the Settings drop-down menu in the Batch settings window to select the settings for your final compressed movie.**

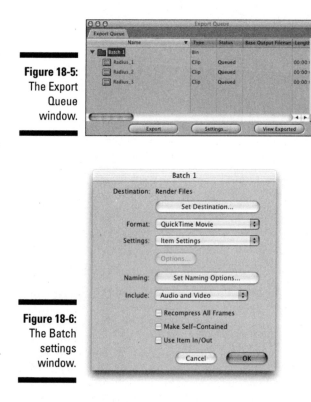

Figure 18-5:
The Export
Queue
window.

Figure 18-6:
The Batch
settings
window.

7. **In the Batch settings window, click the Set Naming Options button and choose the name of your final exports.**

   For instance, you can check the Add Custom Extension and type **.mov** if you're embedding your movie in an HTML document on the Web.

8. **Select the Use Item In/Out check box in the Batch settings window to export the portions of a clip or sequence that you have previously marked with In or Out points.**

   You can mark the In and Out points in your clip or the sequence by pressing the I and O keys, respectively. In absence of In and Out points, the entire clip or sequence is exported. Note that you must mark In and Out points before you take this series of steps to batch-export.

9. **Click OK to close the Batch settings window.**

10. **To begin a batch export, select in the Export Queue window the bin or bins you want to export by clicking them and then clicking the Export button.**

    You can also select individual items within bins in the Export Queue window and then click the Export button.

    The progress of your exports is displayed in a dialog box that appears. You can click Cancel or press Esc to end your export at any time. When an item is exported, the status of the item changes to Done in the Status column of the Export Queue window.

Easy Exporting with the Compressor Application

Final Cut Pro seems to have it all: You can capture, add titles and effects of all kinds, record to tape, and even export to the Web, a CD, or a DVD. But can one software package do everything and still do it well? The answer is "Almost." Fortunately, Final Cut Pro 4 added a new application named Compressor, which improves the flexibility and power of exporting a finished project (or individual clips) to a wide range of formats, including the newly popular DVD format. After all, who doesn't want to watch his or her video masterpiece at its best quality? VHS just doesn't cut it anymore. Now, you can tweak settings to your heart's content and produce that shiny new disc you have always wanted.

One of the best aspects of Compressor is that it features tons of *presets,* which are collections of compression settings that define the image size you want your exported video to take on (for instance, DVD video is sized at 720x480 pixels, but Internet-destined video is more like 320x240 pixels or even less), and what image quality level it should have as well. There are settings, ready to go, for creating DVD video at various quality levels (the lower the quality, the more video you can fit on a DVD) as well as video aimed at the Internet, or CD-ROMs. What's more, some presets are specifically designed to work with the kind of media your original Final Cut movies use — that is, video that's originally shot on film at 24 frames per second, on video at 30 frames per second (technically, 29.97), in a wide-screen format or in the European PAL format, for instance.

In this section, I take you through the steps of using Compressor from start to finish.

Exporting video from Final Cut Pro using Compressor

You can use Compressor as a stand-alone application for converting video and audio files to other formats, or you can use it directly by choosing File↩ Export↩Using Compressor in Final Cut Pro HD. The main benefit of using Compressor outside Final Cut Pro is that you can import and convert all sorts of clips rather than just projects and sequences. I focus on using it from within Final Cut because that's most convenient.

To export a sequence directly from Final Cut Pro using Compressor, follow these steps:

1. **Select your sequence in the Browser or make the Timeline window active by clicking it, and then choose File↩Export↩Using Compressor from the menu bar.**

   The Compressor application launches and presents you with a Batch window, with the sequence you selected at the top of the list (see Figure 18-7).

2. **Choose a setting from the Preset drop-down menu.**

   Select a setting that most closely matches the needs of your project. You see many presets for DVD. This is the area where Compressor truly excels. If you're producing a DVD for your project with an application like DVD Studio Pro, you can use these settings to choose a suitable encoding option. For instance, if you have a 60-minute video and you don't mind waiting for your video to encode, you can choose the MPEG-2 60min High Quality Encode option and then select All to produce an MPEG-2 file with an accompanying audio file. You should generally choose the shortest time possible (60 rather than 90, for instance) to achieve the best quality. If your clip is 10 seconds long, you should use the 60-minute setting. You should also account for the total running time of all the clips that are going on the DVD. Add their durations and use that number as an indicator to choose your setting. You can also choose to create high-quality video for the Web by using MPEG-4. In this case, you can choose from a variety of options, beginning with the type of source material (24P, which is progressive-frame video that produces motion similar to film, NTSC, or PAL, depending on your country of origin). If you're feeling adventurous and want to modify an existing preset to create your own settings, choose Window➪Presets and then make your adjustments in the more detailed Presets window (see Figure 18-8).

Figure 18-7:
The Batch window in Compressor.

Figure 18-8:
Selecting presets in Compressor in the Batch window and in the Presets window.

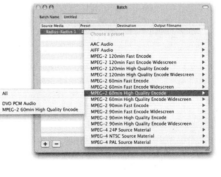

3. **Select a location for your file by clicking the Source drop-down menu, which appears when you click in the Destination column of the Batch window.**

   Choosing Source as your destination places the resulting files in the same directory as your original files (in this case, the `Final Cut Pro` directory). To choose a different folder on your hard drive, select Other and locate another folder.

4. **When you're ready to export your file, click the Submit button in the lower-right corner of the Batch window.**

   A progress bar indicates that your files are processing. Also, a Batch Monitor window displays the progress of your individual files.

The best way to get familiar with Compressor's different presets and their quality-to-data size trade-offs is by repeatedly running a video through Compressor and applying a different preset each time. For instance, if you're compressing a video for the Internet, you may try it with the MP4 NTSC presets for Large Progressive downloads, Small Progressive Downloads, and even for CD-ROMs. Comparing the resulting files that Compressor spits out help you determine which offers the best balance of quality and file size for your job.

Batch-exporting sequences with Compressor

One of the nicest features of Compressor is its ability to easily create and monitor batch lists, either straight from Final Cut Pro or by adding files directly from your hard drive. In fact, you could bypass the Final Cut Pro batch-export features altogether if you decide that you like Compressor's features better. However, if you intend to export individual clips from the Browser (or even portions from your Timeline), you may want to stay with the familiar processes of Final Cut Pro. Compressor allows you to trim a sequence in its Preview window (choose Window⇨Preview in the Compressor software), although you can sometimes do this more easily in Final Cut Pro instead. Also, Compressor allows you to export only sequences, although the Final Cut Pro Batch Export feature allows you to export clips as well.

As I mention earlier, Compressor is a useful application for exporting video for DVDs (as well as for a multitude of other formats). By using the Batch window, you can easily export several MPEG-2 files for your next DVD project without having to adjust the settings for each one individually.

Follow these steps to convert multiple sequences with Compressor using the Batch window:

1. **Select multiple sequences in the Browser by ⌘+clicking or Shift+clicking, and then choose File⇨Export⇨Using Compressor.**

   The Compressor application launches and presents you with a Batch window, and the sequences you selected are arranged in a batch list. You may also add video files that are not in Final Cut Pro (perhaps you have on your hard drive a finished project that you want to convert) by clicking the Add button (it looks like a plus sign) at the bottom of the Batch window. Choose the files you want to import, and click Open.

2. **Type a name for your new batch in the Batch Name field.**

3. **Select all your files in the Batch window by holding down ⌘ and clicking (⌘+clicking), by Shift+clicking, or by dragging the mouse over the files.**

   Selecting several files at one time allows you to apply the same settings to all files without having to specify settings for each one individually. Of course, you may also apply separate settings for each file, as I discuss in the preceding section. If it's difficult to see filenames in the Batch window, expand the window by dragging out the lower-right corner.

4. **Control+click any of the selected Preset drop-down menus, and choose a setting.**

   This preset automatically applies to all the selected files (see Figure 18-9). Remember to select a setting that most closely matches the needs of your project.

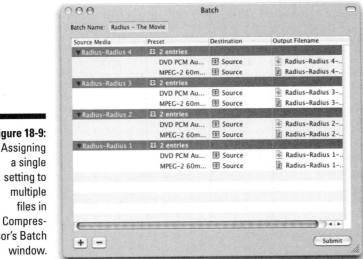

Figure 18-9: Assigning a single setting to multiple files in Compressor's Batch window.

5. **Select a location for your file by clicking the Source drop-down menu, which appears when you click in the Destination column of the Batch window.**

   To send all your files to the same destination, make sure to keep all of them selected as you did in Step 4 and then select the destination. Choosing Source as your destination places the resulting files in the same directory as your original files (in this case, the `Final Cut Pro` directory). To choose a different folder on your hard drive, select Other and locate another folder.

6. **When you're ready to export your file, click the Submit button.**

   A progress bar indicates that your files are processing. Also, a Batch Monitor window displays the progress of your individual files (see Figure 18-10).

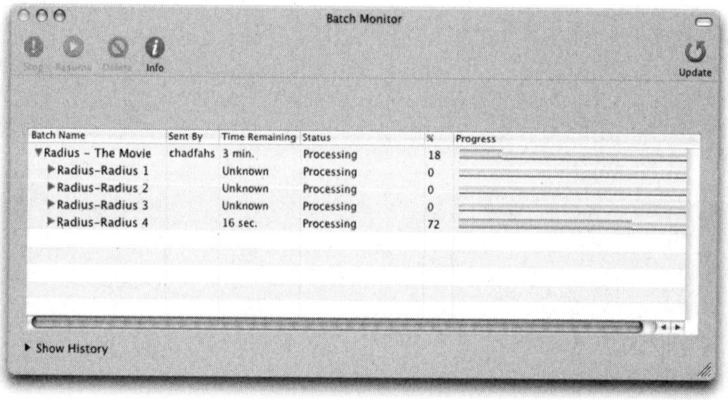

Figure 18-10:
The Batch
Monitor
window.

Part VI
The Part of Tens

The 5th Wave

By Rich Tennant

"Honey—remember that pool party last summer where you showed everyone how to do the limbo in just a sombrero and a dish towel? Well look at what the MSN Daily Video Download is."

In this part . . .

In Part VI, I serve up ten or so simple things you can do to become a more capable Final Cut Pro editor, from honing your creative and technical know-how to upgrading your current Mac setup. I also offer some ten-odd tips for how to manage long projects in Final Cut Pro: everything from establishing a logical bin structure to naming clips intelligently.

Chapter 19

Ten Tips for Becoming a Better Editor

*A*fter you have gotten your feet wet with Final Cut Pro HD, you can do plenty of things to nurture your abilities as an editor. In this chapter, I present a few tips that cover everything from getting a better grip on how the Final Cut Pro features work together to honing your creative instincts, improving your technical knowledge of the editing and postproduction process, and upgrading your hardware and tools.

Try Out the Final Cut Pro Tutorials

Final Cut Pro includes a nice set of tutorials that take you through the basics of editing and effects work, using video and audio clips that are designed just for use in the tutorials. (You probably have to dig up the tutorials CD in your Final Cut Pro box because these tutorials aren't installed automatically with the main application.) Tutorials aren't so useful when you want to pick up a particular skill in a hurry, but they can help you soak in a broad topic, and they make learning easier by providing you with the appropriate media (instead of having to dig it up on your own).

Study (Don't Just Watch) Movies and Commercials

A great way to improve your picture-editing instincts is to carefully study all the professional editing work that you can find on television and in movies. Watch a bunch of features, commercials, and music videos carefully — in fact, a good tactic is to watch with your TV's volume turned off so that you can focus solely on how shots move from one to another. You can see an infinite number of editing styles (fast and slow, superstylized, and subtle), and you can refine your own tastes from there. Finally, when you start to see the conscious design behind movie shots — how the editor uses shots in a particular order to communicate information and set a mood — you start to see a payoff in your own work.

Practice on Someone Else's Real-World Footage

The best way to improve your editing skills is to edit, edit, edit, so try coming up with practice projects so that you can keep honing your skills. Producing new practice footage to edit is difficult. For instance, I used to record practice scenes on a videocamera (using friends as placeholder actors), but eventually ran out of fresh ideas for new footage, and I grew tired of the raw look produced by my handheld video.

But, I eventually discovered a great alternative: I borrowed real-world, professional footage from working editors. For instance, I found a postproduction company that was willing to loan me the source footage for real-world commercials that its professional editors had worked with. It was a perfect solution: I could practice on professionally shot footage that looked great and offered lots of angles and perspectives to choose from (called *coverage*). And, after I had edited this footage, I could compare my work against the real-world commercials that the postproduction company had produced.

If you're looking for good practice material, try asking some established editors to let you "borrow" footage from their finished projects. You can probably find someone who is willing to lend an editor-in-training a hand.

Go Online and Find a Community

I recommend the following helpful Web sites, which can help expand your technical grasp of Final Cut Pro and help improve your general editorial knowledge:

✔ **2-Pop.com (**www.2-pop.com**):** This world-class site focuses on all things for Final Cut Pro. You can find news of Final Cut Pro–related products, reviews of the latest Final Cut Pro updates, how-to tutorials, and, most important, a variety of message forums where fellow users can answer just about any Final Cut Pro question you can conjure up. (2-Pop also has a couple of forums dedicated to other digital media topics.)

✔ **Creative Cow (**www.creativecow.net**):** A solid runner-up to 2-Pop, this fun site has a strong Final Cut Pro message forum and tons of other active forums dedicated to other digital video applications and topics. Creative Cow also has some helpful tutorials and product reviews written by real-world users.

✔ **Apple Discussion Forum (**http://discussions.info.apple.com/**):** Few people know that Apple hosts a thriving discussion forum dedicated to Final Cut Pro. To join, go to this link and choose the Final Cut Pro option.

✔ **EditorsNet (**www.editorsnet.com**):** This great site has daily news about the editing business and new products, but it really shines for its interviews with professional editors (usually, film and television editors) about their latest projects. These interviews and other articles give you a useful perspective on both the art and the craft of real-world editing.

Join a Final Cut Pro User Group

You can join (or just drop in on) a growing handful of user groups that are dedicated to Final Cut Pro editors. The members of these groups typically meet monthly for product demos and helpful question-and-answer sessions. You can find some of the most active groups in the following locations:

✔ Boston (www.bosfcpug.org)

✔ Los Angeles (www.lafcpug.org)

✔ San Francisco (www.sfcutters.org)

✔ Chicago (www.chifcpug.org)

To find a Final Cut Pro user group near you, visit the following Apple site:

www.apple.com/software/pro/resources/usergroups.html

Upgrade Your Hardware

Adding a few optional, affordable pieces of hardware can really enhance your editing experience with Final Cut Pro. Check out the following suggestions:

✔ **Speakers or headphones:** A good pair of speakers or headphones can help you pick up the subtle details in your audio.

✔ **Television or monitor:** Get a decent TV or dedicated video monitor so that you don't have to watch your clips and Timeline sequences in the Final Cut Pro smallish Viewer and Canvas windows. It's not only helpful to see your video on a bigger screen, but it's also much easier to spot problems with color accuracy and to find other small glitches in video.

✔ **Second display screen:** Getting a second computer monitor or LCD display gives you more space to comfortably spread out the numerous Final Cut windows and palettes. (Most PowerBooks and PowerMacs can "drive" two monitors at one time, but iBooks, iMacs, and eMacs can't.) For instance, with a second monitor, you can place the Final Cut Browser window on its own screen and set it to display clips as large thumbnail images so that you can easily spot the clip you're looking for. If you're working in HD video, you can use a second monitor (like the 23-inch Apple Cinema Display flat screen) to preview HD imagery in its high-resolution glory.

✔ **More RAM:** If your Mac has 384 MB of RAM, boosting it to 512 MB, 640 MB, or more can make Final Cut Pro run faster overall. You may not see *major* speed gains, but you see the OS X spinning cursor less often — especially if you tend to keep other applications open at the same time (for instance, a Web browser or the Final Cut Pro secondary applications, such as LiveType and Soundtrack).

✔ **Programmable mouse or trackball:** A programmable mouse or trackball sports extra buttons that you can program to invoke the Final Cut Pro features you use often. Taking advantage of these extra buttons means that you don't have to spend as much time moving your mouse around the screen or reaching for some keyboard shortcuts.

Upgrade Your Software

I recommend the following third-party software, which either adds new features to Final Cut Pro or helps with digital video production in general:

✔ **Final Cut Pro plug-ins:** You can add new visual effects and text-generation features to Final Cut Pro by installing custom plug-in software. A dizzying array of plug-ins is available — some to create flashy effects and others for more subtle work, such as tweaking colors or giving footage shot on video a more filmlike look. To sample some of the best plug-ins, check out the plug-in demos on the CD that comes with this book.

✔ **Sorenson 3 Professional Edition:** If you edit lots of video projects for CD or the Internet, you obviously need to compress all that video into smaller, more manageable file sizes. One option is to compress the video with the MPEG-4 codec, which is included free with QuickTime and which the Final Cut Pro Compressor application is ready to work with immediately. If you want the *best* image quality at the smallest file sizes, though, skip MPEG-4 and use the Sorenson 3 Pro Edition compression codec instead. (Don't confuse this product with the standard Sorenson 3 codec, which is also included free with QuickTime.) At $399, Sorenson 3 Pro is expensive, but it gives your projects a polish that sets them apart. (For instance, most online movie trailers are compressed with Sorenson Professional Edition.) Unfortunately, Sorenson 3 Pro doesn't work with Compressor. However, it ships with the Sorenson Squeeze software, which lets you tweak all your encoding settings and create batch-processing lists. Check out www.sorenson.com for more details.

✔ **DVD Studio Pro:** If you want to memorialize your movies on DVD and your Mac has a DVD-burning SuperDrive (or third-party equivalent), consider using DVD Studio Pro 3. Sure, it costs a hefty $499 and the lighter-weight iDVD from Apple is free (or $49 with the Apple iLife software suite), but DVD Studio Pro 3 can make DVDs with custom menus, highlights, commentary tracks, multicamera angles, and advanced scripting. Plus, its interface is similar to Final Cut Pro's, so you can be up and running quickly.

Curl Up with a Good Book

The following books can help raise your editing skills and general postproduction knowledge to the next level:

✔ *In the Blink of an Eye: A Perspective on Film Editing,* by Walter Murch: If you read just one book on editing theory, make it this one. It's short and informal, and you find little technical stuff here. Instead, Murch focuses on editing from a creative standpoint, with an emphasis on telling a story and setting emotion through editing. The book also has a section on digital editing and its effect on the aesthetics of editing. Murch knows a thing or two about editing: His editing credits appear on such films as *American Graffiti; Apocalypse Now; The Godfather, Part II* and *The Godfather, Part III; Ghost; The English Patient;* and *The Talented Mr. Ripley.*

✔ *When the Shooting Stops, the Cutting Begins: A Film Editor's Story,* by Ralph Rosenblum and Robert Karen: This book is another gem about the aesthetics of editing and the flow of the editing process as a film goes from raw dailies to rough cut to final cut. Rosenblum did most of his cutting in the 1960s and '70s and goes in depth on his experiences working on classic films like *The Pawnbroker* and *Annie Hall.* (I recommend renting these films at a video store to get the most from the book.)

✔ *Understanding Comics,* by Scott McCloud: Okay, it's not about editing per se, but it's still surprisingly helpful for filmmakers (directors, storyboard artists, and especially editors). Written in comic-book form, *Understanding Comics* explains how comics are composed, read, and understood. As you read it (it's a quick read), you realize that the principles behind comic design apply to visual language in general — and what is film if not a visual language? Give it a try; you won't regret it.

✔ *The Film Editing Room Handbook: How to Manage the Near Chaos of the Cutting Room,* by Norman Hollyn: If you're using Final Cut Pro as a one-stop, all-in-one filmmaking machine (for not only editing but also outputting your final projects), this book isn't so useful. But, if you're working in a more conventional postproduction atmosphere, where different parts of your film are handled outside Final Cut Pro (for instance, your film's negative may be assembled for theatrical projection, or its sound, music, and dialogue may be mixed elsewhere), this book is a great primer for navigating this sometimes-minefield.

✔ *Practical Art of Motion Picture Sound,* by David Lewis Yewdall: If you find yourself working with audio quite a bit, check out this volume. It's a helpful introduction to postproduction audio topics from both the technical and artistic standpoints. Topics include planning an audio strategy for production and postproduction, gaining tips for recording better production audio (something that many all-in-one filmmakers using Final Cut Pro can appreciate), making preliminary versions of your score, recording sound effects, and editing dialogue.

Chapter 20

Almost Ten Tips for Managing Big Projects

A nice thing about Final Cut Pro is that it's really good at editing projects as short as TV commercials or as long as feature films. But, if you're working on longer-form projects (features and documentaries come to mind), you run into some particular challenges. For instance, you can easily get overwhelmed by all the media that you have to keep handy (possibly *thousands* of separate video and audio clips!). You can also easily fill hard drive space quickly, to the point where you no longer have room for additional media that you have to capture.

This chapter gives you a few tips to keep those big projects under control. I cover each of these topics in detail elsewhere, but it makes sense to point them out again, in one place, with big projects in mind.

Keep Your Media Files Organized

After you import your media into the Browser, Final Cut Pro remembers where each clip of media is located on your hard drive. That is, you only have to find a clip in the Browser to work with it; you don't have to fish through lots of folders on your hard drive to find the right file. That's a helpful feature, but it doesn't mean that you should get lazy or careless about where you store original media clips on your hard drive. These clips shouldn't be strewn among random folders on your drive (or on multiple drives) because, at some point, you probably will need to work with those media files outside of Final Cut Pro. For instance, you may need to clear some space on your hard drive without affecting your movie's media. If the media is stored in a variety of folders and mixed with unrelated media or files, figuring out what files can stay or go becomes difficult (and accidentally deleting some important media is much easier). Some tips for organizing the media files on your drive are as follows:

✔ **Keep media files for different projects in different folders.** Don't capture media for Film A into your Film B folder. (You can target these media folders when you capture — refer to Chapter 4.)

✔ **Divide media logically between multiple hard drives.** Keeping your media on a single hard drive is always handy, but if you have too much media to fit on a single drive, try to organize your drives in a logical way. For instance, keep Scenes 1 through 50 on Drive A, 51 through 100 on Drive B, and so on.

✔ **Keep your source videotapes on hand and organized.** Just because you have captured video from your original tapes, you shouldn't let those tapes out of your sight. You may need them to do an online edit or in case some of your captured media gets lost. (Occasionally, QuickTime files get corrupted, or your entire hard drive could crash.) To make life easier, keep your source tapes clearly labeled, make sure to note any timecode breaks that occur within a tape (refer to Chapter 4 for more information about timecode breaks), and store your tapes in a safe, secure place that you can easily get to.

Use Bins — Lotsa Bins!

When you're importing media clips, don't let them clutter the Browser window — the more clips you have there, the harder it gets to find a particular one (check out Figure 20-1). Instead, create bins for each of your project's scenes (for instance, Scene 1, Scene 2, Scene 3, and so on), and store your video and audio clips in their scene's bin. (If your film doesn't have traditional scenes, figure out some other theme you can use for organizing clips.) If you're dealing with lots of clips per scene, you can even create sub-bins within your Scene bins — for instance, for video, music, dialogue, and sound effects.

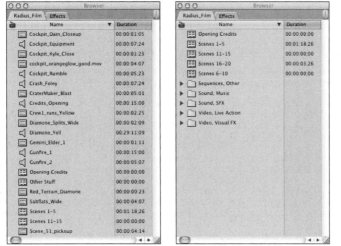

Figure 20-1: A cluttered browser versus one that's organized neatly into bins.

You can drag files and folders directly from your Mac's desktop to the bin of your choice in the Browser.

You can capture video clips from tape directly into the bin of your choice — just designate that bin as the logging bin for your project. (Refer to Chapter 4 for more information on logging bins.) You can also import a clip directly into the bin of your choice rather than import it straight to the Browser and then drag the clip into a bin. Just double-click a bin to open it in its own window; then choose File➪Import to send a clip right into that window.

Keep Your Clip Names Informative

Important: When you're importing or capturing media, try to name your clips in a consistent, systematic way. When you're disciplined about this strategy, you make finding a given clip much easier because a quick look at its name can tell you a great deal about the clip. For instance, don't name one clip `Dan's Closeup at the Dinner Table`, another clip `Everyone at the Dinner Table`, and a third clip `Medium Shot of Pam`. Instead, use `DinnerTable_Dan_Closeup`, `DinnerTable_Group_Wideshot`, and `DinnerTable_Pam_Medium`. Naming the clips with this kind of systematic approach makes spotting media easy, either in the Browser or after it's on the Timeline.

Document Your Clips

In addition to naming clips, Final Cut Pro lets you thoroughly document each clip with an FBI–like dossier. For instance, you can detail a clip scene and its take, describe its contents, add several additional comment lines, apply labels (best take and alternate shot, for instance), and more. You get your first opportunity to add this kind of info when you capture a clip from videotape (refer to Chapter 4 for more information on capturing), but you can also add these helpful details to clips later on. To do so, select the clip in the Browser, choose Edit⇨Item Properties⇨Logging Info, and type your data into that tab (as shown in Figure 20-2).

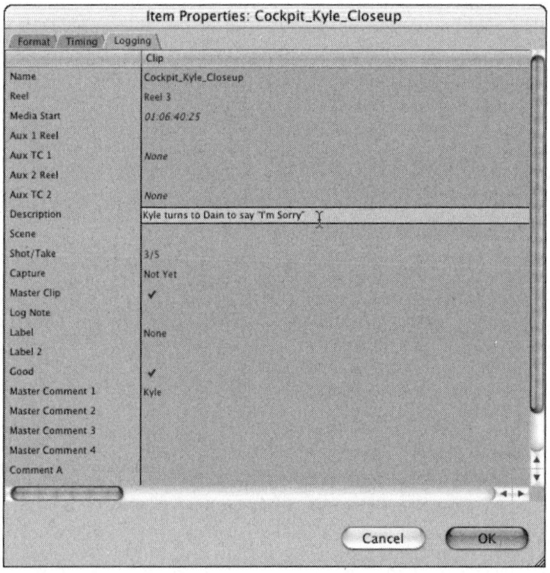

Figure 20-2: Use the Item Properties box to document important clips.

Of course, I'm the first to admit that documenting clips to this extent is a bit of a pain (you're an editor, not a librarian!), and I wouldn't blame you if you didn't go all out. But, doing a little advance legwork here can save you lots of time when you're sifting through hundreds of clips and looking for just the right one. For instance, you can quickly organize the Browser to show clips by their comment fields, or you can dig up clips (using the Final Cut Pro Find feature) by looking for keywords in clip descriptions or comments. Refer to Chapter 6 for more about labeling and documenting clips.

Use the Find Feature

The powerful Final Cut Pro Find feature can pull the proverbial needle out of a haystack when you're looking for a particular clip or group of clips. (This is something that any editor who works on long projects can definitely appreciate.)

To search for a clip, make sure that the Browser window is active and then choose Edit⇨Find. The Find dialog box, as shown in Figure 20-3, lets you specify tons of different search criteria. You can search for keywords in a clip's name, description, or comments (another reason that you should carefully name and document your clips!), by labels you have applied, or by the clip's scene, log tape, or a number of other criteria (even the compression codec that the clip uses or its frame size). You can also combine different search results — for instance, to find only the clips in Scenes 48 and 56 that you labeled as best or good takes and that feature the actress named Pam.

Figure 20-3:
The Final
Cut Pro Find
dialog box.

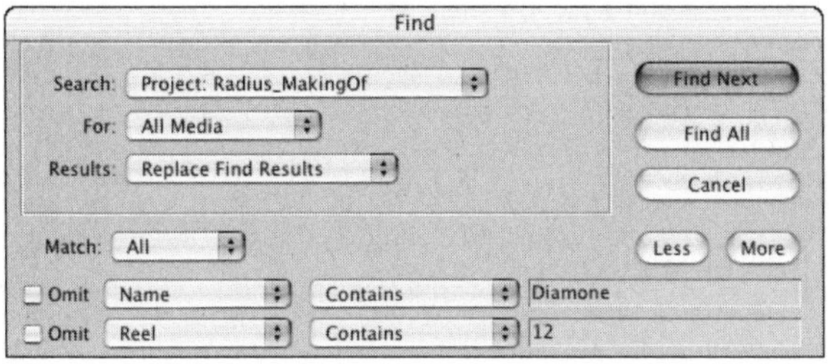

Stay Oriented with Markers

You can place markers to highlight important moments in your individual clips or Timeline sequences. Using markers makes finding these moments easier when you're in a hurry.

You can set two kinds of markers. The first variety is a Timeline marker, which you place in your Timeline sequence (maybe at the beginning of a new scene on the Timeline or at some notable event within a scene), as shown in Figure 20-4. The second variety is a clip marker, which you set within a single clip. Clip markers are especially handy for breaking long clips into more manageable morsels. For instance, when you set markers within a clip, each marker becomes a subclip of the master clip, and you can open a subclip by clicking it in the Browser (as shown in Figure 20-5) or move it exclusively to the Timeline.

Figure 20-4:
Sequence
markers on
the Timeline.

Markers in the Browser

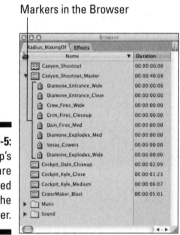

Figure 20-5:
A clip's
markers are
recognized
in the
Browser.

You set Timeline markers in the Timeline window and set clip markers while looking at a clip in the Viewer window. Just position the playhead in either window at a frame you want to mark, and then press M. (You see a marker symbol appear at that point, as shown in Figure 20-4.) To give the marker a name, choose Mark➪Markers➪Edit.

To search for Timeline markers, hold down Control, click the Timecode box (refer to Figure 20-4), and choose from the pop-up menu that appears the marker you want to jump to.

To search for clip markers, you can use the Final Cut Pro Find feature. Make the Timeline window active and choose Edit➪Find to search for markers in clips that are already on the Timeline, or make the Browser window active and choose Edit➪Find to search through all your project clips.

To find out more about these handy tools, check out Chapter 9.

Break Scenes into Sequences and Nest 'em Together

If you're working on a long project — anything more than 30 minutes — I advise against editing the project in a single Timeline sequence. You not only get disoriented by staring at an endless string of clips on the Timeline, but also spend lots of time scrolling around the window and zooming in and out to find a particular spot in your jumbo-size sequence.

Instead, break a big movie into smaller scenes (or acts or other kind of division), and build each of those smaller morsels in its own Timeline sequence. Then, whenever you want to watch your whole video, you can easily assemble it by creating another sequence (it becomes the master sequence) and nesting all your scene sequences into the new sequence, as shown in Figure 20-6.

Figure 20-6: Nested sequences, with a clip of background music running beneath.

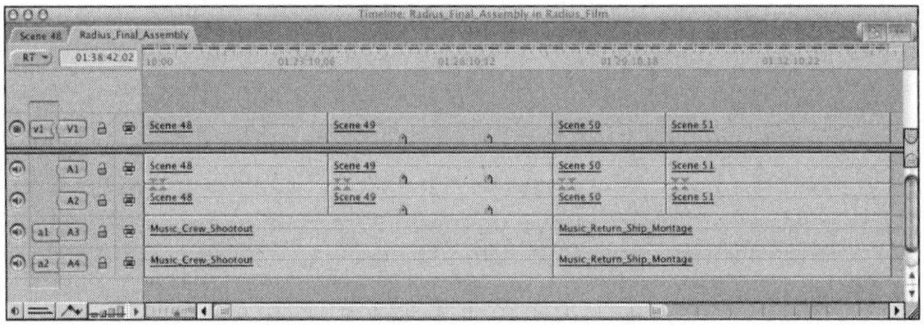

In other words, just drag your scene sequences from the Browser window into the master sequence (as though they were individual media clips) and arrange them on the Timeline in the order you want them to play. Refer to Chapter 9 for more details.

Save on Hard Drive Space

Long projects tend to eat up lots of disk space. This tendency is fine if you have endless hard drive storage space, but it can become quite a problem when you don't. (**Remember:** You need roughly 13 GB (gigabytes) to store an hour of DV footage, and about 50 GB for footage using DVCPRO HD.) If you find yourself running out of space, I recommend the following strategies to ease the shortage:

✔ **Save space with the OfflineRT codec.** Final Cut Pro lets you capture video by using a special codec named OfflineRT, which takes about 10 times less hard drive space as video captured in the DV codec. (You would normally use the DV codec to capture video, unless your system sports a fancy add-on capture card from a company such as Aurora or Pinnacle.)

What's the catch? (There's always a catch, isn't there?) OfflineRT's picture quality isn't nearly as good as DV — its video is sized at only 320 × 240 pixels (rather than DV's 720 × 480 pixels). The video, therefore, features more compression artifacts — that is, little imperfections in the imagery — than DV delivers.

Here's the good news: OfflineRT's lower quality is often a moot point because you're not expected to record your final movie by using video in the OfflineRT format anyway. Instead, you use OfflineRT to capture *preliminary* versions of all your source footage (saving lots of disk space in the process) and edit your movie to perfection. Then, when you're done, you can quickly recapture only the video you ended up using in your final cut — but this time using a much higher-quality codec, such as DV. Refer to Chapter 4 and Bonus Chapter 3 (on this book's companion Web site — see the Introduction for the Web address) for more about capturing video in OfflineRT.

✔ **Clean out old rendered files.** When you render video in your project — for instance, special effects, video transitions, color corrections, or superimposed titles — Final Cut Pro creates a new version of the clip, called a *rendered file.* Over time, these rendered files can pile up on your hard drive and hog lots of disk space (especially if Final Cut Pro is set to render clips at a high resolution). Of course, you want to keep some of these rendered files because you're using them in your final movie, but you may no longer need others that are just taking up valuable space. Fortunately, you can use the Final Cut Pro Render Manager to skim through and delete all unused rendered files for your projects. See Bonus Chapter 1 on this book's companion Web site (refer to the Introduction for the Web address) for more details on rendering.

✔ **Use Media Manager to trim projects.** When you finish editing a sequence, you can use the Final Cut Pro Media Manager to toss out all the excess video and audio that you imported but ultimately never used. This file removal frees some disk space for your next sequence. See Bonus Chapter 3 on this book's companion Web site (refer to the Introduction for the Web address) for more details about Media Manager.

✔ **Use the Edit to Tape feature.** If you're running low on hard drive space, you can finish a sequence (or a set of sequences) and then use the Final Cut Pro Edit to Tape feature to record that sequence to videotape — perhaps to a DV tape or maybe a higher-end format, such as Betacam SP or Digital Betacam. After the sequence is on tape, you're free to clear your drive of all the media the sequence used and then start a new sequence. When that sequence is done, you repeat the same steps to add the new sequence to the same videotape, right after the last sequence you recorded.

Editing to tape is an extreme solution to the hard drive space problem, and it can cramp your editing style. Given today's low hard drive prices, you may just want to bite the bullet and buy a new, larger drive. If not, refer to Chapter 17 for more details about the Edit to Tape feature.

Index

FOR DUMMIES®

The easy way to get more done and have more fun

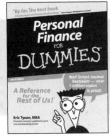

FOR DUMMIES®

A world of resources to help you grow

HOME, GARDEN & HOBBIES

0-7645-5295-3

0-7645-5130-2

0-7645-5106-X

Also available:

Auto Repair For Dummies
(0-7645-5089-6)

Chess For Dummies
(0-7645-5003-9)

Home Maintenance For Dummies
(0-7645-5215-5)

Organizing For Dummies
(0-7645-5300-3)

Piano For Dummies
(0-7645-5105-1)

Poker For Dummies
(0-7645-5232-5)

Quilting For Dummies
(0-7645-5118-3)

Rock Guitar For Dummies
(0-7645-5356-9)

Roses For Dummies
(0-7645-5202-3)

Sewing For Dummies
(0-7645-5137-X)

FOOD & WINE

0-7645-5250-3

0-7645-5390-9

0-7645-5114-0

Also available:

Bartending For Dummies
(0-7645-5051-9)

Chinese Cooking For Dummies
(0-7645-5247-3)

Christmas Cooking For Dummies
(0-7645-5407-7)

Diabetes Cookbook For Dummies
(0-7645-5230-9)

Grilling For Dummies
(0-7645-5076-4)

Low-Fat Cooking For Dummies
(0-7645-5035-7)

Slow Cookers For Dummies
(0-7645-5240-6)

TRAVEL

0-7645-5453-0

0-7645-5438-7

0-7645-5448-4

Also available:

America's National Parks For Dummies
(0-7645-6204-5)

Caribbean For Dummies
(0-7645-5445-X)

Cruise Vacations For Dummies 2003
(0-7645-5459-X)

Europe For Dummies
(0-7645-5456-5)

Ireland For Dummies
(0-7645-6199-5)

France For Dummies
(0-7645-6292-4)

London For Dummies
(0-7645-5416-6)

Mexico's Beach Resorts For Dummies
(0-7645-6262-2)

Paris For Dummies
(0-7645-5494-8)

RV Vacations For Dummies
(0-7645-5443-3)

Walt Disney World & Orlando For Dummies
(0-7645-5444-1)

Available wherever books are sold. Go to www.dummies.com or call 1-877-762-2974 to order direct.

FOR DUMMIES

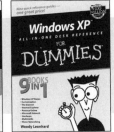

Plain-English solutions for everyday challenges

COMPUTER BASICS

PCs FOR **DUMMIES**

0-7645-0838-5

The Flat-Screen iMac FOR **DUMMIES**

0-7645-1663-9

Windows XP ALL-IN-ONE DESK REFERENCE FOR **DUMMIES**

0-7645-1548-9

Also available:

PCs All-in-One Desk Reference For Dummies (0-7645-0791-5)

Pocket PC For Dummies (0-7645-1640-X)

Treo and Visor For Dummies (0-7645-1673-6)

Troubleshooting Your PC For Dummies (0-7645-1669-8)

Upgrading & Fixing PCs For Dummies (0-7645-1665-5)

Windows XP For Dummies (0-7645-0893-8)

Windows XP For Dummies Quick Reference (0-7645-0897-0)

BUSINESS SOFTWARE

Excel 2002 FOR **DUMMIES**

0-7645-0822-9

Word 2002 FOR **DUMMIES**

0-7645-0839-3

Office XP 9 IN 1 DESK REFERENCE FOR **DUMMIES**

0-7645-0819-9

Also available:

Excel Data Analysis For Dummies (0-7645-1661-2)

Excel 2002 All-in-One Desk Reference For Dummies (0-7645-1794-5)

Excel 2002 For Dummies Quick Reference (0-7645-0829-6)

GoldMine "X" For Dummies (0-7645-0845-8)

Microsoft CRM For Dummies (0-7645-1698-1)

Microsoft Project 2002 For Dummies (0-7645-1628-0)

Office XP For Dummies (0-7645-0830-X)

Outlook 2002 For Dummies (0-7645-0828-8)

Get smart! Visit www.dummies.com

- **Find listings of even more *For Dummies* titles**

- **Browse online articles**

- **Sign up for Dummies eTips™**

- **Check out *For Dummies* fitness videos and other products**

- **Order from our online bookstore**

Available wherever books are sold. Go to www.dummies.com or call 1-877-762-2974 to order direct.

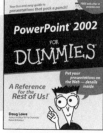

FOR DUMMIES®

The advice and explanations you need to succeed

SELF-HELP, SPIRITUALITY & RELIGION

0-7645-5302-X

0-7645-5418-2

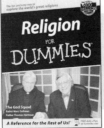
0-7645-5264-3

Also available:

The Bible For Dummies
(0-7645-5296-1)

Buddhism For Dummies
(0-7645-5359-3)

Christian Prayer For Dummies
(0-7645-5500-6)

Dating For Dummies
(0-7645-5072-1)

Judaism For Dummies
(0-7645-5299-6)

Potty Training For Dummies
(0-7645-5417-4)

Pregnancy For Dummies
(0-7645-5074-8)

Rekindling Romance For Dummies
(0-7645-5303-8)

Spirituality For Dummies
(0-7645-5298-8)

Weddings For Dummies
(0-7645-5055-1)

PETS

0-7645-5255-4

0-7645-5286-4

0-7645-5275-9

Also available:

Labrador Retrievers For Dummies
(0-7645-5281-3)

Aquariums For Dummies
(0-7645-5156-6)

Birds For Dummies
(0-7645-5139-6)

Dogs For Dummies
(0-7645-5274-0)

Ferrets For Dummies
(0-7645-5259-7)

German Shepherds For Dummies
(0-7645-5280-5)

Golden Retrievers For Dummies
(0-7645-5267-8)

Horses For Dummies
(0-7645-5138-8)

Jack Russell Terriers For Dummies
(0-7645-5268-6)

Puppies Raising & Training Diary For Dummies
(0-7645-0876-8)

EDUCATION & TEST PREPARATION

0-7645-5194-9

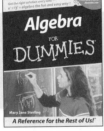
0-7645-5325-9

0-7645-5210-4

Also available:

Chemistry For Dummies
(0-7645-5430-1)

English Grammar For Dummies
(0-7645-5322-4)

French For Dummies
(0-7645-5193-0)

The GMAT For Dummies
(0-7645-5251-1)

Inglés Para Dummies
(0-7645-5427-1)

Italian For Dummies
(0-7645-5196-5)

Research Papers For Dummies
(0-7645-5426-3)

The SAT I For Dummies
(0-7645-5472-7)

U.S. History For Dummies
(0-7645-5249-X)

World History For Dummies
(0-7645-5242-2)